Expressionist Architecture

Wolfgang Pehnt

EXPRESSIONIST ARCHITECTURE

with 519 illustrations

THAMES AND HUDSON

Translated from the German
Die Architektur des Expressionismus
by J. A. Underwood and Edith Küstner

Frontispiece: pen drawing by Hans Scharoun, 1920

First published in Great Britain in 1973 by
Thames and Hudson Ltd, London

© 1973 Verlag Gerd Hatje, Stuttgart

English translation © 1973 Thames and Hudson Ltd, London
and Praeger Publishers, Inc., New York
Originally published in the United States
of America in 1973 by Praeger Publishers, Inc.
First paperback edition in the United States of America
1979 published by Thames and Hudson Inc.

Library of Congress Catalog card number 79-63888

Printed in Great Britain by
BAS Printers Limited,
Over Wallop, Hampshire

Bound in Great Britain by
H. Brooks, Cowley, Oxford

Contents

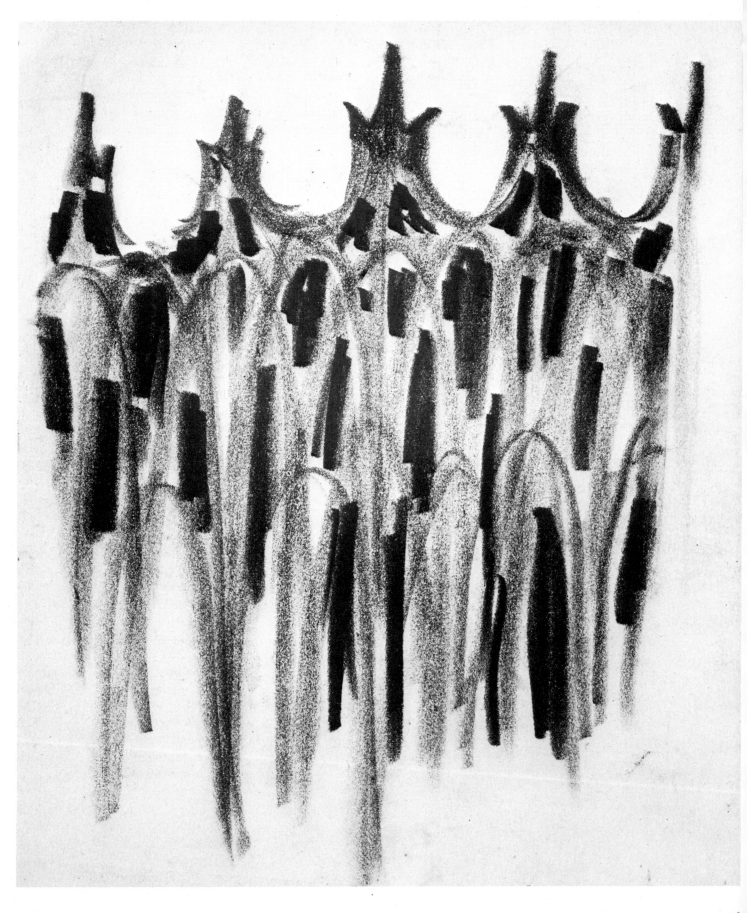

Foreword

I have been preoccupied by the subject of this book since 1958, but circumstances have prevented me from coming to grips with it. I remember my astonishment at the arbitrary way in which historians of modern architecture ignored completely an epoch to which their own heroes – Peter Behrens, Walter Gropius, and to a certain extent Mies van der Rohe – had belonged. What kind of objectivity was that, I wondered, when historians disregarded everything that did not agree with their premises?

The protagonists of the 'New Architecture' (see pp. 144ff.) themselves took a highly selective view of history in order to preserve the polemical force of their arguments. Their historians can invoke no such excuses. They continued to ignore Expressionism long after it had been rediscovered by architects themselves. Until the late 1950s the history of modern architecture was an attempt to trace the line of descent of what was regarded from the outset as an inviolable ideal. Sir Nikolaus Pevsner – himself not entirely innocent of this kind of historical simplification-by-violence – suggests in one of his later works, with a touch of self-mockery, how a new history of the origins of modern architecture might be written using only those works and personalities that had once been ignored.[1]

This unsatisfactory situation has now been put right. The kind of architecture which we shall be referring to in this book as Expressionist has found its place in a number of works on modern architecture – in Henry Russell Hitchcock's richly informative compendium, *Architecture, Nineteenth and Twentieth Centuries* (1958), for example, and in Reyner Banham's brilliant *Theory and Design in the First Machine Age* (1960). At the same time as Göran Lindahl's essay *Von der Zukunftskathedrale bis zur Wohnmaschine* ('From the Cathedral of the Future to the Living-Machine') came Ulrich Conrads and Hans G. Sperlich's *Phantastische Architektur* (1960): in this stimulating illustrated study they recalled the thinking behind the Berlin group of architects centered around Bruno Taut, a subject to which Conrads has returned in later works. There are two books specifically on the period of Expressionism: a brief survey by Dennis Sharp, *Modern Architecture and Expressionism* (1966), and a more extensive and detailed work by Franco Borsi and Giovanni Klaus König, *Architettura dell'espressionismo* (1967). In England and Italy the architectural press has also turned its attention to the architecture of Expressionism, with *The Architectural Review*, *Architectural Design*, *Casabella* and *L'architettura* publishing essays on particular aspects. Even though far less attention has been paid to Expressionist architecture than to Expressionist visual art and literature, a number of individual architects, including Peter Behrens, Erich Mendelsohn, Bruno Taut, Antoni Gaudí, and above all the Bauhaus school, have been the subject of admirable monographs. Marcel Franciscono's study of the prehistory of the Bauhaus (*Walter Gropius and the Creation of the Bauhaus in Weimar*, 1971), which deserves detailed analysis, reached me only after my own manuscript was completed.

The study that follows concentrates on the architecture of the German-speaking countries, the area where art and literature between about 1910 and 1923 bore the mark of Expressionism. The situation in the Netherlands, which was closely linked to the German scene, and also – despite the evident risks involved – the Futurist movement in Italy, are adduced as parallels. In spite of its uninhibited affirmation and acceptance of modern technology and urban life, in spite of its undeniably greater affinities with 'modernity', Futurism dealt to some extent with the same arguments which arise in any discussion of Expressionist architecture.

Certain characteristics of Expressionist architecture are not uncommon outside this narrower compass, particularly the use of individual elements to determine form at the expense of all others. This disturbance of harmony, which appears

1. Hans Poelzig. Charcoal sketch, c. 1920. Wolfgang Pehnt Collection, Cologne.

as deliberate strangeness, as the result of dogmatism or of a compulsion to expressiveness, is found not only in the work of Expressionist architects but also (with a different content) in some of the work of Charles Rennie Mackintosh, for example, or of Frank Lloyd Wright, or of the Russian Constructivists with their glorification of the machine. Nevertheless the term 'Expressionism' can still be validly used to refer specifically to a particular phenomenon that occurred within a particular area over a certain period of time. The features which characterize a style are not, taken individually, confined exclusively to that style; but the frequency with which such features occur and the way in which they are related to one another can justify us in marking off a particular stretch of the continuum of development and giving it a stylistic label. The label used in the present work, then, should not be taken to imply anything more than the fact that the designs and buildings here discussed bear more resemblance to one another than they bear to other designs and buildings. To demand an absolute correspondence between the thing and the term is to ask too much of any stylistic label – or of any term at all, for that matter.

'Expressionism could have no influence on architecture', declared Sigfried Giedion in his famous book *Space, Time and Architecture*. Giedion took the view that architecture, being an applied art, was too strongly conditioned by such tangible factors as utility, materials, construction and economics to be able to heed the Expressionist call. However persistently it may be advanced, this view is still open to question. First of all architecture, in all cases where it does more than fulfill the simplest physical need, is never entirely determined by external conditions. These merely provide the framework: within that framework the architect disposes of a practically unlimited number of possibilities. Secondly, the tangible conditioning factors are themselves to some extent dependent on the given style of the

2

period. This is proved by a glance at the preferred architectural subjects of the period 1910–23 – the *Volkshaus* or community centre, the *Stadtkrone* (literally 'crown of the city') or urban centrepiece, the sacred building; and also at the preferred building materials – wood, brick, concrete, stained glass and other decorative materials, but not stone, particularly not expensive stone.

The kind of distortion of the objective world practised in Expressionist painting and sculpture was quite obviously not susceptible of application to architecture. But was it not a kind of distortion when architects rode roughshod over or subordinated to their own expressive needs the specific content of their particular experience – tradition, architectural type, construction, material, purpose, etc.?

In a way architecture even seemed to have a certain advantage over all the other arts. It is much easier for architecture, as the articulation of interior and exterior space, to eliminate that element of remoteness that attaches to the aesthetic. Pictorial art, poetry and music one can ignore, but not space, not buildings. 'Architectural objects embody . . . a mental process which is repeated in the mind of each person who sees and ex-

periences them' (Heinrich de Fries).[2] Like theatre, with which it was often allied, architecture offered a way to the total artistic experience. Unlike theatre, it guaranteed this a certain permanence. Consequently in their more optimistic moments the architects of Expressionism were confident of their ability to fulfill in their entirety the ideas of the new art and to embody the 'eruption of the soul' (Theodor Däubler) and the 'belief in mind as the divine element in man' (Wilhelm Worringer)[3] in a more forceful manner than could their colleagues in other artistic disciplines.

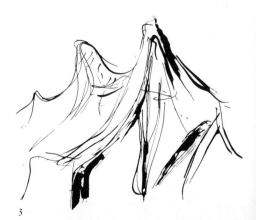

3

The conflict between utilitarian and artistic considerations, between 'could' and 'would', remained of course something of which the architects of that time were continuously and painfully aware. Many of them were tempted to break out of it, at the very least to a realm of wishful thinking. As early as 1909 the architect Otto Kohtz (1880–1956) wrote hopefully, 'It is highly possible that later generations will achieve such mastery of materials and technique that they will construct a building or a landscape for no other purpose than that of contemplation, simply out of a desire to create in a particular mood, rather in the way that many pieces of music are written today. Just as the composer can already, through sound, move thousands to joyful exuberance or to sorrow, so the architect will be able to do the same through form and colour.'[4] He illustrated his predictions with drawings which went so far as to show gigantic growths, serving unimaginable purposes and constructed of quite inconceivable materials (ill. 2).

The critics of the period, for their part, did not scruple to apply to architects the same term as they used for revolutionary writers, painters, sculptors, and composers, referring to them as 'expressionists'. Did they not collaborate with the latter in the same associations, at the same schools, and on the same newspapers? The term 'expressionism' began to be applied to pictorial art in the course of the year 1911,[5] but it was not used in connection with architecture until somewhat later – a delay which corresponds to the time lag governing the arts. It was only once Expressionist architecture had established itself after the First World War that people began to talk in terms of a pre-war Expressionist architecture. When Adolf Behne used the term 'expressionist architecture' in 1915 he had to back it up with extensive argument and reference to the interrelatedness of all the arts. Two years later, however, Bernhard Hoetger's design for Bahlsen's TET town (ills. 304–306) was already

being described in the popular press as 'an extraordinarily interesting piece of expressionist architecture'.[6]

After 1918 the references are numerous. Walter Müller-Wulckow spoke in 1919 of the 'individualistic expressionism' of architectural ideas, and in 1920 Hans Hansen called Expressionism the 'active architecture of the future'. The Hamburg *Baudirektor* Fritz Schumacher, certainly no youthful hothead, believed he could feel in architecture the same pulse as beat in Expressionist painting. Henry van de Velde, on the other hand, who was possibly afraid of being invoked as the father of the new style, condemned this kind of art as 'vaguely reminiscent of the eccentric expressionism of Gothic or Indian architecture'.[7] An architect like Hans Poelzig was continually being mentioned in the same breath with the Expressionist painters, as an Expressionist among Expressionists. So if contemporaries had no hesitation in speaking of an Expressionist architecture, we must be permitted to use the term as a working hypothesis and to examine what it really means.

But is this the right moment for an investigation of Expressionist architecture? The period shortly before and after the First World War has shown that a particular stylistic situation can exert a powerful influence – and one which is subsequently often found to have been unfortunate – on the course and the objects of art historians' studies. There was a boom in scientific and speculative works on Gothic, Baroque, and eastern Asian art. Architects were able to cull from them a mass of illustrations and to feel confirmed in their inclinations. Assuming that art history could exert a similar influence again, is a concern for Expressionist architecture desirable in our present situation?

In 1959, when Conrads and Sperlich finished their book, *Phantastische Architektur*, a good deal of which is devoted to the architecture of Expressionism, they expressed the hope that the apparently odd achievements of the latter might

4

5

2. Otto Kohtz. Sketch from *Gedanken über Architektur*, Berlin, 1909.
3. Giovanni Michelucci. Project for San Giovanni, near Florence, 1961.
4. Virgilio Marchi. 'Musical monument', from *Architettura futurista*, Foligno, 1924.
5. Tokuchika Miki, designer. Tower of Peace, Osaka, 1970.

9

6

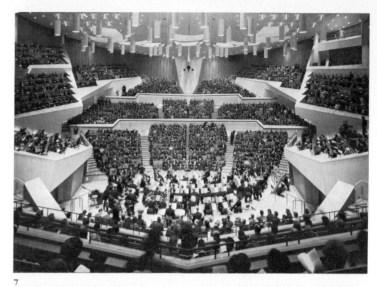

7

8

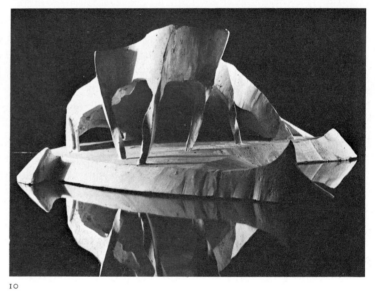

10

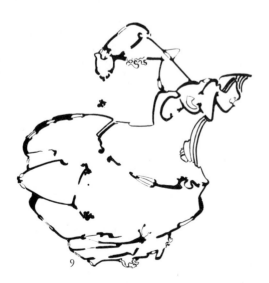

9

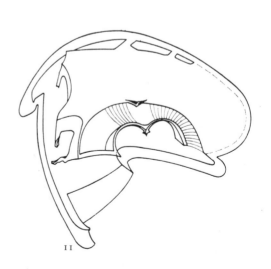

11

furnish an essential element for the architecture of the future. At the conference on Expressionism in Florence in 1964 Bruno Zevi maintained that Expressionism was a permanent feature of modern architecture. More recently, Borsi and König considered the Expressionist experience in terms of a possible alternative to rationalism.

There is no doubt that today we need imagination more than ever before. But over the last decade architects' enthusiasm for discovery has turned to the past rather than to the future. For architects whose clients held their purses open and their mouths shut, Expressionism was a source of inspiration on which they drew enthusiastically. Their motives were honourable and understandable. A modernism now grown old called for its opposite, for space with character instead of a negative enclosure between rectangular panes of glass, for an openly picturesque quality instead of the rationality of the screen, for an experiential approach to materials in place of the smooth perfection of office-building façades or the – highly *im*perfect – plastered walls of local-authority housing. The architect's joy in creation, repressed in terms of the whole, came out all the more strongly in details.

Hence those churches that have grown up beside our trans-European motorways, competing with filling stations and restaurants for the driver's eye (ill. 3). Hence the late Expressionist jokes with which firms and nations try to shout one another down at mammoth world exhibitions. Knobbly tower buildings of the kind that in Virgilio Marchi's case never got off the drawing-board and in Antoni Gaudí's case required months of laborious stone-masonry to build can now be cast effortlessly in reinforced concrete (ills. 4, 5). Hermann Finsterlin's cave-homes (ills. 8, 9) have found many successors, from Juan O'Gorman's fantastically decked-out grotto, André Bloc's inhabitable sculptures (ill. 14), and Frederick Kiesler's 'endless house' to the inventions of the young Berlin architect

Engelbert Kremser, who with his concrete bowls on pre-formed earth embankments has shown a practicable way to realize irregular ground plans (ills. 10, 11).

Is it an accident that the first major example of this earth architecture, a playhouse for children, was constructed in a residential quarter – Berlin's Märkische Viertel – that has achieved a sad notoriety for its architectural and social shortcomings? Or that in the holiday camps of the French Riviera itinerant holidaymakers are offered playful sculptural forms to live in, by way of relaxation from the pressures of the workaday world? The exceptional and the banal provide an alibi for one another – a dialectic for which historical Expressionism is in part to blame. The architects of Expressionism themselves drew a sharp distinction between the dull jobs that did not leave much scope for imagination and the big chance that would enable them to give vent to their delight and intoxication with form to the full.

The original Expressionist architecture is recent enough for numerous traditions based on personal or idealistic factors to be with us still. Anthroposophical architects in Switzerland, Germany, and Great Britain piously preserve the architectural legacy of Rudolf Steiner. In the person of Hans Scharoun the Expressionist heritage was until recently present at first hand. In the many commissions which he received after the late fifties he was able to draw upon the reservoir of ideas represented by his unexecuted projects (ills. 6, 7). Gottfried Böhm, who began by working with his father Dominikus Böhm, has gone beyond any early Expressionist architecture with the reinforced concrete masses of his later sacred buildings. In his Bensberg children's home he grouped the individual houses for the children round a central church, rather in the way that Bruno Taut did in his Folkwang School in Hagen (ills. 12, 13). His communal buildings are part of a world in which people are subject to artistic dictatorship. It is not an inspiring

12

13

6. Hans Scharoun. Watercolour, between 1939 and 1945.
7. Hans Scharoun. Philharmonie, Berlin, 1956–63.
8. Hermann Finsterlin. Plaster model, c. 1920.
9. Hermann Finsterlin. Plan, c. 1920.
10, 11. Engelbert Kremser. Project for a pavilion in the Tiergarten, Berlin, c. 1967. Plaster model and plan.
12. Bruno Taut. Project for the Folkwang School, Hohenhagen, Hagen, 1920. Site plan.
13. Gottfried Böhm. Children's Village, Bensberg, 1968. Site plan.

14

15

14. André Bloc. Habitacle no. 2, Meudon, 1964.
15. Gottfried Böhm. Old people's home, Düsseldorf-Garath, 1966–68. Stairway.
16. Antoni Gaudí. Crypt of Santa Coloma de Cervelló, chapel of the Colonia Güell, 1898–1914.

16

spectacle to see the inhabitants of his old people's home in Düsseldorf-Garath walking through a Lilliputian landscape *à la* Gaudí (ills. 15, 16).

The genius of the creative artist and the mediocrity of the cross-section that identifies with society's conventions, the bizarreness of the exceptions and the barrenness of the rule – is one justified in feeding this apparently insoluble conflict with fresh material? What in 1920 was a conservative Utopia of belief in the redeeming quality of all art, in the creative potential of artisan craftsmanship, in the regenerative power of the people, appears half a century later as self-satisfied ambition on the part of individual artists. We need imagination today not for the isolated building that one individual erects for another. We need it for the systems by which we are seeking to come to terms with our existence. One of the secondary aims of this book – and one that is by no means unimportant – will have been achieved if it succeeds in showing how the Expressionist blueprint is bound to its particular historical moment and to no other. What I mean is that there is no hope for a revival of Expressionism.

My thanks are due to many individuals and institutions. Information was generously supplied by Frau Suzanne Klingeberg, Itzehoe; Frau Lina Krayl, Güsen near Magdeburg; Mrs Louise Mendelsohn, San Francisco; Frau Marlene Poelzig, Hamburg; Herr Cornelius Brust, Leinfelden; Professor Hermann Finsterlin, Stuttgart; Professor Fred Forbat, Vällingby; Dr Alberto Longatti, Como; Dr Wassili Luckhardt, Berlin; Herr Wilhelm Teichmann, Hamburg; Professor Oswald Mathias Ungers, Ithaca, N. Y.; Heer H. T. Wijdeveld, Amsterdam; and Heer D. van Woerkom, Amsterdam. The following institutes, their directors and staffs have also been particularly generous in furnishing material and information: the Akademie der Künste, Berlin; H. Bahlsens Keksfabrik, Hanover; Bauhaus-Archiv, Berlin; Die Böttcherstrasse, Bremen; Deutsches Institut für Filmkunde, Wiesbaden; Deutsche Kinemathek, Berlin; Goetheanum, Dornach; Istituto di Storia dell'Arte, Pisa; Museo Civico, Villa Comunale dell' Olmo, Como; Städtisches Karl-Ernst-Osthaus-Museum, Hagen.

I dedicate this book to my wife: she knows the reason.

Wolfgang Pehnt

Introduction: the Theatre of the Five Thousand

'Let us rather be impractical, if we wish a ray of our creative activity to strike the human soul.'

Hans Poelzig, speaking at the conference of the Deutsche Werkbund, Stuttgart, 1919.

Coup de théâtre

On 28 November 1919 the Grosse Schauspielhaus in Berlin's Friedrichstadt (ills. 17–21, 28) was inaugurated with a performance of Aeschylus' *Oresteia*. Max Reinhardt (1873–1943), the brilliant impresario and director, had fought hard for the 'Theatre of the Five Thousand'. He had purchased a dilapidated building, the Zirkus Schumann, a considerable portion of which was incorporated in the new theatre, notably the rectangular arena ending in a semi-circle and the amphitheatre-like auditorium. Even before the war, Reinhardt had studied the scenic possibilities of circus architecture, noting that it preserved the classical orchestra and the classical amphitheatre. Hence his decision to convert the old circus building and make it the home of the Reinhardt theatrical empire. The arena and the auditorium undivided by balconies suited his fondness for vast, colourful productions and an atmosphere of festivity and magic.

As far as the public was concerned the spectacular aspect of the new building lay not so much in its importance in terms of the history of theatre architecture as in the unmistakable form which the architect hit upon for it, and the time at which it was built. The most that anyone considered doing in Berlin at that time was to modernize some of the older commercial façades. Yet out of the remains of the old circus arose the large and mysteriously compact building, with an interior like a magic cave. It was a *coup de théâtre* in every sense.

Part of the surprise effect derived from the speed with which the work was done. The stalactite dome above the arena was only designed in July 1919, yet four months later it was already finished. And if we take into account the strikes that continually interrupted building operations and the shortage of building materials, this rapid completion becomes little short of miraculous. No other building or projected building in the Germany of those years captured the public imagination to the same extent as Reinhardt's Grosse Schauspielhaus. It was the first prestige building of the young republic, an exotic bloom in the grey landscape of the post-war period. To the conservative critic Karl Scheffler the great building, painted a burgundy red, seemed 'a threatening image of red revolution'.[1]

Two points on which Reinhardt particularly insisted did not make the architect's and later the directors' work any easier: first there was the panoramic stage, thirty metres wide, which provided an acting area beyond the orchestra and the fore-stage and which called for a greater degree of illusionism than the action taking place within the auditorium, i.e. nearer the audience; and secondly there was the dome, which was to vault the auditorium and arena as the sky vaulted the classical theatre, but which could not of course take in the main stage and the stage tower. This ambiguity between axial and centralized space had a disturbing effect. But because Reinhardt wanted to produce plays written for a proscenium stage as well as for an open arena the compromise was unavoidable.

The difficulties were further increased by the decision to retain the fabric of the old building. This had originally been erected by Friedrich Hitzer as a five-aisled market hall, and was only later converted for a circus. The iron framework of the auditorium walls and of the front part of the building had to be retained. (The stage tower of the circus building had collapsed in May 1918.) Several architects had already had a go at the job before Hans Poelzig, then architectural advisor to the city of Dresden, was called in.[2]

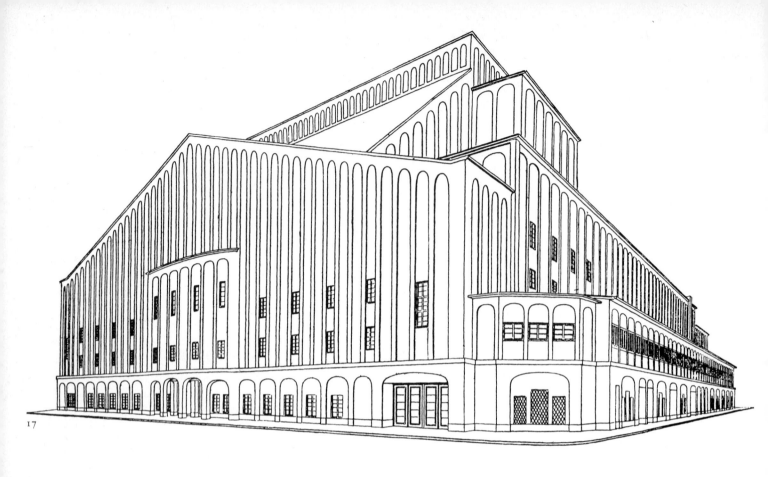

17

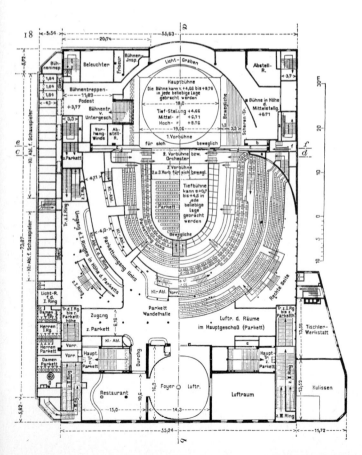

18

19

14

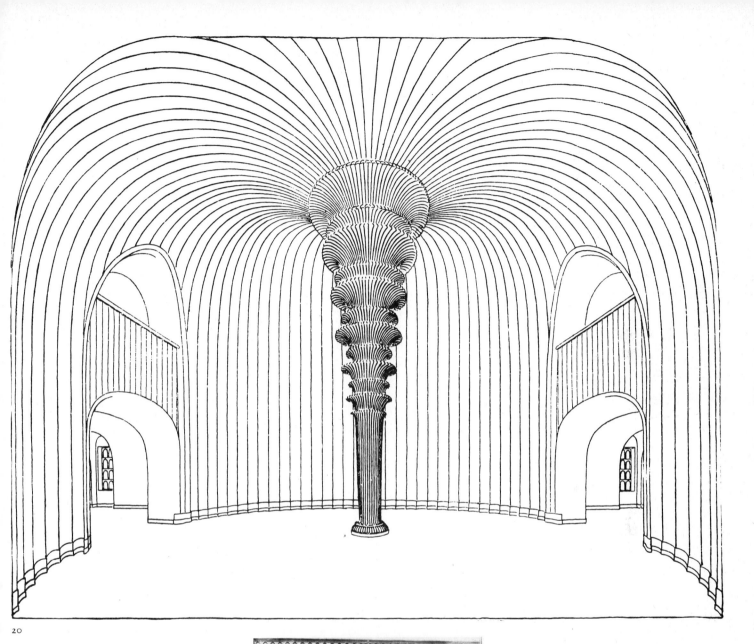

20

21

17–21. Hans Poelzig. Grosse Schauspielhaus,
Berlin, 1918–19.
17. View from the Schiffbauerdamm.
18. Plan at stalls level (left) and upper tier level
(right).
19. Auditorium.
20. Main foyer.
21. View from the south.

Hans Poelzig

In his earlier industrial buildings Hans Poelzig (1869–1936) had come as close to neutrality as was possible for an architect of his generation (ills. 144–150). Yet in spite of this he already had a reputation among the most diverse critics as a dynamic designer, an Expressionist of the more vital kind. Comparisons were drawn that took in Michelangelo. Art meant everything to Poelzig. He frankly acknowledged that he 'glorified the almost impracticable': 'what matters to me is form and form alone.'[3] But he only spoke in this way in the early post-war years. Architecture as *ars magna* was his aspiration – an aspiration of the time.

Poelzig behaved in the manner of the genius. He worked on a large number of canvases at the same time; he designed everything from large buildings to small appliances; he moulded models of his architectural projects; and his speech was salted with the racy Berlin slang of the time. The first idea for the Schauspielhaus exterior was jotted down during a meal on his paper napkin. In the case of other designs, this *furioso* element might only emerge when work was already under way: for the Dresden fire-station (1916), he began with a sober statement and ended with a powerfully surging mass.

The young were impressed by Poelzig, even though his loud, booming self-confidence did not appeal to them – that was not their style. Erich Mendelsohn told with grudging respect of a visit to the Schauspielhaus in Poelzig's company, when he was unable to resist the effect of the vast interior and what he described as the 'experience of concrete'. Bruno Taut, the spokesman of the younger generation, attacked Poelzig on many an occasion, and indeed it was because of him that Poelzig wanted to leave the Berlin Arbeitsrat für Kunst, or Working Council for Art (see pp. 89ff.).[4]

In letters to friends Taut complained of Poelzig's habit of doggedly repeating similar or identical motifs: 'Poelzig calls it resonance when he goes on hitting the same note, sometimes loudly and sometimes softly.'[5] Poelzig's attitude to form was in fact inflationary. He used tautology as a means of suggestion. His drawings give the impression that the architectural form of his buildings was often the outcome of a kind of compulsive copying-out of whole strings of ornaments.

There are thus grounds for regarding Poelzig's Schauspielhaus as an idiosyncratic invention. With the exception of Erich Mendelsohn and Rudolf Steiner, none of his contemporaries in the German-speaking world ever had the opportunity of executing such a highly personal piece of work. Whatever the difficulties Poelzig might have had, he spent money on a scale more reminiscent of the imperial past than of the post-war period. Yet there are also good reasons for seeing the Schauspielhaus, whose form would have been unthinkable five years earlier or five years later, as a product of its time. The categories that are applicable to this building are also applicable, to a greater or lesser extent, to a large number of projects and a smaller number of buildings actually executed.

Food for the hungry

The passion for building theatres dates back to the years before the First World War. For Peter Behrens the theatre was – in 1900 – the 'highest symbol of civilization', an estimate which is reflected in the figures: whereas in 1896 there were 302 permanent theatre buildings in Europe, by 1926 there were 2,499![6]

The 'People's Theatre' movement, which went back to the late nineteenth century, played an important part in this development. In the years immediately following the war its attempt to attract new classes of people to the theatre became extremely topical. Artists of all disciplines were concerned to break down the barriers between art and the people. The 'People's Theatre' movement emerged as 'the most commanding expression of a new society, its mind and its voice', as Romain Rolland put it. Reinhardt himself, over-rating his profession in the characteristic way of the period, went so far as to describe the stage as 'food for the hungry'. Thousands, hundreds of thousands of people who had never been inside a theatre before would become acquainted with the repertory of classical and modern drama in his new Schauspielhaus.[7]

This conviction of the social usefulness of art was something architects shared with the other artists of Expressionism. The more individual and subjective the design, the firmer the architect's belief that he had acted on behalf of and indeed at the dictate of society. The Grosse Schauspielhaus fulfilled these ideas in two respects. First, Poelzig's formal solutions, with their powerful, almost vulgar effects, were calculated to dazzle the crowd rather than to satisfy the taste of an élite. Secondly, this giant amphitheatre embodied a programme which earlier popular theatres – with the exception of the Théâtre du Vieux-Colombier in Paris – had failed to achieve, namely the renunciation of a differentiated seating plan and the reduction in ticket prices made possible by the house's enormous capacity.

The popular theatres that were laid out axially on the basis of a proscenium stage had to have one or more balconies (despite the fundamental antipathy to such feudal relics as tiers and boxes) if they were to accommodate a sizeable audience: the stalls area would otherwise have to be far too deep. Only in the arena theatre, as realized by Poelzig and Reinhardt in the Grosse Schauspielhaus, did the community of actors and audience, of givers and receivers, become a visible reality. Such a theatre was thought to epitomize the people as an emotionally affected whole. Reinhardt spoke (in connection with the Salzburg project) of the 'sacred character' of his theatre.[8]

In this respect Poelzig's building constitutes a high point in the development that goes back to the teachings of Ruskin and Morris, to the manifold efforts of reformers in the direction of a new popular culture, and to nineteenth-century Utopian socialism. The idea behind 'People's Theatre' was no longer that of educating the lower classes but of identifying with the people as a whole. Stage and auditorium ought to form a unity 'in which everyone, actors and audience, is caught up in the enchantment of togetherness' (Bruno Taut).[9] Theatres occupied a central position in town-planning projects during these years, not only with Taut but also with Bernhard Hoetger, and even as late as 1927 in Walter Gropius' project for a *Stadtkrone* for Halle an der Saale.

In practice the 'enchantment of togetherness' turned out to be something that was not to be achieved without some additional help. Reinhardt admitted with naïve candour that capturing the audience's emotions required a certain amount of manipulation: 'The spectator must not have the impression that he is a mere uncommitted outsider, but must be fed the suggestion that he is intimately bound up with what is happening on the stage and that he too has a part to play in the unfolding of the action.'[10]

Where Reinhardt spoke of 'suggestion', Poelzig spoke of 'coercion'. This desire to involve the spectator in a situation which is foreign to him has long survived Expressionism as a factor in the aesthetics of theatre architecture. The total theatre developed by Walter Gropius and Erwin Piscator in 1927 – one of a number of contemporary variants of the single-space theatre – was intended, according to Gropius, to 'catch [the audience] unawares and force it into experiencing the play from within' by 'mobilizing every spatial means'.[11]

Cave and tower

With Poelzig this psychological coercion of the spectator began even before he entered the building. The exterior was given a vertical emphasis by the use of soaring pilasters culminating in round arches, a motif which Poelzig had already tried out in previous designs and which was to be much imitated in subsequent years. Between these projecting strips of wall the windows were squeezed down to the size of dormers, thus preserving the sinister impenetrability of the façade. In the context of the street the theatre loomed up like some alien, threatening mass, as mysteriously alluring as it was gloomily forbidding. The foyers and corridors provided a 'state of suspense far removed from any utilitarian considerations' (Fritz Stahl).[12] The squat proportions, the indirect lighting emanating from the fan-like supports, and the green colour chosen for the main foyer all contributed to the effect of some unredeemed, submarine world. In this empire of art the spectator must feel himself far removed from the everyday, secular life of the city. A typical feature of this enveloping character of the interior was the fact that walls and ceiling were merged together to create a continuous form. In the main foyer a single support sent out a sheaf of fluted mouldings that

22

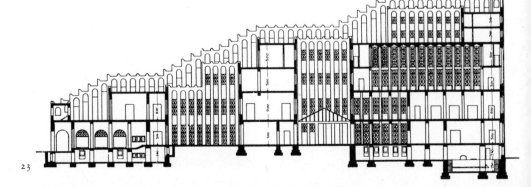

22, 23. Hans Poelzig. Project for the House of Friendship, Istanbul, 1916. Isometric view and longitudinal section.

23

24

glided over ceiling and walls until they reached the floor (ill. 20).

After the sombre, oppressive proportions of the foyers came the liberation of the amphitheatre – a pale yellow, to which the indirect lighting seemed to impart an inner glow. If in the foyers there was some question as to whether the palmate columns grew upwards or downwards, here in the amphitheatre the whole magnificent stalactite formation quite clearly grew downwards from the ceiling into the slender supports that had the appearance of exposed roots. This interior too was a cave – the light and lofty grotto after the tunnels of the low corridors.

Poelzig's cave theme became a *leitmotiv* of the period. Architects imitated him even in the kind of projects that were not conceived as sculptural models, that were not treated 'stereotomically' (as the architectural theorist Paul Klopfer described this kind of design) but 'tectonically', in opposition to the law of load and support. In this case opaque coloured glass was often used for the outer plane, or the building was so constructed that the load-bearing members appeared to the eye to merge into a single surface. An example of such a 'tectonic cave' is Bruno Taut's Glass Pavilion at the Werkbund Exhibition in Cologne in 1914 (ills. 163–167).

A second central theme of Expressionism, complementary to the cave theme, preoccupied the 'stereotomic' Poelzig: this was the theme of tower and pinnacle, the *Stadtkrone*, 'alpine architecture'. Poelzig was only commissioned actually to build one tower: the water tower cum exhibition hall in Posen, now Poznan (ills. 144–146). But his passion for tower-shaped buildings went much further than this. As long as he was numbered among the Expressionists he dreamed of building mountains. His House of Friendship in Istanbul (ills. 22, 23) he pictured as a gigantic, free-standing flight of steps, an autocratically assertive form into which the architectural programme was skilfully integrated. Designed to stand on the ridge of the hill of old Istanbul, as seen from the Bosphorus the building would have continued the slope of the hill above the crest of the city, turning its tall, narrow rear wall towards the Sea of Marmara. A mountain on top of the mountain – and a brusque, even brutal intrusion into the silhouette of this city of domes and minarets. Almost everyone who took part in the competition had visited the site in Istanbul; Poelzig, who entered the most self-assured design, did not.

Poelzig took up the momentum of the landscape in order to give it dramatic emphasis in many of his projects. His building projects – and those of many other Expressionists as well – do not look like artificial structures at all, but like an extension to nature, like 'human hills' (Joseph Ponten). 'It is the earth itself that builds with our hands', wrote Otto Bartning.[13] These buildings squat solidly on the ground on broad bases. Poelzig's design for the Bismarck monument near Bingerbrück (ill. 25) looks like an eroded sandstone cliff that some titanic heaving of the earth's crust has thrust up in the middle of the Schiefergebirge. His daring plans for a Festspielhaus in Salzburg envisaged a towering elliptical cone connected by a system of arcades to a smaller theatre building, with the whole thing looking as if it were worked in natural rock rather than constructed in brick and concrete on an anything but impressive hill in the Hellbrunn Park (ill. 24). In giving his building a corkscrew movement Poelzig managed to combine upward thrust with the feeling of enclosure – the tower with the cave.

Mendelsohn, who was later to build a tower of his own – the Einstein Tower – even saw the Grosse Schauspielhaus as a tower-building: 'Here we no longer have storeys stacked up one on top of another like steps but the individual components of the architectural mass hurled against

24. Hans Poelzig. Project for the Festspielhaus, Salzburg, 1920. First version.
25. Hans Poelzig. Project for the Bismarck monument, near Bingerbrück, 1910. Second version.
26. Hans Poelzig. Page of pencil sketches, *c.* 1920. Marlene Poelzig Collection, Hamburg.

25

one another and thrusting upwards to form a tower.' Karl Scheffler even found 'a certain tower-like quality' about Poelzig himself.[14]

The total work of art

Common to both the tower and the cave is an effect of physical oppression on the spectator. Buildings such as Reinhardt's theatre were loaded with artistic expressiveness to an extent which made it possible to talk of the eclipse of pictorial art by architecture, the more powerful medium. 'Buildings are in the highest degree alive; in them the concept of the picture as work of art is immeasurably deepened and enhanced. We can only guess at the extent to which the art of spatial articulation will one day transcend the art of pictorial creation . . . The end of painting as an independently valid art seems to be approaching; its eclipse by the far greater power of expression of architecturally structured space appears to be an immediate possibility' (Heinrich de Fries).[15]

Expressionism knew nothing of the dialectic of exterior and interior which was to become increasingly important during the twenties. If the buildings of this period are sealed off from their surroundings it is because the unstructured environment was unworthy of the structured inner world of their architecture. The tendency of Expressionist architecture, on the other hand, was to try to draw into itself the earth as a whole. 'The artistic permeation of the world through spatial creation is now only a question of time', thought de Fries. Bruno Taut spoke of 'earth-crust architecture'. 'Important to remodel the earth's surface sculpturally', runs a note found among Poelzig's papers.[16]

In the Expressionist context the word *Gesamtkunstwerk*, or 'total work of art', had a double meaning. As normally used it meant the union of all the arts in architecture, but it also referred to the total environment that called upon more than one of man's senses. Expressionist

architecture appeals to the eye, to the touch, to the synaesthetic sense. It awakens heterogeneous associations both in time and space. Poelzig drew inspiration from the most culturally diverse sources without his borrowings being recognizable – as they were in the case of nineteenth-century architecture – as quotations. His Schauspielhaus dome may have been based on a memory of Islamic stalactite vaulting, a similarly illusive architectural form unrelated to construction (ill. 27). The same motif was echoed in Wilhelm Kreis' Rheinhalle in Düsseldorf (ill. 29). The way the supports fan out towards the top seems to have been inspired by Egyptian umbellate or palmate capitals; the round-arch articulation stems from Romanesque architecture.

With Poelzig – and with others too – the new went hand in hand with a determined use of the old. In other projects – the designs of his Dresden period or the Salzburg Festspielhaus plans – he drew inspiration from the tradition of the surroundings and raised

superstructures of Baroque exuberance above fluidly curving ground plans. His House of Friendship for Istanbul illustrates Diodorus' description of the Hanging Gardens of Babylon. The fact that most of these borrowings from the history of art were themselves allusions to natural formations – to stalactitic caves, ribbed leaves, or rock formations – made them all the more welcome. The formal material supplied by history and nature was indistinguishable as to treatment. Enthusiastic observers described the Grosse Schauspielhaus – surely in accordance with Poelzig's intentions – as an attempt 'to furnish in architectural form an image of the cosmos that is more direct, more immediate, and more embracing than any furnished by earlier times.'[17]

The system of indirect lighting with its elliptical and parabolic reflectors and the picturesque use of powerful colours contributed further to the amalgam of motifs and means employed in the Schauspielhaus. The red of the façade became lighter towards the top, and

26

27

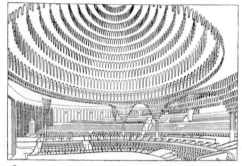

28

29

27. Stalactite vault in the Sala de los Aben-
cerrages, Alhambra, Granada, 1354–91.
28. Hans Poelzig. Grosse Schauspielhaus, Berlin, 1918–19.
29. Wilhelm Kreis. Rheinhalle, Düsseldorf,
1925–26.

tonal values differentiated the blind arches from the wall surface. Synaesthetic creations tend to overstep the bounds of good taste as well. In the Schauspielhaus the bulbs attached to the 1,200 wired-plaster stalactites were connected in such a way that, when lit, they reproduced different stellar constellations; they were also variously coloured – in shades of yellow, green, and red – to resemble the actual stars in the night sky. In contrast to formally strict, 'pure' stylistic periods, Expressionism did not hesitate to resort to popular gimmicks. It was not inappropriate that Reinhardt, having soon lost enthusiasm for his work, handed over the theatre to the music-hall impresario Eric Charell.

What distinguished Poelzig as a professional architect from the architecture-struck dilettante was his capacity for finding a common denominator between artistic and utilitarian demands. The terraces of the Salzburg Festspielhaus project, for example, were not only an artistic feature: they functioned as a promenade area and provided access to the tiers and boxes of the auditorium. In the Berlin Schauspielhaus the rings of stalactites in the dome proved to have acoustic advantages: they had the effect of dispersing sound and shortening echo-times. The stalactite motif could also be justified on constructional grounds as an echo of the suspended dome, held up by an invisible framework.

This example illustrates how the Expressionists saw the relationship between form and function. Static function – or non-function – merely provided the starting point for a *capriccio* of forms which then ran its course until the starting point was forgotten. 'It is still better to do violence to the purpose and create a true work of art than to let the purpose, i.e. cold reason, get the better of you' (Hans Poelzig).[18] Expressionism was heavily criticized later by the disciples of the New Architecture on the grounds that this relationship between form and the formative impulse was untruthful. Dishonest it certainly was, if we take as

our criterion of form that it should appropriately illustrate structural conditions. The Expressionists, however, did not accept such premises.

Yet even within the aesthetic accepted by its creators the Grosse Schauspielhaus showed certain inconsistencies. In part these were caused by the building's history. The wreaths of stalactites, at the point where they form the transition between the dome and the flat ceilings around it, looked more like cardboard cut-outs than three-dimensional forms. Even more uneasy were the transitions from the circle of the room under the dome to the single plane of the proscenium. In order to open up the stage as widely as possible it was necessary – at the cost of considerable technical ingenuity (e.g. changing the ties in the proscenium arch) – to remove some of the supports of the old building. Although the dome was represented by its detailing as a suspended dome it seemed to tilt towards the unsupported, stage side. At such critical points as these it becomes evident how imperfectly the intention of giving the building a sculptural form was in fact realized. Up to a point even this completed project remained 'on paper' – a fate which was reserved for the majority of Expressionist projects anyway.

The Grosse Schauspielhaus
as Expressionist architecture

As one example of a whole group of buildings and projects, Poelzig's theatres suggests some provisional conclusions.

The Grosse Schauspielhaus was conceived as a work of art. Bruno Taut asserted, 'Architecture is art and ought to be the highest of the arts. It consists exclusively of powerful emotion and addresses itself exclusively to the emotions.'[19] Never again since Expressionism have architects insisted so categorically on the artistic character of their creations. Fritz Höger's Chilehaus in Hamburg (ills. 300, 301, 499) was protected by a preservation order as soon as it was finished.

30

As was only to be expected in an art that recognized no canon, Expressionism was concerned not with harmony but with character. In architecture too, Expressionism ennobled the ugly. It did not – as, say, Mannerism had done – delight in contrasting the ugly and the beautiful but merged the two into a whole which transcended both ugliness and beauty. The expressive element occupied first place among the factors determining a particular design, whether expressive of the ideal destiny of the building, of the nation, of the period, of the 'World-Spirit', or of 'subjective aliveness'.[20] Expression in this context was not understood as reflection or elucidation of objectively demonstrable design elements but as a kind of super-elevation, a symbolic synthesis of heterogeneous elements. Characteristically Poelzig saw the two colossal gables of his Schauspielhaus (ill. 17) as symbols of the dome – with which all they had in common was the round-arch decoration – purely on the grounds of their enormous size.[21]

This was 'expressive architecture', an *architecture parlante*, like the so-called 'Revolutionary Architecture' of the eighteenth century. Unlike the designs of Ledoux and Boullée, however, the hybrid solutions of Expressionism could seldom be reduced to a single concept. They retained their diversity even when they were moulded by the motifs of mountain and cave, of tower and vault, or their intensification and combination in the crystal one could walk around in. In every case the conveyor of the expression – the building – must appear as a fully sculptured architectural entity. A sculptural effect was also usually aimed at in the demarcation between solid and void, divided between light and shade. Enclosed space itself was treated as positive sculptural form.

When it came to the actual building techniques used, German and Dutch Ex-

30. Hans Poelzig. Sketch (Festspielhaus, Salzburg), 1920.
31. Hans Poelzig. Porcelain wall light, *c.* 1920.

31

32. Hans Poelzig. Watercolour sketch, 1921.
Marlene Poelzig Collection, Hamburg.

pressionists preferred the arts and crafts tradition to modern technology. Relatively modern construction techniques might in fact be used, but they were always subordinated to the overall impression of uniqueness and individuality. Any suggestion of repetition and hence of industrialized manufacturing methods and rationalization was taboo. The Grosse Schauspielhaus was not reproduceable. It did not constitute a type. It was only itself. The 'addressee' of this kind of architecture was not – so the theory ran – the private employer, the individual institution, or a specific social class but a new (though not further defined) social conception of the people as a whole. In their most subjective creations, it was in the name of this concept of the people that Expressionist architects believed themselves to be acting.

This belief implied numerous contradictions. The architects of Expressionism wanted to be close to the people yet produced a highly individualistic 'art for artists'. They attempted to break through to an anonymous kind of architecture with which anyone might identify, yet their approach to this task led not to anonymity but to the kind of striking idea that was capable of catching the public eye. Like the reform-conscious members of the Jugendstil movement they wanted to right their period's most urgent wrongs. Yet they employed means which at best could only satisfy the sophisticated artistic needs of connoisseurs. That their architecture rested on insecure foundations is certain; but it is equally certain that the often bizarre and often extravagant imaginative power of their designs could have developed in no other way.

Background

1 Politics and society

'*Chaos is with us; there is a new and convulsive stirring abroad; spirits are awakening; souls are rising to responsibility and hands to do great deeds; may the fruit of revolution be rebirth.*'

Gustav Landauer, *Aufruf zum Sozialismus*, Foreword to the second edition, 3 January 1919

Architecture in the reign of Wilhelm II

In the years shortly after 1900 there emerged in Central Europe a condition of mutual tolerance, not to say outright complicity, between the leading classes of society as a whole and the avant-garde of architects and designers. Art Nouveau – in Germany Jugendstil – had had to rely on the sophisticated tastes of a few wealthy patrons. A good deal of the English Arts and Crafts movement and almost all the major achievements of continental Art Nouveau had been financed by individual members of the upper middle classes who had recognized no criterion of judgment outside their own subjective taste.[1] The desire for social reform which moved certain of the creators of this style was either tolerated or regarded as an added charm. Victor Horta may have designed a Maison du Peuple; he was nevertheless primarily the architect of the elegant town houses of Brussels. The fact that Art Nouveau was created by the two most highly industrialized nations of Europe, England and Belgium, had nothing to do with those countries' social problems – except in so far as the wealthy there were more open to new ideas, more active, and of course richer than anyone anywhere else.

The patrons of Art Nouveau – cultured and wealthy bankers and shipowners, aristocrats, gentlemen of private means, and the successful writers and artists who doubled as customers of their colleagues – dealt entirely on their own account and not in any way as representatives of the public. The physical delicacy and dubious morality of many products of the Art Nouveau movement – and these the most costly – was in almost direct proportion to the private standing of the people who had commissioned them. Without this air of fragile luxury the interest of such a clientèle would never have been captured. The most important architectural commissions of the period were private houses, the villas of wealthy patrons of the arts. In them all the other arts were involved as well.

The fact that this sociogram no longer holds good for the period 1900 to 1914 is something that has not escaped the notice of attentive observers of the German scene. (With certain differences of emphasis, the same could be said of the Netherlands.) The minority of outsiders began to give way to the opinion-forming and economically determinative managerial minority. The English architect, teacher and writer William Richard Lethaby saw German science and German architecture as marching side by side with German industry, on the road to world dominion, driven on by the desire to beat the competition on the world market.[2] State and culture in the Germany of Wilhelm II appeared to him to be identical. The spokesmen of the German Arts and Crafts movement did everything in their power to give substance to such assumptions.

Lethaby was writing as an Englishman under the influence of the early German successes in the First World War. But his viewpoint was shared by many. In a small provincial town in Switzerland, La Chaux-de-Fonds, the young Le Corbusier, a graduate of the local art school, was commissioned to write a study of the German reform movement. The impression of Germans that he gathered in 1910–11 was not unlike that of the older and more experienced Lethaby: 'During this period of creative development [of German crafts, the Germans] showed a great capacity for enthusiasm and enterprise, but most of all they showed discipline, an admirable sense of the practical and an intelligent opportunism . . . They posed as nationalists, socialists or im-

33

34

35

33. Peter Behrens. Mannesmann building, Düsseldorf, 1911–12.
34. Wilhelm Kreis. Rheinische Metallwaren- und Maschinenfabrik building, Düsseldorf, 1917.
35. Hans Hertlein. Wernerwerk M, Berlin-Siemensstadt, 1915–17.
36. Bruno Schmitz. Völkerschlacht memorial, Leipzig, 1898–1913.
37. Peter Behrens. AEG light engine factory, Berlin, 1910–11.
38. Peter Behrens. German Embassy, St Petersburg (Leningrad), 1911–12.

perialists, depending on the circumstances, and thus proved themselves at the same time shrewd speculators.'[3]

The individual promoter of the arts remained of course as important as before. His role, however, was now thought of in a different way. The most important patrons in 1910 were not concerned merely with satisfying their own inclinations; they saw themselves as responsible to the public, as an opinion-forming élite. Catering to their own taste for luxury, they believed themselves at the same time to be performing a culturally and politically worthy action, the benefits of which, thanks to the lower classes' propensity for imitation, would redound to the good of all. Aside from private collectors there were also such astute organizers as Eberhard von Bodenhausen, Count Harry Kessler and Walter Rathenau who provided a link between art and economics, and between art and politics. Many of these managers in the service of the muses were just as good at presiding over armaments factories as over art museums.

The new type was embodied at its most striking in the person of Karl Ernst Osthaus (1874–1921). This banker's son and millionaire from Hagen, with his Folkwang Museum, the touring exhibitions and lectures of his German Museum for Art in Commerce and Trade, the books put out by his publishing house, his architectural commissions, and his many contacts in industry and the political administration, had a highly impressive propaganda machine. Even the revolutionary artists who in 1918 banded together to form the Berlin Arbeitsrat für Kunst believed they could not get by without him. 'A fantastic metabolism. Despotic in taking – that he might be more generous in giving; strongly centered on his ego because it was an ego of his time', wrote a colleague after Osthaus' death.[4]

Under the influence of this active élite, big business started to take an interest in 'utilizing' artists. Anonymous firms began to hand out commissions. It is

significant that in the case of the most spectacular of these employments, the appointment of Peter Behrens (1868–1940) as artistic advisor and architect to the AEG or Allgemeine Electricitäts-Gesellschaft, it is impossible to determine who exactly was responsible.[5] A series of large and countless small firms followed suit, including Mannesmann and Continental with head offices also by Behrens; Siemens with the appointment of Hans Hertlein; and the Leonhard Tietz department store chain with commissions for Joseph Maria Olbrich and Wilhelm Kreis. The firm of Wertheim had already provided a much-copied example in Alfred Messel's loosely Gothic frame-building for their department store on the Leipziger Platz in Berlin. The heavily monumental, corporeal treatment of the building as a whole (rather than merely of the façades) for which the majority of these architects plumped seemed better suited than historicism both to the new scale on which such buildings were being erected and to the new context of competition and power that they represented (ills. 33–35).

The Kaiser and art

One name that was missing from the circle of patrons and promoters was that by which this period of German history is known – the name of Kaiser Wilhelm II (1859–1941). The Kaiser saw himself as the great protector of the arts, a Maecenas in the Renaissance mould. His bias in favour of a euphemistic type of art whose task it was to educate the

36

37

38

people towards ideals blinded him completely to the artistic strengths of his time. The sculptures of the Siegesallee, the new north-south axis of the Tiergarten in Berlin, were remarkable only as a piece of systematic political propaganda in favour of the Hohenzollern dynasty.

Wilhelm II's architectural ventures were no less unfortunate. Julius Raschdorff's Berlin cathedral, with its excessive detail and its poorly proportioned dome, and the prestige buildings erected in Berlin by the chief architectural advisor to the imperial court, Ernst von Ihne, were already condemned as signal failures by the more critical among their contemporaries. A church-building programme for the capital under the patronage of the Empress led to the creation of churches situated for maximum optical effect at the points of intersection of major vistas, rarely corresponding to the actual needs of the areas they had to serve.

The monuments erected by Bruno Schmitz (1858–1916) translated Wilhelm II's dashing imperial gestures into architectural terms. Schmitz was one of those talented men born out of their time.

Spoiled by success, full of ideas and a feeling for the magnificent, he did at least break out of the convention of stylistic imitation in his colossal monuments on the Kyffhäuser, on the Wittekindsberg near the Porta Westfalica, and on the Deutsche Eck, the tongue of land between Moselle and Rhine in Koblenz. In his Völkerschlacht memorial in Leipzig, commemorating the Battle of the Nations in October 1813 (ill. 36), Schmitz erected on an artificial mound a towering structure which is hollowed out inside in a vertical series of domed chambers – a combination of tower and cave that was to become a favourite of the Expressionists.

The Leipzig monument, complete with artificial lake, arena, and a seemingly endless approach axis, was intended as a temple of fame and a symbol of national power. Together with the tower-monuments to Kaiser Wilhelm I and Bismarck and the Jahrhunderthalle or Centennial Hall at Breslau, now Wroclaw (ills. 128, 140–142), it formed part of the architectural expression of a new political mythology that went back to the war of liberation of 1813 or to the founding of the Reich in 1871. In its monumental

effect and its illusive use of materials (reinforced concrete construction with porphyry facing) the Völkerschlacht memorial is a fitting embodiment of the spirit of Wilhelmine Germany.

Following the Kaiser's enforced abdication in 1918, artists and architects felt themselves liberated from an artistic dictatorship that had been directed against everything modern. In terms of their formal repertory, however, architects had thoroughly conformed to the imperial demands of the Reich. Fritz Hoeber, in his intelligent biography of Peter Behrens, is right to speak of national conservatism as constituting the soul of the St Petersburg embassy building (ill. 38).[6] From the sanctification of work which Behrens aimed at in his AEG buildings in Berlin to the sanctification of the state was but a step. The same colossal half-columns robbed of any kind of organic corporeality march along the St Petersburg embassy as along the AEG light engine factory in Berlin (ill. 37). Behrens asserted, 'German art and technology will thus work towards the one end: the power of the German nation.' So strongly was the embassy building regarded abroad as a provocation that the German business world feared a reaction in the export market.[7]

If the Kaiser failed to identify with the new kind of monumental art that emerged from the reforming efforts of the Jugendstil movement and confined his interests to the Academicists, the decision was purely a matter of the monarch's personal taste. Between the way the Reich was developing, with its urge to self-representation, and the aims of the Jugendstil designers there was no contradiction. The two could easily have reached a *modus vivendi*.

Even without the protection of the court and in spite of their differences of opinion with the traditionalists, the architects and craftsmen then regarded as progressive were able to feel altogether accepted and involved. Names like Behrens, Billing, Endell, Kreis, Möhring, Olbrich, Pankok, Paul, and Riemerschmid figured prominently in the German entries to the international exhibitions in Paris (1900), Turin (1902), St Louis (1904), Brussels (1910) and Ghent (1913). The Deutsche Werkbund, an association of artists, craftsmen, and industrialists founded in 1907 – the principal promoter of these architects' interests – put forward in a large number of discussions and publications the idea of artistic design as a factor of rising profits. The import and export quotas of the expanding German economy in the period immediately before the First World War exceeded those of England, France, and even the USA. The Werkbund, representing German arts and crafts, saw its mission as to consolidate and increase those quotas.

This argument had a certain tactical (though not only tactical) value as regarded manufacturers who were sympathetic to the Werkbund and who had to be won over to beauty of form. But if the artists concerned believed in the social effect of beauty of form on both the worker who produced it and the consumer who purchased it, they also believed in the legitimacy of the ambitions of the new German *imperium*. In the immediate pre-war years the conviction was widespread that the political and economic mastery of the world was about to be decided for a long time to come.

In a pamphlet distributed by the Werkbund, the liberal politician Friedrich Naumann spoke of economically decisive battles. The introductory essay in the Werkbund's first yearbook sought to establish the German 'taste industry' as a world power, and in an unfortunate moment in 1915 Hermann Muthesius (1861–1927), the driving force behind the Werkbund, allowed himself to be swayed into saying that German form must do more than conquer the world: it must give the world its image.[8] After the collapse of the Reich the Werkbund was rightly reproached for having acted not as the conscience of the nation but as a hustler for its industry.[9]

39. Johannes Itten. Announcement of the *Utopia* anthology, 1920.

Non-political socialism

In 1918 the hope of a rosy future as architects of a world power was finally destroyed. Dismissed from the service of the bourgeoisie, commerce, and industry, architects found themselves with no employers, no commissions, and no social standing. A new and greater hope then emerged, that of a rebirth of communal life which would involve at the same time a rebirth of architecture. If at first a considerable number of architects, particularly of the younger generation, gave their allegiance to the young republic, it was because they saw it not as a state represented by its privileged classes but as the people as a whole, the brotherhood of all creative workers. The political revolution and the artistic revolution were in their eyes one and the same. Architectural ideas were to spring from the consciousness of the masses. At times it is hard to avoid the impression that the political changes of November 1918 were regarded by artists merely as an opportunity to introduce the new style they had so long yearned for and demanded.

In the circumstances the new style appeared to be Expressionism. 'Expressionism is like socialism – the same outcry against materialism, against anti-mind, against the machine, against centralization, for mind, for God, for the human in man' (Herbert Kühn). The artist was regarded as the executive organ of the people's will, which did not prevent him being simultaneously and by the same authors cast in the role of leader and seer. 'Truly, invention has been taken entirely out of the architect's hands', wrote Adolf Behne. 'He stands there with an awesome freshness of mind and *builds*, builds what the masses as builders determine: he simply gathers together like a magnet the architectural images that emerge spontaneously from the people and makes them into a clear and holy vision.'[10]

This flush of enthusiasm in the first months following the revolution had nothing to do with any insight into political aims and strategy. The activist among the *literati*, Kurt Hiller, defined socialism as a sense of brotherhood rather than as a party doctrine. In this sense many architects were left-wing. The Taut brothers were involved in the trade-union movement. Bruno Taut hoped to be invited to join the cabinet of Kurt Eisner, the Independent Social Democrat prime minister of Bavaria, while advocating a 'socialism in the non-political supra-political sense'.[11] Taut's close friend and successor as chairman of the Berlin Arbeitsrat für Kunst, Walter Gropius, had already appropriated the maxim 'No politics for export' even before the party-political battles that broke out around the Bauhaus in Weimar and later in Dessau. Socialism he found 'so sullied by this mean and vulgar era and so utterly made a fool of that it will be a long time before it has removed this stain upon its name'.[12]

Erich Mendelsohn dreamed in similar terms of such a socialism as was not to be found in the commonplace round of party politics: 'Solidarity as combination of individualism and socialism.' 'Not party-political, whether Bolshevik or anything else, but human', was how Otto Bartning imagined the new community of men. Even Hans Poelzig spoke of the

rth-pangs of a new era – though he
mmediately dissociated himself from any
nd of political position, for 'the real
okesmen of a revolution are the weak'.
ernhard Hoetger, who within the space
 only a few years was responsible for
opagating a tribute to Hindenburg and
ecting a monument to the revolution,
fused to burden 'the pure genesis of
rm with a lot of sophisticated prob-
ms'.[13]

In strong contrast to these ideal
onceptions of a new society were the
ean little wishes to which architects
ave expression with regard to the state.
he universal brotherhood of man and
arrow sectional interest were by no
eans mutually exclusive. It was typical
f these artists' non-political way of
inking that they set all their hopes on
e people yet regarded the state as a
ecessary evil. For them it was good only
 the addressee of a long list of demands.
he state must provide the means yet
ostain from exercising any kind of con-
ol over the way in which those means
ere used. It must provide for the artist's
eeds, take care of his education, guaran-
e him commissions, place at his dis-
osal communal workshops in the form
f colonies, and establish 'experimental
tes'. But, Adolf Behne declared, 'Even
 the socialist state the artist is an
utsider. He belongs in the socially alive
ntity of the people! ... We for our part
ant to build as if the state did not exist
 all.'[14]

In its early years the young German
tate could do practically nothing for its
rchitects – and for the architects this
ircumstance was made even more
erious by the fact that their professional
risis dated back to the war years. Except
here directly related to wartime needs,
uilding had come to a more or less
omplete halt. An estimated average of
00,000 new homes were built per year in
he pre-war Reich; in 1918 the figure was
,800. In Berlin not one single residential
uilding was erected during 1917. Even
e subsidies voted by the Reichstag and
e Weimar National Assembly to ensure

that home-building would continue in
spite of inflationary building costs
changed little at first. There was a shortage of raw materials, especially coal. Of
the 18,000 brickworks in operation in
Germany before the war, only about 200
were still working in 1919. Although in
all other branches of the economy there
was full employment after the end of the
war and the total number of employed
was up to the pre-war figure, even as late
as 1924 the building industry was em-
ploying only 1.24 million workers, as
compared to 1.63 million in 1913.

Private architects were particularly
hard-hit by this development. 'My outward life is suspended in thin air like
Mohammed's coffin', Gropius wrote to
Poelzig in December 1918. 'I have
nothing to design with which I might
earn a penny. It's all come out the way I
said it would that time: we fools who
went out there and fought are having to
foot the lion's share of the bill.' Bruno
Taut's letters of 1919 reflect a picture of
dire distress: we find him not knowing
how he is ever going to make a living,
sitting 'all alone again, lost in the middle
of Berlin, at my drawing-board, now
become more of a desk', while his brother Max has three men – three! – in his
employ. Exile seemed the only way out.[15]
Architects who already enjoyed a measure of fame at that time took it. For men
at the beginning of their careers the
chances were virtually nil.

To these real difficulties were added
worries about the future structure of the
profession. The fear that the status of the
independent architect might be threatened by the architectural offices of building firms and of the governmental authorities preoccupied the Guild of Architects then as it had done for many
decades. At the end of 1918 – with the
prospect of a socialist republic and a
planned economy – it was particularly
acute, and it stood in the way of German architects' commitment to socialism
in these early days.

The Utopian projects that proliferated
in the immediate post-war years were the

result of this enforced idleness. The pressure of ideas that had been building up
for four or five years, ideas which stood
no chance of becoming a reality in any
foreseeable future, now finally erupted.
However deep their commitment, these
architects could not seriously believe that
they would ever come more than a step
or two closer to the exaggerated future of
their designs. Yet on the other hand a
lively imagination was necessary to come
to terms with the reality of a defeated
post-war Germany, politically as well as
economically disorganized.

The schizophrenic character of this
situation comes out in most of the
designs. The architects of Expressionism
believed in artistic, social, and sometimes
even religious rebirth, and at the same
time they had their doubts. Resignation,
and even occasionally a touch of black
humour, were mixed in with their highflown plans. 'May this be a magnet, the
snowflake that starts the avalanche!' was
how Taut harangued his friends as he
started the 'Glass Chain' exchange of
letters at the end of 1919 (see pp. 92ff.). But
he added, 'If it is no more, if I am wrong,
then it will at least be, for each of us, a
beautiful memorial.'[16]

This totally unrealistic kind of imagination, without which we cannot talk in
terms of an Expressionist architecture at
all, was again, in the last resort, dependent upon the wealthy patrons and influential firms who had supported the
monumental reformist art of the pre-
war period. The Hanover cake-manu-
facturer Bahlsen and the Bremen coffee-
importer Roselius, who made Bernhard
Hoetger's architectural career possible;
the Mosse newspaper concern that scent-
ed the publicity potential of Erich Mendelsohn's brilliant signature; the Berlin
building-contractor and timber-mer-
chant Adolf Sommerfeld, who took part
in the high jinks of the Bauhaus rite;
Max Reinhardt, owner of private theatres; the Farbwerke Hoechst and the firm
of Stumm in Düsseldorf in whose service
Behrens and Bonatz forged the vocabulary of Expressionism into imposing

commercial prestige buildings; the Hamburg group that erected a new office quarter; the wealthy patrons of the Anthroposophists; the Kröller-Müllers, with their feudal building projects, in Holland – where in all this was 'the people' whose 'total will' architects wished to realize? Only in the Netherlands did local authorities commission architects to any notable extent in the immediate post-war years. In Germany the few residential buildings erected during this period were simply continuations on an extremely modest scale of projects begun before the war.

Back to the soil

All the experts agreed, however, that low-cost housing should be given priority. There must be a housing drive as a kind of 'internal colonization'. The Guidelines for the Treatment of Subsidy Applications of 6 July 1919, which governed in Germany the granting of subsidies to cover the increasing cost of building, laid down that small houses and low-rise buildings were to receive preferential treatment. At the beginning of the same year the government had passed a law allowing for the resettlement of a large part of the population in rural areas. No less than a million new agricultural enterprises were planned to cater for approximately six million inhabitants.

There were reasons for the pessimism that found expression in these measures. There seemed to be no future for the industrial city; in fact it even appeared to be doomed to decay. The German economy had become more than unstable. It was threatened with endless reparation payments and had to accept the loss of important sources of raw materials. By the Treaty of Versailles Germany lost almost 75% of all its iron-ore deposits and 26% of its coal.

Thus psychologically, a return to the land seemed the only practicable solution. Village-style settlements, economically autonomous agricultural townships or rather residential quarters where the workers produced a part of their own food themselves, were now the goal to be striven for. 'Only a rural resettlement movement on a massive scale can save us now!' thought Hans Kampffmeyer, general secretary of the German Garden City Association.[17] The memory of the 'turnip winters' of the war years was so much in everybody's bones that slogans like 'Be self-supporting!' achieved a measure of popularity. They were none the less unrealistic. When, following the inflation, the market took a turn for the better for a few years and the economy of the republic appeared to be finding its feet, it was not thanks to the efforts of the agricultural sector but to those of industry.

However explicable in terms of the current emergency, the social and town-planning programme of 1918–19 had a long background of preparation behind it in the garden city movement, with the same conflicting motives underlying both. The garden city style settlement of freehold homes was among the aims of far-seeing capitalists as well as committed socialists. Alfred Krupp was just as enthusiastic an advocate of it as Karl Liebknecht. It is significant that in his book *Die Auflösung der Städte* ('The Dissolution of Cities') of 1920 Bruno Taut was able to call upon witnesses of the most diverse origins. He quoted not only the liberal-socialist protagonist of the garden city idea, Franz Oppenheimer, but also the French politician Jules Méline, an opponent of any kind of 'agrarian socialism'. The one was for the workers' government resorting to expropriation which, by bringing about a redistribution of agrarian property, could lead to a renewal of society as a whole. The other hoped that capitalists would come round to the view that they could get a higher return on agricultural investment than they could on investment in industry.[18]

Hatred of existing cities, those 'demonic deserts of stone', in Spengler's phrase, was the rule as far as the right wing was concerned but it was also strongly present among men of the lef Ebenezer Howard, who started the ide of the garden city, had only objected t overpopulated cities and not to cities a such. Here the German Garden Cit Association followed him: its statute spoke of 'urban type' and 'urban life But manufacturers like Lever and Cad bury in England and Krupp in German had seen another side to the garden cit type of settlement. Their fear that work ers who did not own the land they live on might be more accessible to revolu tionary ideas was still present in th consideration that was given to the gai den city at the end of the war. A contem porary commentary on the trend fo firms to move out into the countr noted: it 'must not be forgotten that th over-politicization of the worker in th big city through frequent shop-floc meetings and strikes makes it much ha der to maintain a constant level of pro duction than in places where anxiet regarding food and lodging is less pro minent.'[19] Similar fears governed th beginnings of national life in post-wa Germany. It was not merely for symboli reasons that the National Constituer Assembly of the Weimar Republic wa summoned at the scene of Goethe's an Schiller's finest hours; this comfortabl central German town was a safer place t meet than the politically turbulent capi tal.

The marriage of the garden city move ment and the heightened need for expres sion that now preoccupied architects an their employers was not without conflic In his Egyptian-influenced designs fo the TET town that Hermann Bahlse wanted to build in Hanover (ills 304–306), the sculptor and amateu town planner Bernhard Hoetger base the residential quarter rigorously on th symbolic devices of the firm in a way i which the capitalists of the post-187 'Gründerzeit' period, for all their ex perience in dealing with dependents would never have dared to do. Th ideologically-oriented community a Dornach (ills. 332–358) came in for a n less severe piece of stylistic constraint. A crowning monumental building drawing the residential areas together into an aesthetic unit and a symbolic commitment was something that neither Hellerau near Dresden, nor Dornach, nor the plans for Osthaus' garden city Hohenhagen were without.

The stylistic inclinations of this generation, its delight in the vertical and its predilection for loading things with meaning, conflicted with the pragmatic conception of the garden city spreading in the horizontal plane. Architects probed and pounded the rational arguments of the garden city tradition for their irrational overtones. In the garden city expert Hans Kampffmeyer's publication *Friedenstadt*, for example, the landscape-architect Leberecht Migge spoke of the 'rejuvenation of the ancient, sacred soil'. Bruno Taut struck the same solemn note in *Die Auflösung der Städte* and *Alpine Architektur*. The title vignette of Kampffmeyer's 1918 edition depicts the sun of the future rising; in Taut's *Die Stadtkrone* of 1919 it beams with even greater promise; and on both occasions what it glorifies is a towered silhouette that has little to do with the reality of the garden city (ills. 40, 41).[20]

This tension between the demand for re-agrarianization and the fascination with the city and all it meant is clearly traceable in Taut's publications (see pp. 78 ff.). However highly people of the period extolled the restorative power of rural life, even critics of the city succumbed to the attraction of metropolitan life. The modern age is permeated not only by a tradition of hostility to the city, but also by a delight in romanticizing the city as the work of the Devil – witness the countless reports of German travellers returning from visits to New York and Chicago after the war, Oswald Spengler's *The Decline of the West*, and Fritz Lang's film *Metropolis* (ills. 43, 44, 415).

The art historian Fritz Burger, for example, let himself be carried away by a vision which is the German Romantic counterpart to the Italian Futurists' idea

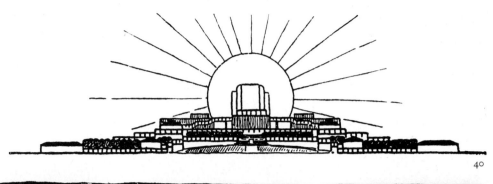

40

41

40. Bruno Taut. Illustration from *Die Stadtkrone*, Jena, 1919.

41. Title vignette from Hans Kampffmeyer's *Friedenstadt*, 2nd ed., Jena, 1918.

of the city (ill. 42): the new generation's 'fairy-tales are no longer set in the mysterious gloom of the lonely forest but in the labyrinthine bustle of the big city, where the buildings become gigantic Towers of Babel, in an ocean of stone where millions of people utilize the miraculous forces of nature to fly with dizzying speed from one place to another and the mind of man takes its daily stroll in the deepest recesses of the earth and out among the stellar expanses, daily returning, heavy-laden with discoveries and treasures, to tell the astonished world of the magical power of organized intellect.'[21] In the pages of the *Handbuch der Kunstwissenschaft*, in which Burger's essay appeared, such intemperate flights of fancy look strange indeed.

Not until the period of political, economic, and intellectual sobering-down

around 1923–24 did the tangle of ideas to which every advocate of the garden city of whatever school had contributed his particular thread begin to sort itself out. The architects who subscribed to the new architectural ideals of the late twenties freed themselves from the anti-technological and anti-urban climate of opinion which had been the natural consequence of the first fully technological war in history. The kind of modern settlements that were built at this time no longer denied their urban character. For all their green, sunny, and airy character, these are urban residential areas, renouncing all spectacular excesses in the shape of crystal houses or anything of the kind.

The coalition of unequal partners in which during the second decade of the century such traditional builders as Bes-

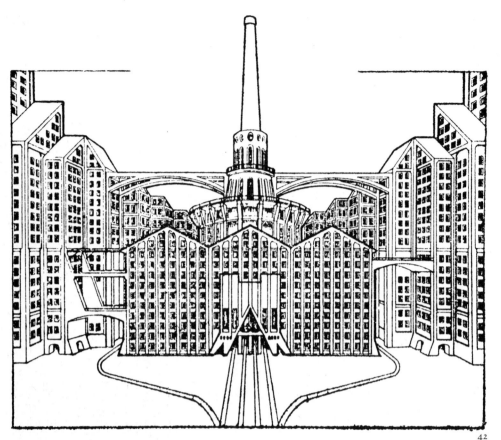

42. Virgilio Marchi. Factory, from *Architettura futurista*, Foligno, 1924.
43. Otto Hunte, Erich Kettelhut and Karl Vollbrecht. Film set for *Metropolis*, directed by Fritz Lang, 1926.

43

telmeyer, Bonatz, Theodor Fischer, Schmitthenner, Schultze-Naumburg, Fritz Schumacher, and Tessenow, and such politically left-wing planners as Hans and Bernhard Kampffmeyer, May, Bruno Taut, and Martin Wagner sought apparently identical goals (ills. 45–48) broke up again during the twenties. The catchword of fidelity to the soil and the belief in the regenerative power of rural resettlement now moved over into the conservative camp from which they were picked up by the National Socialists. Heralded by the emergency decrees of the Brüning cabinet in 1931, re-agrarianization became one of the first demands of the Nazi Kampfbund of German architects and engineers. Bruno Taut's call, echoed by his like-minded friends, for a dilution of the great cities, and even for their dissolution, cropped up again in the vocabulary of the Nazi Commissar for Resettlement, Gottfried Feder.[22]

The new craft romanticism

In the period following the First World War; a chance of survival seemed to be offered not only by a return to the soil but also by a revival of handicrafts. Expressionist architecture went hand in hand with a boom in the craft industries; when the avant-garde later began to lose interest in the craft industries, Expressionism's days were also numbered. The attitude of the Jugendstil artists towards this question had been ambivalent. They extolled the aesthetic of the machine, yet they designed principally for manual methods of production. In the period that followed, the propaganda of the Deutsche Werkbund brought about a greater acceptance of industrial production in Germany. 'Our whole national export planning is dependent on the machine because the world market will tolerate only standardized goods... What we need is large-scale industrial production, not the magic of the small workshop, the zeal of the individual craftsman, and the good old craft traditions' (Friedrich Naumann).[23]

In 1920, however, having dealt in its previous yearbooks with industry, commerce, and transport, the Werkbund devoted its sixth yearbook to *Arts and Crafts Past and Present*, as something of topical importance. The very same Peter Behrens who in 1910 had denounced all romantic day-dreaming and as late as 1919 had spoken out against a 'retrogression from industrial mass-production to handicrafts' was by 1922 promoting handicrafts and romanticism as the things that made life bearable.[24] This attempt to turn back the clock constituted Expressionism's reactionary side. Its progressive aspect was yoked to a pessimism about the future of civilization – something the Expressionists shared with critics of the modern period.

The motives behind this revaluation of handicrafts, made urgently topical, in Otto Bartning's phrase, by the 'holy and bitter suffering of these times [of war]',[25] go back a long way. That hand-made products gave more satisfaction to both producer and consumer than industrial products had been one of the tenets of the English Arts and Crafts movement. Handwork was to abolish the ill-effects of industrial production with its excessive division of labour and the evils of the competitive economy and the quantitative output principle: it was to do away with exploitation. The argument was of course illogical: exploitation lay not in the separation of design from execution, but in the control of the means of production and ownership of the goods produced.

At the same time intensive manual processing of the material available was thought to offer a way out of the calamitous situation whereby, despite the shortage of raw materials that followed the war she had lost, Germany had to export more than before. Already before 1914, the best opportunities for export had been seen to lie in the labour-intensive industries. Then, however, the stress had been on the solidity and design quality of mass-produced goods. The fact that individually finished, expensive works of craftsmanship

could only count on the interest of connoisseurs and stood no chance whatever on the world market was simple economic common sense. But now, after the war, the voice of common sense was seldom heard. In an almanac of 1919, where Chancellor Philipp Scheidemann rightly recommended work-saving methods and scientific, technological planning as weapons against the crisis that threatened, Walter Gropius extolled the people's native resilience as a source of inspiration for future production.[26]

Rational and irrational arguments were closely bound up together. Delight in the personal; the beauty of the simple and noble; handicrafts as a question of outlook, as a safeguard against the swindle of civilization; spiritual enrichment through working with the hands – such were the catchwords of the period. Such different temperaments as Hans Poelzig, Josef Hoffmann, and the Futurist Virgilio Marchi all subscribed to the opinion that the challenge to the worker represented by original work depending on thoughtful co-operation led to increased output and, as Poelzig put it, to 'playing as part of the orchestra'.[27] The long-term goal was to lead the worker by way of handicrafts to art, and to transform art from something which a few specialists produced for the benefit of a few enthusiasts to something which everyone produced for the benefit of all. Anyone who got left by the wayside still had the possibility of earning his daily bread as a skilled, high-quality craftsman.

In this way, it was hoped, the problem of the artist-proletariat which had been raised as early as the eighteenth century and had preoccupied the whole of the nineteenth century would be solved.[28] There have been complaints about the excessive numbers of artists and the inability of the art market to support them all in every country in Europe in every century. In an era of threatened poverty these inevitably took on a special urgency. Handicrafts were to free the artist from worry as to where his next meal was coming from. Art was no

44

44. A vision of New York in the future, from Erich Mendelsohn's *Russland Europa Amerika*, Berlin, 1929.

longer distinguished from craft in principle but only in degree. In handicrafts art was to hibernate through the winter like the butterfly in its cocoon. Kurt Eisner, prime minister of Bavaria in the winter of 1918–19, saw the existence of the new artist-craftsman in these terms: '[I have] begun to wonder whether the creative artist ought not in fact to take as his point of departure his own craft, whether he ought not to found his economic existence on that – the sculptor, for example, as stone-mason – turning his attention to works of art only in the leisure-hours of his inspiration, when he need be under no obligation to complete them in haste within the space of twenty-four weeks in order to earn his living, but could often work on them for years at a stretch.'[29]

In the context of this climate of ideas the spotlight of topicality fell on those art-educational reform proposals which attached importance to craft training. These applied both to art schools and to general schools. 'Ultimately our children will build us as craftsmen a world of small towns that will be characterized by great external modesty and yet be the product of the highest skill, a world so rich and splendid and wonderful that nothing can compare with it', dreamed Heinrich Tessenow.[30] The Bauhaus became the most publicized exponent of this craft-based teaching (see pp. 107ff.).

Surprisingly, the question whether the social problem had not merely been shifted from one professional bracket to another never cropped up in these debates about artists and craftsmen, about academies and masters' workshops. A craftsman-proletariat threatened to take the artist-proletariat's place. Possibly the policy of protection of craft industries and small businesses which had been pursued in Germany since Bismarck's time contributed to the exaggerated overestimate of the economic efficiency of production by hand.

The chief reason why handicrafts were so highly regarded by artists and architects was that they seemed to guarantee contact with the people. This *Volk*, closer sociological examination of which was never attempted, was to be the soil from which the culture of the future would spring. To it were attributed, by Adolf Behne, a 'hearty and vigorous feeling for form', 'bold, powerful colour', a pleasure in 'attractively alive outlines', and a 'delight in the novel and surprising'. The fact that these qualities had been abstracted from works of folk-art which had long since passed into history was ignored. Like the return to the soil, the return to handicrafts implied a romantic search for origins, a reversion to the conservative Utopia. Thus for example people believed they could detect an increased use of dialects, an increase in provincialization, and they regarded this as something positive. Many shared the opinion of Eckart von Sydow, one of the first chroniclers of Expressionism, that the precondition of renewal lay in this 'return . . . to the earliest origins . . . to the primitive roots of mankind, in order to arrive on this basis at a higher and truer culture'.[31]

In the creative arts these demands took the form of an interest in folk-graphics, glass-painting, and exotic cultures. In architecture they led to an emphasis on the craft element which went beyond any kind of rational argument. Whereas the Italian Futurists and later the Russian Constructivists, starting from different national experiences, sang the praises of the machine and of technology, in Central Europe it was the preachers of a dignified poverty and a modest simplicity who made their voices heard.

In Germany the chief of these voices was that of Heinrich Tessenow (1876–1950), whose designs for houses were thought to be 'like folk-songs'. In his Spartan or idyllic drawings, with their sparsely distributed dots and dashes, and in his treatises that even the layman could understand he taught his contemporaries what a doorstep, a door, a window, a staircase, and a portico were (ills. 45, 49). And although his discipline and asceticism with regard to anything 'out of the

45

46

47

48

49

dinary' were not to the taste of the irited younger generation, his doctrine at redemption lay in handicrafts and at the workshop was more important an the studio echoed their own convic-ons.

Conformity of opinion on this ques-on went so far that even an architect as nsitive to the dynamics of modern life Erich Mendelsohn fitted out the Al-ed Einstein astrophysical laboratory at otsdam with little rooms which would ve provided the ideal set for a Ufa film out the life of Copernicus (ill. 50). ter Behrens, in his 'Scholar's Study', mbined such 'technological' details as ms suspended by wires from the ceil-g with other elements of grotesque edievalism (ill. 51).

During the twenties Behrens lost his ce sure feeling for avant-garde posi-ns. The crudely assembled and carved rnishings of his Study, displaying ces of their hand-made origins, date m 1923, the year in which Gropius mmitted the Weimar Bauhaus to the w formula 'Art and Technology' (rath-than 'Art and Handicrafts'). How arly the Bauhaus, which had itself len for it, now saw the problems of the ndicrafts renaissance, is apparent from marks made by the painter Oskar hlemmer as early as June 1922: 'We

can and may practise only what is most real . . . Away with medievalism, then, and the medieval concept of handicrafts and ultimately with handicrafts them-selves, as mere training and means for the purposes of form.'[32]

One practical result of socialist reform-ing efforts and the cult of medievalism was the appearance of socialized building firms, which arose out of the initiative of the building unions. A model was pro-vided by the medieval masons' lodges, from which the new corporations derived their evocative name, *Bauhütte*. Gropius even called his Weimar institute a 'lodge' at first.[33] The principle of free competi-tion was maintained. Workers and em-ployees, however, were represented on management bodies and received a share of the net profits. The first *Bauhütte* was formed in Berlin in 1919. It and all subsequent foundations were regarded with suspicion by private building con-tractors. Most of their jobs came from communal resettlement co-operatives.[34]

The hope of cultural improvement which was associated with the new lodges met of course with only a modest fulfilment, and the expectation of full socialization in the future came to nothing at all. All that remained was a legacy of union involvement in the build-ing trade.

50

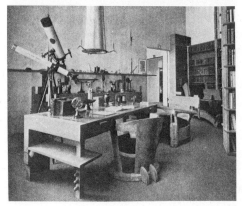

51

50. Erich Mendelsohn. Einstein Tower, Pots-dam, 1917–21. Living room.
51. Peter Behrens. Scholar's Study, 1923.

2 Beliefs and writings

'Life wants to raise itself on high with pillars and steps; it wants to gaze into the far distance and out upon joyful splendour – that is why it needs height!'

Friedrich Nietzsche, *Thus Spake Zarathustra* ('Of the Tarantulas')

The architect as lord of the arts

Expressionism constituted a decisive phase in the history of the architectural profession. It was probably the last time when the members of the profession felt themselves to be a community of the chosen, probably the last time when they surrendered themselves to the cult of genius with a clear conscience. Two of the major architects who carried the message of the New Architecture into the second half of the century, Le Corbusier and, to an even greater extent, Frank Lloyd Wright, did invoke for themselves the myth of the chosen artist. But Le Corbusier and Wright were solitary figures. Their isolation derived – it seems today – not least from the anachronistic elements in their work.

In the Expressionist period, a whole generation held the view that the architect worked under the influence of inspiration. There was a boom in irrationalism. Biographies adopted the pattern of hagiographies. Hermann Obrist, a Munich Jugendstil artist who had some influence on the Expressionists, suffered from his student days until the end of his life from hallucinations, in which individual buildings and even whole towns appeared to him and an inner voice enjoined him to 'Go and build this!'. The painter and architectural visionary, Hermann Finsterlin, received his call in the traditional setting for the prophetic vocation: in the remote solitude of the mountains, the moonlit Watzmann near Berchtesgaden. In the case of Otto Bartning, who in 1917 referred to the silent hours of work as a 'mystery', inspiration came with musical accompaniment: for a

52. Erich Mendelsohn. *Domine te*, pencil sketch, 1920s. Louise Mendelsohn Collection, San Francisco.

whole day during a trip round the world made in his youth he heard the message, 'Build towers, build towers'. With Erich Mendelsohn too, music – preferably Bach – served to stimulate the flow of ideas (ill. 52). In his letters from the trenches he tells of inspirations received from a 'supramundane' source. 'The visions are once more behind every ring of light and every corpuscle in my closed eye.'[1] Eye-witnesses of the erection of the first Goetheanum at Dornach describe work on the site in terms of a second miracle of Pentecost.

The patterns of experience employed were not always of so obviously sacred a character. But it was generally held that the great achievements of architecture had not been attained by rational means, and neither could they be so judged. 'Beethoven and norms! That for me represents the complete denial of any kind of higher thought in architecture and town-planning', was Osthaus' horrified reaction to the demand that town-planning should take account of statistical data. Hans Poelzig, visiting Mirabell and Hellabrunn and contemplating the panorama of the Salzburg Alps, felt himself caught up in 'a more or less mild frenzy that drove everything from his mind save the thought of how he could contribute to this world of shapes something of the same character, even an intensification'.[2]

It was not only the young who hoped for this great art-architecture to come: even the older practitioners paid at least lip-service to the idea. The proclamation 'Deutsche Architekten!', of 1919, which demanded in almost identical terms as Gropius that the architect be re-enthroned, 'as once in great days gone by', as 'leader and lord of all artists', bore the signatures of, among others, Peter Behrens and German Bestelmeyer.[3]

The architect as lord of the arts – the thought may be found in almost every proclamation of the period. It arose naturally out of the belief in the artist-architect's supernatural endowments. The man who appealed to higher inspiration must inevitably demand the place that matched his calling. 'He who will not be a leader is no architect', wrote Adolf Behne in 1919, praising Bruno Taut.[4] The blend of humility and presumption which characterizes the manifestos on this subject has its origin in the double function which architects attributed to themselves. They regarded themselves as mediums who, as the philosopher Henri Bergson – an important figure for the Expressionists – put it, grasped the forces of life in a 'state of perfect submission'.[5] From this experience they drew their active role as chosen executors of the life-will. The fact that this missionary consciousness was not matched by any real influence led to frustration, which moved the more active and critical of the architects to revise their position.

Similar demands were also put forward by artists in other disciplines: writers, painters, and sculptors had no less exalted a view of their role. 'Long live the leader! Long live the man of letters!' cried Ludwig Rubiner, and the painter Ludwig Meidner wrote, 'We are light and wise and must wave like banners before our heavy brethren' (the workers).[6] The architects, however, had an advantage over their colleagues: they were able to back up their claim to leadership with a striking example from history. The figure of the medieval cathedral-builder was more vivid than the models cited by writers and artists – the poet-priest of antiquity or the carver of primitive idols.

Added to this there was the argument that architecture is more closely and effectively related to life. The Expressionists were not only convinced of the power of expression of the architectural medium: they also placed a high value on the psychological effect of their buildings. It was a creed of the Expressionist Utopia that the well-built town ennobled those who lived in it. 'In the last analysis every art is a sculpting of the human being. Architecture is most powerfully and obviously so', observed Adolf Behne, again in the context of a eulogy of Bruno Taut.[7]

Mysticism and the religious Utopia

Architects had much too high an opinion of their mission to believe that it could be fulfilled in the immediate present. An unknown religion of the future in which the new art would find its first true realization was a theme treated by poets and painters, by philosophers and critics alike – Kasimir Edschmid and Franz Marc, Gustav Landauer and Leopold Ziegler, Adolf Behne, Walter Curt Behrendt, Paul Fechter, and Herman Sörgel; and of course by architects – Bartning, Berlage, who nourished the hope of a 'Christendom of this earth', de Bazel, Mendelsohn, Migge, Bruno Taut, Wijdeveld. 'Wherever a new saving truth, a new religious idea is born, there too the swing to art is most likely to take place, for art is none other than the transforming of supramundane thoughts into objects of sensory perception' (Walter Gropius).[8]

This type of thinking led easily to the old tripartite pattern of eschatology: 1, the lost Paradise, which in the eyes of architects was represented by India or the Gothic period (see pp. 50ff.); 2, the chaotic present, marred by intellect, competitive strife, and profit-oriented thinking; 3, the new era to come, the rebirth,

the age of the spirit, of faith, of love, the communion of peoples, and all the other chiliastic expectations of the post-war period. Significantly, the images used to describe the age to come were taken from the fund of religious metaphor. In his book *Die Stadtkrone* Bruno Taut took up a text of Erich Baron, who saw shining before him the 'battlements of the eternal city', the New Jerusalem of the Apocalypse. Hans Hansen, who was active in the Berlin Arbeitsrat für Kunst, mentioned in his *Das Erlebnis der Architektur* (ill. 53) the guiding star in the Christmas story, which he believed he could see.

It was Walter Gropius above all who thought about the present, the in-between period. His contribution to the pamphlet that accompanied the Arbeitsrat für Kunst's exhibition in April 1919 drew a distinction, despite its incantatory language, between 'longing for the stars' and 'day-to-day work'. Ideas might be condemned to death if they once became compromises, but their *un*compromising realization was something he saw no

53. Title vignette from Hans Hansen's *Das Erlebnis der Architektur*, Cologne, 1920.

chance of at that moment in history. He did not expect to see the 'better times to come' in his own lifetime.

As guiding maxims in what Gropius called the 'night of chaos', the artist-architects of Expressionism looked for preference to the pronouncements of the mystics. In this choice they again followed the writers, who had, out of a variety of motives but with unvarying intensity, been pursuing a dialogue with mysticism since the time of the Symbolists. 'Renounce yourself! Destroy yourself!' was Hans Hansen's formula for the mystical *terminus technicus* of the 'dark night', that painful condition of alienation from God which the mystics saw as the test and precondition for the renewal of mind and spirit. For Gropius it was a question of wiping out 'the curse of presumption in spiritual things'.[9]

The teaching practices of those years, particularly Johannes Itten's preliminary course at the Bauhaus, can be seen in terms of techniques for this 'renunciation of self' (see p. 110). Bruno Taut regarded his glass houses of prayer (ills. 55, 159, 160) as the empty vessels of a faith yet unknown, because in the view of the mystics the return of the divine presupposed emptiness and silence. Taut referred explicitly to Meister Eckhart: 'Were I empty and pure, God would have to come to me out of his own nature and be enclosed within me.'[10]

In these years Taut often called upon the mystics as witnesses – Eckhart, Henry Suso, Jakob Böhme, Sister Hadewych. What he found in their works, and also in the popular *Das Büchlein vom Leben nach dem Tod* by Gustav Theodor Fechner (1836, fourth edition 1900, English translation 1882), was a feeling of universality and timelessness that removed the boundaries between life and death. Taut related this to the specific experience of the inspired artist. In negative theology the concept of nothing describes the Absolute, the totally Other that eludes all positive assertion. For Taut this Other was also the New to which the true artist aspired. Death as the end of limitation is

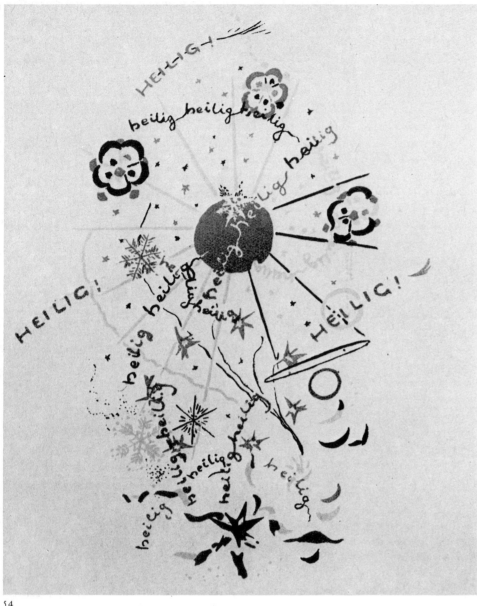

the true life. 'Art seeks to be an image of death', he wrote, 'to furnish the threshold at which mean preoccupation with earthly things dissolves in contemplation of that which opens up beyond death.' Beyond this 'mean preoccupation with earthly things' the artist was granted the vision of a union with each and all. The artist 'assigns everything to its place ... Light casts its radiance over all ... The earth itself sparkles with the New; as the impossible becomes possible, "hard" reality yields up miracles'. Poelzig, who disagreed with Taut in many respects, here concurred: 'Form arises out of the mystic abyss.'[11]

This feeling of an all-embracing unity – an anticipation of what a more circumspect mind like Walter Gropius attributed only to a future epoch of world history – gave rise to a pragmatic faith that took the form of earth – and star – worship. The penultimate page of Taut's *Die Auflösung der Städte* (ill. 54) shows a dance of orbiting spheres and stars that might as easily represent the microcosm of the atom as the macrocosm of the universe. Incorporated in the drawing are the words from the *Sanctus:* 'Holy, holy, holy!' But with Bruno Taut they applied to the world, not to the Lord God of Hosts.

A shrine of gleaming crystal

Sister Hadewych, the medieval Flemish mystic quoted by Taut in his magazine *Frühlicht* ('Early Light'), saw in visions a crystal cross and a seat set on three columns which suggested precious stones. She interpreted the vision as symbolizing eternity and the three persons of the Godhead – one of the many 'precious-stone' teachings that have cropped up in the wake of mysticism since the Middle Ages. The Biblical basis was provided primarily by the Song of Songs and the final chapters of the Revelation of St John which depict the new Jerusalem – 'the city was pure gold, clear as glass' – and 'the river of the water of life, bright as crystal'.

54

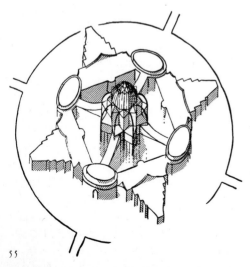

54. Bruno Taut. *Heilig! Heilig! Heilig!*, from *Die Auflösung der Städte*, Hagen, 1920.
55. Bruno Taut. Crystal building, from *Stadtbaukunst alter und neuer Zeit. Frühlicht*, 1, no. 1, 1920.
56, 57. Wassili Luckhardt. 'Crystal on the Sphere', *c.* 1920. Project for a religious building (second version), wax crayon. View and section. Wassili Luckhardt Collection, Berlin.

55

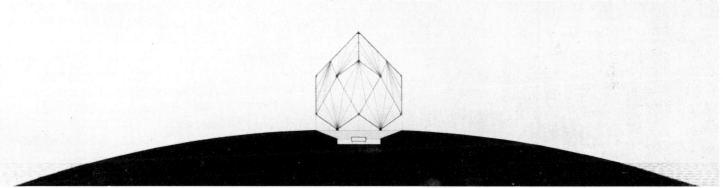

For the Expressionists the crystal, whatever they may have understood by the word, represented the ultimate, the supreme. In Ernst Toller's play *Die Wandlung* ('The Transformation'), of 1919, there opens before us 'The lofty vaulted door of the cathedral of mankind / The youth of all nations step ablaze / Up to the shrine of gleaming crystal glimpsed in the night'. The playwright Lothar Schreyer, who taught on occasion at the Bauhaus, mentions a whole range of things which the prismatic dissection of natural appearances in the crystal meant to him: annunciation of the 'world of symbol', landscape of the soul, bridge to the supernatural, vessel of the divine.[12] Architects and architectural writers too – Bartning, Behne, Gropius, von Sydow, Taut – used the word 'crystalline' in this vague, ecstatic sense. As late as 1924 the Dutch magazine *Wendingen* devoted a double issue to the crystal (ill. 59).

The iconographical meaning of the crystal symbol is best illustrated in a passage by the editor of *Wendingen*, Hendrikus Theodorus Wijdeveld. Wijdeveld speaks of the crystal's property of showing its inner core in the facets of its external form: the core, he maintains, consists of no more than its form. The crystal conceals nothing. Its secret lies in its transparency. Its surfaces reflect the light of the external world. 'We want to crystallize the infinity of the cosmos and give expression to it in form.'[13] The crystal is the emptiness in which the Whole is mirrored – a suitable symbol not only for the Expressionists' penchant for mysticism but also for that specifically Expressionist non-religious religiousness. In Bruno Taut's crystalline temples man seeks in his 'great perceptions' to embrace the universal and is at the same time overwhelmed by the object his vague belief has conjured up (ills. 55, 159, 160). He is the great solitary and the tiny speck of dust lost in the cosmos.

58

There were precedents for the crystal-mania of Expressionism. In the nineteenth century there was a revival of interest in the legend of the Grail, which in several of the medieval epics was characterized as a mysterious, miracle-working stone. In the Romantic period, the writers Fouqué and Uhland and the artist Sulpiz Boisserée had turned to the subject of the Grail. With the first performance of Richard Wagner's *Parsifal* in 1882, the motif became familiar to a wider public. In Art Nouveau and right up into the twenties the Grail legend enjoyed great popularity: there were Grail leagues, Grail societies, Grail foundations, and even a Grail press.[14] The ancient epics of the Grail were brought out in new editions or translated into modern German, among them the *Jüngere Titurel*, in which the Grail is represented as an enormous, cosmic, circular temple.

At the opening ceremony of the Darmstadt artists' colony in 1901 a 'prophet' bore a mysterious object referred to as 'The Sign'. This turned out to be a large crystal, and was clearly intended as a symbol of the miracle-working nature of art. Peter Behrens used the crystal motif several times in his book-illustrations of this period, and even used it as a symbol in his own ex-libris (ill. 58). This interpretation as confined to art was completed in a moral sense primarily by the writer Paul Scheerbart. Scheerbart and the architects and critics of Bruno Taut's circle were tireless in their praise of the

58. Peter Behrens. Ex-libris, *c.* 1920.
59. B. Essers. Vignette, from Wendingen, VI, nos. 11–12, 1924.

59

purity, clarity, precision, ennobling effect, and redeeming power of crystalline matter – and at a pinch even of glass.

The purely aesthetic properties of crystalline structures fascinated artists – and architects of course included themselves in this category. Wilhelm Worringer, in his influential book *Abstraktion und Einfühlung* ('Abstraction and Empathy') of 1908, wrote of absolute form that it finds expression in life-denying, inorganic, crystalline form. Geometrical regularity he regarded (wrongly, as Kandinsky was very soon to show) as abstraction pure and simple. In it, he maintained, man strove for deliverance from all fortuitous contingency.

Crystalline forms, star-shaped plans, and decorative elements drawn from the mineral world are legion in the years of Expressionism (ills. 60–68). Wenzel August Hablik, a member of the Arbeitsrat für Kunst, was particularly systematic in his use of forms based on crystals. He joined cubes, hexahedrons, and octahedrons, linking them by other prismatic shapes, and thus designed novel towers and domes (ills. 220–222). Hablik wanted to replace the verb 'to build' by 'to crystallize'.

Within Taut's circle of friends it was Hermann Finsterlin who rebelled against the supremacy of crystalline stereometry, because he felt that even this constituted a limitation. Underlying his criticism was the suspicion that regular, repeatable polyhedrons lent themselves all too readily to integration in a rationalistic architecture. But rationalism in architecture was itself not free from irrational elements. A good many designs which can hardly be reckoned as Expressionist show traces of the mystical concept of the 'crystalline world edifice'.

The building erected for the London International Exhibition of 1851, with an iron frame filled in with ordinary glass, had been called the Crystal Palace; so were its successors in Europe and the United States. For the Arts Décoratifs exhibition in Paris in 1925 Peter Behrens erected a glass building where the interpenetra-

60, 61. Paul Gösch. Pilgrimage chapel, from *Ruf zum Bauen*, Berlin, 1920. Elevation and plan.
62. Peter Behrens. IG Farben building, Höchst, 1920–24. Skylights over the main hall.

63, 64. Wassili Luckhardt. Country house, from *Ruf zum Bauen*, Berlin, 1920. View and plan.
65. Wassili Luckhardt and Rudolf Belling. Publicity building on the Avus, Berlin, 1922–23.

66. Walter Würzbach and Rudolf Belling. Scala restaurant, Berlin, 1921.
67, 68. Peter Behrens. Exhibition pavilion for the Association of German Mirror Manufacturers, Cologne, 1925. View and plan.

tion of diagonals (roof-ties, metal cross-pieces) and orthogonals resembled the fault-patterns in minerals. Mies van der Rohe's studies for tower blocks of 1919–21 (ills. 72, 73), whose form derived from the way light is refracted by the surfaces of a prism, were meant to look 'like a crystal, like a polished crystal'.[15] Hans Soeder's project for a tower block at the Friedrichstrasse station in Berlin (ills. 70, 71), with its six-point radial layout that takes no account of disturbing heat effects or of the incidence of reflection, also exhibits that fascination for the crystalline which architects of later office blocks have signally failed to realize.

The shadow of Nietzsche

In the ideas of the solitary genius and the expectation of a new Man, the sacred character of the world of sensory perception and the prophecy of a Dionysian Age, the long shadow of Friedrich Nietzsche (1844–1900) lies across Expressionist architecture as it lies across Expressionist poetry. The sketches of Bruno Taut and Josef Emanuel Margold are annotated with quotations from his works. *Thus Spake Zarathustra* (1883–85) was a canonical text for the Expressionists. Nietzsche's rejection of the bourgeois world, history, and established authority and his scorn of the state for the people's sake made him appear the only liberated German of his time. His description of the creative act in terms of ecstatic revelation corresponded to the Expressionists' view. And if the majority of them did not approve of Zarathustra's anti-social attitude, his scornful opinion of neighbourly love and belief in an aristocracy of the spirit, what the anonymous author of the pamphlet *An alle Künstler* ('To all Artists') wrote in 1919 was largely true: 'The world catastrophe has not made such a nonsense of Zarathustra that a storm has not swept in on the wings of the Holy Ghost.'

With its many architectural metaphors, *Thus Spake Zarathustra* met architects

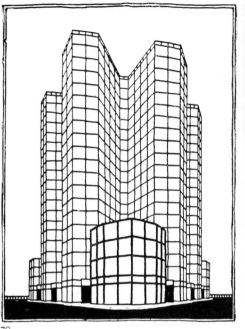

70

72

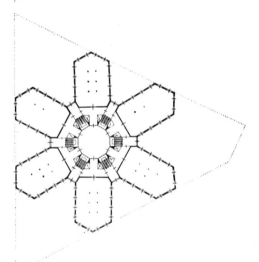

71

73

69. Uriel Birnbaum. The city of glass, from *Der Kaiser und der Architekt*, Leipzig and Vienna, 1924.
70, 71. Hans Soeder. Project for an office building at Friedrichstrasse station, Berlin, 1921. View and plan.
72, 73. Ludwig Mies van der Rohe. Project for an office building at Friedrichstrasse station, Berlin, 1919. First version. View and plan.

Karl Schmidt-Rottluff – an expert on Nietzsche – painted himself a mountain retreat atop a towering pile of cubic masses, César Klein a colourful city of rock by the sea with pyramids of golden glass, miraculous gardens of flowers, and 'dematerialized' people.[16] Another favourite motif of Expressionist architects, the cave, played a part in Nietzsche's topography as Zarathustra's dwelling-place.

The attraction of the Alpine world reached its culmination in Expressionism but in fact it went back much farther. Joseph Maria Olbrich was a passionate mountaineer, and Hermann Finsterlin's vision on the Watzmann has a parallel in the moment of truth which Henry van de Velde experienced in 1905 in the mountains above Kaprun. It was particularly in student projects, where there was least constraint upon the imagination, that peaks tended to rear heights crowned by architecture. Drawings of the Otto Wagner school and studies by Hermann Billing and his pupils are full of solemn flights of steps or daring bridges leading to fantastically hollowed-out or

half-way, as it were. The sage, standing before a row of new houses, is amazed at how small they are, as if symbolic of the smallness of the souls that inhabit them. The Expressionists took this reproach very much to heart in their megalomaniac designs. The topographical schema underlying the book was particularly evident to architects whose profession it was to think in spatial terms. Zarathustra lives in the perilous solitude of the mountains. He brings his message down from the heights into the lowlands. But he has no liking for the plain and passes the swamp of the big city by. Up and down here signify positions of the spirit. The icy heights of the peaks are contrasted with the flatlands of the contemptible mob, an anticipation – although admittedly a not unambiguous one – of the hostility to things urban which characterized the period. 'He who perceives, let him learn to build with mountains', was

quoted by Walter Müller-Wulckow in his book *Aufbau – Architektur!*. 'Alpine architecture', by no means confined to Bruno Taut's book of that name published in 1919, found in Nietzsche its philosophical justification. The scenery of the Alps of course found expression not only in current literature but also in the new generation's preference for angles and polished surfaces, for all the precipitous ruggedness of mineral structures. But its elevation by Nietzsche to the status of a *Weltanschauung* confirmed artists in their inclinations. The dreams of architects and artists around 1918 were set against a background of mountains.

74. Wenzel August Hablik. Etching from the *Schaffende Kräfte* series, 1909. Hablik Collection, Itzehoe.
75. Hermann Billing. Architectural fantasy, from *Stadtbaukunst alter und neuer Zeit*, 1, no. 11, 1920.

monumentally stratified rocks or cliffs ills. 75–77, 328, 425, 426). Billing's pupils included both Hans Luckhardt and Max Taut.

Cosmic architecture

The many sects and schools of redemption which had sprung up since the end of the nineteenth century as a reaction against materialism and positivism found particularly fertile soil in the restless years after 1918. The Christian churches were as incapable of satisfying the burgeoning religious feeling of the time as the political parties were of pinning down in their programmes the urge towards new forms of human coexistence. At the Bauhaus in Weimar, the Persian-American gnosis of Mazdaznan, Theosophy, Anthroposophy, neo-Buddhism, and Neoplatonism were all so widespread that the institute was forced to try and channel this tendency to sectarianism with a Bauhaus rite of its own (see p. 110). Max Berg, architectural adviser to the city of Breslau (Wrocław), is said to have referred to the Bauhaus as an 'alchemists' kitchen'. Berg himself was in touch with people who dealt in occult phenomena and apparently had himself pensioned off from his job because a clairvoyant friend of his had prophesied the destruction of the city of Breslau in the next war.[17]

The Theosophical Society, founded in 1875, and the Anthroposophical Society which grew out of it were the most important religious communities outside the churches. Theosophy, which attempted to discover the basic esoteric truth behind all religions, was largely based on Buddhist and Hindu teachings. It found a following among artists of the most diverse schools. Both Dynamic Abstraction and Aesthetic Constructivism took their stand on Theosophical ideas: both Kandinsky and Piet Mondrian had a tendency to equate matter and mind. Mondrian, a member of the Theosophical Society from 1909 onwards, took up the challenge inherent in Dr Schoenmak-

76

77

76. Emile Hoppe. Architectural study, 1902. From *Wagner-Schule 1902*, Leipzig, n.d.
77. Hermann Billing or one of his pupils. Architectural study. From Hermann Billing, ed., *Architektur-Skizzen*, Stuttgart, n.d. (1904).

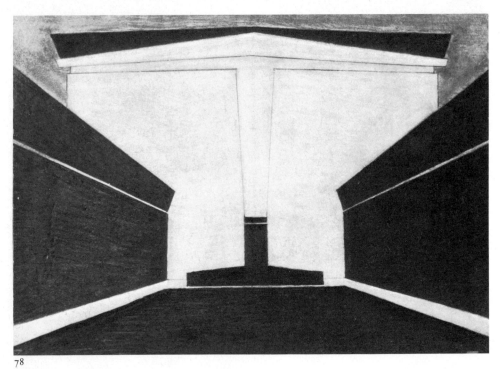

78

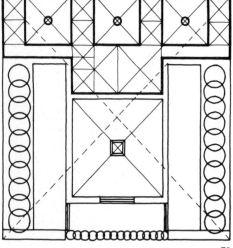

79

78, 79. Paul Thiersch. House of the Architect, 1914. View (charcoal and chalk) and plan.

er's 'positive mysticism' of realizing a *unio mystica* between mind and matter. The laws of cosmic creation being based on mathematical structures, harmonious numerical proportions ought also to lie at the basis of the new art.[18]

There was a growing interest in arithmetical and geometrical principles of design during the latter part of the nineteenth century. Art historians tried to discern the secrets of the proportions of Egyptian architecture, the classical Greek temple and the Gothic cathedral. In the monastery of Beuron, Desiderius Lenz, founder of the Beuron School of Art, derived basic numerical units for art from the proportions of the human body. His *Urmass* or 'primal measure', the equilateral triangle, he related to the essence of the Godhead.

Of great practical importance to architects was August Thiersch's restrained article on 'Proportions in Architecture' in the *Handbuch der Architektur* (1883). Renouncing all eccentric speculations on triangulation, quadrature, and the golden section, Thiersch fell back on the thesis of similar figures. Harmony stems from the repetition of the work's principal figure in its subdivisions. The 'House of the Architect' designed by his son Paul in

1914 shows this theory in application (ills. 78, 79). Both plan and elevation of this group of buildings are based on a square module. The silhouette of the main building, vaguely reminiscent of a sarcophagus, testifies also to the kind of stylization of their own lives that architects of the period expected. Paul Thiersch (1879–1928) belonged to the circle of Stefan George and later became director of the School of Arts and Crafts at Burg Giebichenstein, near Halle, a friendly rival to the Bauhaus.

Nevertheless mathematical principles of composition were still so little known outside Holland that the great Dutch architect Hendrik Petrus Berlage was able to introduce them abroad as something new. Other Dutch designers practising or promoting geometrical design methods included Cuijpers, de Bazel, Lauweriks, and particularly Jan Hessel de Groot. Berlage treated these methods as a means of achieving pleasing effects. He even saw in the introduction of mathematical calculation a way to a new style which would be based on necessity rather than arbitrary decree. But he attributed no symbolic meaning to numerical relationships. In his *Grundlagen und Entwicklung der Architektur*

44

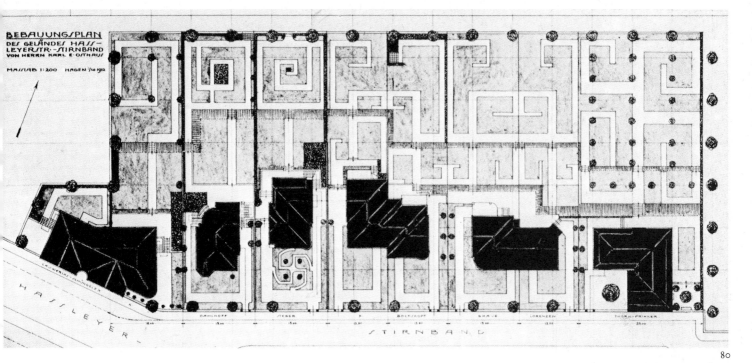

('Foundations and Development of Architecture') of 1908 he quoted with approval a warning of Hegel, who saw in numerical symbols an arbitrary game having no deeper significance.

The key man in this connection was Berlage's younger countryman, J. L. Mathieu Lauweriks (1864–1932). In 1904 Behrens, who had taken over as director of the Düsseldorf School of Arts and Crafts the year before, appointed Lauweriks as his lecturer in architecture. In 1909 Lauweriks moved to Hagen, where he directed a seminar in handicrafts training and contributed a group of nine dwellings to K. E. Osthaus' Hohenhagen development (Am Stirnband, ills. 80, 81). Lauweriks was not like other architects content to draw a grid of lines on the plan and elevation to order his measurements. For him geometry constituted a form-creating system, 'the primary cell of the building . . . on which everything else is erected'.[19]

From a basic modular arrangement of a variable pattern of squares, cubes, circles, and spheres Lauweriks arrived at his favourite motif, the labyrinth of rectangular spirals (ill. 82). These rectangular spirals governed the whole of his architecture. In the Hohenhagen complex they can be seen in the advancing and receding line of the row of houses, in the layout of the gardens, in the rising and falling line of the blocks and strips of natural stone on the façades, contrasting with areas of brick, and in the uniform though repeatedly interrupted line of the roof-ridges. The labyrinth was more to Lauweriks than a fascinating motif: it symbolized man's struggle for freedom as he pressed forward from darkness to light.

After Lauweriks – whose achievements as a teacher far outweighed his slender corpus of architectural work – there were two different lines of development. The systematic method he promoted made possible the standardization and consequently the industrialization of the whole building process. In this respect the Theosopher Lauweriks belongs as much in the tradition of scientific, rational architecture as the Parisian architect J. N. L. Durand, who in his lectures at the Ecole Polytechnique a hundred years earlier had taught techniques of design using combinations of modular elements.

Lauweriks' influence as a pacemaker of rationalization can be shown and verified in terms of personal contacts. Peter Behrens, under the influence of his colleague

80. J. L. Mathieu Lauweriks. Plan of the Am Stirnband housing development, Hohenhagen, Hagen, 1912.
81. J. L. Mathieu Lauweriks. Steger and Bockskopf houses, Am Stirnband development, Hohenhagen, Hagen, 1910–14.
82. J. L. Mathieu Lauweriks. Visiting card, 1912.

83

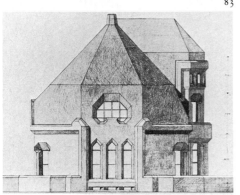

84

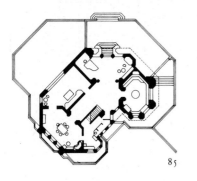

85

86

83–85. Fritz Kaldenbach. Country house, 1914.
From *Ruf zum Bauen*, Berlin, 1920. Views and
plan.
86. Fritz Kaldenbach. Villa or music school,
1914. From *Stadtbaukunst alter und neuer Zeit*.
Frühlicht, 1, no. 13, 1920.

at Düsseldorf and of his knowledge of the work of August Thiersch, whose son worked in his studio in 1906–7, evolved a system of parallel diagonals which can be clearly seen in the façades of his buildings designed between 1905 and 1907. Adolf Meyer, who later went into partnership with Gropius, studied under Lauweriks. And Gropius himself, a friend of Lauweriks' patron Osthaus, also knew the Dutchman's work at first hand.

Not only rationalism, however, but also its counterpart could appeal to Lauweriks. His idea of art was the same as that of the Expressionists, except that according to him the 'expression' was removed from the subjective creative urge of the individual artist. He regarded the work of architecture as a symbol of a harmony that was not to be experienced by sensory perception but rather through a spiritual phenomenology. His number-symbolism was to reflect the objective order of the universe. 'Art is a representation of the cosmic drama: it embodies cosmic events symbolically in stirring pictures and eloquent, profoundly convincing acts. The history, the drama, the image, the architecture, in short the harmony of the cosmos as a whole concentrated in a single statement, rather as a small photograph reproduces the entire picture.'[20] For Lauweriks, art was religion become perceptible to the senses.

Lauweriks passed this theory on to his pupil and colleague Fritz Kaldenbach (1887–1918). Theosophist philosophy, Kaldenbach claimed, gave him a feeling for the coherence of life. 'I am convinced that the whole complex business of life can in the long run be traced back to a few quite simple forms, in the same way as a beautiful, uniform building develops out of a standard unit of measurement, out of a single basic form.'[21]

Kaldenbach died of influenza in the last days of the war. His reputation at the time as one of the most gifted of the younger generation of architects rested on two designs for villas dating from 1914 (ills. 83–86). They were published in Bruno Taut's *Frühlicht* and in the organ of the Berlin Arbeitsrat für Kunst, *Ruf zum Bauen*. They are prismatic buildings based on a standard square module and its diagonals. The lines of the ground plan relate at an angle of 135°, and this angle also determines the line of the facings and the profile of the cornices. Strips of wall bent at right angles and reminiscent of Lauweriks draw the hollowed-out volumes together optically. One of the projects, a country house, is intelligently developed out of two axes, the entrance axis and the central axis of the living room, which meet at 45°. The other house, which Osthaus wanted to have built as a music school, was governed by a symmetry which was only slightly varied. The enormous roof-hoods and also the powerful central motif, a kind of vast keyhole containing the entrance door and hall windows, are recalled in Rudolf Steiner's second Goetheanum ten years later (ills. 86, *353*).

Behind both the revolutionary architects of Berlin and the Anthroposophists of Dornach lay similar ideological presuppositions. Of Bruno Taut's friends at least Paul Gösch, who devised architectural forms in the spirit of the first Goetheanum (ills. 87, 88), and Hermann Finsterlin were sympathetic to Theosophy or Anthroposophy. Lauweriks and Rudolf Steiner must have been in contact. When Steiner left the Theosophical Society in 1913 Lauweriks took over from him as director of the German section. Steiner may not have used a modular system but he attached far greater importance than even Lauweriks did to number symbolism (see p. 140).

87

87. Rudolf Steiner. First Goetheanum, Dornach,
1913–20. Detail of the west façade.
88. Paul Gösch. A portal, 1920 or earlier. Pen
drawing. Oswald Mathias Ungers Collection,
Cologne.

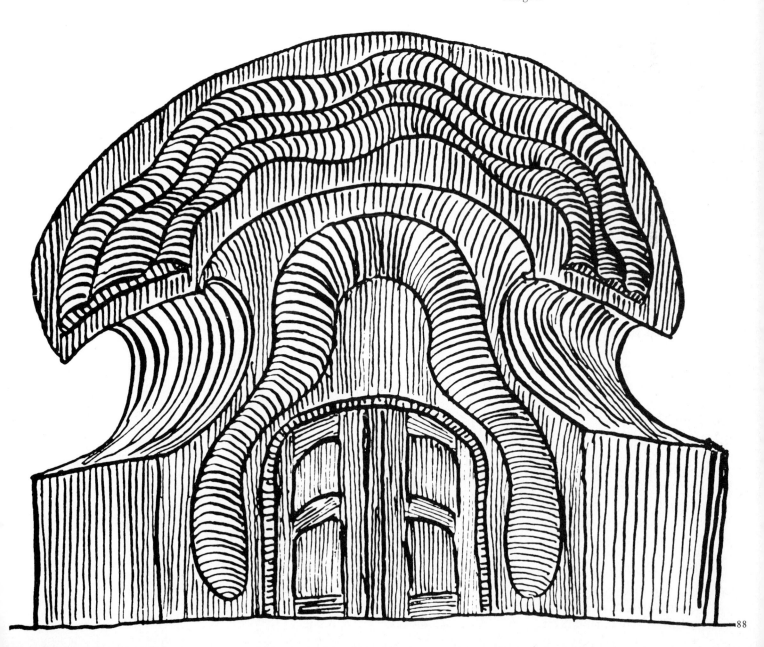

88

3 Art and architecture

'We badly need something excessive again, something that will spark off the purely musical.'

Karl Scheffler, 'Henry van de Velde und der neue Stil', in *Kunst und Künstler*, 1910

The longing for style

All through the nineteenth century artists and critics were continually expressing the wish for a style of their own. Again and again we find them saying that their particular period is a period of transition, characterized by a confusion of aesthetic terms and a temporary paralysis of creative talent. Gottfried Semper looked forward to the 'mysterious Phoenix-birth of the new life of art out of the annihilation of the old', but was pessimistic enough to add that this hypothesis was a practical one because it was encouraging; whether it was also justified was something he did not presume to decide.[1]

After the Jugendstil had failed to produce the great synthesis it promised, the call for a new style became all the more urgent. In the period during and after the war the motives behind this demand were by no means purely aesthetic. Unity of style was regarded as proof of a healthy whole, of a spiritual unity, of a living community that admitted and adhered to certain norms. 'Did the longing for style really spring only from the psychical and physiological need for quiet and order, for clarity and security in impressions received from outside?' asked the critic Walter Müller-Wulckow in 1919. His reply was of course in the negative: 'After the battles of the most extreme forms of individualism and the makeshift of a borrowed, subjective convention there must be a reasonably secure guarantee that only those things will be recognized as important that bear a firm relationship to the whole.'[2]

As an approach to history Karl Friedrich Schinkel had offered the following advice (not his last word on the subject): a meaningful selection, modification, and

89. Ziggurat depicted on a Sumerian cylinder-seal, *c.* 3000 BC.

90. Otto Kohtz. Architectural study, from *Gedanken über Architektur*, Berlin, 1909.

completion of such things from the past as might be usable in the present. Since the end of the nineteenth century only conservative artists and architects had adopted this recommendation entirely. The groups that at one time or another regarded themselves as progressive showed an increasing tendency to question this positive attitude to history. In fact the 'decay of all current categories of art' as precondition of the new (Gottfried Semper), an emphasis on such moral virtues as honesty, naturalness, and spontaneity, and a religious dedication to novelty and originality constituted the basic polemical equipment of almost every avant-garde.

It was not until the International Style, however, that history was rejected as a source of inspiration and point of reference (and then not entirely, in practice). The architects of Expressionism did not go so far. They felt no contradiction as yet between their demand for originality and their appeal to particular periods of history or to exotic cultures. What they looked for in history was not models that they could copy but confirmation of what they themselves wanted to do. They had no respect for tradition at all. They just took what they could use, transforming what they had taken into something else. They treated the achievements of the past as a yardstick for measuring their own strength. 'A growing knowledge of primitive, Eastern, and Far Eastern art gave the new movement an awareness of its far-reaching ancestry and thus strengthened it in its instinctive feeling for development' (Wilhelm Worringer).[3]

The new choice of models was determined by single-minded stylistic intentions. Architects rejected periods that had been compromised by excessive exploitation in the nineteenth century, with the exception of Gothic and German Baroque, which would seem to have found a follower in Hans Poelzig. The periods and cultures they preferred were those in which the fine arts served the collective artistic goal of decorated architecture, in which the ideal of the natural truth of life

had disappeared from circulation, in which superabundance of means, spatial ideas and ornament was the rule rather than economy, and in which the people could be seen as patron and commissioner of architectural work and the architect as anonymous servant of the community as a whole. Clearly, with regard to the realities of history, such an outlook demanded a very considerable capacity for abstraction.

The architecture of ancient Egypt

There is a striking difference between the sympathies of art historians in the years before 1914 and in the post-war period. In the first fifteen years of the century, as the Jugendstil passed its peak and massive buildings with less and less ornamentation began to dominate the scene, there was a vogue for Egyptian architecture. Whenever there has been a desire for simplification or monumentality or both, the eyes of European architects seem to have turned towards Egypt. In the second half of the eighteenth century, for example, Jacques-François Blondel spoke (unfavourably) of a *simplicité mâle* and Claude-Nicolas Ledoux of *surfaces tranquilles* in connection with Egyptian architecture. And in the period after 1900 solid surfaces, linear precision of outline, and stereometric basic elements came to the fore once again. Peter Behrens talked about Rameses II as a 'venerable older colleague'. The inner room of the Egyptian temple came to be regarded as a crystal, the inner structure of which was 'in a magical way' made visible in the exterior of the building (Ludwig Coellen).[4]

The square pillars and weighty corporeality of a series of Behrens' designs in the period 1908–10 are indeed reminiscent of ancient Egypt. His former colleague Walter Gropius drew comparisons between the 'huge, tightly-bound form' of North American silos and 'the architecture of ancient Egypt',[5] and in the administration building of his model factory in Cologne he himself used pylon-

91

92

93

94

91. Walter Gropius and Adolf Meyer. Administration building for a model factory, Werkbund Exhibition, Cologne, 1914. Entrance.
92. Temple of Horus, Edfu, Upper Egypt, first century BC.
93. Paul Bonatz and Friedrich Eugen Scholer. Main railway station, Stuttgart, 1911–28. View from the side.
94. Enclosure wall of the funerary district of King Zoser, Saqqara, c. 2650 BC.

95

96

95. Max Taut. Marble cathedral, from *Stadtbaukunst alter und neuer Zeit. Frühlicht*, 1, no. 12, 1920.
96. Wenzel August Hablik. Fantasy, from *Ruf zum Bauen*, Berlin, 1920.

like flanking towers, small pylons beside the main entrance, and a solid facade wall (ills. 91, 92).

Large masses were articulated with pillar-like, projecting vertical strips that recall the enclosing wall of the temple area at Saqqara, for example in the main railway station in Stuttgart by Bonatz and Scholer (ills. 93, 94). Bonatz's trip to Egypt during the designing stage was made for good reason. A too-literal use of Egyptian 'quotations', as in Bernhard Hoetger's design for a town for the Hanover firm of Bahlsen, tends in the context of such monumental buildings to look like frivolous whimsy (ills. 304–306).

As the national art of a hierarchically organized sacerdotal monarchy, Egyptian art was not the kind of thing to arouse the enthusiasm of artists after a revolution. It was no coincidence that Kaiser Wilhelm II, president of the German Oriental Society and a passionate amateur archaeologist, had shown a marked interest in the monumental art of Assyria, Babylon, and Egypt. Such architecture conspicuously embodied imperial pretensions, and the architects of the Kaiser's cyclopean monuments and factories, both those that were built and those that were only dreamt of, were able to find kindred spirits in Egypt and Assyria (ills. 89, 90).

The spirit of Gothic

On the other hand the new social and revolutionary ideas could very easily be read back into the medieval period. In his book *Mutual Aid, a Factor of Evolution* (1902) the anarchist Prince Kropotkin had accounted for the artistic heights reached in medieval architecture by the idea of brotherhood and neighbourly love which he believed was fulfilled in the guilds and brotherhoods of the later Middle Ages. The Gothic style was credited with freeing man from petty self-interest, whether the egocentricity of the individual became annihilated through submission to one's neighbour – as Kro-

potkin maintained – or through a transcendental yearning for God. Gropius remarked: 'The entire people *built*, created: that was its principal occupation, with commerce only secondary. That was how it was in Germany at the height of the Gothic age and that is how it must be here again now.'[6]

Expressionism's receptiveness to Gothic was reflected in the attitudes of two authors, Wilhelm Worringer (1881–1965) and Karl Scheffler (1869–1951). Both found a far wider audience than the professional circle of art historians. Worringer's *Abstraktion und Einfühlung* ('Abstraction and Empathy'), published in 1908, was already in its eleventh edition by 1921; Scheffler's *Geist der Gotik* ('The Spirit of Gothic'), of 1907, was in its twentieth thousand only two years after publication, and by 1925 had reached its fortieth thousand.

In Worringer's antithetical schema Gothic occupied a curious and significant central position. The word empathy *(Einfühlung)* he took over from the aesthetic theorist Theodor Lipps. He associated the organic with man's capacity for empathy, contrasting it with an urge towards abstraction which he saw – debatably – as motivated by a fear of space and a feeling of insecurity before the diversity of the external world. With this need for abstraction Worringer associated the inorganic as object. According to Worringer, Gothic transmitted this capacity for empathy to objects which did not naturally possess it, to matter which was ruled by mechanical laws. He spoke of heightened expression on an inorganic basis, of the uncanny pathos of the abstract become expressive, of sublime hysteria.

Worringer's contemporary commitment is clear even without his later references to the causal connection between his theory and the art of Expressionism:[7] 'Caught up in the intoxication of this mighty crescendo of orchestrated mechanical forces proceeding from all the ends of the earth and striving heavenward [man] felt himself convulsively

eized and raised up in a blissful dream,
drawn high above himself into infinity.'
In a further work, *Formprobleme der Gotik*
(translated as *Form in Gothic*, 1927),
of 1911 Worringer extended his psychological treatment of style. He compared
the basic type of primitive and classical
man with Oriental man – a hint of the
coming Oriental boom – whose insight
into the unfathomable mysteries of Being
he saw as surpassing the imaginative
power of Europeans.

Scheffler's essay was written not only
in a more popular vein but also more
simply. It was an eloquent apothesis of
the Gothic style, which Scheffler regarded as equal to the style of classical
Greece: he set the two side by side and
contrasted them in an endless series of
opposing pairs – verticalism as against
horizontalism, modelled mass against
tectonic structure, will-power and aspiration against balance and discipline, symbolic against representational purpose,
barbarism against civilization, pained
striving against gay enjoyment, and so
on. Of great importance subsequently
was Scheffler's attempt to establish
Gothic as an eternal type in the history of
art. Worringer himself spoke of a 'secret
Gothic' which he believed he could see at
work before and after the Gothic period
as such. Scheffler expressed himself in
rather less cautious terms. Prehistoric,
Egyptian, Indian, Chinese, and Baroque
art, even Impressionism, he summarily
classified as 'Gothic' styles.

It was ironic that Scheffler, who built
up his magazine *Kunst und Künstler* as a
defensive bastion for Impressionism
against Expressionism, should have
given the Expressionists so much ammu-
nition in his book. A reader who did not
share Scheffler's prejudice must inevitably in 1917 see a sentence like 'The most
revolutionary is always the most Gothic
as well' as a justification of Expressionism. Critics could now attach the 'Gothic'
label to Wilhelm Kreis, Hans Poelzig,
and even Frank Lloyd Wright.

Even before the revolutionary years
brought with them this enthusiasm for

97

97. Dominikus Böhm. St Johannes Baptist,
Neu-Ulm, 1921–26. View towards the pulpit.

98

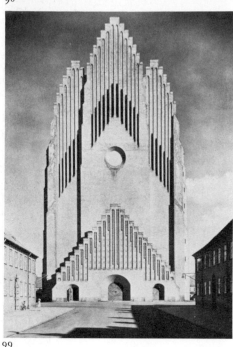

99

98. Peder Vilhelm Jensen-Klint. St Hans Tveje, Odense, 1919.
99. Peter Vilhelm Jensen-Klint, completed by Kaare Klint. Grundtvigs church, Copenhagen, 1921–40.

Gothic, metaphors from religious architecture had been applied to contemporary secular buildings. The modern factories and administration buildings that emerged from the studies of the celebrated artist-architects were frequently referred to as 'cathedrals of labour'. Joseph Maria Olbrich even called the great inner court of his Tietz department store in Düsseldorf a 'cathedral'. The Futurists attacked both the word and the thing when they denounced *pesantezza* and *cattedralismo*.

The cathedral became the new image for the period following 1918, but what was intended was not any pseudo-sacred treatment of secular themes. The glass houses and crystal castles (ill. 96) were to constitute the 'powerful witnesses of a unity' that was 'founded once again on human feeling for community, far from the lamentable strife of the present' (Herbert Eulenberg). Paul Scheerbart declared that the Gothic cathedral lay behind his experiments in glass architecture, from which a new Europe would emerge. Karl Ernst Osthaus interpreted the pile of rock and buildings that is Mont Saint Michel as 'the yearning of a community [whose] final gesture is heavenward'.[8] Gothic meant many things – the triumph of expression over purpose; the predominance of a single unified art over many arts, all isolated from one another; the guarantee of a new community exalted high above the shopkeeper-mentality of the present.

The 'Gothic spirit' affected painting and sculpture more than it did architecture. Gothic sculpture and late Gothic woodcuts influenced German Expressionist artists, and the motif of the Gothic church entered into the iconography of such different artists as Delaunay, Mondrian, and Kupka. In architecture the new enthusiasm for the Gothic style was naturally focussed on ecclesiastical building, from Peder Vilhelm Jensen-Klint's monumental 'village Gothic' to Behrens' mannered 'cathedral masons' lodge' at the Munich fair (ills. 98–101). Behrens allowed his second biographer, Paul

Joseph Cremers, to talk of this romantic brick and timber jewelbox quite seriously in terms of a witness to 'the spiritual brotherhood of religious artists' and to the 'metaphysics of his search'.

This Expressionist Gothic was also reflected in the sacred atmosphere of interiors that did not at all serve sacred ends. It engendered a whole repertory of neo-medieval forms: arcades, loggias, balconies, pointed arches, crenellations (though these could also have been derived from Islamic architecture), and the vertical patterning of the wall by breaking it up into piers, a process which was in any case suggested by the steel and reinforced-concrete skeleton. Peter Behrens even got excited about the 'exposed roots', the downward-tapering sheafs of supports, in early Gothic cathedrals (ill. 136).

Ex oriente lux

'At no time has Europe come so close to the Orient as during the Gothic period', wrote Adolf Behne (1885–1948), the architectural critic in Bruno Taut's circle. If there was one style, one cultural context, which was valued even more highly than Gothic, it was the Orient – by which was meant India and South-east Asia, though the word occasionally took in China and the Near East as well. Gothic was 'nothing but a marvellous dream of the Orient, dreamt by the crusaders after their return.' No one embellished this dream more richly than Behne. For him Indian architecture was 'the ultimate in architecture, the peak'. 'And what is this ultimate? It is an architecture that bursts all human bonds, that raises up before men a great and miraculous form into the stature of whose splendour and magnificence men may grow. A work that is the incarnation of the human will to cosmic love. Such a concept is no Utopia. Such buildings exist in this world – the temples of India!'[9]

As Behne put it, 'Light perpetually comes from the East'; as Taut put it, *Ex oriente lux*. 'What mellowness of form, what fruitful ripeness, what coherence and rigour and what an incredible fusion with sculpture! The decoration bubbles over, transcending all frontiers, tender with the fervour of surrender and strong and sonorous in the extreme. Tense, angular stratification, a massiveness both strong and gentle, a mighty, heavenward towering, and the greatest delicacy conceivable – *ecstasy!*'[10]

Every committed architect offered at least verbal homage to Indian art during these months. Otto Bartning came back from his travels intoxicated by the Javanese stepped temple of Borobudur, 'hardly by the hand of man, but rather as if the earth, sunk in dream, had depicted itself with its waking gesture'. A sheet of paper has survived on which Walter Gropius jotted some notes for a speech in the early days of the Bauhaus: 'To build! To give form! Gothic – India'. Erich Mendelsohn, in the issue of *Wendingen* devoted to him, spoke not only of the Greek temple and the Gothic cathedral but also of the 'formal ecstasy' of the pagodas that 'enchanted the world with the native originality of their jungle life'. Hans Poelzig went so far as to maintain that the frontier between East and West ran straight through the middle of Germany, and that whenever Germans had turned their backs on the West to accept the mystic art of the East they had become stronger and more themselves.[11]

This yearning on the part of architects for things Asian was part of the mystical wave of renewal that flooded Europe in the first decades of this century. Where nineteenth-century Orientalism had derived unknown delights and new forms from the exotic East, twentieth-century Orientalism looked for nothing less than the rebirth of the inner man. Annie Besant, president of the Theosophical Society and herself born in India, travelled about the world with Krishnamurti, an Indian youth in whose body a new 'World Teacher' was to take up residence. The diaries of Count Eduard Keyserling, the literary result of Hermann Hesse's Indian trip, and the

Asian themes that run through the poetry of German Expressionism (Kasimir Edschmid, Alfred Döblin, Alfred Brust) all testify to the attraction of the mysterious East. Architectural journals came out with essays on highly specialized aspects of the Orient. The publisher Bruno Cassirer issued a series entitled *Die Kunst des Ostens* ('The Art of the East'), and the house of Folkwang brought out another series called *Geist, Kunst und Leben Asiens* ('The Mind, Art, and Life of Asia'). In The Hague, capital of a country whose colonies made it receptive to the Far East anyway, a Society of the Friends of Asian Art was founded.

For the architects of Central Europe who longed 'in their souls for that great and distant work' (Bruno Taut),[12] Indian art was a means of loosening the imagination (ills. 103, 104). As a source for imitation, however, it was rather less suitable than Gothic. Even in the Netherlands, where interest was concentrated on the East Indies, Eastern influence was noticeable not so much in details as in the general exuberance of design – although of course the two-dimensional fantasy world of Indonesian motifs had been a stimulus for the arts and crafts of Dutch Art Nouveau and hence also for the graphic and decorative works of architects like Berlage, de Bazel, Lauweriks, van der Meij, Kromhout, and later Wijdeveld (ills. 105, 106). In architecture the curved roofs of some smaller buildings, the odd forward-leaning gable, and the occasional piece of brick ornament suggestive of wicker-work might have been derived from Malaysian domestic architecture (ills. 107, 108). Yet even the eight tapering towers in Berlage's project for a Palace of Peace or Pantheon of Mankind, so strongly reminiscent of the bullet-shaped pinnacles of Siamese temples (ills. 105, 106), also have European parallels – in the shell shapes used by Otto Wagner and his pupils, in Theodor Fischer's Gedächtniskirche (1911) in Ulm, and, under the influence of the Wagner school, in Antonio Sant'Elia (ills. 329, 422, 430).

100

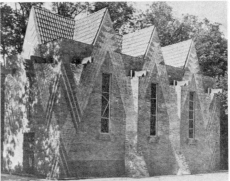

101

102

100, 101. Peter Behrens. Cathedral masons' lodge at the Gewerbeschau, Munich, 1922.
102. Clemens Holzmeister. Crematorium, Vienna, 1922–24. Arcaded passage.

103

104

103. Hans Scharoun. Pen drawing, 1920.
104. Mukteshvara Temple, Bhuvaneshvar, Orissa, late ninth century AD.

Expressionism and Jugendstil

Expressionism naturally stood in a different relationship to the Jugendstil movement than to movements further removed in time and place. For the architects of Expressionism the Jugendstil was not, like Gothic or the Orient, an example which they could either choose or reject. It was, for better or worse, a part of themselves. Peter Behrens had been one of the Jugendstil's most outstanding figures. Bernhard Hoetger had worked as a sculptor on that collective work of art, the Mathildenhöhe in Darmstadt, before he turned to architecture and designed houses that reminded Behrens of his own Darmstadt beginnings. Futurism drew its Art-Nouveau inspiration from the Italian *stile floreale* and from the school of Otto Wagner (see pp. 175–76). In Holland the tradition of *de nieuwe kunst* was even more abiding. The magazine *Wendingen* published, along with contemporary works of architecture by the school of Amsterdam, posters by Toorop, pictures by Klimt, and Josef Hoffmann's Palais Stoclet in Brussels as if they were products of an immediately relevant present.

Jugendstil architecture did indeed anticipate many of the features of Expressionist architecture. The latter, after a divergent phase lasting from 1900 to 1914, looks like a continuation of the former on a more exalted level. Jugendstil buildings were also seen as three-dimensional bodies characterized by uniformity of outline and sculptural treatment of mass. In them as well glass and colour played a dominant part, though Jugendstil designs remained harmonious ensembles, without any extravagant, expressive solo passages. They too had been intended as total works of art *(Gesamtkunstwerk)*, in which painting appeared as an element in the architecture, and architectural perspectives had the look of paintings.

In the few years since the turn of the century, however, the cultural climate had changed fundamentally. Expression-ism addressed itself to the people, and this called for a loud and violent language that could not be ignored. It did not seek to improve taste but to alter society, and this called for aggressive methods and a rhetoric aimed at breadth of effect. Whereas the Jugendstil had been based on the world of plants, with its supple forms and smooth transitions, Expressionism went back to the crystal. In Expressionist architecture it was beam and angle rather than curve and loop, uncompromising hardness rather than complaisant flexibility. The spatial units in Jugendstil architecture flow into one another through numerous slurring transitions, which it is impossible to infer from the plan; in Expressionist designs and buildings the geometrical figures of the plan are generally followed with rigid precision.

These differences apply to the fundamentals of the two styles. In practice there was much overlapping. It was not merely through the short-sightedness of contemporaries that the drawings by Mendelsohn which Paul Cassirer exhibited in 1919 were ascribed not to an architecture of the future but to the Jugendstil past, or that the Utopian architectural designs of Bruno Taut's friends were compared to van de Velde, Endell, and Obrist.[13] Both Mendelsohn and Taut acknowledged their debt to Jugendstil sources: Taut wrote that he had had Olbrich's 'delightfully drawn sketches' in mind when writing his *Alpine Architektur*.[14] In the Glass Pavilion at the Cologne Werkbund exhibition Taut prominently exhibited the metallic-sheened glass vessels of the American Art Nouveau artist Louis Comfort Tiffany. Even Hermann Finsterlin's biomorphic designs made it difficult not to think of the Jugendstil – of the glacier formations in the paintings of Hans Schmidthals, for example (ills. 109, 110).[15]

Continuity between the turn of the century and the time of the First World War was provided by the great father-figures who straddled both epochs: Henry van de Velde, Hermann Obrist, and Antoni

Gaudí. Young artists' sense of kinship with these older men was so strong that there was a plan to give it organizational form in a new foundation, which would be set up in competition to the Deutsche Werkbund and would exclude the middle generation on the grounds of its readiness to compromise. In a letter to Gropius, Poelzig referred to van de Velde and Obrist as comrades in outlook and went on: 'These older men and the younger men in fact [take their stand] spiritually and stylistically upon a Gothic foundation.'[16]

Henry van de Velde (1863–1957) was one of the more problematical of these father-figures. Anyone seeking to understand him must come to terms with numerous contradictions as integral parts of a complex personality and a dynamic temperament. His theoretical pronouncements were difficult enough to reconcile with one another, let alone with his practical work. The principle of logical structure which he advocated implied a functionalism in which form was the expression of a need, and beauty consequent upon utility. In fact, however, this 'logical construction' led him to solutions which approached the Expressionist aesthetic. In his autobiography he wrote that he had always pursued the one goal, 'to channel the stream of my own life towards the objects to be created'. Ornaments and architectural elements were to mirror the whole scale of human

sensory experience and 'become mimic bearers of an abstract expression'.

In an essay of 1920 in which he denounced the mystical exuberance of the young, van de Velde defended his 'original formative principle of *Sachlichkeit*'. Nevertheless he clearly regarded it as a requirement of objectivity that the work created should be informed with 'organic strength' and that the material used should be dematerialized.[17] Form for van de Velde was a product of the individual's feeling for life and symbolic representation. To be worthy of living in his houses required training in the art of living – and a readiness to submit willingly to the demands they made upon one.

In the few large commissions van de Velde received after his enforced retirement from his Weimar job – the museum he planned for the Kröller-Müllers (ill. 111) and the Jewish old people's home in Hanover (ill. 112) – he accepted certain features of the International Style such as the flat roof and the corner window. Yet the play of ramps, terraces, and projecting and receding elements remained dominant. Chamfered corners and polygonal lateral terminations illustrate how he tried to combine the smooth plasticity of his earlier work with the greater strictness of prismatically stratified masses. His Weimar pupil, Thilo Schoder, continued not only this later phase of van de Velde's work (ill. 113) but also the softly

105. Hendrik Petrus Berlage. The Pantheon of Mankind, 1915. Vignette from *Schoonheid in samenleving*, 2nd ed., Rotterdam, 1924.
106. Wat Arun, Bangkok.
107. G. F. La Croix. Forwarding agent's office, Amsterdam, before 1924.
108. Hendrik Petrus Berlage. Sketch made on a journey to India, 1923.

rounded corporeality of the theatre built for the 1914 Werkbund exhibition in Cologne.

Another father-figure, difficult in a different way, is Hermann Obrist (1862–1927). The generation that felt in 1918 that its great hour had come inevitably saw this 'old, serious artist of the future' (as Wilhelm von Bode called him) as an early martyr to their cause. Mendelsohn saw him as a lonely and forsaken man, victim of an overflowing imagination that was regarded as irrelevant and anachronistic. The young, however, were all for him, as they had been in the days when he had aroused their enthusiasm as co-founder and teacher at the Debschitz School in Munich. Bruno Taut hoped to get him to serve on the Arbeitsrat für Kunst. In the Exhibition for Unknown Architects which the Arbeitsrat organized in April 1919 there were references to a 'spiritual forefather', with photographs of tombs by Obrist (ill. 115).[18]

Obrist saw himself as an ancestor who outstripped his descendants: 'in the silence [I] design fantasies [in paint and drawing] which, I believe, go far beyond ... Expressionism. They are mere sketches, dreams, skimmings, which I shall not show for a year or two. Then, however, I hope to be able to offer a surprise.' Apart from this, the sixty-year-old artist was without illusions. The excited nature of his visions contrasted with the sceptical clarity of his thought. In 1918 many people believed the brotherhood of man and art to be a possibility: Obrist had shrewdly dismissed it as early as 1903 in his book *Neue Möglichkeiten in der bildenden Kunst* ('Fresh Possibilities in the Fine Arts'). He made short work of other clichés of the artists of the Arbeitsrat für Kunst as well. Their practical demands, he said, could never be met: the Social Democrats were more

109. Hans Schmidthals. Composition in blue, *c.* 1900. Pastel. Bayerische Staatsgemäldesammlungen, Munich.
110. Hermann Finsterlin. Study X-2, before 1924. Pencil and watercolour.

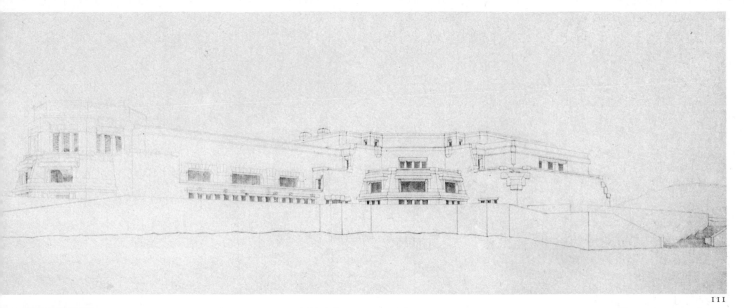

111. Henry van de Velde. Museum, Otterlo, *c.* 1921. Preliminary design, pencil. Rijksmuseum Kröller-Müller, Otterlo.
112. Henry van de Velde. Jewish old people's home, Hanover–Bemerode, 1929–31.
113. Thilo Schoder. Housing estate, Hermsdorf, Thuringia, 1925.

hostile to art than the bourgeois civil servants of pre-war times, true artistic work shunned any kind of organization or committee of artists, and private initiative was more necessary than ever.[19]

It is not surprising that architects sought Obrist's patronage. In his wilder inspiration he saw fairy-tale cities and interiors and religious buildings of inconceivable beauty which he attempted to capture in drawings and models (ills. 114, 116, 392). Even his fountains, which he regarded as examples of an architecture specifically adapted to the life of water, appeared, in spite of their doughy softness, to be based on architectonic if not urbanistic ideas. The spiralling towers and solidly based domes, the aqueducts meandering like snakes, and the capitals that throw out broad, flowing fronds suggest how his demand for 'deepened expression and an intensification of life'[20] in architecture might have been met.

Modernismo, the distinctive Catalan form of Art Nouveau, came so close to Expressionism as to be indistinguishable from it. Its most influential representatives, Lluís Domènech i Montaner and Antoni Gaudí, only died in the twenties: Gaudí (1852–1926) was killed in an accident when he was in the midst of work on his masterpiece, the still unfinished church of the Sagrada Familia in Barcelona. His colleagues and disciples – who included Francesc Berenguer, Lluís Moncunill, Josep Puig i Cadafalch, and above all Josep Maria Jujol – were building long after what is generally accepted as the end of the Art Nouveau period (ills. 117–120). It was only after the turn of the century that Gaudí himself fused the wild and ingenious inventions of his early work into large sculptural masses that appeared as coherent formal statements, and thus as finished works of art (ills. 121, 122, 348).

Unlike Germany, where Jugendstil ran into strong opposition after 1900, in Barcelona there was no break between the architecture of the late nineteenth century and that of 1910. The power of drawing things together into a unity grew, but the elements to be united remained as disparate as before. The most faithful naturalism and the boldest liberties are present in Gaudí's early and later works alike. Both in youth and in age Gaudí loved combining heterogeneous materials: rough masonry, freestone worked until it lost its identity, brick, cast iron, clear and coloured glass, ceramics, and – in the Güell Park, built in 1900–1914 – the most improbable series of *objets trouvés*, from bits of scrap metal to dolls' heads. Architectural members of similar function might be constructed of different materials. In the crypt of Santa Coloma de Cervelló, the chapel of the Colonia Güell outside Barcelona, some of the supports are of brick, others of natural stone masonry, and yet others are monoliths. Unity is achieved not by the use of similar elements, but by the inten-

114

sity with which the architect forces seemingly incompatible elements into the service of his idea. After 1900 Gaudí was searching for a synthesis, and in his late works historicist allusions to Gothic or Moorish architecture disappear.

Many features of Modernismo make it appear to be both a variant and continuation of Art Nouveau and also a parallel to Expressionism. In its products the arts are integrated in a more literal and forceful way than they ever were in the Expressionist designs of Central Europe. It promoted a cult of the ugly: numerous illustrations can be found in the work of Gaudí and his pupils, and also of Domènech i Montaner, with his interest in technology. In this it went further than the architecture of Central Europe, which would not and could not escape the quality of harmony which it had cultivated for so many centuries. Modernismo charged form with religious symbolism to an extent which was only possible in a culture dominated by an active Catholicism. There were many architects in Germany who wanted to build crystal shrines for an unknown faith. But not one of them would have crowned an upper middle class apartment building on a busy avenue with a more than life-size statue of the Virgin, as Gaudí planned to do at the Casa Milá (ill. 121). The statue was never put in place, but the attic storey of the street façade still bears the inscription *Ave gratia plena Dominus tecum*.

Modernismo's distinctive blend of sophistication in the invention of forms and naïveté in their use can only be understood in terms of the political and social background of Catalonia. In the nineteenth century it was the only part of Spain where the level of industrialization was comparable to that of the countries of Western and Central Europe. The Catalan *renaixença* set up the cry for political autonomy for Catalonia, and in the second half of the century it helped Catalans to become aware of their economic and cultural achievements. In Modernismo this new patriotic self-esteem found an apt form of expression.

The Catalan renaissance was a regionalism with its eye on the world: it drew nourishment from folk and local historical traditions, and at the same time it was aware of the latest import from London, Glasgow, Paris or Vienna. The middle class, become prosperous thanks to industrialization, produced the style. Unlike international Art Nouveau, however, Modernismo appealed not only to wealthy and adventurous connoisseurs but also to the general public. Gaudí's church of the Sagrada Familia, a 'temple for the poor', was paid for (as much of it as was built) in part out of collections and donations. Other commissions of his – projects and buildings for the co-operative Societat Obrera Mataronense and the garden-city housing colony for the textile manufacturer Eusebio Güell – testify to the extent to which Modernismo was permeated with social ideas. This broad social basis explains the coherence of Modernismo and its comparatively long life-span.

In Germany the 'new Catalan style' was known more by rumour than by fact. Photographs with vague captions were published from time to time in the architectural press. An exception was made by the magazine *Die Böttcherstrasse*, which in June 1928, probably at the instigation of its co-editor Bernhard Hoetger, published an essay on the church of the Sagrada Familia. Bruno Taut and his circle also knew what was going on. Taut noted Gaudí in his *Neue Baukunst* (1929), along with Eliel Saarinen, Pankok, Billing, and Möhring. In his magazine *Frühlicht*, however, he confined his attention to buildings which gave no hint of Gaudí's decisive late work. Hermann Finsterlin was sufficiently in the picture to sense in Gaudí a fellow spirit, and about 1920 or later the two men were in correspondence. He found Gaudí's ground plans too timid, however, and too dominated

114. Hermann Obrist. Winding viaduct, *c.* 1895. Charcoal. Staatliche Graphische Sammlung, Munich.
115. Hermann Obrist. Tomb of Karl Oertel, Munich, before 1910.
116. Hermann Obrist. Monumental building on a rock, *c.* 1908. Plaster. Kunstgewerbemuseum, Zurich.

117

118

by symmetry, and he recommended that his successful colleague make big buildings of his chimneys and turrets.[21]

Finsterlin and the other Expressionists overlooked the fact that Gaudí, in the luxuriant vegetation-forms of his ground plans of the Casa Batlló and Casa Milá, moved further away from traditional architecture than any Expressionist ever did in anything that was actually built. They also failed to see that Gaudí's 'Gothic without crutches' – without flying buttresses – succeeded in overcoming the problem of load and support by means of a construction that followed the paths of force. This meant that he could subject the entire architectural organism to an expressive will that need take no account of the usual principles of construction. The supports of the walkways in the Güell Park, of the crypt of the Colonia Güell chapel (ill. 16) and of the Sagrada Familia church were all worked out partly through diagrams, partly through models, and partly by improvisation on the spot. Gaudí's statics relied on intuition backed up by experience. Work on the site proceeded with an endless series of spontaneous decisions: the final appearance of the building was not something that could be determined until the last workman laid down his tools. This method was beyond the scope of the Jugendstil and Expressionist archi-

119

tects alike: this was action-building, architecture as a happening.

Gaudí's way of going about things would have been unthinkable but for the exceptionally high level of craftsmanship in the Catalan building trade. The creative potential of handicraft, so often hailed in Central Europe, was actually to hand in Catalonia and was something of which the architects of Modernismo made full use. What elsewhere meant a regression to conditions of the past in Catalonia meant progress, artistic experiment there made use of available talent as a matter of course.

'Architectural Cubism' in Prague

The understanding of architectural volume in terms of monumental, cubic shapes, an attitude which emerged in Central Europe soon after the turn of the century, was compared by contemporary critics with Cubist painting. The two things in fact had no more in common than a preference for straight lines and right angles. The true principles of analytical Cubism only took effect in architecture after the Expressionist phase. The most that can be said is that the apparently indeterminate architectural compositions of the twenties, that both permeate space and are permeated by it, play the same kind of subtle, thoughtful, and

120

121

122

intelligent game as Picasso's and Braque's pictures of 1910 to 1920.

The year 1911, however, saw a premature and superficial attempt to harness Cubism in the service of architecture. It was confined to a single city, Prague, and to a period of about a decade. A group of artists in their thirties, who belonged to the Skupina výtvarných umělců (Avant-garde Artists' Union) and contributed to the magazine Umělecký měsíčník ('Art Monthly') that appeared from 1911 to 1914, employed prismatic and, later, cylindrical and spherical forms as well in the façades of their buildings (ills. 123–126). The experiment was closely connected with the influence of Parisian Cubism upon Czech artists, an influence which was furthered primarily by the collector and art historian Vincenc Kramář.

In an essay on a new approach to façade design, the theoretician of the group, Pavel Janák, defined the wall as a sculptural termination of space which in turn determines the movement of space.[22] The buildings and projects of Janák himself and of Josef Chochol, Josef Gočár, Vlatislav Hofman and Otakar Novotný to some extent bore out this contention. The façade appears as an autonomous sculpture, but it also reflects

123

117. Francesc Berenguer. Bodegas Güell, Garraf, 1888–95.

118. Josep M. Jujol. Chapel of the Sacrament, Vistabella, 1923.

119. Josep M. Jujol. Torre dels Ous, San Joan Despí, 1914.

120. Josep Puig i Cadafalch. Casarramona, Montjuic, Barcelona, 1911.

121. Antoni Gaudí. Casa Milá, Barcelona, 1906. Façade elevation showing proposed statue of the Virgin in the central gable.

122. Antoni Gaudí. Project for an American hotel, 1908. Pencil drawing by Juan Matamala. Catedra Gaudí Collection, Escuela técnica superior de arquitectura, Barcelona.

123. Josef Chochol. Private house, Prague-Vyšehrad, 1912–13.

124. Otakar Novotný. Apartment building, Prague, 1917.
125. Josef Gočár. Private house, Prague, 1911–12.
126. Vlatislav Hofman. Façade detail, 1914. Linocut from *Der Sturm*, v, no. 6, 1914–15.
127. Marcel Breuer. Technological Institute of New York University, 1964–69. Detail of the façade.

the horizontal movement of the space it screens. 'Shifts occur on [the] surface [of the inner mass] rather as if we were pulling out of or pushing into it in various directions prism-like drawers and interpenetrating slabs' (Josef Čapek).[23] Even when the intention succeeded, the Cubist quotations retained a purely ornamental character. Segmentation was restricted to the outer shell, and the ground plan remained unaltered.

The reaction of the avant-garde artists of Prague in one respect resembled that of the Catalan Modernists: they used their international contacts to increase their regional independence from the political centre. Stimuli from Paris were used in Prague as weapons against Vienna and the Austrian Sezession which, as a result of Otto Wagner's success as a teacher, had also influenced the architects of Bohemia, most of whom were pupils of Wagner.

Though this Cubist interlude in architecture was brief, it did not go unnoticed. At the Werkbund exhibition in Cologne in 1914, the Bohemian Werkbund exhibited in the Austrian pavilion works that sought 'beauty in plans and solids by means of sharp-edged contours and daring angles' (Peter Jessen). Herwarth Walden published material about the group in his magazine *Der Sturm*. The knock-kneed, spiky furniture and architectural details of Pavel Janák and Josef Gočár (ill. 125) seem to have attracted attention as early examples of the fashion for zigzags and triangles. The Czechs' call for an 'architecture of noble forms and high emotion' and for animation of materials (Josef Čapek) coincided with the aspirations of many German architects.[24]

4 Around 1910

'Monumentality produces the same effect as great wars, or popular uprisings, or the birth of nations: it liberates, consolidates, and is as much dictator as endorser of fate.'

Arthur Moeller van den Bruck, *Der preußische Stil*, Munich, 1916

The search for imposing effect

'Where do we stand?' asked Hermann Muthesius in a lecture delivered to the Deutsche Werkbund in 1911.[1] Where did the German arts and crafts movement stand? The answer he gave was that it was under way rather than at its destination. The feeling for quality had gained ground, he said, but had still not got through to the public at large. Muthesius believed there was a danger of a return of historicism. The Heimatschutzbewegung or national conservation movement, and publications like Paul Schultze-Naumburg's *Kulturarbeiten* (1904–10) and the book *Um 1800* ('Around 1800') published by Paul Mebes in 1908, had brought the Empire and Biedermeier styles back into favour. A further return to what Mebes called the 'sanctified and traditional paths of the art of our forefathers'[2] was indeed to be feared.

Muthesius argued for an architecture that should be conscious of its time and should strive to typify it. Suppression of individual elements and stress on essentials were what determined the institutions of big business and the state. Muthesius wanted to see art organized in a similar manner; he wanted an architecture founded on purpose, materials, and function, yet not slavishly dependent on them but rather crowned and justified by the strict discipline of form, by the 'spiritual'. Muthesius' lecture was dynamite, not only in its implied polemic against the Heimatschutzbewegung but also in its demand for the *Typisch* – for architectural 'types', norms or standards: as early as 1911, but more particularly in the famous Werkbund debate of 1914, this ideal was held up against the idea of architecture as the product of the artist's individuality. Nevertheless the theses put forward in the lecture fell well within the general lines of Werkbund ideology, upon which indeed Muthesius had for several years had a decisive influence.

In the period around 1910 monumentality was the order of the day. 'Monumental art is the highest and most individual expression of the culture of an age', wrote Peter Behrens. Architecture is by its nature a social art: monumental architecture can express, in addition to the physical facts of its construction, the aspirations and mood of the time in which it was built. The subjects of monumental art will naturally be found 'at the point which a people holds in highest esteem, which most deeply affects it, and by which it is animated and moved. It may be the place from which power is exercised, or that which receives the most fervent adoration.'[3]

128. Wilhelm Kreis. Bismarck tower, Lössnitz, Dresden, 1902.

129

130

The search for imposing effect was expressed in a series of public buildings for which the literature of the time offers the apt term 'Cyclopean style'. They are characterized by solid silhouettes, simple contours, horizontal skylines and flanking pylons or towers with dome-like superstructures (which, by accident or design, often recall the mausoleum of Theodoric at Ravenna), and by the use of solemn axes of symmetry and rough undressed masonry. Echoes of historical styles are to be found as a rule only in details. The general design is dominated by a crude originality.

Bruno Schmitz's Völkerschlacht memorial at Leipzig, of 1898, is an early example of this trend (ill. 36). Wilhelm Kreis (1873–1955), who from his 1900 design for the Burschenschaft memorial in Eisenach onwards was the expert on tower-monuments to Bismarck (ill. 128), proved himself a 'Cyclops' not only in his numerous memorials but also in the Museum für Vorgeschichte in Halle (ill. 129): its massiveness recalls the Porta Nigra at Trier, which Kreis counted among his prototypes. He renounced a thoroughly sculptural treatment of the wall, however, in the interests of the stereometric effect of the building as a whole. A certain Cubist solidity suggested itself in museum building, partly because of the need for top-lit interiors and partly as a consequence of the idea of a place set aside for art and shielded from the profane, day-to-day world. Hermann Billing's Kunsthalle in Mannheim is a striking confirmation of this tendency.

Fritz Schumacher (1869–1947) defended his claims to monumentality in a more discriminating way than Kreis with his architectural poster-style. As a teacher at the technical university in Dresden, Schumacher had Heckel, Kirchner, and Schmidt-Rottluff, who later founded the group of painters called 'Die Brücke', among his architectural students. In the case of his Dresden crematorium (ill. 130) the very nature of the commission called for solemn ceremonial, for even as late as 1908 cremation was still a highly controversial subject.

The declamatory spirit in which architects conceived their monumental buildings is clear from their impassioned ink- and charcoal-drawings, tortured works in which towering masses loom threateningly in front of stormy horizons. This architecture of bound and embossed masonry can be seen in the National Romanticism of Finland and in the buildings of Henry Hobson Richardson in the United States.[4]

129. Wilhelm Kreis. Museum für Vorgeschichte, Halle, 1913–14.
130. Fritz Schumacher. Crematorium, Dresden, 1908–11.
131. Paul Bonatz. Project for a war memorial, 1915.
132. Paul Bonatz and Friedrich Eugen Scholer. Main railway station, Stuttgart, 1911–28.

131

132

Picturesque monumentality

The main railway station in Stuttgart, by Paul Bonatz (1877–1951) and Friedrich Eugen Scholer, is one of the principal exemplars of the new monumentality (ills. 93, 132). The fact that it took so long to build, work being interrupted by the war, made it a contemporary of the Dessau Bauhaus, although in concept it dated from the monumental phase of 1914. Despite the fact that Bonatz and Scholer's competition design, with its asymmetrically placed clock-tower, had its prototypes in nineteenth-century station architecture, particularly in Eliel Saarinen's main station at Helsinki (1904–14), it was rightly regarded as being something out of the ordinary. The uncompromising horizontal terminations, the casing of rough limestone that makes the rustication on Florentine Renaissance palaces look delicate in comparison, and the lofty proportions of the halls and colonnades produced an effect of austere dignity. The halls Bonatz admitted to having 'consciously intensified beyond the useful and secular'.[5] In 1915 he submitted a design for a war memorial that looks like one of the portals of his Stuttgart station (ill. 131). The Stuttgart painter Willi Baumeister wondered why, to purchase such a small thing as a railway ticket, one had to pass through such vast and stately halls.

For all its brash rhetoric of 1914 Stuttgart station does contain elements that make a comparison with the modern architecture of the twenties meaningful. The individual components of the building could be combined in a variety of ways, so that the design was easily adaptable to changing conditions. In the original plan the tower and the main portal stood close to one another; but a new street that they were to have terminated failed to materialize, and their position was changed. The building's individual components, even if out of proportion to the occasion, are clearly related to their respective functions: the portal of the main-line entrance hall is considerably larger than the portal of the suburban hall.

The ambiguous situation of these years can also be seen in the grouping of volumes. On the one hand Stuttgart station met the demand for picturesque impressiveness which in Germany was associated with the name of Bonatz's teacher, Theodor Fischer. On the other hand the asymmetrical grouping of masses gave rise, with every change of viewpoint, to the kind of optical displacement of the different parts of the building that was called for by the 'space-time architecture' of the International Style. Indeed the realization that architectural form cannot be developed independently of the rhythms of big-city movement by no means originated in the Dessau Bauhaus days. Peter Behrens wrote in 1914 that the speed of city traffic demanded broadly expansive surfaces, series of evenly sized details, and 'clear contrasting of prominent features'.[6] These criteria might have been derived from Stuttgart station as much as from Behrens' own work.

Behrens himself was much more strongly influenced by classical ideas of organization and was indebted in detail to the legacy of Schinkel. Yet he too combined the monumental with the picturesque, sometimes in one and the same building. His light engine factory for AEG on the Humboldthain in Berlin is dominated by the even rhythm of gigantic half-columns along the two-hundred-metre street frontage (ill. 37); the rear of the building, by contrast, is treated in a more relaxed

133. Peter Behrens. AEG works on the Humboldthain, Berlin-Wedding, 1909–12. North-west entrance. Watercolour by W. Obronski, 1912.
134. Peter Behrens. Gas-works in Osthafen, Frankfurt am Main, 1911–12. Water tower and cylindrical containers.
135. Peter Behrens. Gas-works in Osthafen, Frankfurt am Main. Site plan. A instrument house, B cylindrical containers, C–F factory buildings and workshops, G–I social, administrative and residential buildings, K furnace houses, L gasometers.

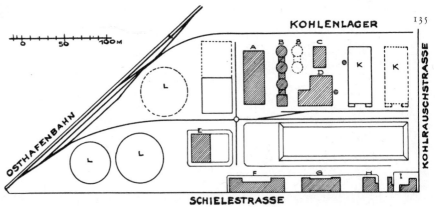

136

fashion with lateral wings, staircase towers, and windows of varying sizes. The informal arrangement of the AEG buildings, which is in such opposition to the strict principles of serial arrangement that governs the individual façades, was of course the result of the programme. On the Humboldthain site, where 13,000 workers were employed, only a few buildings could be rebuilt or converted. Work areas were to be kept free from vertical circulation, which thus required extra structures of its own – hence the staircase towers. Unification by means of a consistent plan was not possible. Nor, however, was it desired.

Behrens in fact went out of his way to heighten the impression of diversity by staggering his building lines, stressing individual parts of the complex, and using a variety of formal motifs. The north-west entrance to the complex appears to lead into a gigantic, but none the less idyllic, works yard (ill. 133). Grouped in depth along the entrance diagonal are towers, halls, temple-like portals, and neutral surfaces of glass. In one of the many irritating about-faces of his career, after the war Behrens advocated a new Romanticism. The move was not entirely unheralded. The irrationalism of the Hoechst office-building – a post-war building, free of symmetrical relationships, with balconies, a bridge, a clock tower, a belfry, parabolic windows, tapestry-like wall textures and a cathedral-like main hall (ills. 136, 137) – was anticipated in the loose layout of the AEG buildings, if not in their harder, more sober individual forms.

The extent to which the big buildings of the late Wilhelmine period were intended as artistic utterances was demonstrated in a complex where one would have expected function to dictate form: the gas-works in Frankfurt's Osthafen (ills. 134, 135). The individual buildings

136, 137. Peter Behrens. IG Farben building, Höchst, 1920–24. Main hall, and bridge with clock tower. Charcoal drawings. Archives of the Farbwerke Hoechst.

were arranged without the use of rigid axes. The plant buildings and the residential buildings for employees were each treated – by means of pilasters and wall-panels, different types of roof, and the use of polychrome stone – as largely independent elements and, in the eyes of the architect and his contemporaries, raised to the level of art. This attempt to give artistic value to buildings of practical necessity took on a surrealist character in the cylindrical containers for water, tar, and liquid ammonia. They are decorated with a scroll frieze and joined by flying buttresses, and with their projecting upper parts they suggest the stout 'rampart towers of old Nuremberg', as Behrens' biographer remarked with satisfaction.[7] As a base for the slimmer water tower Behrens used a kind of Romanesque block capital – upside down! It is a conceit worthy of Ledoux, and with it the classical or rudely stereometric formal material turns fantastic.

The dispute over architectural 'types'

The historians of modern architecture have passed varying judgments on the architects of this monumental phase. Behrens got off quite lightly. The method of composing with isolated or independent architectural masses, even if they were on a gigantic scale, heralded an openness of system which was admittedly only put into practice by other men and not by Behrens himself. Behrens' habit of drawing a distinction in his buildings between load elements and supporting elements appeared to be an important step in the direction of transparency of form in relation to construction. In practice, however, Behrens rarely expressed structural relationships. On the contrary, he sometimes deliberately concealed them. In the end wall of the famous turbine factory it is the lightest visual elements, the delicate uprights of the windows, that bear the load. The heaviest visual elements, the concrete corner-piers that lean inwards as if under a tremendous weight, are only infill.

137

The tectonics of their elevations and the isolation of their architectural masses distinguish these buildings from those of Expressionism. But Monumentalism did pave the way for Expressionist architecture. Function and construction stood in an irrational relationship to form. Wherever it appeared possible to achieve powerfully massive effects, logic had to take a back seat. Rough surface textures or contrasts between rugged and delicately wrought are as sought to stimulate the sense of touch. Even the many façades of Behrens' buildings that look as if they have been stamped out are made up of differently toned and graded brick and iron clinker.

In their combination of 'painterly' details and an impressively large scale, these buildings resolved a conflict that had divided contemporary theoreticians, with the pupils of Fischer on one side, and the disciples of Ostendorf on the other. Theodor Fischer (1862–1938), the proponent of cosy, comfortable architecture, taught liberation from the constraint of academically articulated façades and adaptation to nature as a principle of town planning. All form, he said, sprang from life. At the opposite extreme, Friedrich Ostendorf (1871–1915), professor at the technical university in Karlsruhe, contended that truly architectonic designs were only possible on the basis of easily accessible mental images. Such images must be reduced to their simplest manifestation. A building based on a mental image was simple, clear, and legitimate; a design conceived on paper, on the other hand, was complicated, unclear, and arbitrary. Ostendorf illustrated his *Bücher vom Bauen* ('Books about Building') of 1913–20 partly with historical examples and partly with designs of his own based on the simpler town and country houses of the eighteenth and early nineteenth centuries.

Ostendorf's polemic was aimed at several targets. He disapproved of the architects of the school of Fischer, who strove towards an architecture freed from the yoke of symmetry, and also of the architects of the English 'free planning' school which, thanks to the publications of Hermann Muthesius, had gained some ground in country-house architecture. Muthesius himself accused his Karlsruhe colleague of wanting to put the clock back. The accusation was justified where Ostendorf's own formal inclinations were concerned. It is however characteristic of the paradoxical nature of this transitional period that even Ostendorf with his historical orientation had the

138. Hermann Muthesius. Stave house, Lübeck-Marly.

139. Friedrich Ostendorf. Corrected version of the Stave house by Hermann Muthesius. From Ostendorf's *Sechs Bücher vom Bauen*, Berlin, 1913.

future on his side. For one thing, his idealistic exaltation of the architect's vision anticipated the ideas-architecture of Expressionism, which as a rule departed similarly from preconceived formal images. The Expressionists' mental images of form may have differed radically in content from Ostendorf's retrospective thinking, but both parties stood in the front line against 'naturalistic' architecture based on a free ground plan.

In a second argument, however, Ostendorf, while publicly criticizing the buildings of Muthesius, played into his opponent's hands (ills. 138, 139). Ostendorf believed in the binding nature of tradition as a coiner of 'types'. In his view the work of art was not the personal creation of a great architect but an achievement in which several generations might have a hand. Muthesius shared this conviction when he demanded an architecture of stability, repose, and longevity, of evenness of proportion, clarity, and consistency in the as-

semblage of masses. Muthesius, who as an architect was by no means committed to one particular direction, may have been thinking of the new industrial architecture as represented by Behrens; Ostendorf of a simplified Baroque palace. The *typical* was something both regarded as desirable.

The thoughts that Muthesius had advanced in favour of norms in his 1911 lecture *Wo stehen wir?* ('Where do we stand?') led, three years later, at the Werkbund conference in Cologne, to a row that threatened to blow the Werkbund apart. Muthesius saw the formation of types as a precondition of a consensus of taste, a harmonious culture. Although by 'typical' he did not mean to imply standardization or industrialization, the artists mobilized a powerful opposition against him. To the ten theses which Muthesius had advanced Henry van de Velde put up counter-theses, in which he had the support of August Endell, Hermann Obrist, Karl Ernst Osthaus, and Bruno Taut. In the heated discussions, declarations, and exchange of telegrams behind the scenes, none represented the artists' cause with greater zeal than Gropius. Gropius, though he had been working since 1909 towards the standardization and industrialization of house-building, felt much too deeply indebted to the 'great and simple manifestation' and the 'harmony of architecture, sculpture, and painting' of which artists were the guarantors to be able to recognize how Muthesius' lecture in fact formulated his own intentions.[8]

Essentially, the positions were much closer than the parties to the dispute believed. Muthesius did not for a moment think of encroaching on the artist's freedom. The 'orderly' architecture he was talking about was largely realized in the monumental 'artists' architecture' of the years preceding 1914. The violence of the Werkbund quarrel, which flared up again in 1919, is not to be explained by its apparent cause. Personal antagonisms had something to do with it. Partly, too, the artists' protest was

aimed at the political 'mercantilism' of the Werkbund, despite the fact that even Muthesius' opponents, people like Osthaus and Gropius, had long accepted it. But above all it was due to the apprehensive reaction of these artists – and with them the architects – against their growing isolation. As accomplices of modern capitalism, interpreters of given aims and demands, architects were able to experience a measure of integration. As 'glowing individualists' and 'free, spontaneous creators' (Henry van de Velde) they were beginning to feel frustrated.

In the fine arts this crisis in artists' understanding of themselves soon came out in Dada and Surrealism, where it took the form of increasing introspection. The self-confidence of artists in the applied arts apparently remained intact. In the conditions obtaining in 1910 architects were able to work with greater originality and greater independence in matters of form than they had been able to in the nineteenth century, and than they were to be able to in the New Architecture of 1920. When van de Velde advocated brilliant fantasy and Bruno Taut demanded a dictatorship in artistic affairs, nominating van de Velde or Poelzig as dictator, they were prompted by a sense of mission which was to find fulfilment again in Expressionism.

Seen in the larger perspective, however, this dispute was still a retreat. Behind the bitterness with which it was conducted lay scruples and conflicts which could not in the end be repressed.

Berg and Poelzig

The trend towards the monumental in architecture just before the First World War was expressed not only in the aesthetics of the buildings erected, but also in their size. The Jahrhunderthalle, or Centennial Hall, in Breslau was designed by Max Berg (1870–1947) and completed in 1913. It exceeded what had hitherto been the biggest dome in the world, that of the Pantheon in Rome, by half its span – 67 metres as against 43 (ills. 140–142).

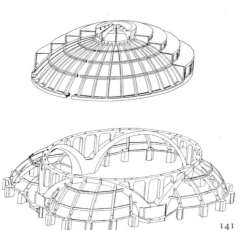

Unlike Friedrich von Thiersch's somewhat older Festhalle in Frankfurt, of 1909, it was built of reinforced concrete. The choice of material was, in the words of Berg and Trauer, the building's engineer, to ensure that it should 'bear witness to the culture of our time even after the passage of centuries'. This reinforced-concrete structure constituted a literal embodiment of Horace's *monumentum aere perennius*, 'a monument more lasting than brass'. No other building of the pre-war period more strikingly overplayed its secular purpose without resorting to stylistic trimmings. Erich Mendelsohn saw in this symbol of patriotism – ceremonially opened with Gerhart Hauptmann's pageant in memory of the 1813 'War of Liberation' and intended for congresses, song festivals, gymnastic displays, etc. – both 'earthly and heavenly audacity'. 'One day we too will have to extend our technical thinking to cover sacred ends.'[10]

What made Berg's Centennial Hall one of the buildings of the century was the way monumental effect was derived from the very explicitness of the construction. In his book *Formprobleme der Gotik*, published two years earlier, in 1911, Wilhelm Worringer had spoken of the 'superfluous construction mania' of the

Gothic style in which construction and artistic intention were, for no immediate practical purpose, made one. The same applies to the magnificent dome of the Jahrhunderthalle. The corporeality of the supporting structure is the outcome of statical necessities. It derives chiefly from the fact that the powerful main arches of the supporting structure stand on a circular plan and are consequently bent out of line. They also become thicker towards the abutments, which heightens their sculptural effect. Just as in Gothic buildings the thrust of the vault is countered by flying buttresses, in the Jahrhunderthalle the flying buttresses of the four apses take up the lateral thrust (ill. 141). Above the supporting structure thirty-two ribs shoot up to a pressure ring at the top of the dome on which a smaller cupola rests. The exposed concrete, on which the marks of the forms are apparent, would certainly have appealed to Le Corbusier.

Yet even this building is not completely free from convention and compromise. Berg wanted to avoid a glass roof on acoustic grounds. So he decided in favour of side-lighting through vertical bands of windows in the walls and tiers of windows between the ribs of the dome. Seen from outside, the superstruc-

ture is terraced, and gives no hint of the flow of forces in the dome inside. Inappropriate also was the timid attempt to relate this centralized structure to one of the main axes of the exhibition site (ill. 142) by means of a portico.

The second important architect working in Silesia at the time, Hans Poelzig, was also associated with the Breslau exhibition. Poelzig designed the exhibition hall itself, a square building consisting of four domed rooms, and also a temporary administration building and a long colonnade around an artificial lake (ills. 142, 143). The stocky columns in these buildings are the result not so much of classical revival as of Poelzig's desire for an *architecture parlante*, in which architectural forms would symbolize a building's meaning or purpose. Here Poelzig wanted to suggest the period around 1813, which the exhibition was commemorating. The columns were cast in

140, 141. Max Berg, Jahrhunderthalle or Centennial Hall, Breslau (Wroclaw)-Scheitnig, 1911–13. Interior, and diagram of the dome and its support system.
142. Max Berg. Design for the exhibition grounds, Breslau (Wroclaw)–Scheitnig, showing the Centennial Hall, Poelzig's exhibition building, and unexecuted auxiliary buildings.

143. Hans Poelzig. Colonnade and exhibition building, Breslau (Wroclaw)–Scheitnig, 1913.

concrete, and Poelzig departed from traditional proportions and simplified the details, so that apart from their historical symbolism they also symbolize the material of which they are made.

Like Max Berg, Poelzig erected a building which drew its monumental effect from its construction. His water tower in Posen (now Poznan) was the steel counterpart of Berg's concrete hall (ills. 144–146). The expression of the material used was here even more obvious than in Poelzig's buildings at Breslau, because until the installation of the reservoir the tower functioned as an exhibition pavilion for the Upper Silesian mining industry (the top level served as a refreshment area). On the façade the iron framework was left exposed. The textile-like patterning of the brickwork showed that it was mere filling. Inside, the steel supports and diagonal braces produced labyrinthine perspectives. The 'scattered sticks' that had irritated Gropius in early iron or steel constructions[11] did not worry Poelzig, the artist, in the least. On the other hand, undogmatic as he was, he gave the staircase closed sides and banisters, making it wind its way up to the gallery like some prehistoric reptile, a vast showpiece romanticizing technology (ill. 146). The lean-to roofs of the sixteen-sided building do not correspond to the structure, because Poelzig was concerned to have a building that sat solidly on the ground and was built up in terrace-like layers. The Posen water tower is stocky and powerful; in spite of the generous distribution of windows the building forms a solid mass, like everything Poelzig designed during his Breslau period – country houses, blocks of flats, an office building, a church, a town hall, and some factories.

Among the things which Poelzig demanded of modern industrial architecture at the time were a quietly austere silhouette and a solid wall-plane, in which the windows are not sculpturally emphasized as penetrations of the wall but related to its surface by their frames.[12] He used these features himself in his design for the Werder mill in Breslau (ill. 147) and in the buildings he erected for the chemical works at Luban, near Posen (ills. 148–150). In coming to terms with the architectural requirements of industry, Poelzig did not make things easy for himself. He believed in the possibility of the engineer's emancipation in artistic matters, and he realized that industrial buildings are built not for eternity but at most for about fifty years.

Nevertheless the essence of his thinking turned out to be no different from that of Behrens or Gropius. Industrial buildings, being least subject to preconceptions and hence more open to the new, ought to be the most powerful and typical expressions of the age. It was a

144–146. Hans Poelzig. Water tower, Posen (Poznan), 1911. Exterior, interior with exhibition spaces, and staircase.

145

144

146

question of finding new symbolic forms. In the façade of his design for the Werder mill Poelzig sought to achieve this kind of symbolic effect by setting glass sections side by side with solid areas of wall. Gropius, who admired Poelzig's buildings,[13] used what is essentially the same device in his Fagus factory at Alfeld and in his office building for the Cologne Werkbund exhibition. Unlike his Berlin colleagues, however, Poelzig effortlessly combined diverse elements in a unified architectural whole. Where Gropius and Behrens placed their staircases in distinctive parts of the building, Poelzig enjoyed the apparent arbitrariness of variously sized wall-apertures placed at varying heights, determined by the heights of the storeys and the courses of the staircases, in a single architectural unit.

Poelzig saw no fundamental contradiction between the demands of art and the demands of function. In his eyes the architect was – for the time being, at least – superior to the engineer in that he could take a particular set of constructional and economic demands and from them evolve new formal relationships and powerful rhythms. The Luban site, for example, owed part of its romantic strangeness of atmosphere to the varied treatment – justifiable on constructional grounds – of the openings: round-headed windows in a load-bearing wall, and rectangular windows where vertical and horizontal metal bands had been incorporated in the courses of brick masonry (ill. 148). And of course there was no lack of motifs, such as the medievalizing stepped gable, with no functional basis whatever.

The House of Friendship

Berg's Jahrhunderthalle and Poelzig's Posen water tower suggested the possibility of an Expressionism under the spell of technique. This development was not followed up. Poelzig's entry in the competition for a 'House of Friendship' in Istanbul (ills. 22, 23) was already charac-

terized by a monumentality which, though it did not disregard function and construction, did not make any aesthetic capital out of them. Poelzig's drawing of the terraced building gives away as little about its internal arrangements as it does about the building's relationship to town planning. The idea of the slope of the hillside being extended architectonically triumphed over all other considerations, even diplomatic ones (see p. 18). It is in fact highly questionable whether any nation has the right to impose itself upon an alien culture in so violently authoritarian a manner as Germany would have done had Poelzig's design been built.

The competition, which the German-Turkish Union organized in 1916 and in which, on the advice of the Deutsche Werkbund, it invited twelve architects to participate, provided in the middle of the war a resumé of German architecture as represented by its most distinguished practitioners (ills. 151–154). Invitations went out to Peter Behrens, German Bestelmeyer, Paul Bonatz, Hugo Eberhardt, Martin Elsässer, August Endell, Theodor Fischer, Bruno Paul, Hans Poelzig, Richard Riemerschmid, and Bruno Taut. Walter Gropius failed to obtain leave from the front and was prevented from taking part. Erich Mendelsohn, at the age of thirty still a relative beginner, seems to have been inspired by the competition or by the resulting Werkbund publication to a Utopian design, as the title and appearance of one of his sketches suggest (ill. 279).

Although privately financed by interested industrialists, the House of Friendship was conceived as an instrument of imperial foreign policy. It was to cement the alliance between Germany and Turkey both culturally and politically. With the end of the war the project was naturally abandoned. Many an imposing gesture had its origin in the thought of an imperial show-piece in the Near East. The fact that most of the participants nevertheless settled for an articulated complex rather than for a rigorous formal entity was due to the

147

147. Hans Poelzig. Project for the Werder mill, Breslau (Wroclaw), 1906.
148–150. Hans Poelzig. Chemical works, Luban near Posen (Poznan), 1911–12.

148

149

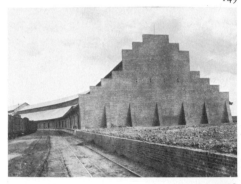

150

heterogeneous nature of the programme. This required facilities for theatrical performances, lectures, festivals, concerts and exhibitions as well as flats for students, a library, and a restaurant.

Apart from Poelzig it was above all Bonatz and Taut who were inspired by the unusual nature of the project. Whereas other designers manipulated various reminiscences from Early Christian church architecture to columned halls in the style of the Italian Renaissance to domestic motifs from the German past, Bonatz piled up powerful cubic volumes (ill. 152). The interiors were all solemnity, and on the exterior the effect was further heightened by stately verticals. The roofline was finished off with toothed crenellations, soon to become one of the most popular formulae in representational architecture.

Bruno Taut was the only one to use a dome; its pierced concrete structure made for an interesting silhouette (ill. 151). The idea of the Oriental setting appears to have had a liberating effect on Taut. No one group of motifs in his gay assortment of forms resembles another. Symmetrical relationships govern only parts of the ground plan and elevation. In the context of Taut's work, the House of Friendship was the first of the many magnificent architectural creations with which he sought to 'crown' cities and mountains.

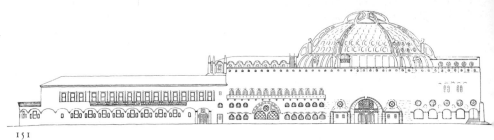

151

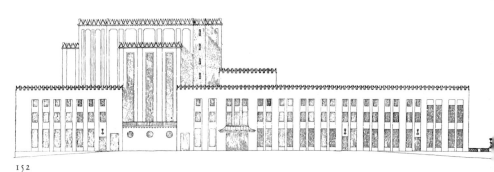

152

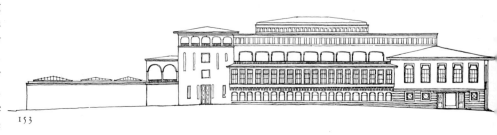

153

151–154. Projects for the House of Friendship, Istanbul, 1916.
151. Bruno Taut.
152. Paul Bonatz.
153. Peter Behrens.
154. Martin Elsässer.

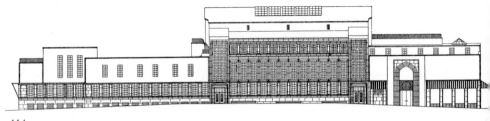

154

Bruno Taut

My torch dazzles me, but I am determined to carry it.'

Bruno Taut to Karl Ernst Osthaus, 14 November 1919

The call for a leader

The fact that he was invited along with the leading members of his profession to take part in the competition for the German-Turkish House of Friendship testifies to the kind of reputation that Bruno Taut (1880–1938), the youngest participant but one, enjoyed among his colleagues. When Taut took up his role as spokesman of the young German architects of the post-war period he had a considerable amount of practical experience behind him. Expressionist architecture was by no means the work of fanatics ignorant of the ways of the world. The buildings Taut erected before the outbreak of the First World War hinted already at the kind of problems which were to occupy him in later life. A rest-home at Bad Harzburg (1909–1910) shows his social commitment. In the twenties he concentrated his attention on residential architecture: before the war he was already concerned with a number of apartment buildings in Berlin and the two garden cities of Falkenberg near Berlin and Reform near Magdeburg. Taut's pavilions at the 1913 building-trade exhibition in Leipzig and the 1914 Werkbund exhibition in Cologne showed his no less strong didactic interests.

Architecture alone was never enough for Taut. He was a born organizer, a keen experimenter with words and actions, a leader of men and a maker of enemies, the author of numerous appeals and circulars, a man who was always taking the initiative with fresh ideas, an avid reader and a tireless writer. A 'delicate bundle of nerves' was how Paul Bonatz described him. Though he did not like Taut, Bonatz assisted him in 1933 on his adventurous escape from Russia through Nazi Germany to Japan.

Taut, Bonatz felt, made everything unhealthy by his habit of exaggerating.[1]

In Taut we find almost every one of the ideas that moved his colleagues in the architectural profession – and moved them, in many cases, precisely because they had received the ideas from him in the first place. Artistically, there were undoubtedly more powerful figures than Taut: his drawings are not entirely free of dilettantism and their effectiveness is due more to their content than to their graphic quality. But as a communicator of ideas Taut was a key figure in the architecture of the post-war period. Around 1920 he was a one-man encyclopaedia of all the ideas then in vogue about building, about art, about society, and about the future.

A love of polemics was an essential part of the make-up of this sensitive and easily excitable man; and so was an unmistakable Messianic streak. 'I believe firmly in my mission . . . marvellous that the young, the twenty-year-olds, have such belief in me.' He saw himself in 1919 as a leader aloof from the commonplace world of everyday life: 'but the call for a leader did not come.'[2]

Taut's personal sense of mission matched perfectly his conception of the task of the architect as such. Here again he put at its clearest what some of his colleagues in the profession sensed as well: 'Building, when all is said and done, is the recognition of matter and the abolition of all contradiction between it and mind'.[3] The architect becomes demiurge, the demiurge architect. Taut's 'architecture play', a scenario he drafted in August and September 1919 and in which he sought to represent the creative principle at work, was entitled *Der Weltbaumeister* – 'The World Architect' (ills. 155, 156). As depicted in a series of twenty-eight charcoal drawings which were published in book form in 1920, the action takes the form of the interplay of different colours and shapes as they appear and disappear. A deep stage was needed to allow the effects of a cathedral rising up and crumbling to the ground,

stars approaching and retreating, plants growing wild, the earth's crust splitting, and the gleaming crystal house emerging in the crimson light of evening, opening up, and gradually unfolding: 'Architecture – night – space . . . all one'.

It is revealing that, for the music to accompany his work, Taut had his eye on the late-Romantic composer Hans Pfitzner, who had treated this same theme of creativity in his opera *Palestrina*, first performed in 1917.[4] In Taut's schema, which is as it were a permanent cosmogony of the 'holy' world, man was excluded on the grounds of his aesthetically disruptive individuality. He was only indirectly present in the manifestations of this continually self-renewing realm of nature and art – as the point of crystallization at which the building wave of creation took shape, as architect.

It is possible to interpret these wild speculations as an interiorization of external troubles, because in addition to the worries that afflicted all German architects in the post-war period, Taut had special cause for concern. He was afraid that his reputation as a 'visionary architect', a 'high flyer', would harm him, and if one looks at what his contemporaries wrote about him this fear seems to have been not without foundation. In the hope of improving his financial position, Taut worked simultaneously on a large number of different publication projects – three volumes for the Folkwang Verlag, *Die Stadtkrone* for Diederichs, a magazine to be entitled *Bauen* which he, Behne, and Gropius wanted to produce for the general public, and the (later independent) supplement *Frühlicht* which was to find its way into architects' offices as part of the magazine *Stadtbaukunst alter und neuer Zeit*. At times he appears to have regarded his journalistic activities as a substitute for the architectural commissions which failed to materialize; yet he enthused about the 'nights of passionate activity in which I build the new world' and was 'almost intoxicated' by the vision of his *Die Weltbaumeister*.[5]

155

156

Paul Scheerbart

Taut dedicated *Der Weltbaumeister* to the poet Paul Scheerbart (1863–1915), who had died five years before the book's publication. His Glass Pavilion at the Cologne Werkbund exhibition of 1914 had also been dedicated to the poet, and Scheerbart in turn included in his book *Glasarchitektur* (1914) a dedication to Taut. Scheerbart's influence can be seen throughout Taut's work. Taut found the same inspiration in the curious, cosmic novels of this successor to Cyrano de Bergerac, Swift, Rabelais, and Brentano as he found in the texts of the mystics – the joy in change that turns every death into a rebirth.

In the last years of Scheerbart's life and after his death Taut, along with Adolf Behne, was one of his most ardent propagandists and it was thanks to Taut's persistence that Scheerbart gained a certain posthumous reputation among architects. His visions of sapphire towers and emerald domes, diamond castles and suspended restaurants, mountain-top buildings and crystalline stars gave his disciples the 'certainty of a far-off home'. Taut and the members of his circle actually used them as texts for their drawings. In this way Scheerbart gradually became the 'true patron saint of genuine architecture', 'a St Paul'.[6]

Scheerbart also had suggestions of a more concrete nature for architects. His book *Glasarchitektur* contained 111 paragraphs of arguments in favour of glass: like all Scheerbart's work the book was sloppily put together, but it did contain real facts. He quoted precedents, from the Gothic cathedral to the palm-house at Berlin-Dahlem, stressed the importance of double-glazing for thermal insulation and colour effects, and argued for a combination of steel supports and lighting tubes. 'The whole structure gives a much freer effect – as if everything were self-supporting.' The entire world was to become a single source of light, with lighthouses for the airship traffic, gigantic steel and glass windmills, floating glass buildings, and mountain illuminations. 'On Venus and Mars they will raise their eyebrows in astonishment as the surface of the Earth changes beyond recognition.' Scheerbart even foresaw the competition to glass of plastics.

Scheerbart may have had some contact with Taut before the publication of his *Glasarchitektur*, but the ideas were essentially Scheerbart's own. He had been interested in the problem of building in glass long before he met Taut. An essay written as early as 1898 contains an analysis of the window as source of light, means of ventilation, and point of contact with the outside world, with Scheer-bart arguing in favour of the separation of the three functions.[7] He thus anticipated the fully air-conditioned buildings of a later period, although he would have found their stereotyped character repellent.

What Scheerbart, Taut, and Behne hoped for from the new 'glass culture' was nothing less than a new morality. 'A person who daily sets eyes on the splendours of glass *cannot* do wicked deeds. *Dixi*.' What Scheerbart proclaimed light-heartedly became with Behne a dogma. For him glass stood for a brighter awareness, clearer determination, and that 'utter gentleness' which glass possessed in spite of its sharp edges. More far-reaching moral effects have probably never been attributed to aesthetic causes. Taut himself, who signed his letters to friends with the pseudonym *Glas*, added a cosmological perspective in the spirit of Scheerbart. Glass was the material in which mind and matter were reconciled: 'Glass – molten, liquid earth only afterwards becoming solid and yet transparent, shimmering, sparkling, flashing, teeming with endless reflections in the light of space'.[8]

In addition, the enduring precision of glass distinguished it from natural materials such as brick and timber which, being affected by weather, were subject to decay. (The fragility of glass was gnored.) Taut continued to propagate what was virtually a mythology of glass throughout his life, though the emphases changed. In an essay of 1925 he stressed the power of glass to open up spaces and to enclose them. Glass here appears not so much as something that brings about a change in people as a material that promotes communication. In architecture where much glass is used, people will no longer peer out of the window-openings like imprisoned grasshoppers'.[9] The excessive use of glass in modern architecture is incomprehensible without this irrational background.

Projects for crystal buildings

Adolf Behne, who had hailed 'the alluring beauty of the ideal' – the ideal of glass architecture – saw 'a delightful fragment' of his ideal in the pavilion which Bruno Taut built for the glass industry, at the entrance to the 1914 Werkbund exhibition in Cologne (ills. 163–167).[10] Taut had received a similar commission a year before, for the 'Monument to Iron' which he built as the pavilion of the German steel industries at the building-trade exhibition in Leipzig (ills. 161, 162). In Leipzig Taut had superimposed four tapering octagonal shapes, with the top one, an open steel framework, surrounding a dome of gilded zinc that crowned the building. Despite this unusual piling up of stereometric bodies the building retained a classical air. This was due to the rectangular frame construc-

57

tion, the design of broader main views and narrower side views, and the careful differentiation of load-bearing and non-load-bearing cylindrical girders.

Centralized ground plans were part of the convention of exhibition pavilions in Germany. They were used above all by Behrens, to whom Taut was indebted in his early exercises in the genre. The Glass Pavilion in Cologne followed this tradition (ills. 163, 164): an addition at the back with stepped roofs – aesthetically the weakest point – was significantly concealed in most of the contemporary photographs. Yet in the construction of his glass building Taut was highly original. A three-dimensional framed structure rises above a concrete base and a fourteen-sided drum. The rhombic mesh of the pineapple-shaped dome consists of reinforced-concrete ribs, the shuttering for which was extraordinarily difficult to make. The octagons of the Leipzig steel building gave no hint as to the layout of the interior; the three upper prisms concealed a two-storey-high cinema auditorium, the dome of which was formed of eight curved steel supports. In the Cologne Glass Pavilion, on the other hand, the identity of form and construction, a key dogma of post-Expressionist architecture, was already a reality.

The Werkbund exhibition had a mixed reception, but three buildings won immediate approval: Taut's Glass Pavilion, van de Velde's theatre and Gropius' factory. Scheerbart, author of the rhyming inscriptions on the plinth, saw the pavilion as the beginning of a new age in architecture. Others found it 'as delicate as a flower', referred to its 'fine spirituality', and called it 'a little jewel', 'captivating in its individuality and completeness'.[11] These comments were prompted by the interior, where a succession of rooms managed to give a foretaste of the delights of the prophesied glass architecture.

The path which the visitor to the pavilion had to follow was characterized by seductive anticipation and an increasingly intense experience of space. From

158

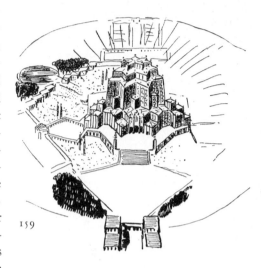

159

160

155, 156. Bruno Taut. Illustrations from *Der Weltbaumeister*, Hagen, 1920.
155. '[It] reveals its halls – – – multicoloured light – – – bells – – –'
156. 'The gleaming crystal building – in the crimson stage light of evening – –'
157. Paul Scheerbart. Vignette from *Revolutionäre Theaterbibliothek*, Berlin, 1904.
158. Bruno Taut. Project for a religious building on a centralized plan, 1905.
159, 160. Bruno Taut. House of Heaven, from *Stadtbaukunst alter und neuer Zeit. Frühlicht*, 1, no. 7, 1920. View and section.

161

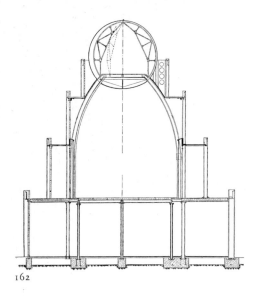

162

the main staircase two outside staircases, one on each side, led up to the upper hall 'vaulted like the inside of some sparkling skull' (ill. 167). In accordance with Scheerbart's prescriptions the dome was double-glazed, with coloured prisms inside and reflecting glass outside. At night it was lit by a bouquet of electric light bulbs and by frosted-glass spheres to the sacred number of seven. A circular opening in the glazed floor led the visitor's eye down to the next stage – the cascade room on the floor below, again reached by two staircases, on the inside this time, with glass steps and glass walls, an 'unreal, unearthly flight of stairs that one descends as if through sparkling water' (ill. 166). Down on this lower floor the visitor found a rotunda with a pool in the centre (ill. 165). The water came bubbling down a cascade of pale yellow glass, terminating in a recess of deep violet in which pictures were projected from a kaleidoscope.[12]

Taut had already begun to explore the possibilities of light-shows in his Leipzig Monument to Iron. There the dim main room on the ground floor had contained photographs on glass which were illuminated by indirect lighting. Various artists designed the different images for the kaleidoscope in the Cologne pavilion, thus contributing to the kind of kinetic light experiments conducted in the second half of the decade by the Russian composer Alexander Scriabin, with his 'light piano', and the Dane Thomas Wilfried, with his 'Clavilux'. The kaleidoscope and waterfall occupied the annex with the stepped roof.

Taut's view was that every building which was not built for an individual but was commissioned by a collective body must be made of glass.[13] The Glass Pavilion at Cologne he regarded merely as a modest beginning (see ills. 55, 159, 160). We can see from Taut's books, *Alpine Architektur*, *Die Auflösung der Städte* and *Die Stadtkrone*, the kind of tasks he expected of glass architecture, but we can also see this from an actual project, the Folkwang School which he

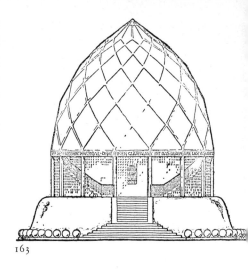

163

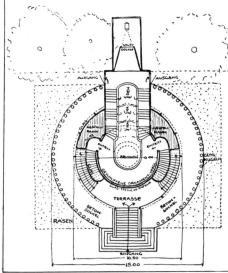

164

165

161, 162. Bruno Taut and Franz Hoffmann with Fa. Breest & Co. Steel Industries Pavilion at the building trade exhibition, Leipzig, 1913. View and section.

163–167. Bruno Taut. Glass Pavilion at the Werkbund exhibition, Cologne, 1914.
163. Elevation.
164. Plan.
165. Cascade room on the ground floor.
166. Staircase leading from the domed hall to the cascade room.
167. Domed hall.

designed for Karl Ernst Osthaus (ills. 12, 168–170). Osthaus had bought a piece of wooded land to the east of Hagen, in the neighbourhood of Eppenhausen, which he named Hohenhagen. Here he planned to erect an architectural complex which, had it ever been completed, would have rivalled Darmstadt's Mathildenhöhe.

Osthaus chose the architects for his garden city with an unerring instinct: Henry van de Velde, Peter Behrens and J. L. Mathieu Lauweriks. He also discussed the Hohenhagen project with Josef Hoffmann, August Endell, Gropius and Taut. Gropius worked on the site plan and hoped to get commissions for the offices of the publishing house, Folkwang Verlag, as well as for two residential buildings.[14] Taut submitted a plan for a residence and a large-scale project that captured the imagination of client and architects alike. Hohenhagen lay at a considerable distance from Hagen, and could not be seen from the city centre; its population was tiny. In spite of this, Taut wanted to erect one of his *Stadtkronen* or urban centrepieces: all the splendour of a New City was to fall upon this little colony that was eventually to total thirteen buildings! For the highest point of land in the Hohenhagen settlement Taut designed a complex that was to include not only a new school complete with farm, workshops, and observatory, the offices of the publishing house, and the Folkwang Museum, but also a towering crystal to be known as the 'House of Prayer'. It was soon apparent that even without the crystal building the project would be impossible to finance. But, Osthaus declared, 'nothing is so important today as to set our sights as high as our imaginations will reach'.[15]

The Hohenhagen crystal-building was no more precise in its programme than were the 'houses of heaven', the 'shrines of the radiant ones', the crystal temples and the enormous churches that appear in Taut's books of the period. In his description of the project Osthaus therefore confined himself to repeating Taut's statement that the plan – a figure composed of two interpenetrating seven-pointed stars – was particularly suitable for pageants and theatrical performances. Taut was thinking of the dramatic cos-

168

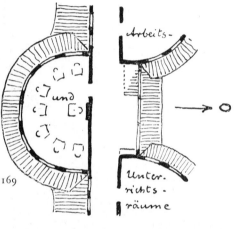

169

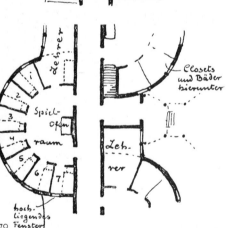

170

168–170. Bruno Taut. Project for the Folkwang School, Hohenhagen estate, Hagen, 1920.
168. View showing the crystal building and observatory.
169, 170. Plans of the residential and school pavilions.

mogonies of Alfred Brust and August Stramm, of dramatizations of the works of Paul Scheerbart, or of his own *Der Weltbaumeister*.

'*Das Licht will durch das ganze All | Und ist lebendig im Kristall*' ('Light seeks to penetrate the whole of space | And is alive in crystal') – so runs one of the rhymes which Scheerbart composed for the plinth of the Cologne Glass Pavilion. To capture, split up, and multiply the light of the cosmos was the true mission of Taut's building: 'All great and fervent feelings shall here be called to life when the full light of the sun overflows the lofty room and breaks up into countless delicate reflections, or when the setting sun fills the vault of the ceiling and deepens with its crimson glow the richly coloured glass pictures and the sculpture . . . Suffused with the light of the sun the crystal pavilion reigns like a glittering diamond over all; a symbol of the highest serenity and the purest peace, it sparkles in the sun.'[16]

Taut's interest in social matters turned out to be the most consistent element in his thinking. It determined his entire activity in the late twenties, when he built large residential estates for Gehag, a Berlin building society, and in 1932 it took him to the Soviet Union, where he hoped – in vain – to see realized his ideal of a popular architecture that should be 'close to the earth'.

In this field too Taut's 'restlessly speculative mind' (Scheffler)[17] assimilated many influences. The Hohenhagen project shows him under the spell of the educational theories that had been developed by the so-called 'free school' movement. A number of country boarding schools had been founded in Germany on the English model, including the Odenwaldschule (founded in 1910), from whose staff Osthaus drew the headmistress of his experimental school. Among the aims of the school reformers were an emphasis on creative activities and practical handicrafts, a considerable degree of self-government, and the division of the school into small communities known as 'families' or 'fellowships'. Rejection of the city was also part of the ideology, and a rural environment was preferred.

Such a platform could not fail to appeal to Taut. Concurrently with the project for the Hohenhagen school he was working on his Utopian picture-book *Die Auflösung der Städte* ('The Dissolution of Cities'), which incorporated a part of this theory of education: 'The child works where he wants to, in the workshop, in the fields, in the garden; he moves about – with no one trying to bend him to his will or put a stamp on him. He is able to live his own life.' Taut's school consisted of a number of pavilions set in a circle around a wide lawn (ill. 168). The individual buildings, semicircular in plan, and connected by an extremely long corridor, were to serve as dormitories, living rooms and classrooms for the different 'families' (ills. 169, 170). The pavilion system anticipated here was later widely used in school building.

Taut himself realized that the Hohenhagen complex, with its round houses, its crystal-shaped glass building and its museum with an Orientalizing façade, contained some arbitrary elements.[18] Divergent concepts gave rise to a divergency of forms. The crystal building represented the urban centrepiece; the pavilions constituted a miniature 'dissolution of cities'.

Taut's book *Die Stadtkrone*, begun in 1916 and published in 1919 (ills. 40, 171–173, 508) contains a comprehensive catalogue of the visual stimuli that inspired his work at the time. Indian and Gothic architecture occupy first place. Three particularly revealing choices from his architectural history of the world are a reconstruction of Solomon's Temple in Jerusalem, to which the site-plan of Taut's *Stadtkrone* bears some similarity with its principal and subsidiary axes, the Karlsruhe scheme with its segmental organization of urban functions, and Hans Kampffmeyer's Friedenstadt project (ills. 40, 41). Although he criticized Ebenezer Howard's garden city for its rational plan, Taut quite rightly admired its urban character. In his ideal plan for a garden city (ill. 174) Howard had included a central ring which, containing the town hall, concert hall, theatre, library, hospital, museum, and 'crystal palace', was a prelude to Taut's own *Stadtkrone*.

Taut criticized another example of a *Stadtkrone*, Berlage's design for a national monument (ill. 105), for the way in which the architecture was overloaded with symbolic significance. Yet when Berlage went in for towers of love and courage and enthusiasm and prudence, Taut by no means lagged behind. The interior of his House of Heaven, for example, was to feature a Pillar of Prayer and a Pillar of Suffering, both to be carved by the painter Karl Schmidt-Rottluff.[19] The solar-energy power station in *Die Auflösung der Städte* even labours under a double symbolism. It is

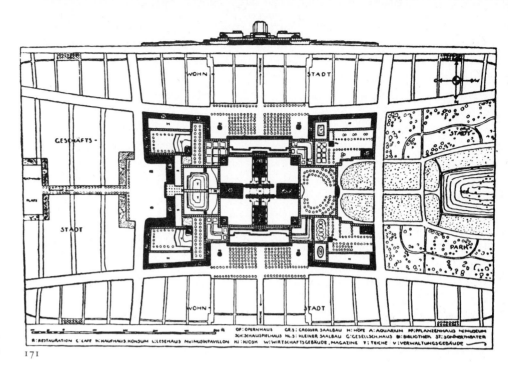

171

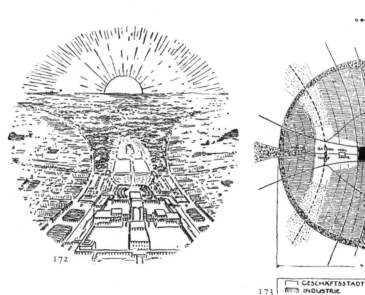

172

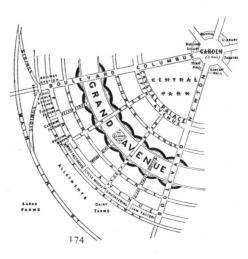

174

173

171–173. Bruno Taut. Illustrations from *Die Stadtkrone*, Jena, 1919.

171. Site plan and silhouette.

172. Bird's-eye view.

173. Diagram of the city.

174. Ebenezer Howard. Ideal plan of a garden city (detail), from *Tomorrow. A Peaceful Path to Social Reform*, London, 1898.

at the same time 'a great flower', a phallus and a vagina (ill. 178). The designs of other architects of the period had a similar tendency to become sex symbols (ill. 175). This was symptomatic of a period that equated the architectural process with the creative processes of nature, and consequently turned the result of that process – the building itself – into a sexual metaphor.

Taut's theoretical sources are revealed in *Die Auflösung der Städte*, begun in 1919 and published in 1920 (ills. 54, 176–179). The book puts Taut firmly in the tradition of such Utopian social reformers as Robert Owen and Filippo Buonarroti. It contains an anthology of texts which includes Rousseau ('The breath of man is death'), Nietzsche, Walt Whitman's then extraordinarily popular pioneer mythology, the inevitable Paul Scheerbart, who had advocated the radical decentralization of residential settlement as early as 1897 in his novel *Ich liebe Dich!*, and a commanding array of social theorists and political economists taken from all parts of the political spectrum.

Apart from Taut's sceptical attitude to the city, another criterion of selection in this *pot-pourri* of quotations was a commitment to land reform, which accounted for the presence of Tolstoy, Gustav Landauer (Kropotkin's translator, who had been a member of the first soviet government in Munich in April 1919 and had been murdered in the following month), and the law of the soviet republics concerning the socialization of land. In *Die Stadtkrone* Taut had listed capitalistic land-speculation as one of the motives behind the move away from older cities, without however going any further into the question of how it was to be avoided in the foundation of new cities. Irrational arguments were ranged side by side with rational ones, not only in the passages Taut quoted from other authors but also in his own text and illustrations. The goddess Demeter was played off against the idol of the machine; the book preached the great exodus, from the deserts of stone domi-nated by war and the competitive economy, into the countryside where the land was still 'the good earth'.

Taut's most impressive witness, as it were, was the Russian Communist and anarchist Prince Peter Kropotkin (1842–1921). Kropotkin's vision of the society of the future stemmed from his reactions to two theories – Darwinism and Malthusianism. Darwin's law of the survival of the fittest he countered with the principle of mutual aid in nature and history. Against Malthus' theory of the arithmetical progression of food production and the geometrical progression of population increase he put forward the idea that, given the right kind of social organization, agricultural output could be stepped up sufficiently to keep pace. Mutual aid, the intensification of agricultural production, renunciation of exports and profits, and the abolition of the division of labour were to determine the social forms of communal life.

Unlike the Romantic reactionaries of post-war Germany, Kropotkin had no wish to return to pre-industrial conditions. He thought in terms of light industry, widely distributed, using the most modern equipment, and powered by electricity. Factories and workshops would be out in the country, surrounded by fields and gardens, with the exception of course of those industries which are bound to a particular locality (steel, coal, ship-building). Kropotkin's goal was the whole, integrated man whose happiness was not based on the misery of others: 'each individual is a producer of both manual and intellectual work; [and] each worker works both in the field and in the industrial workshop.'[20] It was Kropotkin's ideas, from the abolition of the state right down to the electrification of household technology, that Taut illustrated in *Die Auflösung der Städte*.

Cities, those 'great spiders', are dead. Yet in marked contrast to this hypothesis of *Die Auflösung der Städte* is the fact that, only a year before, Taut had published plans for cities on the unprecedented scale – for new towns – of 300,000 and 500,000 inhabitants. New cities of this size did not begin to occupy the drawing-boards of architects until after 1945, with Brasilia (500,000) and the English New Towns of the 'third generation' (Milton Keynes, 250,000).

This ambivalent attitude to the city was common to both Taut's books, the highly Utopian *Die Auflösung der Städte* and the less Utopian *Die Stadtkrone*. Even in the thinly populated country-side, following the dissolution of the cities, there were to be numerous cult-centres and public buildings in which the labouring multitudes might gather together. This kind of thing appears to have interested Taut just as much as the idyll of the economically self-sufficient

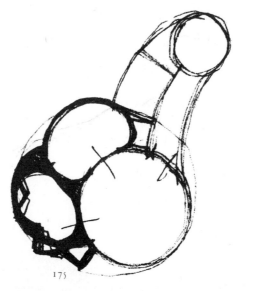

175

175. Paul Thiersch. Project for a private house, Munich-Nymphenburg, 1923. Plan.
176–179. Bruno Taut. Illustrations from *Die Auflösung der Städte*, Hagen, 1920.
176. 'A working community of 100 houses – 500–600 people'.
177. *Volkshaus* (community centre).
178. The great flower.
179. The great church.

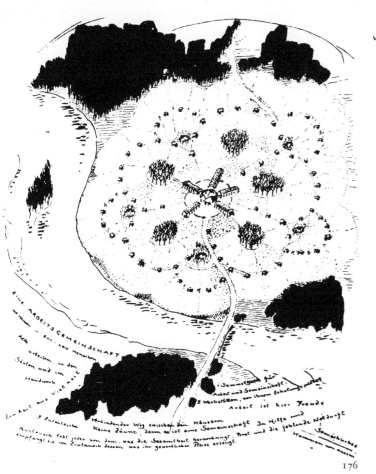

Eine ARBEITSGEMEINSCHAFT

Arbeit ist hier Freude

Wer wollte jetzt Grenzen ziehen!

Welche Gemeinschaft dürfte jetzt sagen: Halt! nicht über diesen Bach oder jenen Berg! Gleichmässig durch Aller Mühe ist die Erde bebaut, berieselt – überall hingestreut wohnt man – zwischen den Ozeanen von Wasser und Wald –

Die grossen Spinnen – die Städte – sind nur noch Erinnerungen aus einer Vorzeit, und mit ihnen die Staaten. – Stadt und Staat sind eins mit den andern gestorben. – – An Stelle des Vaterlandes ist die Heimat getreten – und sie findet jeder überall, wenn er arbeitet. Es gibt nicht mehr Stadt und Land, und auch nicht mehr Krieg und Frieden.

Man kennt keine Abstraktionen, denen man Macht über Leben, Arbeit, Glück und Gesundheit gibt – Aus der natürlichen Zusammengehörigkeit im Tun und Leben ergeben sich die gemeinsamen Interessen – und sie bilden ihre eigenen Einrichtungen zum Schutz, Austausch, zur Weiterbildung und Entwicklung. z. B:

VOLKSHAUS

DIE GROSSE BLUME

Technik ist jetzt etwas ganz anderes als in der Fabrikschorn-Steinzeit.

Heiligtum zur Aufsaugung der Sonnenenergie mit Glasplatten und Brennlinsen und -spiegeln. Anstauung in Lichttürmen – Flugzeugweiser.

Der Mensch ist so umgebildet, dass er keine Arbeit tun kann, die nicht Freude ist. Es geht an.

Uralte Weisheit ist wieder lebendig:

Die grosse KIRCHE
mit exzentrischem Turm

Gebet u. wachsendes Empfangen

Dank der Gemeinschaften
im Auftürmen von Hallen
zu einer grossen vielgliedrigen
von Generation
zu Generation

neighbourhood that justifies the title of his book. The new city of *Die Stadtkrone*, on the other hand, apart from its centre, is seen as an extended garden city with a population density of 150 inhabitants to the hectare (just over 60 to the acre). This figure is only about twenty-five per cent more than the density figure which Raymond Unwin, the planner of Letchworth, recommended for the very much smaller garden cities planned for England.

The practical problems of both concepts concerned their author hardly at all. In *Die Auflösung der Städte* no mass-transport system is provided. Country-dwellers and artisans reach the great popular assemblies by lorry, motor-boat, or aeroplane. How people whose existence is founded on mutual aid at seed-time and harvest are to lay their hands on such means of transport and how the division into independent living communities is to be reconciled with the establishment and administration of a differentiated infrastructure are questions that remained unanswered. In the same way, Taut ignored the implications of high population density around work centres such as mines and shipyards: like Kropotkin, Taut regarded this concentration as unavoidable, in spite of the fact that it contradicted the basic thesis of urban dissolution.

In the more realistic *Die Stadtkrone*, Taut takes it for granted that residents will walk a distance of up to three kilometers to reach the town centre. With railway stations, industry, universities, and hospitals all removed from the holiday atmosphere of the centre to the periphery, Taut was obliged to provide a local public-transport system; but given the low density of population, it would be impossible to run this system economically. Taut constantly thought in terms of the opposite, the alternative. He wanted the country to have the fascination of the town, and the town the advantages of the country; he wanted the New Jerusalem and the good earth. The first wave of enthusiasm safely over, Taut's mammoth designs were seen to belong to the past: Adolf Behne remarked that a *Stadtkrone*, a city-centre as Taut saw it, presupposed a walled city, an enclosed community whose size and character were determined once and for all.[21]

Taut, a pacifist, did not believe that the embodiment of his social ideals would suffice to contain human aggression. This would require Herculean efforts, a pooling of all available energy. Thus he refers in *Die Auflösung der Städte* to his monumental undertaking in *Alpine Architektur* of 1919 (ills. 180, 181). This 'alpine architecture' was to transform the entire chain of mountains from the lakes of northern Italy to the Monte Rosa into a fantastic landscape of Grail-shrines and crystal-lined caves. In a second stage – 'earth-crust architecture' – all the continents of the earth were to be covered with glass and precious stones in the form of 'ray-domes' and 'sparkling palaces'. With his 'stellar architecture' (the title of the last chapter of *Alpine Architektur*) Taut extended the process into the cosmic sphere.

Taut's first draft of *Alpine Architektur* is dated 1917. Similar thoughts were expressed by Scheerbart, and by other authors as well, of whom the most prominent was Nietzsche (see p. 41 f.). 'The

180

Der
Monte Resegone 1876 m bei Lecco
am Comersee
Aufbauten vorwiegend aus Glas

Tafelberg bei Garda
·· GLASKRISTALL

Der Monte San
Salvatore an
der Bucht von
~ Lugano ~
Ausgebaut durch
Felsanbauten und
-absprengungen
um die Naturform
Terrassen für Flug-
landung und als
Zuschauerraum für Flug-,
Ballon-, Licht- und Wasser-
vorführungen.

Horizontkorrekturen.

time may come when man has the power . . . to play with mountains as a child plays with sand. To create works of art as high as the Himalayas, formed from his imagination as the jeweller forms a casket for his jewels, perforated like lace, with stone used like metal, forest and field like jewels, glaciers like pearls, and water like crystal . . .' So dreamt Otto Kohtz in 1909, designing foaming lace-work not so very different from Taut's own creations.[22]

Illustrated publications in which architects gave their imaginations free rein came out fairly frequently from 1900 onwards. Taut's books differed from others in that each of them formed a coherent whole. The thirty plates of his *Alpine Architektur* were drawn and coloured in a way which made use of all the techniques of the comic strip: time-sequences in the order of pictures; changes from overall view to detail which are reminiscent of film; different scales used in the same illustration; text incorporated into the picture; textual elements exploited visually (colour, capitalization, strength of stroke, rhythmic successions of lines); we even find him using speech-bubbles. In *Die Auflösung der Städte* and in his duplicated exchanges of letters with his friends Taut used similar methods, and he also used them occasionally in his designs for buildings which he wished to publish.

This technique was intended to make what was being said more comprehensible to the layman, and as such was in line with the contemporary demand for an architecture that should be close to the people. In the matter of thematic invention as well, incidentally, *Alpine Architektur*, *Die Auflösung der Städte* and many of the designs produced by Taut's friends are remarkably similar to science-fiction comic strips (ills. 511, 512) – except that the strips they most resemble, the 'space operas' of Dick Calkins or Alexander Raymond, are much later in date: *Buck Rogers* first appeared in 1929, *Flash Gordon* in 1934. We can only guess at the influences at work here.[23]

181

180, 181. Bruno Taut. Illustrations from *Alpine Architektur*, Hagen, 1919.
180. Monte Resegone, and other 'wrought' mountain peaks.
181. Grotesque landscape with wrought mountain peaks.

City Architect of Magdeburg

In the summer of 1921 Taut's period of unemployment came to an end: he accepted an invitation to become City Architect of Magdeburg, where he already had an introduction as architect of the Reform estate. He stopped feeling like a moonstruck sleepwalker and began to feel on his face the 'cool breeze of morning'.[24] He realized quite clearly that the years of fruitless playing about with form were over: it would no longer be a matter of striving to create Utopia and producing only individual, exemplary buildings, but of steering the forces of development along the right paths in a community of 300,000 inhabitants. In his two and a half years in Magdeburg Taut reorganized the planning office, developed types of allotment sheds which could be expanded to form small houses (ill. 182), tried to influence the Magdeburg building co-operatives, and worked on projects for the future development of the city.[25]

Taut, however, would not have been Taut had he not immediately spotted the chance of crowning Magdeburg with a crystal building. It seemed to the author of *Die Stadtkrone* that the silhouette of the city lacked a climax, so on the site of a former fortress, the citadel on the south bank of the Elbe, he proposed a new town hall in a new civic quarter.

Another building which Taut conceived – as spiky as his town hall but more practicable as a building proposition – was a library, to the south-west of the cathedral, which was to be dedicated as a memorial to those who had died in the war (ills. 184, 185). Taut's polygonal reading-niches anticipated the carrels that have become the norm in library-building today. The idea of putting up a building for the living instead of a monument to the dead was not uncommon after the First World War: it was felt that since there was no generally accepted interpretation of the war, any monument would be a failure. The pretentious Gothic style and light-symbolism of Taut's library were, however, excessive for its secular role.

Apart from one or two municipal sales kiosks, oblique-angled wooden constructions covered in colourful posters that brought a breath of Dada into the city's business district (ill. 183), the Halle für Stadt und Land or City and Country Hall was the only building by Taut in the city of Magdeburg itself. The rhombic plan of the original project (ills. 187, 188) was justified by Taut on functional grounds: the oblique positioning of the rows of seats would ensure that everyone had a good view. The steel ties of the framework of the hall were staggered in height as well as in span.

Rising building costs forced Taut to modify his design several times. He did however succeed in developing the roof elevation of the main hall – segment-shaped reinforced-concrete ties with a skylight on top – and the lean-to roofs of the subsidiary buildings into an impressive silhouette. The rhombic figure from the original design was to reappear four years later as one of several formal elements that distinguished Taut's site plan for the large estate of Britz near Berlin (1925–31).

Among the Magdeburg projects that remained on paper were an office block containing a cinema that was to provide a focus in a square that had lost its unity (ill. 186), and a combined hotel and commercial building near the station to be called 'Stadt Köln' or City of Cologne (ill. 189). The office block, in keeping with its homogeneity of purpose, was articulated vertically by shafts and looked like an enormous Gothic stepped gable crowned with pinnacles. In contrast to this medievalism, Taut based his 'Stadt Köln' design on the variety of different purposes the project was to serve and on the use of a different structural system, yet even on parts of the building whose function and construction were identical he used different forms (for instance the balconies and partitions on the upper storeys of the hotel).

Even Taut's smaller buildings were displays of alternatives. In later years he rationalized this delight in juxtaposing things which did not belong together, demanding that 'the body of a . . . house, following the correct solution of its inner functions, emerges naturally and with as little coercion as possible'.[26] As in *Der Weltbaumeister*, it is a case of architecture creating itself: the architect is no more than midwife to the process. Yet even with Taut's buildings of the late twenties a comparison of plan and elevation shows that the ostentatious changes in scale of the wall apertures in no way derive logically from inner function. Often they are not even symbols echoing particular spatial relationships; they are purely and simply ends in themselves.

Compared with Mies van der Rohe's glass buildings (ills. 72, 73), Gropius' entry for the *Chicago Tribune* competition, or the office block that Hans Soeder designed for the Friedrichstrasse competition (ills. 70, 71), Taut's works of 1921–22 appear antiquated, feeble, and even obsessive. In the competition for an office block on the Kemperplatz, on the south side of the Tiergarten in Berlin, Erich Mendelsohn submitted a brilliant project, piling storeys with railway-carriage windows one on top of another, while he casually yet impressively applied to the front of the skeleton of the building on the ground floor a series of portal-like supports (ill. 190). Taut, on the other hand, submitted a timid study with medieval overtones, where the eye has patiently to spell out the axial divisions one by one (ill. 191).

As an architect of the Expressionist avant-garde Taut had manoeuvred himself into a *cul-de-sac* from which his only chance of escape was over the wall. With the benefit of hindsight, of course, we can see certain constants even in Taut's work: the 'thirst for the lightning flash, for the edgy thing',[27] the distinctive power of geometrical figures such as the star, the rhombus and the circle combined with an undoctrinaire pluralism of formal detail, an almost feminine receptiveness to the stimuli in his environment – whether it be exotic Istanbul, Magdeburg with its medieval past, or just somewhere in the countryside – and a predilection for the surprise effect, the showy climax, which he was never quite able to overcome.

Max Taut

Another entrant in the competition for the Kemperplatz office block was Bruno Taut's younger brother, Max (1884–1967). Max Taut's preference at this time was for advancing and retreating masses, sculpturally handled structural frameworks, and tent-shaped roofs – a powerful and expressive architecture already regarded as *sachlich* (objective). His office block for the Allgemeine Deutsche Gewerkschaftsbund (ADGB), the German association of trades unions, in the centre of Berlin (ill. 193) was greeted as a model of clarity and efficiency. The light reinforced-concrete skeleton was determined both by the desire for flexibility and by the difficulty of giving the building a proper foundation: it was to stand on poor ground and had an underground-railway line running beneath it. However, with successive designs Max Taut achieved the requisite lightness of construction and translated it into architectural terms. Stocky supports give the ground floor the character of a

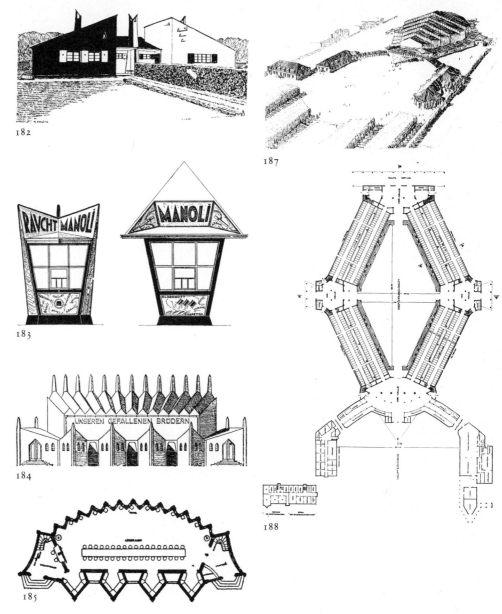

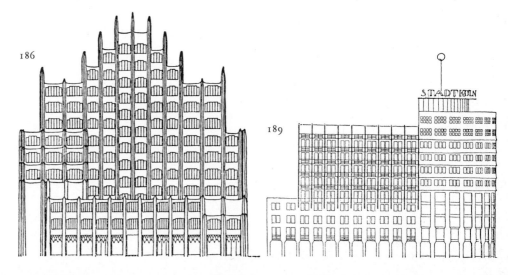

182. Magdeburg City Architect's Office (Karl Schütz). Project for enlarging a garden shed to form a double house, 1921.
183. Magdeburg City Architect's Office (W. Günther). Sales kiosks, 1921.
184, 185. Bruno Taut. Project for a war memorial library, Magdeburg, 1921. View from the north, and plan.
186. Bruno Taut. Project for an office building with shops on Kaiser-Wilhelm-Platz, Magdeburg, 1921.
187, 188. Bruno Taut. Halle für Stadt und Land, Magdeburg, 1921. Preliminary design. View (drawn by Carl Krayl) and plan.
189. Bruno Taut. Project for 'Stadt Köln' hotel and commercial building, Magdeburg, 1922.

190

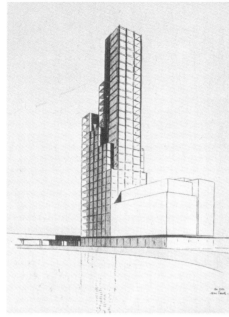

192

191

193

base. The slender piers of the upper storeys become stronger, like ribs around the main cornice. The fact that the top storey on the Wallstrasse side had to be set back because of building regulations and the upper three storeys on the Inselstrasse side had to be set back for structural reasons produced a façade in which the wall relief is of varying depths degrees of shadow, and colour. Particular spatial functions are expressed: the large rooms that rise out of the main axes are stressed by triangular gables. The modelled supports in chiselled concrete and the star-shaped ceilings (in the conference rooms) were sufficiently 'artistic' to impress even prestige-conscious trade-unionists.

Max and Bruno Taut were on friendly terms, but in architecture each would work only with the third member of the partnership, Franz Hoffmann. The analysis of frame construction – logical, despite all its eccentricities – was the personal achievement of the younger brother, Max. Bruno Taut continued until the middle of the twenties to treat each of his designs as something unique, a particular assortment of a variety of components. Max Taut's designs, on the other hand, from the Realgymnasium entrance in Nauen (1913–15) and the Werdandi-Bund pavilion in Leipzig (with Friedrich Seesselberg, 1913) onwards, were based on the equal interplay of vertical and horizontal load-bearing members.

In the years since then modern architecture has used the grid to the point of boredom, though it still remains indispensable as a planning instrument. At that time, however, it was the principle of the future. It guaranteed an orderly whole even where, as in the case of Max Taut's ADGB building, it was filled in a personal manner and did not rule out the possibility of variation. It made it easy to enlarge a building (the ADGB building did in fact allow for extensions) and to connect it to others. These advantages also made Max Taut's design for the *Chicago Tribune* (ill. 192) superior to that of his brother. Max proposed a spatial

190. Erich Mendelsohn. Project for an office building in Kemperplatz, Berlin, 1921. Charcoal. Louise Mendelsohn Collection, San Francisco.
191. Bruno Taut. Project for office building in Kemperplatz, Berlin, 1921.
192. Max Taut. Project for the *Chicago Tribune* building, Chicago, 1922.
193. Max Taut and Franz Hoffmann. Offices of the Allgemeine Deutsche Gewerkschaftsbund, Berlin, 1922–23.

structure which left open the question of the use to which that space should be put; Bruno submitted a monumental, solitary piece of sculpture.

The cry for colour

To most of the citizens of Magdeburg Bruno Taut was neither a famous architect nor a town-planner who was trying to come to terms with some unusual jobs; neither was he the *spiritus rector* of the younger generation of architects or the author of the most important Utopian publications of the period. For them he was the man who had taken it into his head to brighten up their city with a bit of colour. Taut himself recalled, not without pleasure, the day the electric trams stood still in the streets of Magdeburg because the drivers wanted to take a good look at the freshly painted façades.[28] Of all the aims of Expressionist architecture the new emphasis on colour had the most chance of becoming popular.

Taut had already begun to promote colour in architecture in his Munich days under Theodor Fischer;[29] and his commitment corresponded to a desire that was already widespread in the pre-war years. The 'Aufruf zum farbigen Bauen' or 'Appeal for colourful architecture' which he initiated and which was published in September 1919 in the magazine *Die Bauwelt* was subsequently reprinted in numerous other publications. Among the signatories of this manifesto were virtually all the most prominent figures in German architecture. They also included art historians, who had in mind the theories of Jacob Ignaz Hittorf and Gottfried Semper on the polychromy of classical architecture, local politicians, chemists, and of course the Confederation of German Decorators. None of Taut's many other undertakings found such a response as his call for colour: 'Let the dirty-grey house in the open air at last give way to houses in pure and brilliant tones of blue, red, yellow, green, black, and white!'

Both the English reform movement and the Jugendstil had been in favour of colour and against the subdued tones of the nineteenth century. Yet in these movements colour had been confined to particular, carefully chosen combinations; and it had had more success for interior than for exterior decoration. Exteriors were still governed by Ruskin's ideas, which considered colour in terms of the natural colours of materials. The revolt of the Expressionist painters gave impetus to the campaign to extend the use of colour in architecture. Even before the war, when it was only partly built, Bruno Taut's Falkenberg estate was already known as 'the paint-box colony'. The Arbeitsrat für Kunst took up the theme in an inquiry conducted among its members, the ultimate aim of which was seen as the abolition of the *Tafelbild*, or easel picture, in favour of the *Stadtbild* – the image or general aspect of a town or city. The 'Universal Brotherhood of Colour'[30] promptly put forward ideas for street façades in red, green, blue, silver and gold.

An 'Alliance for the Promotion of Colour in Towns' was set up and 'Colour Days' organized, with Bruno Taut among the speakers. In 1925 the teachers of the province of Brandenburg and the city of Berlin issued an ordinance entitled *Farbe in der Schule* ('Colour in the School'). New magazines were founded (*Die farbige Stadt, Das farbige Strassenbild* – 'The Colourful City', 'The Colourful Street Scene'), exhibitions arranged (*Farbe und Raum*, 'Colour and Space', Berlin, 1925), and plans were drawn up for painting entire cities. Other expert voices were raised in protest against what they considered the disfiguring of the urban environment with colour. Yet the demands of the progressives even found an echo among traditionalist architects, and in the ranks of conservationists.

The interpretation of colour changed considerably between the immediate post-war period and the late twenties. Initially colour was regarded as a free

194. Bruno Taut, with colour scheme by Franz Mutzenbecher. Clubroom in the Ledigenheim Lindenhof, Berlin-Schöneberg, 1919–21.

means of expression, independent of form, capable of both arousing and containing the entire range of human emotions. It constituted both expression and summons. 'Every pure colour is like a note sounded by the universe, something final and decisive – something that demands clear decisions from us' (Adolf Behne).[31] One of the things the next generation came to realize was that it was not possible to confront the passer-by with the 'final and decisive' every time he crossed the street.

To this generation, convinced of the moral value of aesthetic considerations, colour made it possible to create what architecture was for the time being prevented from creating, namely a community united by powerful emotion and a shared delight in sensory experience: 'in this way we can give our architecture, which is condemned to an unwilling modesty, an entirely new and joyful resonance' (Walter Curt Behrendt). Colour had the further advantage of being relatively cheap. Even Taut remained realistic for once, speaking of gay and cheerful impulses and seeing the colourfully painted façades of old apartment houses as a summons to dissociate oneself from the dreadfulness of such buildings. Yet he too was a believer in the moral and physical effects of colour, as proof of which he pointed to the behaviour of children; he claimed to have observed that children preferred to play in streets where the houses were colourfully painted than in streets where they were grey.[32]

Nowhere did what Poelzig called the 'cry for colour' ring out louder than in Magdeburg. Taut started things off by painting the late seventeenth-century town hall, giving it a fire-red base with black lines between the courses, green loggias, yellow statues and capitals, and a new coat of paint inside as well. The City Architect's Office offered its services to house owners for colour consultations and organized a competition among artists for posters and brightened façades. Houses began to appear in green, pink and blue, blue and yellow, and sea-green and pale grey – 'jesters' costumes', as the critic Fritz Stahl called them.[33]

The citizens of Magdeburg took up the council's example, for better or worse. The authorities had a say only in the few streets of the city centre which were covered by the terms of a local statute. In many cases, even where the impetus had come from the City Architect's Office, paint was applied with a complete disregard of architectural form: the Karlsruhe painter Oskar Fischer, a colleague of Taut, decorated the façade of the Barasch building with a Cubist-inspired design that took no account of the windows (ill. 513). The enthusiasm for colour in Magdeburg was such that even window-frames were dappled.

Within his narrow circle of influence Bruno Taut handed out even more ambitious commissions. The banqueting hall in his Schöneberg home for single people (1919–21) was entrusted to three artists who were to improvise the decoration without any preliminary studies at all. A clubroom in the same building, where Taut had extended curved niches into an eccentric spiral on the ceiling, was one of the more successful solutions: Franz Mutzenbecher, a member of the Arbeitsrat für Kunst, painted the room with brilliant bands of colour which he shaded off evenly towards the bottom (ill. 194).

The post-Expressionist years were characterized by an attempt to distinguish the physiological, psychological, and aesthetic laws of colour and put them to use. After a period of being treated as autonomous, colour was now disciplined and subordinated to particular purposes. It was used to give individual character, to lend support to cubic forms, to stress static relationships or particular details, to guide the eye and create perspectives, to produce psychological effects. Taut justified the bold colour schemes of his own house in Berlin-Dahlewitz, of 1925, by the phrase, 'The purely aesthetic . . . is here no more than the outcome of what is practical.'[34] Though he gradually came round to this principle in the twenties, his own work never showed a suitably radical application of it. Even in his later work the 'practical' was always arranged with an eye to aesthetic considerations. Still, the formal decisions were at least susceptible of corroboration by functional arguments, so Taut was able to justify his use of colour both as psychological stimulus (with a gradation from cold to warm as you moved from hall to living room) and as symbol of function (with the feed pipes of the central heating painted red and the drainage pipes blue).

In later years Bruno Taut remarked – with exaggerated scepticism – that the increased use of colour was perhaps the only gain of the post-1918 *Sturm und Drang* era.[35] Yet even with its new 'objective' justification the use of colour was still in dispute. Theo van Doesburg, propagandist of the De Stijl group, had in 1922 admitted to noticing himself that the faces of passers-by lit up with joy when they passed coloured houses; yet in the late twenties he pronounced white to be the colour of the new era. White, he claimed, represented perfection, purity, certainty, and spirituality. 'The studio must be like a glass bell or like a hollow crystal. You must be white yourself . . . Cold kills germs.'[36]

Van Doesburg's statement is a variant on the crystal-myth which had once been the rallying point of revolutionary architects; at the same time, it shows how much things had changed. The brightly coloured, sparkling, mysterious abundance of light that streamed from the pages of the mystics and of the novels of Paul Scheerbart, and through the stained-glass windows of Gothic cathedrals, had given way to the clear, dust-free light of the laboratory. For that is where van Doesburg saw the artist – in the laboratory, equipped with the implements of the surgeon. One irrational image had emerged from another; though the new one seemed more easily reconcilable with industrial society's interpretation of itself.

The New Architecture of 1920 certainly did not repudiate colour, but architects became increasingly fascinated by 'white cities': had not Adolf Loos, with ironically halting emphasis, seen in them the New Zion, capital of the kingdom of heaven?[37] White became the background colour, against which only details were picked out in colour, whereas the Expressionist era had sought to turn everyday life into a festival of colour.

'Be young, be joyful and true! And give your all to the one faculty – building.'

Mitteilung an Alle, a prospectus for the magazine *Bauen*, 1919

The Arbeitsrat für Kunst

During the first half of November 1918, workers and soldiers, and sometimes other citizens and farmers as well, began to group themselves into soviets all over Germany, to watch over the provisional government which had assumed power after the collapse of the Empire. They lost their importance in the political sphere with the elections of 19 January 1919, when their function was taken over by the parliamentary group of the National Constituent Assembly.

Professionals and artists began to organize themselves too, along the same lines as the revolutionary workers' soviets, but whereas these were elected, the 'intellectual' soviets had no such electoral mandate. Their formation was described by Kurt Hiller, chairman of the 'Proletarian Council of Intellectual Workers' founded on 10 November 1918 in Berlin: 'No one did any nominating; no one did any electing; the competent parties simply got together one day and said: we are the council.' Gustav Landauer, a member of the revolutionary government of Bavaria, condemned the soviets of 'intellectual workers' as nonsense, since other workers were not 'unintellectual'.[1]

The revolutionary organization of Berlin artists called itself the Arbeitsrat für Kunst – the Working Council for Art, virtually the 'Artistic Soviet'. Similar organizations were set up in other cities of Germany such as Darmstadt, Dresden, Karlsruhe, Cologne and Munich. An Arbeitsrat membership list of March 1919 gives 16 names for the business committee, 19 for the 'artistic working community', and a further 59 as 'friends at home and abroad'. The membership list overlapped with that of another Berlin organization setting itself similar tasks, the Novembergruppe. Unlike the long-lived Novembergruppe, however, the Arbeitsrat für Kunst only lasted for two and a half years.[2]

The climate in the first weeks of the Berlin Arbeitsrat's existence appears to have been stimulating. Gropius commented enthusiastically on its 'congenially radical atmosphere', 'fruitful ideas', and the 'fine, fresh atmosphere'.[3] Around Christmas 1918 the Arbeitsrat came out in public with two pronouncements. The first was the *Architekturprogramm* of its first spokesman, Bruno Taut, and the second was a manifesto calling for a kind of dictatorship of artists: 'Henceforth the artist as moulder of the people's experience is alone responsible for the outward apparel of the new state.'[4] This assertion immediately betrayed the hand of Taut, who had already expressed himself in similar terms at the Werkbund conference in Cologne in 1914. Architectural programme and manifesto both employed the formula of a merging of the arts 'under the wing of a greater architecture'.

The architecture committee, which was chaired by Bruno Taut, obviously played the leading role. On 1 March 1919 Walter Gropius succeeded Taut as chairman of the Council. The Arbeitsrat für Kunst arranged lectures and published manifestos, pamphlets, and two small volumes. The majority of these were concerned with architecture. The second pamphlet prepared by the Arbeitsrat, *Ein Unterrichts-Plan für Architektur und bildende Künste* ('A Teaching Plan for Architecture and the Fine Arts') bore, like the first, the name of an architect; this time it was Otto Bartning. Two exhibitions organized at I.B. Neumann's Graphisches Kabinett on the Kurfürstendamm were devoted to architecture: the 'Exhibition for Unknown Architects' in April 1919, which was accompanied by a pamphlet by Gropius, Taut, and Behne and went on to Weimar and Magdeburg, and the 'New Architecture' exhibition of

195

196

195. Johannes Molzahn. 'Architectural idea', 1919.
196. K. Paul Andrae. Dynamic study (tower block), 1923 or earlier.

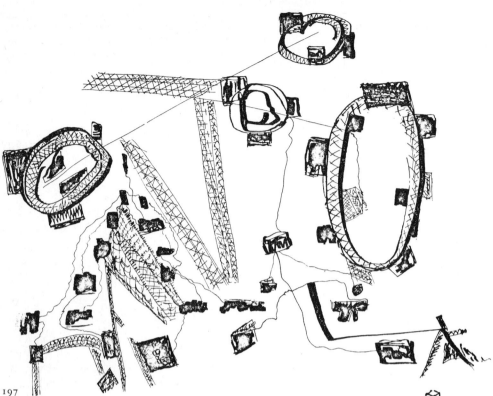

197

tained with 'experimental buildings' which were also thought of as providing new exhibition possibilities. And of course there was no shortage of reform proposals for the competition system, which has been and will continue to be regarded as urgently in need of reform as long as there are private architects for whom winning a competition means a chance of professional independence.

The different points of this platform, all dictated by the professional interests of architects and artists, were generally accompanied by far-reaching preambles couched in the most emphatic terms. These put forward the idea of the *Gesamtkunstwerk*, the total or collective work of art, demanded an 'art for the

197. Jefim Golyscheff. Drawing, *c.* 1919.
198. Carl Krayl. Experimental sketches, from *Ruf zum Bauen*, Berlin, 1920.

May 1920. The Arbeitsrat's first book, published in November 1919, was *Ja! Stimmen des Arbeitsrates für Kunst in Berlin* ('Yes! Opinions of the Working Council for Art in Berlin'); it arose out of an inquiry conducted at the beginning of that year in which most of the questions had to do with architecture. Its second book, *Ruf zum Bauen* ('A Call to Build'), was published in connection with the exhibition of May 1920; the title alone makes clear which of the arts it was concerned with.

In these various declamatory publications the same series of demands is repeated over and over again. The power of established institutions such as building authorities, exhibition juries, national school inspectors, academies and state art commissions is to be abolished and where necessary replaced by corporate bodies chosen from among the ranks of artists. Arts and crafts teaching must undergo a radical transformation with preference being given to workshops training apprentices, and masters' studios. Public housing must be built, and permanent experimental sites main-

198

eople', and expressed the belief that architecture could create a feeling of community between those who designed and built it and those who used it. 'We now that the feeling of brotherhood that arises out of this kind of communal work – on an architecture which, thanks to the many hands contributing to it, will burst into magnificent bloom – is capable of producing in the soul of man that which we all of us long for: the true spirit of socialism ... Man, in going about his business, is transformed.'[5]

The inquiry conducted by the Berlin Arbeitsrat early in 1919 was concerned with 'ideal projects with far-reaching goals' and the 'periodic exhibition of such designs in models and drawings'. A few weeks later, in April, the Arbeitsrat opened its 'Exhibition for Unknown Architects', which had been arranged by Gropius himself. As part of its attempt to rouse public interest for the collective artistic product of architecture, sculpture and painting, the Arbeitsrat expressly invited amateurs to send in sketches or photographs which, in the event of a positive verdict by the selection subcommittee, they were asked to follow up with further work.[6] This was how Hermann Finsterlin, who was not an architect, came into contact with the Berlin group. The work submitted was apparently inadequate in quantity or in quality, because the Arbeitsrat asked the painters among its members to turn their attention to 'ideal projects'.

The pamphlet which was published in conjunction with the exhibition did not include a catalogue, so that to find out who took part one must turn to the reviews (most of them negative).[7] One of the three rooms of the gallery – Neumann's Graphische Kabinett – was devoted to practising architects such as Heinrich de Fries who exhibited projects for small housing estates and designs for functional buildings and skyscrapers. In the realm of fantasy it was the painters and graphic artists who dominated – understandably, since they were not bound by any considerations of practi-cability. Wenzel August Hablik exhibited his juxtaposed polyhedrons, Oswald Herzog a domed temple, Arnold Topp a temple of the dead with walls of coloured glass reminiscent of Scheerbart, and Johannes Molzahn a sacred building made up of 'segments of a sphere and spiky pyramids arranged in fan shapes' (ill. 195). César Klein, Erwin Hass (with a tower consisting of giant masks) and Oscar Treichel had all made use of motifs from Cubist or Expressionist painting. Among other architects represented were Carl Krayl and the Dresden architect K. Paul Andrae, who submitted skyscraper projects (ill. 196).

A particular stir was created by the biomorphic inventions of Finsterlin (who had a whole room to himself) and Jefim Golyscheff. Golyscheff, born in the Ukraine in 1897 and brought up as a musical prodigy, cultivated the kind of cheerful naïveté usually associated with children's drawings. His scrawled, haphazard topographies reminded Adolf Behne of Paul Scheerbart's drawings. Behne noted that they were meant 'to give everyone the feeling he could do the same' (ill. 197).[8]

The 'New Architecture' exhibition of May 1920 included the illustrations from Bruno Taut's *Alpine Architektur* and *Der Weltbaumeister*. Most of the other works were reproduced in the book *Ruf zum Bauen*. Hans Luckhardt told friends that the exhibition was hung by his brother and himself and that it included works by Wilhelm Brückmann, Finsterlin, Paul Gösch, Carl Krayl, the Luckhardt brothers, Hans Scharoun, and Max and Bruno Taut. Some of Fritz Kaldenbach's designs were shown at the Unknown Architects exhibition and possibly at this one too.

Once again, of course, the organizers had to face the charge of being unrealistic, having their heads in the clouds, and even of fostering a new Pre-Raphaelitism.[9] The charge was not unfounded. Bruno Taut encouraged his younger colleagues – in full awareness of what they were doing – to be visionary architects. Gropius declared that the principle of the Arbeitsrat was to ignore the real world. For Finsterlin the retreat into self

199. Hans Hansen. *Bauhof*, or building centre, from *Ruf zum Bauen*, Berlin, 1920.

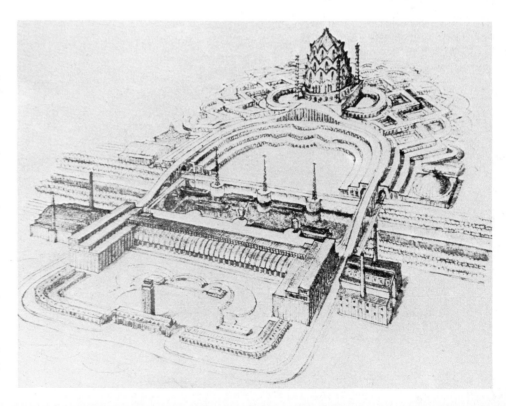

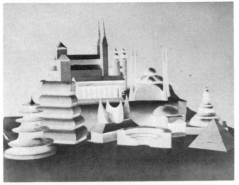

200

201

202

203

200. Hermann Finsterlin. 'The Play of Styles', building blocks, *c.* 1921.
201. Hermann Finsterlin. 'Formdomino', *c.* 1922.
202. Hermann Finsterlin. 'Villayette'. Plaster model.
203. Hermann Finsterlin. Museum of Hygiene, *c.* 1920. Plaster model.

was the very condition of his artistic existence: 'This earth could not begin to give me the wonder and enjoyment I experience in the hours when awareness of the norm is swallowed up in nothingness. I could happily do without the ghastly waking dreams of the earthly day – and would be no worse off than the beggar of Baghdad who was nightly granted the consciousness of the Sultan.'[10]

Gropius' speech on the occasion of his installation as chairman of the Arbeitsrat für Kunst reveals that the Council was not unanimously in agreement with his tactics. There were in fact two opposing parties: the one pressed for a publicly declared artistic policy, while the other thought it advisable that the Council should prepare its work in silence. Gropius supported the second party. He saw the Arbeitsrat group as the tiny minority it really was: 'I regard our association as a conspiracy . . . If we are going to achieve something big we must cherish every point of our programme and brook no compromise, especially not amongst ourselves . . . We need a different spirit which, when at last we have it, will be our own fulfilment.'[11]

Thus Gropius demanded that the Council should for a time forego all propaganda directed at the outside world. It is difficult to reconcile this principle of silence with the practice of the Council, which went on pouring out manifestos. The conspiracy idea was inescapably linked with a tendency to breast-beating – not uncommon behaviour among minorities with a sense of mission.

The Utopian correspondence

The exchange of letters that Bruno Taut organized towards the end of 1919, with every precaution to ensure secrecy – including the use of pseudonyms, and the obligation to return all material if one withdrew from the circle of correspondents – found its way, at least in part, to the public. Taut published excerpts from it in *Ruf zum Bauen* and in his magazine *Frühlicht*, which appeared in the first half of 1920 as a supplement to the magazine *Stadtbaukunst alter und neuer Zeit* and then in four independent issues during 1921–22. Taut kept things going and spurred on the twelve dilatory artists and architects who were involved in this exchange of photostats (ill. 510) and carbon copies: Brückmann, Finsterlin, Gösch, Jakobus Goettel, Gropius, Hablik, Hans Hansen, Krayl, the Luckhardts, Scharoun, and Max Taut. Taut had met most of these people through the Arbeitsrat für Kunst. A fourteenth member, the writer Alfred Brust was adopted by the group after a few months; it was he who thought of the name *Die gläserne Kette* ('The Glass Chain'). Alfred Brust's laconic mystery plays appear to have come to Taut's attention through a remark made by that great go-between, Adolf Behne. They reminded him of his own *Der Weltbaumeister*. Brust was still championing the 'house of glass' in 1927 with arguments which must by then have appeared very odd to Taut and his colleagues, such as his view of glass as an allegory of earthly existence for those who have nothing more to hide . . .[12]

204–209. Hermann Finsterlin.
204. Study III-1, 1916(?). Watercolour, photograph retouched in pencil.
205. Lake-side villa (I-2), 1918. Watercolour, photograph retouched in pencil.
206. *Casa nova* (XI-5), 1920. Watercolour, photograph retouched in pencil.
207. Concert hall (IV-5), 1919. Watercolour, photograph retouched in pencil.
208. *Casa nova* (XI-3), 1923. Watercolour.
209. Study VIII-2, 1920. Watercolour.

204

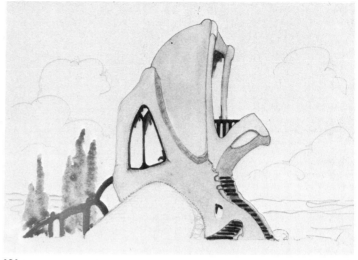

205

206

208

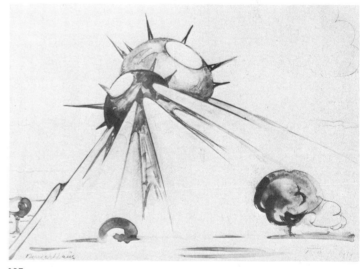

207

209

Most of the correspondents in the Glass Chain felt themselves to be solitaries crying in the wilderness. Some of them did in fact live, if not in the wilderness, at least in outlying parts of the provinces. They regarded the community of their 'magic circle' as a mystery, and spent their time trying to confirm that the magic was still working. Hablik, who lived in Itzehoe in Holstein, wrote: 'What a beautiful thought! – that people, men, should learn once again to have confidence in one another, a confidence that extends so far that each will share with the others his most secret thoughts and vital ideas . . .'[13]

Despite the feelings of sympathy cultivated by most of the correspondents there were differences of opinion. Finsterlin, apart from the constant reproach that he expressed himself in too complicated a manner, was criticized by that apostle of glass, Bruno Taut, on the grounds that his capacious and expansive forms called for large-scale structures that conflicted with the principle of sublimation. Finsterlin for his part was irritated by his friends' mania for all things crystalline. The Luckhardt brothers charged Taut with still thinking too much as a city-dweller. Hans Luckhardt rightly pointed out that even Taut's Utopias of rural and mountain architecture were the Utopias of a city-dweller.

Yet for all the differences, which make this correspondence so readable and at times dramatic, it is the shared convictions that predominate. One thing they all had in common was the wish for a great large-scale project that would bring all the arts together. Hans Hansen (1889–1966), the Cologne painter and architect, who was probably accepted into the circle on the strength of his book *Das Erlebnis der Architektur* ('The Experience of Architecture', ill. 53), which Taut reviewed, applied Taut's *Stadtkrone* ideas to an organism which would at the same time suit current ideas on educational reform. Hansen's *Bauhof* or building centre (ill. 199) was intended as the administrative centre for all building activity within a particular district. It was to contain workshops and schools for the most diverse disciplines, to include an area to be set aside for experimental buildings and exhibitions, and to be 'crowned' by an academy building. In Hansen's design this looks like a decorated cake flanked by minarets. Unlike other German Expressionist architects, who paid no attention to such things, Hansen took an almost Futurist interest in problems of traffic and communications. His *Bauhof* was to be accessible by rail and ship, to have its own radio tower, and, 'as an architectonic synthesis of the whole workshop idea', to be encircled by a road leading over the roofs of the warehouses to a ramp in front of the academy.

Here again reality played a minor part. The large coloured model proposed by Hans Luckhardt and various projects for architectural films were never realized, nor was 'The Book', devised by Hablik. This was to have been a kind of gospel of creativity, comprising both art and literature. The individual members of the circle contributed works to it, and the Bauhaus was to have produced the binding and wrought the clasp – 'preferably no work of art, something quite primitive, simple, and beautiful', wrote Taut.[14] Taut, Finsterlin and Hablik worked on film projects that were conceived as *Gesamtkunstwerk*, total works of art; they too came to nothing.

The 'visionary architects' called themselves radicals, and radical they were in the sense that they sought the *radix*, the root of creative activity. Taut spoke later of a mystic flux that had to do with the origins of the universe.[15] Architecture was seen as emanating from some mysterious, primitive force. Many of the correspondents' thoughts were devoted to the problem of defining what it was that made true architecture a mirror of the cosmos. Wassili Luckhardt sought

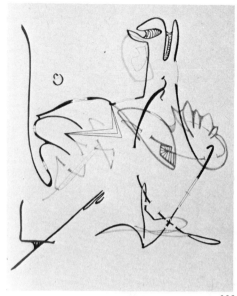

the principle of unity in stirring images from nature – in the heaving of the ocean swell, of dunes and hills and mountain chains, or in crystal clusters with their power of refracting light. Bruno Taut warned against the obvious temptation of copying forms from nature and referred to the numerical proportions of the neo-Platonic tradition. Hans Scharoun appealed to the will of the age, of the people, or even of some *Urmass* or 'primitive mass'.

Hermann Finsterlin

The most noteworthy attempt to find a common denominator for architecture – including the various historical styles – was made by Hermann Finsterlin (b. 1887) with his stylistic building blocks (ills. 200, 201). Toys designed by architects are by no means unusual. Erich Mendelsohn, Bruno Taut and Ernst May all designed building blocks for their children. Finsterlin, however, was more ambitious. Before turning to art he had studied natural sciences and philosophy at Munich University; what he wanted now was no less than to trace the descent of world architecture and parallel the theory of evolution with an artistic 'origin of species'. Indeed, he called himself the Darwin of architecture.

210. Hermann Finsterlin. Play of forms in architecture, from *Wendingen*, VI, no. 3, 1924.
211. Hermann Finsterlin. Plan (V-7). Ink.

213

214

215

Where most of the Expressionists believed in an anonymous *Zeitgeist* or 'spirit of the age' whose tools they thought themselves to be, Finsterlin actually believed that there was a biological creative urge in art which made use of the human medium. The Expressionists' belief in genius was worked out by him in biological terms. But he never actually came up with the proof that the succession of phenomena represented by the history of architecture was explicable by any principle as plausible as Darwin's theory of natural selection.

In dealing with the 'species' of art Finsterlin was not able – as the natural scientists were – to start out from an existing high point. For him the past constituted one epoch – one that had not even exhausted the possibilities of the primary formal elements. In his stylistic box of bricks they were represented by the cube, the column, the pyramid, the cone, the hemisphere, the needle, the onion, the bell and the horn. Using these elements Finsterlin demonstrated the principal stages of world architecture

from temple and amphitheatre to dome and pagoda. In the post-war period he discerned the beginning of the second, geometrical epoch – an opinion in which he may have been strengthened by the works of his crystal-loving friends. He hinted at the architecture of the future in a further box of building blocks, *Formdomino*, with various combinations of organic parts; but he saw this new architecture as coming only with the 'unfathomable, organic fusion of already hybrid formal elements'.[16]

This architecture of the future was Finsterlin's architecture: the totally new, that stood in the same relationship to what existed now as the coral fish to the herring or as the orchid to the buttercup. Some of his five hundred or so watercolours and ink sketches (ills, 9, 110, 204–211, 403),[17] which may have been begun in the last years of the war, depict isolated buildings, often drawn from anthropomorphic patterns. In some cases they display grimacing features or Dada collages of organs – a cross between Bomarzo and Walt Disney (ills. 203,

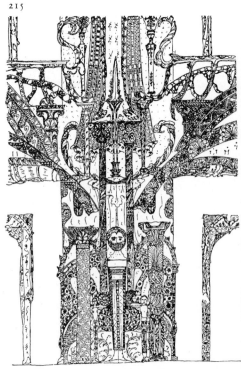

212. Paul Gösch. Town hall. Watercolour. Oswald Mathias Ungers Collection, Cologne.
213, 214. Paul Gösch. Cemetery and illuminated globe, from *Stadtbaukunst alter und neuer Zeit. Frühlicht*, 1, no. 14, 1920.
215. Paul Gösch. Foyer, from *Stadtbaukunst alter und neuer Zeit. Frühlicht*, 1, no. 1, 1920.

216

FORMEN

205). The apogee of Finsterlin's fantasy, however, is represented by a group of works dating from around 1920. These depict sections of a single, exciting form-landscape in which interior and exterior are drawn together into continuous planes and spatial entities (ills. 209, 210). As in Taut's *Alpine Architektur*, the forms of the earth are here extended imaginatively into the realm of a second, artistic nature. *Casa nova, terra nova*. In the Glass Chain correspondence the pseudonym Finsterlin chose for himself was 'Prometh' – Prometheus who stole fire from the gods and brought it to mankind.

One thing Finsterlin shared with Art Nouveau artists was an interest in natural forms as a source of inspiration. He knew the natural philosopher Ernst Haeckel, whose book *Kunstformen der Natur* ('Artistic Forms in Nature'), had appeared so opportunely in 1899 at the crest of the Art Nouveau wave, and though Haeckel's mechanistic monism must have been distasteful to Finsterlin, he may have been heartened by the Jena profes-

216. Carl Krayl. Charcoal drawing. Oswald Mathias Ungers Collection, Cologne.
217. Carl Krayl. Forms, from *Stadtbaukunst alter und neuer Zeit. Frühlicht*, 1, no. 2, 1920.
218. Carl Krayl. Composition, from *Ruf zum Bauen*, Berlin, 1920.

218

219

sor's emphasis on the diversity and artistic value of the forms to be found in nature. Unlike many Art Nouveau artists, however, Finsterlin condemned straight translation of natural into artistic forms. Yet in the issue of *Wendingen* which was devoted to him even he compared his 'dwellings' with rocks smoothed by glacial action and with the joints of animals' bones.

Finsterlin has always denied that he is a Utopian. Form meant everything to him. With the discovery of his 'giant hollow sculptures', he thought the future was already at hand. Architecture's social vocation – a question which occupied a large part of the thoughts of the Expressionist architects – was to him a matter of indifference. Finsterlin saw the true social achievement of architecture as lying in the abundant variety and beauty of its manifestations. He never suspected that the freedom of the artist which he celebrated with such exuberance in his sketches might not be identical with the freedom of the user of the work of art.

'This is a time of struggle such as there has never been before', Finsterlin wrote to his friend Erich Mendelsohn, 'but no mailed fist can shape things any more.'[18] Finsterlin had no feeling for the reality of building, nor did he wish to cultivate one

for fear of losing his freedom of vision. Where materials are indicated in his drawings the reference is to their appeal to the eye or touch rather than to their structural possibilities. The same formal idea bears different functional designations – housing, concert hall, arts centre, vegetarian restaurant, or chapel. Frequently the sculptural mass was evolved without any preconceived ground plan; conversely he drew fantastic ground plans with no suggestions for the structures that they might represent.

Finsterlin has noted with satisfaction that the unease he had expressed long ago in the face of everlasting sameness, mindless accumulation and insipid rationalism is now widespread. He had been one of the first to raise the weapon of his inventive prose against 'God-cages', 'thing-coffins', and 'living-crates'. A feeling of triumph at having been proved right clearly underlies his complaint that mankind has migrated 'to the deserts of Mies van der Rohe rather than to the tropics of Prometheus',[19] and has not played the merry game that he suggested it should play.

The links of the Glass Chain

Taut was the organizer of the Utopian exchange of letters, Finsterlin its theoretician. The interest of the other correspondents lies in the impact of their designs, and in their outspokenness. The luxuriant decorations of Paul Gösch (1885–1940) and the wide-meshed webs – not unlike Golyscheff's – of Carl Krayl (1890–1947) seem to come from the world of daydreams. The hand yields to the slightest impulse; the nets of lines intertwine as if of their own accord. One of Gösch's maxims was 'Above all, don't lie!'[20] Preconceived principles of organization represented a lie. In minutely detailed pen drawings and expansive watercolours Gösch explored architectural ideas derived from the East, and sometimes also from nature, with a childish unselfconsciousness from which one would never guess that he was a trained

219. Wilhelm Brückmann. Fantasy, from *Ruf zum Bauen*, Berlin, 1920.
220. Wenzel August Hablik. 'Cycle of exhibition buildings. Cubes (calcareous spar)', 1921. Watercolour and ink. Hablik Collection, Itzehoe.
221. Wenzel August Hablik. House and studio, 1921. Coloured pencil. Hablik Collection, Itzehoe.

220

221

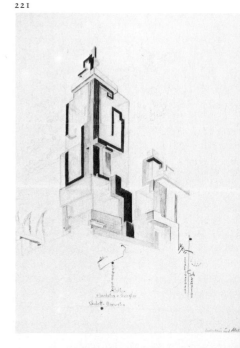

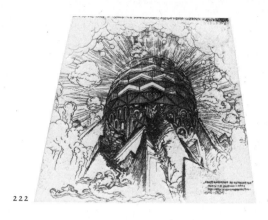

222

222. Wenzel August Hablik. Free-standing construction, 1914–24, from *Cyklus Architektur*,
1925. Etching. Hablik Collection, Itzehoe.
223. Wenzel August Hablik. Crystalline gorge.
Pencil. Hablik Collection, Itzehoe.

architect and one-time government *Baumeister* (ills. 88, 212–215). His is a fairy-tale world where familiar forms like columns, terms, pinnacles and doorways take on unaccustomed shapes. Gösch did in fact also write and illustrate fairy-tales.

Krayl, who worked with Taut in the Magdeburg City Architect's Office from 1921, was different, for in his work there is a clear concern with current architectural problems. His loosely deployed structures seem, as in Taut's *Die Auflösung der Städte*, to be scattered widely over the countryside (ills. 176, 198, 402). Other drawings show Dadaist creations inspired by the construction and typography of big-city advertising structures (ills. 217, 218). Like Taut, Krayl both hated cities and was fascinated by them. He remained in Magdeburg until the National Socialists came to power, building housing estates and office buildings in the modern idiom.

Around the turn of the century many reformist painters had made a dramatic switch from the fine to the applied arts. This did not happen again. Expressionist painters remained painters. Gösch even abandoned architecture for painting. Finsterlin's sketches only got as far as small-scale models. Three of his projects were to have been built, but his clients were unable to carry out their plans. Wilhelm Brückmann, a painter from Emden, dreamed up his schemes on paper – viscous, doughy pavilions or science-fiction scenes which he conceived as projections or gas clouds (ills. 219, 404).

The man most likely to have turned architect was Wenzel August Hablik (1881–1934), who had started life as a carpenter and had moved through a number of trades. He drew fantastic islands in space with crystal citadels and a girdle of rings like Saturn, but he also evolved some imposing ideas with canti-levered domes (ills. 74, 96, 220–223, 511). He was fully acquainted with the technical difficulties of construction and could design for snow-loads and wind pressure. Taut overlooked these elements in Hablik's work when he spoke of his

226

intentions as 'chaotic' and insufficiently 'crystalline'.[21]

In 1925, when many of his former associates had given up the Utopia ideal, Hablik collected his studies, together with some etchings, in a portfolio entitled *Cyklus Architektur* (ills. 222, 511). The ideas behind this collection had interested him for a long time – in one case, he said, since 1908. *Cyklus Architektur* is rich both in allusions and in anticipations. Like Bruno Taut Hablik proposed an 'alpine' architecture, justifying it, as Taut had, on the grounds that it would provide a focus for the energies of the people. The motif of the rectangular spiral favoured by Lauweriks and, after him, by the De Stijl and *Wendingen* artists, appears in Hablik's work, along with space rockets, the space-frames of Konrad Wachsmann and Max Mengeringhausen, and gigantic domes covering entire regions (compare Buckminster Fuller). The trapezoidal shape of the etchings, printed at different angles on the paper, was intended to heighten the dynamic impact of Hablik's ideas. He never actually practised architecture.

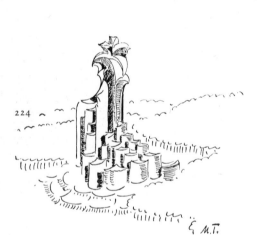

224

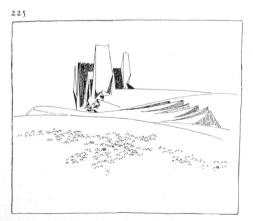

225

The professionals among the Glass Chain correspondents were the two pairs of brothers, the Tauts and the Luckhardts. Some of Max Taut's illustrations are aesthetically among the most successful of the lot (ills. 95, 224–226). Strata of crystal and angular arcades that reveal Max Taut's gift for the tectonic framework are placed in a differentiated light and perfectly integrated into the pictureplane. How much these ideas owe to the techniques of Cubist painting (rather than to purely architectural motifs) is revealed by a comparison with a project that was actually carried out – the concrete frame of the Wissinger family tomb in Stahnsdorf cemetery near Berlin, of 1920 (ill. 227). The sculptural supports, that taper downwards and are linked by pointed arches, take on an anthropomorphic quality and stand about the tombstones like medieval mourners. This motif of an open arcade degenerated rapidly into a formula, as might have been expected (ill. 228).

Finsterlin's phrase 'Utopian crystallists' applied to Max Taut and also to the Luckhardt brothers. Wassili Luckhardt (1889–1972) was excited by the reflections he saw inside crystal clusters, and set himself the task of creating 'a meaningful whole out of the chaos of these primitive forms'.[22] While most of the painters in the Glass Chain produced vague sketches he, an architect, offered solid form thoroughly worked and structured. Luckhardt found his 'meaningful whole' in a balance of variously aligned volumes which were usually governed by a single formal law. The majority of his designs, which he worked out in plasticine, were moraines of mineral masses – the 'Shape-game' and the cinema of 1919, the House for an Architect, and also to a certain extent the Gothicizing country house of 1920 (ills. 63, 64, 232–234). A few projects, most of them of a monumental character, were symmetrical in design – the towering 'Monument to Joy' of 1919, two religious buildings of around 1920 and a theatre of 1921 (ills. 56, 57, 229–231). The fluting and the rib-

construction of some of his projects foreshadowed reality by several decades.

Hans Poelzig made an impression on both the Luckhardt brothers. Wassili described to sceptical friends his experience of the Grosse Schauspielhaus, and Hans Luckhardt (1890–1954) designed a concert hall in which the rooms around the auditorium evolved spirally in the manner of Poelzig's Salzburg Festspielhaus project (ills. 235, 236). The pinnacles that wreathed the exterior dropped from the ceiling of the auditorium like stalactites, recalling the Grosse Schauspielhaus. Applying the principle of crystalline form in a more modest project, Hans Luckhardt designed an estate of detached houses in which square ground floors developed into octagonal upper floors (ill. 237).

The Luckhardts had two chances to translate their formal ideas into reality around 1920: they built a four-pointed advertising structure on the Avus (a practice racing track, whose initials stand for Automobil-Verkehrs- und Übungs-Strasse) in Berlin (ill. 65), and a house in Berlin's Westend district which was a relatively opulent building for the post-

227. Max Taut. Wissinger family tomb, Stahnsdorf near Berlin, 1920.
228. Hans Walter. Tomb, Erfurt, 1922 or earlier.

war period (ill. 514).[23] Here a corner site lent itself to a composition elaborated with all kinds of additional angles and bevelled edges. The apparently axial arrangement of the building is deceptive: access is not in fact on the axis but through a concealed side entrance. This was dictated by the desire to keep the central part of the double-winged music room as a symbolic focus for the house. The composition is forceful and demonstrative, and the colour schemes – in keeping with new ideas – employ strong contrasts.

229. Wassili Luckhardt. Monument to Joy, 1919. Combined techniques. Wassili Luckhardt Collection, Berlin.

230, 231. Wassili Luckhardt. Religious building, *c.* 1920. First version.

Hans Scharoun

The buildings that Hans Scharoun (1893–1972) erected during the late twenties are not unrelated to the functional 'New Architecture'; they are not, however, identical with it. In this 'white period' of his work Scharoun drew inspiration from the streamlined shapes, rows of windows, portholes, bridges and railings of ships, which he would have seen daily as a boy, since he was born in Bremen and brought up in Bremerhaven. Other influences included Erich Mendelsohn, six years older than Scharoun, and, probably, the architecture of the 'Section d'Or'. Scharoun was closer to the progressive wing of his profession during this period than at any other point in his career; yet he kept his distance.

What separated him from many of his doctrinaire colleagues was his irrationalism – the extent to which he had retained his Expressionism. Unbridled by convention, Scharoun's imagination led to results which, though they were susceptible of rational examination, could never

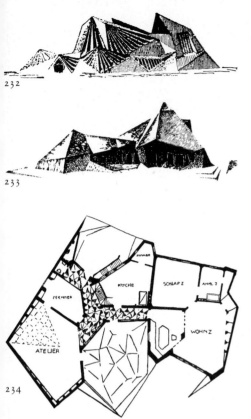

232

233

234

have been arrived at by the mere analysis of needs. Functional solutions are by no means the monopoly of functionalism. Scharoun's timber building for the Liegnitz gardening exhibition of 1927, when he had spent a few months studying prefabrication, was far more flexible and thus superior to the projects of convinced rationalists. The corridor access system for multi-storey flats in his Breslau block was revolutionary.

The late twenties were a highly successful period for Scharoun. For all their effortless variety his buildings possess a homogeneity that he had not aimed at before and which he never repeated. In a dialogue with Hugo Häring (ills. 490–494) Scharoun developed his own conception of organic architecture, a conception in which the successful building is interpreted as a vital organ, as a form obtained from the essence. The 'essential' solution is not meant as a strict tying of form to particular conditions. 'Essence-conditioning' – the objective requirements of the job in hand – and 'intuitive vision' – the subjective contri-

bution of the architect – are closely related to one another. Only 'intuition' will recognize 'essence'; 'essence' will reveal itself only to 'intuition'.

It is a rather different vocabulary from that of the early post-war years. The Scharoun of the Glass Chain had put creation before thought and – probably a swipe at Finsterlin – objected to the 'mazes of intellectual topiary'. But whether the terms used were 'blood' and 'will', 'sensuality' and 'spirit', or the later 'essence' and 'intuition', what underlay them in every case was an ideology in which objective and subjective appeared as phases of a single life-current. At twenty-seven, he spoke of 'our hot blood's ecstatic dream'. Yet Scharoun seems to have believed in some mysterious correspondence between task and execution all his life. 'We think we are living and in fact we are lived.'[24]

The disparate repertoire that Scharoun employed from the thirties onwards, sometimes on a single project, was still divided into different series of forms in the early designs for glass and cultural buildings. One sequence of studies explores the metamorphosis of crystal clusters as they burst open (ills. 103, 240), depicting masses and volumes that appear to have emerged out of an explosion. The violence of style that distinguishes Scharoun's ink drawings from those of his fellow Utopians perfectly matches their subject.

Another series consists of variations on the theme of round forms in violent motion, with the direction often stressed by three or four horizontal slashes or outline strokes (ill. 239). The buildings appear as organisms, yet not in the sense

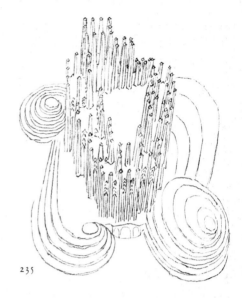

235

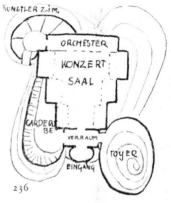

236

232. Wassili Luckhardt. Cinema, 1919. From *Stadtbaukunst alter und neuer Zeit. Frühlicht*, 1, no. 3, 1920.
233, 234. Wassili Luckhardt. House for an Architect, 1920. View and plan. From *Frühlicht*, no. 2, 1921–22.
235, 236. Hans Luckhardt. Concert hall, 1920. View and plan.
237. Hans Luckhardt. Residential estate consisting of detached houses. From *Frühlicht*, no. 2, 1921–22.

237

of the later theory of the building as a living organism. They are much more like zoomorphic creatures invested with a sinister life of their own. No people are shown. The concept of the society that such buildings are intended to serve remains abstract. There are no clues as to either scale or architectural function.

In his competition projects of 1921–22 – and perhaps already in the brilliant if amateurish church designs of his student days, where he drew the mantle of a single, smooth form over a series of heterogeneous parts (ill. 515) – Scharoun sought to synthesize the various possibilities which he had explored individually in the sketches. Designs for a theatre in Gelsenkirchen and a museum of hygiene

238. Hans Scharoun. Watercolour, 1920. Margit Scharoun Collection, Berlin.
239. Hans Scharoun. *Musikhalle*, 1920. Watercolour. Margit Scharoun Collection, Berlin.
240. Hans Scharoun. Watercolour, 1920. Margit Scharoun Collection, Berlin.

239

238

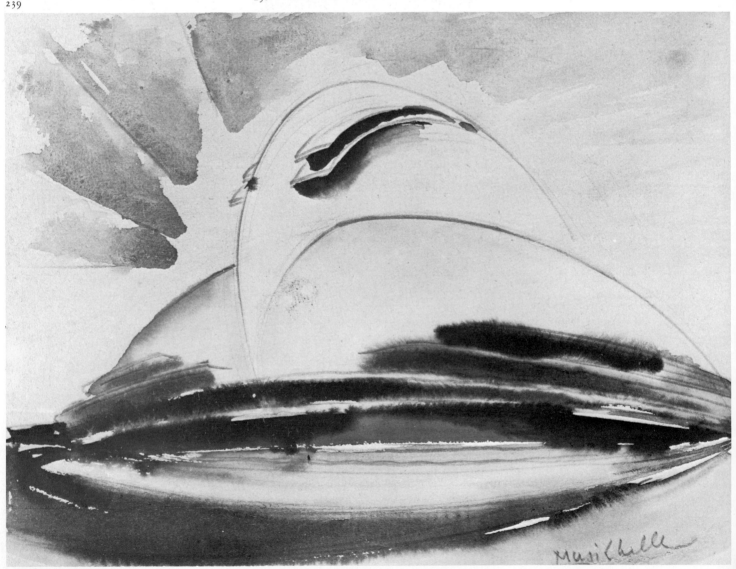

241

242

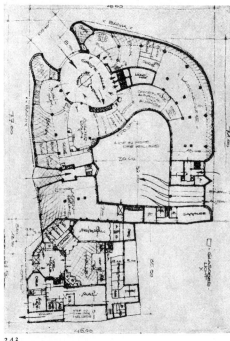
243

241. Hans Scharoun. Project for an office building at the Friedrichstrasse station, Berlin, 1921.
242, 243. Hans Scharoun. Project for the stock exchange, Königsberg, 1922. View and plan.

in Dresden (1920) were much too dominated by jagged decorative motifs, but the projects for an office building at the Friedrichstrasse station in Berlin and for the stock exchange in Königsberg (Kaliningrad) incorporated both flowing and staccato forms side by side (ills. 241–243). Both of these designs illustrate Scharoun's great virtue of bringing out the character of the surroundings and at the same time creating character for his building out of the surrounding conditions. Good taste was sacrificed without qualm – a principle that Scharoun took up again after an interlude with the International Style.

In both competition projects movement is taken into account not only metaphorically, in terms of formal dynamics, but also in real terms, in the organization of flow. It is this real movement or flow of traffic alone that makes completely clear the movement of form. The widths of corridors are dependent on the frequency with which those corridors are used. The Friedrichstrasse building was to be divided by a passage running diagonally through it. The ground plans are as labyrinthine as those of Finsterlin or Gaudí – or as that of Scharoun's own Philharmonie in Berlin, completed in 1963. They allow the interior no hint of transparency, guarantee surprises at every step, and show that Scharoun was not worried about leaving virtually useless areas of space here and there (ill. 7).

After a period of fairly extensive architectural activity – some in East Prussia, more in Silesia and in Berlin – and a spell of teaching at the Breslau Academy, in the thirties Scharoun only built a few private dwellings. It says a lot for the durability of the Expressionist impulse that during the Second World War he made over a hundred visionary sketches in which he went back to his Expressionist beginnings (ills. 6, 244, 245). This time the scale is indicated: a procession of tiny figures makes its way across valley floors carved out in the form of steps, up and down staircases, ramps, and

roofs, and along gigantic tiers and terraces. Roofs that are sometimes like tents and sometimes like sheets of material floating freely in the wind span the different floor levels. Is this wishful thinking – the dream of a free community of men moving securely in a built-up landscape beneath diaphanous sails, dreamt in a blockhouse during the years of peril? Or is even the mighty architecture of these watercolours infected with the hallucinations of a totalitarian regime blind to all sense of proportion?

244, 245. Hans Scharoun. Watercolours, between 1939 and 1945. Margit Scharoun Collection, Berlin.

244

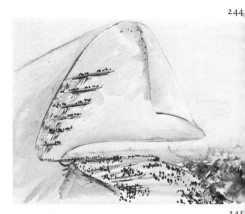

245

7 The early Bauhaus

'No dogma – rather, increased vitality.'

Walter Gropius, 1919 (?). Note in the Bauhaus-Archiv, Berlin

The ultimate, if distant, goal

Expressionism, though it protested strongly against the academies, had one of its own – the Bauhaus in Weimar. From the time of the school's foundation early in 1919 until the exhibition in the summer of 1923 at which Gropius proclaimed the new watchword, 'Art and technology – a new unity', the Bauhaus was regarded by friend and foe alike as a stronghold of Expressionism. Bruno Adler, who was closely associated with it, said later that it worked under the banner of radical late Expressionism. Theo van Doesburg, whose opinion of the Bauhaus was coloured by the scepticism of the rejected reformer, saw himself in Weimar faced with the kind of 'expressionistically distorted abortions' that so suited the Germans. He maintained that because the German people had been so long subjected to a discipline imposed upon them from outside, they had been unable to develop any feeling for clarity, precision, and voluntary self-discipline.[1]

Indeed the remarks that Walter Gropius (1883–1969), the new institute's head, published in 1919 differ only marginally from the lofty utterances of Bruno Taut. Gropius himself confirmed this fundamental agreement with Taut: in an address which he delivered as the new chairman of the reorganized Arbeitsrat für Kunst he identified himself unconditionally with Taut's 'magnificent' *Architekturprogramm*.[2] Architecture as the art that unites all others within itself, the necessity for crafts training, the poverty of all structures that only meet the needs of utility – all these ideas occur both in Taut's writings and in the two manifestos that Walter Gropius published in April 1919. One of these ap-peared, along with contributions by Bruno Taut and Adolf Behne, in the pamphlet which the Arbeitsrat für Kunst brought out in connection with their Exhibition for Unknown Architects; the other constituted the foundation programme of the Bauhaus. Like Taut, Gropius thought true architecture had only been realized in a dim and distant past. Both men had an inkling of how far off the happier future of their hopes in fact lay, the future of a new and greater style, and both invoked the crystal as symbol.

The two manifestos were very timely and well written, and they came out in the same month. Gropius' authorship was questioned at the time,[3] but a comparison of them with his other pronouncements of the period, contained in manuscripts, in correspondence with Osthaus and Poelzig, and in published articles, leaves no room for doubt. These other documents even invalidate Gropius' attempt in later life to explain away the tone and arguments of these manifestos by saying that they were dictated by purely tactical reasons.

Yet even at his most passionate, Gropius showed a certain objectivity. When Bruno Taut invited him in November 1919 to take part in a 'Utopian correspondence' (the Glass Chain, see p. 92), Gropius accepted but expressed reservations. Taut asked all the correspondents to choose pen-names for themselves: in a company that included 'Anfang' (beginning), 'Stellarius', 'Prometh' (the name taken by Finsterlin), 'Angkor' and 'Zacken' (a reference to the jagged ornamental motif so beloved of the Expressionists), Gropius took the name 'Mass', signifying measure, moderation, proportion, which seems to imply a criticism of their highflown idealism. But Taut had good reasons for counting on Gropius' interest. The Bauhaus programme of April 1919 listed as one of the principles of the school the 'corporate planning of comprehensive Utopian designs – communal and cultic buildings – with long-range goals.' Taut may have had this in mind when, nine months later, he drew a 'movement-game for the Weimar Bauhaus' and added the words: 'New architecture: Unusable models held in suspense: Stars and complete and utter fantasy. Things as pure celebration. Enchantment from just being . . . Couldn't Mass's school of building do something of the kind?'[4]

The 'corporate planning of comprehensive Utopian designs' was something the actual teaching programme of the Bauhaus failed to allow for; even practical training in architecture was for years virtually nonexistent – incredibly enough for an institution that went under the programmatic title of the 'House of Building'. Although students soon pressed for an architecture department, it was not until 1924 that a working group for architecture was established, and not until 1927 that Hannes Meyer was appointed as head of the newly founded department of building. Until then Gropius and his colleagues provided only preparatory instruction and let students gain practical experience in the director's private architectural office.

This gap in the curriculum could be justified on the grounds that the course (which consisted of the preliminary course, theory of work and theory of form) took three and a half years and that it would therefore be 1923 before the first generation of students had reached the point where it would make sense to include architecture as a discipline. On the other hand the manifesto of April 1919 was necessarily conceived as a programme for the teaching activity of the Bauhaus in its entirety, rather than in terms of what was immediately practicable. Besides, this programme only mentioned architecture in the passages dealing with principle. The curriculum, it stated, would comprise 'A. Architecture, B. Painting, C. Sculpture including all subsidiary crafts.' But where it went into greater detail it made no mention of either building theory, construction, theory of structures, or practical experience on the site. All we find is, under the heading 'Instruction in Graphics and Painting', 'Exterior, gar-

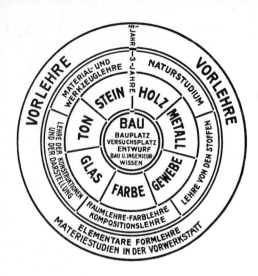

246. Diagram of the teaching program at the Bauhaus. From Walter Gropius, *Idee und Aufbau des Staatlichen Bauhauses Weimar*, Munich and Weimar, 1923.

247. Lyonel Feininger. Woodcut. From Walter Gropius, *Programm des Staatlichen Bauhauses Weimar*, Weimar, 1919.

den, and interior architectural design' – after life-drawing, landscape-painting, ornamentation, and calligraphy!

Gropius chose his teaching staff accordingly. The obvious thing would have been to ask one or more of his architect friends from Berlin to join him in Weimar. Instead the appointments of the first two years went to five painters and a sculptor. This dictum of Adolf Behne's – Gropius' comrade-in-arms from the Arbeitsrat für Kunst – sounds like a justification of Gropius' staff policy: 'In fact painting today holds out more hope of the goal of unity being reached than does the art which is called to the position of leadership, i.e. architecture.'[5]

Like other publications of the period, though if possible with greater scepticism, the text Gropius wrote for the Exhibition for Unknown Architects suggests an architecture so lofty in conception that there was little likelihood, for the present, of its being subjected to reality. Perhaps, then, it was better not to build or teach people to build? In the Bauhaus manifesto, architecture appears only on the horizon: 'The ultimate, if distant, goal of the Bauhaus is *the unified work of art – the great construction* in which there is no distinction between monumental and decorative art.' Sculpture, painting and crafts must be developed as individual entities before they can unite in the 'great construction' for the new man.

Was Gropius, precisely because he saw even less chance of the Utopia of a new architecture becoming reality than did the hotheads of the Glass Chain, fundamentally the greater visionary? He knew that architecture did not change people. 'First man must be well-formed, and only then can the artist fashion a fine garment for him. Today's generation must begin again from the beginning; it must undertake its own renewal.'[6] The moral impulse and sense of mission that emanated from the early Bauhaus, and occasionally went berserk in a form of whimsy, can be explained by the enormity of this claim – as also can the self-restraint implicit in the promotion of handicrafts.

The teaching of crafts

A new art was awaited only with the advent of a new society and a new race of men, but with crafts it was different: they were seen as the contribution which the present could make to the future; they were seen as the epitome of synthesis, combining intelligence with feeling, skill with imagination – the more so as 'handicrafts' meant not the manual mass-production of consumer goods but true crafts – carpentry, wood-carving, pottery, etc.

The emphasis on crafts at the Bauhaus was also dictated by the needs of the Grand Duchy of Saxe-Weimar, later the State of Thuringia, where handicrafts and cottage industries accounted for a large part of the population's income. The 'constant contact with leading figures in handicrafts and industry' to which the Bauhaus programme attached such importance was something which Henry van de Velde had already practised during his directorship of the Weimar School of Arts and Crafts. Van de Velde had been called to Weimar in 1902 to 'raise the artistic level of the craft products and craftsmen of the state'.[7] When Gropius took over in 1919 as director of the united schools, the Academy and the School of Arts and Crafts, Weimar expected the same of him.

The fact that practical instruction in one or more crafts was regarded as the hallmark of progressive teaching must have made it easier for Gropius to meet these conditions. As early as 1852 Gottfried Semper had advocated a studio and apprentice workshop system, recommending a return to the kind of brotherly relationship between the master and his journeymen and apprentices that had existed in the Middle Ages and that had last been favoured by the Nazarene group of German painters at the beginning of the nineteenth century. Semper argued, 'everything depends upon our bringing together again what mistaken theory has separated . . .'[8] The English Arts and Crafts movement and the educational theories of Fröbel tended in the same direction: learning through doing.

In the German-speaking world at the turn of the century the principal teaching institutions paying special attention to craft instruction were the schools of arts and crafts in Berlin, Strasbourg, Vienna, Breslau, and (under Behrens) Düsseldorf, the master-classes given at the Bavarian Craft Museum in Nuremberg, and the teaching and experimental studios of Wilhelm von Debschitz in Munich and Bernhard Pankok in Stuttgart. Le Corbusier, still using his real name of Charles-Edouard Jeanneret, travelled in Germany between April 1910 and May 1911 collecting information on such schools. The tone of satisfaction with which he recorded successful examples is unmistakable.[9] The day was still distant when he was to name his own projects after automobiles, in order to demonstrate his sympathy for economic and automated methods of production.

Immediately after 1918 the demand for more practical instruction – and in the conditions then obtaining this meant handicraft instruction – became general. All proposals for reform called for the old art schools to be transformed into workshops. The Arbeitsrat für Kunst in Berlin devoted a large part of its discussions to ways of winning over the majority of the artist-proletariat to handicraft. In the Arbeitsrat's *Architektur-Programm* Bruno Taut required of the would-be architect that he practise a manual trade as an apprentice in a workshop. The second pamphlet planned by the Arbeitsrat artists was devoted wholly to educational reform. Otto Bartning's *Unterrichts-Plan* or teaching plan, the manuscript of which was edited by Gropius as chairman of the Arbeitsrat für Kunst, was based on the premise that 'handicrafts constitute the core of the people's activity; they are the soil in which speculative technology and the fine arts alike have their roots, and in which architecture as a whole has its foundation.' Bartning saw the Bauhaus as an attempt to put part of his programme into practice, and in his early years at the Bauhaus Gropius defended the pro-

gramme.[10] Yet in doing so he was doing only what was expected of a progressive arts and crafts school director in 1919.

Nor were the other aspects of the teaching programme of the Weimar Bauhaus, in particular the stress laid on the *Gesamtkunstwerk* or total work of art, as unusual as present-day art historians with their Bauhaus-fixation make out. The fact that there were people employed in the teaching profession who 'had absolutely no conception . . . of the unity of art' was a subject of general complaint as early as the turn of the century.[11] The logical consequence was a reorganization of the art school system. Hermann Muthesius, head of arts and crafts schools in the Prussian Ministry of Commerce, was one of the most resolute opponents of the separation of handicrafts, as taught by arts and crafts schools, from the fine arts, for which the academies were responsible, and from architecture, which was the province of the technical colleges. In his book *Kunstgewerbe und Architektur*, published in 1906, he proposed a combined school at which architects, painters, sculptors, students of arts and crafts and gardeners should all be trained on a uniform basis. Weimar, Karlsruhe, Düsseldorf and Berlin all merged their respective academies and schools of arts and crafts at roughly the same time. Seven years before the foundation of the Bauhaus Le Corbusier prophesied in his paper for the school of art in La Chaux-de-Fonds that the foundation of new German schools for industrial arts, interior design and architecture would release undreamt-of energies.

Le Corbusier described other situations that he had seen during his German tour of 1910–11, which seem like anticipations of Bauhaus theory. The Düsseldorf School of Arts and Crafts ran a preliminary course of several terms during which students were taught how to use their eyes as well as the most important artistic techniques, and did studies in composition in the most diverse materials. At the Hamburg school he saw paper cut-outs that were made without preliminary

sketches and were intended to sharpen the students' feeling for colour-harmony and compositional balance (Le Corbusier was reminded of Gauguin) – the beginnings of Johannes Itten's *Vorkurs* or preliminary course at the Bauhaus. The studios of the Stuttgart teaching and experimental workshops were headed jointly by an artistic principal and a technical master, a division of labour which the Weimar Bauhaus also practised. At the Breslau School (later Academy) of Art and Crafts Poelzig set up apprentice workshops which featured collaboration between artists and master artisans. Poelzig himself taught 'theory of material style', as well as other things. A letter from Gropius to Poelzig shows that he took a particular interest in the Breslau institute.[12] At the Weimar School of Arts and Crafts, too – one of the two predecessors of the Bauhaus – all practical work was supervised by master craftsmen: the only difference was that here the director, Henry van de Velde, was himself responsible for the artistic supervision of all classes.

In terms of both organization and curriculum, the Bauhaus thus represented nothing more than a particularly thoroughgoing implementation of ideas and experiments that were current in many minds and many places at the time it was founded. The fact that it developed from a foundation typical of its time into something very much more, the artistic and intellectual centre of the Weimar Republic, was not due to the way the institute was constructed. It was due to the wisdom, the flair, and the courage which Walter Gropius showed in his choice of colleagues. The Bauhaus is an example of the persuasive power of ideas when they are championed by the right people at the right moment.

The joyous ceremonial

There was another aspect to the Bauhaus legend, and that was the fascination of sectarianism. Students, associates, and even one or two masters wore flared trousers of their own design with a shirt that was a cross between a smock and a monk's cowl. Plato, Lao-Tzu, Thomas Aquinas, the mystics, Swedenborg, and of course Stefan George and Rainer Maria Rilke ('Workpeople are we . . .') were read privately or communally; the Epic of Gilgamesh was read aloud by the light of a single candle. Gunta Stölzl, later head of the weaving workshop, wrote of the first Christmas celebrations of 1919: 'Then a great meal. An air of solemnity reigned, and a sense of symbolic significance. Gropius served every single person present personally. A kind of washing of the disciples' feet.'[13]

A joyous ceremonial had been announced in the programme of 1919. In the case of Johannes Itten and Georg Muche it took on the aspect of a cult. Itten (1888–1967) had previously run a private school in Vienna, and he brought a number of students with him when he moved to the Bauhaus, where he was the only person with any considerable experience of teaching. The fact that his preliminary course was compulsory for all students in their first semester gave him a key position in the school. When Itten declared that hair was a sign of sin, his young men shaved their heads. Fasts, rhythmic exercises and purification ceremonies were all practised in Itten's circle, and the mysteries that the master brought back from Herrliberg on Lake Zurich, the European centre of the Mazdaznan movement, and later from the monastery of Beuron were devoutly adopted.

It is impossible to separate Itten's achievement[14] from his personal theories of life and the practices that went with them. Itten believed in an original state of creativity within every single individual. The relaxation and concentration exercises, and even the morning songs and chants that, particularly in later years, seemed so bizarre to the more sober Bauhaus men, were integral parts of his teaching method. Itten not only wanted to explore the objective laws governing formal and structural means: he wanted also to free the creative powers of the individual and to guide him towards an experience of things that was mystical. For him as for the late medieval and Baroque mystics there was no contradiction between self-expression and the most profound experience of matter, or between emotion and intuition. A living representation was always in Itten's view something experienced, and something experienced always a living representation. The world is reborn in receptive people and they in it.

'I must empty my soul that God may enter.' It was not Itten who quoted this dictum but Gropius.[15] Bauhaus students in 1919 saw no apparent antithesis between the theories they were taught in Itten's neo-Gothic 'Templars' Hall' and those expounded in the school buildings on Belvedere-Allee. 'Itten is Gropius', Oskar Schlemmer noted in his diary as late as the summer of 1921. Itten dominated the first romantic, or, as he himself called it, universalist phase of the institute's life. When Itten went, the Bauhaus changed.

To the outside world too the Bauhaus appeared as a place where secrets were cherished. On more than one occasion Gropius invoked the spirit of the medieval masonic brotherhoods, the guilds and lodges. The 'star manikin' that served for three years as the emblem of the Bauhaus was like a stone-mason's sign decorated with symbols of day and night, and runes (ill. 248). Lyonel Feininger's woodcut on the titlepage of the Bauhaus manifesto alludes to the three arts of painting, sculpture, and architecture, but it is also open to more esoteric interpretations (ill. 247). The whole composition is governed by the sacred number three – three portals, three towers, three stars: it is the 'crystal emblem of a new and future faith' of which Gropius speaks in the text. Gropius had some trouble explaining to

248. Johannes Auerbach and Blüthner(?). Symbol of the Bauhaus, 1919. Final version.

the Weimar master craftsmen that a house by Walter Gropius would not in fact be like Feininger's illustration, and was at pains to describe to them how 'simple and sensible' such a house could be.[16]

The buildings of Gropius and Meyer

How 'simple and sensible' were the houses designed in the architectural office of Gropius and Adolf Meyer (1881–1929) after 1918? In the first few years both architects were engaged almost entirely on residential buildings. Designs for estates at the Schwansee and the Belvedere Berg in Weimar, as well as for an estate of small houses for a shoe-factory in Erfurt, were never in fact built. We have to imagine them as being as unpretentious as one that was built (and destroyed in the Second World War), the Stöckle house in the Berlin suburb of Zehlendorf West. As Fred Forbat said, it could almost have been by Tessenow.

Greater elaboration of design characterized the various buildings that the office produced for the sawmill owner and building contractor Adolf Sommerfeld. Forbat tells of a 'highly imaginative project [of 1920] for an office building for Sommerfelds . . . entirely of timber, that was never made public'.[17] Gropius and Meyer did, however, complete a group residence for Sommerfeld in Berlin-Lichterfelde which achieved a certain dynamic effect with its stepped-back façades.

Another building of theirs, close to the group residence, was the Sommerfeld loghouse (ills. 250–256). For architects who had already proved themselves to be the leading specialists in industrial building, this is a truly astonishing piece of work. One critic was reminded of 'the old traditional buildings . . . that still impress one so powerfully today in old Saxony'.[18] Actually the heavy timberwork and the rough granite base were more reminiscent of North American Prairie romantic. The house is like a dramatized reworking, in a rustic idiom, of the very earliest country houses built by Frank Lloyd Wright. Adolf Meyer had the German edition of Wright's work lying open on his desk all the time.[19]

The deliberate primitiveness of the building goes hand in hand with a number of studied artistic effects. The stepped treatment of the wall surface, the entrance with angular projections, the projecting timber balks and the horizontal and vertical movement of the eaves, that cast deep shadows, all serve to break up the volume of the building visually. Inside, the rooms open off a double-height hall, with an angular balcony running round at the level of the upper storey. Sommerfeld was an energetic supporter of the Bauhaus, and helped with purchases of land and loans. His private commissions from the Gropius/Meyer office provided a great deal of work for the school workshops, so that the Sommerfeld house became the first major collective achievement of the Bauhaus community. For Gropius it meant a step in the direction of 'the idea I have been pursuing for many years – the union of all the arts in building'.[20]

The decision to build in timber and to use elaborate teak decor was prompted by Sommerfeld's business activity. The formal appearance of the house, however, was not intended simply as a demonstration of timber building; Gropius himself argued the other way round. A year after Erich Mendelsohn, in an address to the

Arbeitsrat, had sung the praises of reinforced concrete, Gropius was describing timber as *the* material that matched the spirit of the times. The title of his essay was programmatic – *Neues Bauen* or 'New Architecture'.[21] '*The new era calls for the new form*. We have to relive timber anew; we have to rediscover it, refashion it, out of *our own* spirit and not in imitation of old forms that no longer suit our requirements. It is no accident that the younger generation of artists today delights in carving its ideas in logs and balks of timber; artists always instinctively hold the key to the new life. Every material has its beauty and its potential and its time. Timber is *the* building material of the present day.'

The arguments Gropius advanced for timber building were partly practical (there was plenty of timber available), partly artistic, and partly ideological: '*Timber* is a *wonderfully versatile material* and in its nature so suited to the primitive early stages of our renewal of life.' Gropius evolved a kind of philosophy of history in terms of building materials. Stone and iron (!) belonged to the old ways of building, but timber belonged to a time

249

250

that must 'build huts' (*Hütten*, i.e. also 'lodges') as the 'first and most necessary task of a new historical edifice.' The age to come was, in the best tradition of Paul Scheerbart, allocated glass as material. How far even Adolf Sommerfeld's modest timber house was seen as a sparkling, many-pointed creation was revealed by the vignette on the invitations to the *Richtfest*, the celebration which takes place in Germany when the shell of a house is completed (ill. 250).

A few days before Sommerfeld's *Richtfest* (18 December 1920), competition designs were placed on exhibition in Weimar for a monument which the Weimar trade-unionists wanted to erect in the cemetery to the memory of their socialist comrades who had been shot during the Kapp Putsch of March 1920. Bauhaus students had attended the burial of the victims, much to the displeasure of their director, who feared political repercussions. In the competition for a 'Memorial to the Victorious Proletariat', however, Gropius also took part. Even more than the sculptured architecture of the Sommerfeld house, the architectural sculpture of Gropius' monument design shows how completely he accepted the formal ideas of Expressionism (ills. 257, 258). Gropius' monument strains in a single direction, and demands that the spectator see past its material substance to

249. Otto Lindig. Temple of Light, 1921–22. Fired clay.
250. Vignette from the invitation to the *Richtfest* for the Sommerfeld log-house, Berlin, 18 December 1920. Bauhaus-Archiv, Berlin.

251

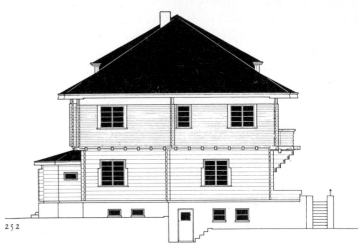

252

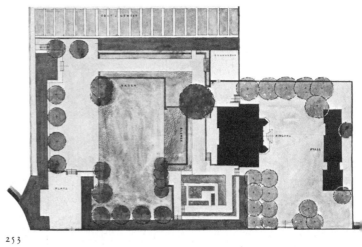

253

254

255

something beyond: it is a kind of fissure in space. The monuments proposed by Max and Bruno Taut, on the other hand, were solemnly statuesque. Gropius' design seems to have been modelled on the spiky termination of Karl Schmidt-Rottluff's Pillar of Prayer (ill. 260), which Gropius must have known.[22]

'For feeling is the source of invention, of creative power – in short, of form.'[23] This pure Expressionist credo, formulated by Gropius and acted on by Johannes Itten in the Bauhaus preliminary course, could only find limited application in the other, more tightly programmed commissions of the Gropius/Meyer office. The house for Dr Otte in Berlin's Zehlendorf West (ills. 266, 267) owed its individuality to predominantly mannerist features: from the garden site it appeared as two separate masses, whereas from the entrance courtyard it was a single mass; the windows on the entrance front were either quite large or quite small; and the axial layout of the house itself contrasted with the diagonal access to the courtyard.

In the design for a house for Dr Kallenbach of November 1921, which was never built, diagonals play an even more important role (ills. 261, 262). Diagonally placed rectangles in the entrance court provide a formal *leitmotiv* for the whole ground plan, relating to the obtuse angles of the walls and the sharply thrusting alcoves of the garden fronts. These too can be found in the houses that Frank Lloyd Wright built in Oak Park, Illinois, shortly after 1900. Wright himself, incidentally, returned to these forms several times during the post-war years, evolving star-shaped plans by superimposing squares.

In the Gropius/Meyer studio the Kallenbach project was regarded as of extreme importance. Adolf Meyer, who had a decisive role in the design, saw it as a chance to do 'something really uncompromising for once',[24] probably not least because the client was willing to spend quite a lot of money, and had also agreed to a flat roof. Dr Kallenbach's adviser was Laszlo Moholy-Nagy, who thus came

256

251–256. Walter Gropius and Adolf Meyer. Sommerfeld log-house, Berlin-Lichterfelde, 1920–21.
251. Garden front.
252. West elevation.
253. Site plan.
254. Staircase windows (by Josef Albers), 1922. Stained glass.
255. Staircase.
256. Door (by Joost Schmidt). Carved teak.

into contact with Gropius. On Moholy-Nagy's advice Kallenbach had asked three architects to draw up plans – Gropius, Ludwig Hilberseimer, and J. J. P. Oud. Oud's design (ills. 263–265) was extremely dry in its forms, and less well orientated, yet it shows quite clearly how, in terms of architectural development, the De Stijl architects were far ahead of the Bauhaus men. It was only later that the Weimar architects made their breakthrough, with a design for a house for a Berlin client; the brilliantly resolved machine factory at Alfeld for Gebrüder Kappe, of early 1922; the much-publicized *Chicago Tribune* design; and the serial-housing development of the summer of 1922.

Before that the Bauhaus had come into direct contact with a member of De Stijl, and thus with its simple vocabulary of elements, its concept of absolute purity, and its idea of universal harmony, when Theo van Doesburg, the eloquent spokesman of De Stijl, moved to Weimar in April 1921. One of his keenest supporters seems to have been Adolf Meyer, though it is doubtful whether Meyer supported the proposal to invite him to join the Bauhaus staff (he was not in fact invited).[25] Such a commitment on Meyer's part should not not be taken to mean that there was stylistic disagreement in the Gropius/Meyer office. Both architects worked within the context of an Expressionist architecture. Meyer clearly played a large part in the Sommerfeld projects and in the house for Dr Kallenbach, whereas the workers' memorial was exclusively the work of Gropius: Forbat modelled it from a free-hand sketch by Gropius.[26]

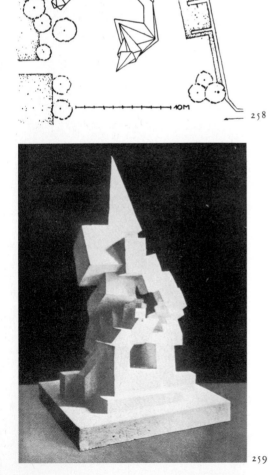

257, 258. Walter Gropius. Memorial to the March victims, Weimar, 1920–21. Rebuilt after destruction in the Second World War. View and plan.
259. Johannes Itten. Composition of cubic forms, 1919. Plaster.
260. Karl Schmidt-Rottluff. Pillar of Prayer. Designed for Bruno Taut's House of Heaven, 1919 (detail).

The source of form

Was this romantic phase an interlude that bore no relationship to the two architects' early work? In putting form and expression first both in theory and in practice in the period between 1918 and 1922, Gropius was doing exactly as he had done in the period before the First World War. The only difference was that in the pre-war years the 'expression' part had been related to an objective content: 'The architect is able . . . to give worthy expression to the inner value of the particular arrangement and method of work.' Such limiting factors as economics, construction, and the organization of flow are 'material for symbolic representation'; the artist's forms find their meaning in 'poetic exaggeration'. After 1918 Gropius at first made expression absolute, 'for feeling is the source . . . of form.' But Gropius' rejection of a purely purposive architecture did not date from the Sommerfeld log-house or the workers' memorial. It was already implied in his very earliest writings and buildings, and in fact it was part of the legacy from Behrens. It was no accident that Gropius changed the title of his Hagen lecture, 'Art and Industrial Architecture', to *Monumental Art and Industrial Architecture*.[27]

Even the ardent aspiration towards a distant future can be found in Gropius' early work: 'Only when mankind is again granted the great happiness of a new faith will art too fulfil its highest aim once more and be capable of reinventing, as proof of a deep purification, joyful decorative forms for the austere forms of the beginning.' This sentence occurs not in any proclamation made by Gropius as Bauhaus principal in 1919, but in the 1914 yearbook of the Werkbund.[28]

Gropius' attitude to the value of crafts, on the other hand, did change appreciably between 1914 and 1919, and then again in 1923. Before the First World War he had little interest in crafts; he saw as inevitable the elimination of the slight individual variations due to manual work and the increased productivity which the machine

261

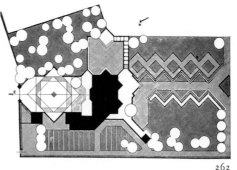

262

261, 262. Walter Gropius and Adolf Meyer. Project for a house for Dr Kallenbach, Berlin, 1921. View from the garden and site plan.
263–265. J. J. P. Oud. Project for a house for Dr Kallenbach, Berlin, 1921. Rear, front and side elevations.
266, 267. Walter Gropius and Adolf Meyer. House for Dr Otte, Berlin-Zehlendorf West, 1921–22. Entrance front and garden front.

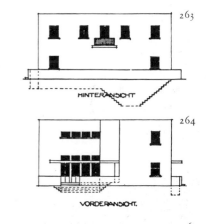

263

264

265

266

267

made possible. It is significant that in the memorandum he sent to the Ministry of State of the Grand Duchy of Saxe-Weimar in January 1916, containing proposals for the establishment of an artistic advisory board in Weimar, he spoke of cooperation between artist, businessman and technician. No place in this triumvirate was given to the craftsman, although the ministry had expressly inquired into the possibility of fostering handicrafts.

After the war Gropius' attitude to crafts changed briefly: he saw in crafts a foundation on which it might be possible to build a community of all creative workers, whatever their social background. It was to the people, however, and not to artists that he looked for a new and spontaneous originality in art. 'New strata of the people, spiritually as yet unawakened, are thrusting upwards . . . Their instincts, fresh and intact, are still rooted in nature. It is to them that the artist of the future will turn.'[29]

The return to crafts had been one of the demands of the first Bauhaus manifesto in 1919. Five years later, when the new orientation of the Bauhaus had been decided, Gropius asserted that 'a conscious reversion to the crafts of the past would be . . . an atavistic error.'[30] From this time onwards crafts were regarded merely as a way of training the spatial/sculptural imagination, a way of preparing the apprentice for the more complex processes of industry, and a field of experiment for industrial production. By 1922 the role of crafts was under heated discussion at the Bauhaus, and the idea of a house as a 'living-machine', proclaimed by Sant'Elia eight years earlier, had caught on in Weimar.

As the attitude of the Bauhaus to crafts changed, so did its attitude to the outside world. The cultivation of art, and a sectarianism that looked to a millenium, were to be replaced by a keen participation in the present, active intervention in the world around, and a systematic mastering of all the techniques of industry. 'Nothing can happen to us if we make ourselves independent of the outside world', Gropius had once noted, and in a letter to his friend Osthaus he had said something very similar: 'The only thing left for us is to ignore the real world and build ourselves a separate, inner world of our own.'[31] Retreat into this inner world for as long as the outer world should fail to coincide with it was now regarded as inappropriate.

Remarks by Feininger, Marcks, and Kandinsky – and also Schlemmer and Muche – show how precarious this change of course seemed to the Bauhaus artists themselves. Theodor Heuss expressed their misgivings in 1923: 'The Bauhaus is after form and standardization as used in industry – a worthy enough goal. Will its path be smoothed by a subjectivism that, in experiments with form and material, gives free play to the imagination?'[32] The way the Bauhaus artists understood themselves and their task continued to give rise to fresh conflicts as long as the school remained in existence, for unlike the members of De Stijl, they were not united behind a strict discipline that could be transposed into other media. On the other hand this unresolved tension – between art and technology, between the claims of artistic individuality and social responsibility, between the openness of method that was asked for and the actual bias in favour of a particular formal canon that was laid down – kept the Bauhaus, throughout all its phases, from becoming complacent.

8 Erich Mendelsohn

'What happens is of value only when it is born in an ecstacy of vision.'

Erich Mendelsohn, *Das Problem einer neuen Baukunst*, 1919

A revolutionary and a success

The career of Erich Mendelsohn (1887–1953) was different from that of the other architects of his generation. Along with Mies van der Rohe, Bartning, the Luckhardts and the Tauts, he belonged to the Berlin Novembergruppe; indeed, he was a founder-member of this revolutionary league of artists, and he sat on its central committee. The Arbeitsrat für Kunst invited him to repeat the speech he had made at the first exhibition of his drawings at Paul Cassirer's gallery. He took an active part in the founding of Der Ring, the league of Berlin architects, in 1925. He contributed as much to the new style of the twenties as any other progressive Berlin architect – possibly even more; but he remained a lone wolf.

He was only a few years younger than Gropius and Bruno Taut, and only one year younger than Mies van der Rohe, yet this difference in age was significant. Mendelsohn built virtually nothing before the First World War,[1] so that his visionary designs come not at an interim stage in his career, but at the beginning (as with Scharoun); and there is thus continuity between his early and late work. The sketches he sent home from the front, some of them literally the size of postage stamps, were the basis for all his works, though they were to be enriched with other elements. Mendelsohn acknowledged the comment that he was the only born revolutionary of his generation[2] – implying that the others had merely acquired their revolutionary spirit.

If Mendelsohn was lucky with history, he was also lucky with his patrons. For his first large commission, the Einstein Tower in Potsdam, he was able to carry through, without any essential modification, a formal idea that had interested him for years. What this meant to the thirty-year-old architect in terms of self-confidence must have been considerable. His stroke of genius helped attract a clientèle that had a feeling for the grandeur of his designs, as well as the money to build them. Both the publisher Mosse, who had seen the Einstein Tower on the front page of the *Berliner Illustrierte Zeitung*, and the department-store owner Schocken, were the kind of clients that figure only in young architects' boldest dreams. It was they who made it possible for Mendelsohn to develop his dynamic horizontals and three-dimensionally felt masses.

Mendelsohn made modernity popular, without any hint of compromise (at least in his Berlin period). His feeling for the total effect was firmly controlled by good taste: he seemed to enjoy a charmed immunity from the kind of blunders that Poelzig's wild imagination sometimes led him into. Mendelsohn's buildings had the quality of images; they sold themselves, their builders, and their architect. He was consistent in considering publicity as a legitimate problem of architecture rather than as a distasteful burden on the architect's imagination. He designed lighting and lettering, and devoted whole areas of wall to publicity – sometimes even overdoing it, as in the disproportionately large lettering of the Schocken store at Stuttgart.

The one architect of the twenties who had a reputation for success was Mendelsohn. At times he employed as many as forty men, an exceptional figure at that

268. Erich Mendelsohn. Ink sketch, 1914–15. Louise Mendelsohn Collection, San Francisco.

269. Erich Mendelsohn. Ink sketch, 1917. Louise Mendelsohn Collection, San Francisco.

period. Unlike Gropius, he did not have to struggle in the provinces with master craftsmen and narrow-minded municipal officials; he was spared the necessity of having to take on jobs to survive. Humorous and self-confident, he was a sound businessman and employer – yet on occasion, as Richard Neutra remembered, he could behave like a young office-boy.[3]

Mendelsohn spent his student years in Munich, in the interim between late Jugendstil and early Expressionism. His association with the members of the Blaue Reiter group of painters may explain the cryptic abbreviated style of his later architectural sketches. It is striking that he was particularly attracted to sculpturally moulded form in architecture: he admired Henry van de Velde's Werkbund Theatre in Cologne for its strong contours, its layered masses and its organic unity. But he knew the theatre from photographs only;[4] and indeed publications played a large part in stimulating his imagination, in particular the Frank Lloyd Wright portfolios published by Wasmuth and the Werkbund yearbooks, from whose 1913 and 1914 volumes he drew many illustrations for his lectures. The reinforcement of perspective with receding sculptural units, illustrated by the American silos in the 1913 yearbook, is reflected in many of Mendelsohn's sketches. When in 1924 he went to America (on a Frank Lloyd Wright pilgrimage), he found that much of what he saw 'seemed to have been shaped interim to my silo dreams',[5] and offered perspectives very much in harmony with his own architecture at the time (ills. 270, 271).

The real hero of Mendelsohn's teaching and travelling years was an architect whose portrait hangs in one of the more

270

271

272

273

274

275

obscure corners of the ancestors' gallery of modern architecture – Joseph Maria Olbrich (1867–1908). Though Mendelsohn alluded to many architects in his 1919 lectures, Olbrich was the only one he named. Olbrich's work was usually dismissed as 'Viennese charm', but Mendelsohn saw other qualities in it: 'Early law, sharply austere and great, appears to emerge, give the world its blessing, and build it anew.'[6] What Mendelsohn liked about Olbrich's Hochzeitsturm in Darmstadt (1905–8) was its 'impregnable surfaces' and the cubic solidity of the tower itself – the horizontal rows of windows, sharply defined by cornices, cut into the surface and, by continuing round the corner, stress the building's three-dimensionality. With Mendelsohn this became a *leitmotiv*. Olbrich's Gebäude für Flächenkunst in Darmstadt (ill. 275), a timber building with a keel-shaped section, made an even deeper impression on him. There is a quality of furniture about many of Olbrich's buildings, which seem to lean against an imaginary wall like giant showcases, and this quality sometimes occurs in Mendelsohn's work as well (ills. 272, 273).

Mendelsohn judged even Olbrich's eccentricities with an indulgence that he never showed towards other architects. Of the curious decoration of the hall of the Gebäude für Flächenkunst, which recalls the prows of Viking ships, and which recurs in his own early drawings (ills. 274, 275), Mendelsohn wrote: 'It seems to me that this is simply an inkling of future associational possibilities; it seems to me that their embracing of the formal entity simply implies a desire to make visible constructional possibilities, even though the right building material is not yet available.' Mendelsohn perceived in Olbrich's work a rhythm which could be realized only with the uninhibited use of reinforced concrete. Olbrich was a kindred spirit for whom Mendelsohn obviously had a special feeling – and that went for his 'bill-posting attitude' too: 'With unerring artistic instinct it just avoided striking a pose and instead created a monument.'[7]

270. Erich Mendelsohn. Sketch, 1923.
271. Grain elevator in Chicago (detail), from Erich Mendelsohn, *Amerika, Bilderbuch eines Architekten*, Berlin, 1926.
272. Erich Mendelsohn. Ink sketch, 1914. Louise Mendelsohn Collection, San Francisco.
273. Joseph Maria Olbrich. Project for a studio building on the Mathildenhöhe, Darmstadt (?), 1899. Pencil. Staatsbibliothek, Berlin.
274. Erich Mendelsohn. Exhibition hall, 1914. Ink. Louise Mendelsohn Collection, San Francisco.
275. Joseph Maria Olbrich. Gebäude für Flächenkunst, Darmstadt, 1900.

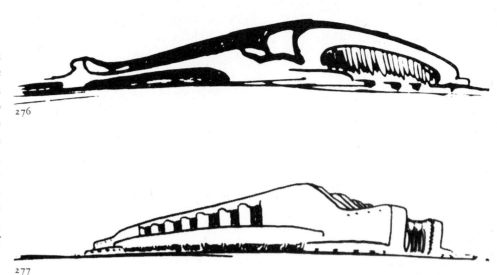

276

277

Mendelsohn's extensive graphic work began in 1914 and reached a climax in the sketches he sent home from the eastern front during 1917. These designs fall into a number of groups which often overlap ills. 268, 269, 272, 274, 276–282). Some motifs interested him for a few years, others troughout his life. Most of the designs are based on what appears to be a limitlessly extendible series of wave-like bays with slanting or upright piers, unified under a great curved roof, pairs of pylons, or portal-like superstructures. Buildings are often spanned with steel girders, on reinforced concrete piers, that serve also as tracks for travelling cranes. Mendelsohn's centralized compositions, like the observatories that initiated the concept of the Einstein Tower, have powerfully projecting elements.

Mendelsohn described the essence of these sketches, which were redrawn and enlarged for an exhibition at Paul Cassirer's gallery early in 1919, as uniformity of outline and the gradation of similar parts. They have something else in common, though: their symmetrical development about a single axis, obscured by the diagonal viewpoint from which they are drawn. Mendelsohn realized that 'the perspective angle certainly has a lot to be said for it'.[8] The Futurists chose similar views in their drawings to suggest movement in symmetrical and uniform buildings.[9] It was not until the highly imaginative doodles of 1920 in which Mendelsohn came closest to the 'original art' of finsterlin (ill. 283),[10] and the somewhat later variations of blocks and projecting plinths (ill. 270), that Mendelsohn's graphic work broke free of symmetry. Another feature common to most of the designs is a pronounced horizontality. Even in the skyscraper projects the horizontal is dominant, due to Mendelsohn's use of low auxiliary structures and his emphasis on the *load* rather than on the vertical load-bearing elements (ill. 190).

Mendelsohn justified the horizontality of his work by claiming that there were

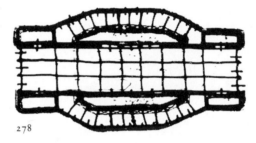

278

276. Erich Mendelsohn. Railway station, 1915. From *Wendingen*, III, no. 10, 1920.
277. Erich Mendelsohn. Central airport for airships and aeroplanes, 1914. From *Wendingen*, III, no. 10, 1920.
278. Erich Mendelsohn. Central airport for airships and aeroplanes. Plan. Ink. Louise Mendelsohn Collection, San Francisco.

divisions in all the hierarchies of politics, economy and culture. In his idiosyncratic concept of civilization, the 'one-on-top-of-anotherness *(Übereinander)* of the pillars of state' was dissolving into a 'horizontal side-by-sideness *(Nebeneinander)* of the individual elements of the race'. In the economic sphere the vertical formation of trusts went against the grain, and would give way in the future to production organisms consisting of parallel units. Mendelsohn clearly equated administrative and technical (production) organizational forms, as if a firm organized as a hierarchy could not work with production methods organized on a linear basis. Even the vertically-structured sovereignty of faith would give way to a pluralistic *Nebeneinander* of religious elements – 'elements of mysticism, esoteric doctrine, and miracle'.[11]

There can be no doubt that in his sketches, which were unrelated to any commission, Mendelsohn thought in terms of volume and only secondarily in terms of function. Descriptions like coach-building works, central airport, goods shed, blast-furnace, and chemical factory are more or less interchangeable; they merely hint at concepts he derived from technology and industry. Mendelsohn had none of that distaste for technology shared by so many of his contemporaries. Though his visions used striking motifs, they went beyond the purely visual. Even where a plan is not given, it can be worked out. This quality distinguishes his sketches from those of Sant'Elia: Sant'Elia's designs are impenetrable fragments of an impenetrable labyrinth of technology; Mendelsohn's sketches are impressive images of isolated and in

279. Erich Mendelsohn. House of Friendship,
1918(?). From *Wendingen*, III, no. 10, 1920.
280. Erich Mendelsohn. Silo over a harbour,
1914. From *Wendingen*, III, no. 10, 1920.
281. Erich Mendelsohn, Sketch, 1917.

almost every case easily comprehensible
buildings. In this sense he already had a
clearer eye for reality than Sant'Elia, even
though his designs would have failed to
meet the specific needs of a more complex
production process in the way that his
later Luckenwalde factory did.

The power of these sketches derives
from a further abstraction, which is that
the surroundings are irrelevant. In the
early sketches the urban or topographical
context is completely suppressed. Mendelsohn also refused to heighten the effect
by distorting the surroundings. No rising
suns transfigure his architecture; no
plunging perspectives over plains or
mountains awaken alpine or cosmic emotions. All the passion is in the forms
themselves, not in the accessories.

How strange Mendelsohn's works appeared even to well-disposed observers is
shown by Hermann Obrist's reaction. He
recognized the 'artistic impetus towards
the splendid mass, the mighty curve', yet
had his doubts about Mendelsohn's
talents in the field of practical architecture. Obrist advised him to confine himself to designing imaginary buildings, but
there to give his imagination free rein.[1]
What seemed to the older teacher to be a
dilemma between brilliant ideas and practical thinking turned out to be the young
architect's strong point – the future synthesis in potential form.

Beginnings in a career

Mendelsohn was a believer in the correct-
ness of intuition. When, in the Einstein
Tower, the 'tellurian and planetary'[1]
character of his drawings proved compa-
tible with the demands of the scientists,
this was proof to him that his gift of visual
imagination covered practical needs. It
was not the commission for the Einstein
Tower that gave rise to the sketches but
the sketches that, thanks to his personal
contacts among associates of Einstein's,
brought him the commission.[14]

The programme of the Einstein Tower
(ills. 284–291) was easily accommodated
within Mendelsohn's formal conception

Financed partly by the state of Prussia and partly from private sources, the building combines telescope and laboratory. The stocky tower, originally intended to be slimmer but subsequently (and not at all to its disadvantage) altered in its proportions, is crowned by a dome housing the coelostat. The light of the stars is transmitted through a system of mirrors and lenses from the coelostat down to the laboratory, which lies underground. There, a further mirror, set at an angle of 45°, reflects it into the spectrum analysis instruments which are housed in a room maintained at a constant temperature (providing a justification for the broad base of the building). Between base and shaft, on the southern side, are a study and sleeping quarters. To the north the external stair and projecting part of the building, which contains a staircase giving access to the second main floor, lead into the tower structure. The upward-surging movement of the approach to the lower main floor is so powerful that it forces the tower wall into a concave profile.

Mendelsohn had a free hand in the organization of access to the tower and of the subsidiary rooms; he also took every kind of artistic licence in the details – rounded corners, punched-out walls, angular window frames and sculptural 'gargoyles' such as were not to be used again until Le Corbusier built Ronchamp thirty years later.

Mendelsohn first conceived the tower as a reinforced concrete structure. Reinforced concrete constituted in Mendelsohn's eyes the true, artistic building material, unlike steel, with its insubstantial appearance. Concrete gave solidity to a building's surface, offering the eye and the hand something to rest on. Above all, concrete made possible the avoidance of a purely technical character, which even Mendelsohn felt to be incompatible with the architectural work of art.

Ironically, however, this monument to the sculptural potential of concrete was only partially made of that material. Due to a delay in the delivery of cement, the Einstein Tower was built in brick and covered with a layer of concrete – involving the builders in endless trouble. Had the building been executed entirely in reinforced concrete, however, the problems of moulding and reinforcing might have been even more formidable. This experience ensured that Mendelsohn never again attempted a monolithic structure, or even one of monolithic effect.

The Einstein Tower is one of the most impressive of German Expressionist buildings. It looks as though it was kneaded by some godlike hand, to create a dramatic play of light and shade – the light modulated by the curved surfaces, and the shade cutting deep into the mass of the building, forcing it open. No other building of the period invites such anthropomorphic epithets – grim, threatening, defiant . . . It crouches on the ground like a sphinx, with paws flexed ready to spring.

Mendelsohn had been able to learn at first hand about the importance of research along the lines developed by Albert Einstein, and he translated it not into a symbol of the scientific/technological age but into an emblem of Promethean power. What he built was not merely a laboratory: it was a monument. One contemporary thought to relate the building's monolithic form to its namesake, and called it *Ein Stein* ('a single stone').[15]

Architects who were concerned about the social responsibilities of architecture saw the Einstein Tower as a homage to the past rather than to the future. This was the view expressed by Jan Frederik Staal, in the issue of the magazine *Wendingen* devoted to introducing Mendelsohn as an architect of German Expressionism.[16] Mendelsohn's critical attitude towards his Amsterdam colleagues (see pp. 125–26) was reciprocated: the *Wendingen* people had reservations about Mendelsohn. Nor were these reservations surprising; Mendelsohn expressed the hope that places of forced labour would become places of work once the 'constraint of capitalist calculation' had been removed, but he was not particularly interested in the social and urban context of his time: he thought

282

283

282. Erich Mendelsohn, Sketch, 1923.
283. Erich Mendelsohn, Fantastic sketch (pleasure pavilion), 1920.

284

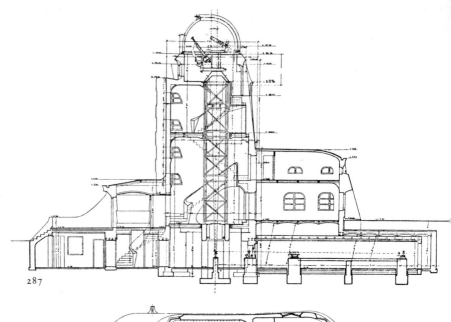

287

285

286

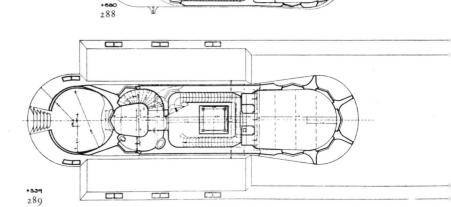

+680
288

+339
289

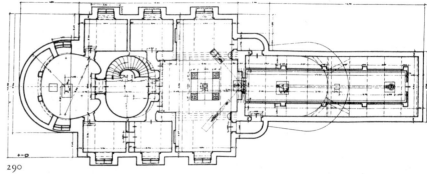

290

284–291. Erich Mendelsohn.
Einstein Tower, Potsdam, 1917–21.

284–286. Views.
287. Section.
288. Plan at 6.8 m level (staircase and sleeping quarters).
289. Plan at 3.39 m level (entrance hall, staircases and living room).
290. Plan at ground level (laboratories).
291. General view.

292

293

294

295

largely in terms of individual buildings. He even made this statement, which sounds like Peter Behrens: 'Expressing the power of an age has always been the best task for art.'[17]

In two jobs during his early years in Berlin Mendelsohn had to take existing buildings into account. He was commissioned to build a new façade for the head office of the Hausleben insurance company on Dorotheenstrasse (ill. 292) – a common enough commission in post-war Berlin, where the urge to build was limited by economic constraint. Mendelsohn's formal compositions recall the efforts of those Czech architects who took up themes from pictorial art (in their case Cubist painting) and applied them to building façades. Characteristically, Mendelsohn tried to suggest monumental sculpture, by surrounding the windows in the façade (painted blue-grey and red) with frames that appear to thrust out of a uniform mass and turn inside out.

A more important job was the extension of the Mosse building on the corner of Jerusalemer Strasse and Schützenstrasse (ill. 293). Above the old sandstone façade he placed two and three extra storeys, which at the corner are welded into the old building right down to street level. The building not only served an advertising firm; it was a piece of publicity in itself. The shock effect was calculated: the ruthless contrast was part of Mendelsohn's intention. Horizontal is set against vertical, plaster against stone; ceramic friezes sharply divide old from new. There is movement in all directions. In all the window surrounds the lintels project beyond the sills, and the extra storeys

292. Erich Mendelsohn. Conversion of the Hausleben insurance building in Dorotheenstrasse, Berlin, 1920.
293. Erich Mendelsohn with Richard Neutra and R. P. Henning. Conversion of Rudolf-Mosse-Haus in Jerusalemer Strasse, Berlin, 1921–23.
294, 295. Erich Mendelsohn. Hat factory for Hermann & Co., Luckenwalde, 1920. Front and side elevations.

terminate at the sides in decorations that are like symbolic wings.

'In this case the building is not an indifferent spectator to the whizzing cars and the ebb and flow of traffic, but has become a receptive and contributory element in the movement around it', wrote Mendelsohn, he added with some amusement that, particularly on account of the long rows of windows, the design was known in his office as 'The *Mauretania* docking in Berlin West'. Mendelsohn's amusement, however, seems rather inconsistent because in the same 1923 lecture in which he told this joke he had previously stated, using the very example of an ocean liner, that the form of a ship was derived from the laws of *real* motion, 'so that it would constitute an utter misunderstanding of the nature of architecture to try and translate those laws of motion into architectural terms'.[18]

In 1920 Mendelsohn built a steel-framed building in Luckenwalde for the hat manufacturers Hermann & Co.; its strict right angles and grid-like structure were relieved only by sloping windows, roofs and cornices (ills. 294, 295). A year later, however, he began to build a large hat factory, also in Luckenwalde, for Steinberg-Hermann, and here the requirements of the programme themselves suggested a vigorous silhouette (ills. 296–298). In the dye shop, fumes had to be removed largely without mechanical means; Mendelsohn achieved the required ventilation with a broad, funnel-shaped building in which the foul air was drawn off through louvres at the top (ill. 296, left). The dye shop and a power plant, arranged on the transverse axis of the site, dominated the production shop, a large low building divided into four aisles which could be extended in both directions along the longitudinal axis.

How much free expression Mendelsohn allowed himself at Luckenwalde, in spite of the rational and economic layout of the whole, can be seen from a comparison with the textile factory for 8,000 workers which he designed for Leningrad in 1925 (ill. 299). The varying pitches of the dye-shop roofs, their banks of sky-lights set at acute and obtuse angles, the projecting corners, the slanted window strips of the production-shop gables which bear no relationship to the three-piece, reinforced-concrete supporting arches, and the ribbed brick fans which Mendelsohn used at Luckenwalde, indicate a self-willed temperament intent on preserving as much of its vision as possible.

In the course of the twenties Mendelsohn reduced the number of ideas admitted purely on the grounds of 'emotional content'. Nevertheless the strong shadow-casting cornices are still present in his department-store designs of 1926–27; and the asymmetrically-placed, glazed circular towers, that conduct real movement (staircases) or gather up the imaginary movement of horizontal strips of window or brickwork, can be found as late as 1950–51 in the Russell house at Pacific Heights. Even buildings that fit into the style of the late twenties, like the Schocken department store in Chemnitz (1928–29) and the Columbus-Haus (1929–31) and Universum cinema (1926–31, ill. 419) in Berlin, are conceived as single plastic volumes. In this they differ fundamentally from spatial systems made up of articulated members such as Gropius' Bauhaus at Dessau and Mies van der Rohe's German pavilion at the Barcelona Exhibition. Whereas these spatial systems were extensible and theoretically reducible as well, Mendelsohn's kind of architectural continuum was governed by his own definition of an organism: 'You

296

297

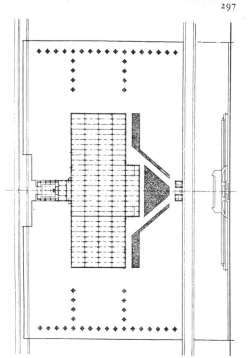

298

296–298. Erich Mendelsohn. Hat factory for Friedrich Steinberg, Hermann & Co., Lucken-walde, 1921–23.
296. View from the south, by the porter's lodge, looking towards the dye shop (left) and production shop.
297. Interior of the spinning works in the production shop.
298. Site plan and view from the south; from right to left: porter's lodge, dye shop, production shop, power plant. The south elevation is shown, vertically, at the right edge of the plan.
299. Erich Mendelsohn. Krasnoye Snamya textile factory, Leningrad, 1925. Model.

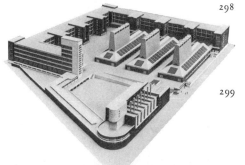

299

cannot . . . remove a single part without destroying the whole, whether of its mass, its movement, or its logical issue.'[19]

Functional dynamics

The opinions Mendelsohn voiced on Dutch architecture have been interpreted as an early repudiation of his Expressionist beginnings.[20] A misleading statement by Mendelsohn himself led to these opinions being attributed to his first trip to Holland; in fact they date from 1923. 'Amsterdam is betraying the faith: it abandons the new discoveries in favour of overdrawn, emotional, romantic irrelevancies and loses itself in variegated modern trifles. Only what is simple can be understood collectively: what is individualistic remains, in the last analysis, meaningless.' Nor did Mendelsohn think the Rotterdam school – which may have inspired his prismatic buildings and projects of 1922–23 – was right. He stood by what he called his 'reconciliation programme'. 'Oud is . . . functional. Amsterdam is dynamic. A union of both concepts is conceivable, but cannot be discerned in Holland. The first puts reason foremost – perception through analysis. The second, unreason – perception through vision. Analytic Rotterdam rejects vision. Visionary Amsterdam does not understand analytic objectivity . . . If Amsterdam goes a step further towards ratio, and Rotterdam does not freeze up, they may still unite. Otherwise both will be destroyed; Rotterdam by the deadly chill in its veins, Amsterdam by the fire of its own dynamism.'[21]

The formula Mendelsohn put forward was 'functional dynamics'. Of course he did not define either 'function' or 'dynamics' precisely, preferring to leave them a certain emotional latitude. He did, admittedly, make a point of refusing to equate dynamics with vitality, but this did not stop him from using the term later as a synonym for feeling and imagination. In his 1923 lecture he called dynamics the expression in movement of the forces inherent in building materials. This 'expression in movement', however, was not, as with the machine, to be reduced to a forced dependence as a 'utilitarian function': it must emerge as a free play between form and its postulates – purpose, material, and construction.[22] The resultant building thus became an image of function. The function it should symbolize Mendelsohn saw in the broadest terms possible; a newspaper building, for example, would reflect not the editorial and administrative work of the paper itself, but the tempo of modern life as distilled in the metropolitan press.

Mendelsohn, like so many of his contemporaries, felt that behind the responsibilities of architecture, behind the introduction of steel, reinforced concrete and glass as building materials, a stylistic principle was at work. If the architect accepted new building techniques and sought to resolve new problems – techniques and problems which were themselves expressions of the times – he could regard himself as the instrument of a will 'that knew and established the law'. The 'new will has the future on its side in the unconsciousness of its chaotic impetus and the spontaneity of its universal embrace.'[23]

In 1919, understandably, Mendelsohn tended to stress the common impetus behind the new awakening. In 1923 – probably to some extent under the influence of the split in Dutch architecture – he saw opposites that needed to be drawn together. Just as he sought to reconcile Amsterdam and Rotterdam, dynamics and function, so too he believed that his concept of architecture combined both Expressionism and Constructivism. He did not regard Expressionism as a stylistic phase that was finished, or as an error that had been corrected; for him it was a continuous process which needs must evolve.

In later years Mendelsohn showed a like predilection for reducing experience to a polarized schema. His trips to America and Russia provided an intensified version of the Dutch experience: Amsterdam became Moscow, Rotterdam New York. Europe, between the two, was to find the balance between the vehemence and impulsive religiosity of Russian nature on the one hand and the rational good sense and uncomplicated energy of the United States on the other[24] – or so Mendelsohn wrote five years before Europe forced him into exile.

'The bolts of a new age flew open. Yet the age had a greater ambition, a deeper yearning – it had set its sights beyond the moment and fixed them on eternity.'

Kasimir Edschmid, 'Bernhard Hoetger', in *Der Falke*, August 1916

The Hamburg *Kontorhaus*

Berlin architects were international in outlook. They knew about American skyscrapers, Frank Lloyd Wright, Russian Constructivism, the schools of Amsterdam and Rotterdam, and even – thanks to the efforts of Herwarth Walden – about the literature and art of Italian Futurism. Contacts with artists abroad were resumed as soon as possible after the war, and appeals were made for cooperation (for instance in the publications of the *Clarté* movement, led by Henri Barbusse and Romain Rolland). International pacifism formed part of almost every 'revolutionary' architect's political credo.

Hamburg architects differed from their Berlin colleagues in many respects. In this ancient Hanseatic city, local tradition counted for more than outside stimulus: the architects considered themselves upholders of a tradition stretching back to North German Gothic, not as innovators. So strong was this tradition that even outsiders, like Fritz Schumacher, who was appointed *Oberbaudirektor* in 1909, willingly submitted and adapted themselves to it. In the Hamburg of the postwar years it was office buildings which came closest to Expressionism. The type of the Hamburg office building, the *Kontorhaus*, had been developing for some decades already; indeed the earliest purpose-built structure housing nothing but commercial offices was the Dovenhof, by Martin Haller, of 1885–86.

The fact that at the planning stage the future tenants of a *Kontorhaus* were as yet unknown called for flexibility. The utili-

ties had to be kept together so that the office area could be divided up as required. The plans that resulted anticipated future practice. Johannes Friedrich (Fritz) Höger (1877–1949), the most important of the Hamburg office block architects, as early as 1910 grouped his vertical access and sanitary installations in the middle, in a way characteristic of so much office building today. Frame construction was a further consequence of the need for freely disposed floor areas.

The consequences of a purely commercial city in terms of town planning made themselves felt earlier in Hamburg than anywhere else in Central Europe. The eastern part of the old city, one of the districts that had decayed and become notorious in the cholera epidemic of 1892, was demolished and replaced by darkly impressive office buildings. The city council's original intention had been to reserve the area for residential accommodation: this proved impracticable in the face of pressure from private developers. Thus Hamburg began to experience the wave of demolition and office building that was later radically to change almost all city centres.

Hamburg's office blocks owe their homogeneity to the fact that they are built in brick. The city's damp climate is unsuitable for plaster and favours brick building; but there were other, less practical reasons for the use of brick, set out in Fritz Schumacher's *Das Wesen des neuzeitlichen Backsteinbaues* of 1917. This apologia for brick in modern building, written by an expert and connoisseur of the subject, forms a counterpart to Paul Scheerbart's *Glasarchitektur*. Building in brick represented the sort of craft tradition in which progressives and reactionaries alike saw salvation: 'it is', Schumacher asserted, 'the craft mentality that architecture needs today if it is to recover fresh life.' The fact that very little brick was still manufactured by hand and that its use in office building was confined to filling in or facing a steel or reinforced-concrete skeleton was not held to be a valid objection. Brick, especially vitrified brick, suited

300

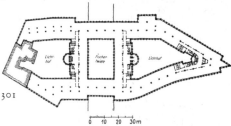

301

300, 301. Fritz Höger. Chilehaus, Hamburg, 1923–24. View from the east, and plan of a standard floor.

the current taste for colour. Ranging from a yellowy tan to a purple brown, from orange to bottle-green, and from a rich mat effect to an iridescent glaze, brick offered a finely shaded spectrum which could be accentuated by laying alternate courses in different colours. Variety and richness of surface effect were what counted with the architects close to Expressionism: to many of them brick appeared a particularly suitable material. Fritz Höger (whose staff were required to call him 'the master') extolled its virtues as 'architecture's precious stone'. They preferred irregular, second- and third-grade bricks because these gave added animation to the wall texture.

Moral and sometimes even irrational arguments were adduced in favour of building in brick. The genuineness, honesty, sincerity, 'intimacy of soul' and 'German temper' allegedly associated

302

303

with brick were all made much of, as was the austere monumentality which brick and vitrified brick could generate. 'Anyone aspiring to a stern and stringent simplicity', wrote Schumacher, 'will find its full and lively realization in this material.' In the late twenties indigenous brick building was upheld as the antithesis of 'white' or International Modern architecture. Höger wrote of the rough peasant whom he preferred to the powdered *salon* fop.[1] The polemical battle over brick versus plaster found a parallel in the argument over pitched or flat roofs; these arguments were waged not for the sake of the thing itself but for the ideology behind it.

Fritz Höger

The qualities of the 'rough peasant' which Höger had praised belong more to his background (he was the son of a Holstein farm labourer) than to his architecture. His office buildings of before the First World War are, like Schumacher's, marked by an austerity which admits few stylistic quotations and limits decorative elements to mere accessories. They are in the tradition of the framed buildings articulated with giant pilasters erected in Hamburg by Erich Elingius, Henri Grell, Georg Radel and others. Windows between the vertical members are gathered together in groups not unlike the famous 'Chicago windows'. Supporting columns and mullions become closer and closer in size and profile until the whole façade is treated vertically with close-set piers between the windows. This produced a uniform façade which, during the twenties, was very often transformed into a single vast decorative pattern.

Among the many office buildings in the Hamburg style,[2] Höger's Chilehaus enjoyed a high reputation (ills. 300, 301, 499). This was due mainly to the acute angled, knife-edge corner, and the broad, overhanging eaves of its dramatic eastern end, which in this maritime city inevitably evoked the prow of a ship. Its crystalline sharpness has a parallel in Mies van der Rohe's famous 1919 design for a glass building (ills. 72, 73). The literary associations of Expressionist building inspired the writer Rudolf G. Binding to a whole string of comparisons: the 'house-body' (*Häuserleib*) of the Chilehaus seemed to him to be 'as slender as a trout, as lean as a ship, as billowing as a pinion, as unbroken and uninterrupted as the orbit of a star, as uncannily light and as uncannily strong as an eagle's wing, and as flowing as a flag in the wind'.[3]

One is inclined to attribute the wilful shape of the Chilehaus, with its S-bend to the south, its dead-straight north side, its pointed eastern corner, and the double bridging of a street, Fischertwiete, to the awkward nature of the site; yet to some extent Höger created the complications himself. The swinging line of the south façade was entirely his decision; Schumacher's office smoothed the way by property deals and special permissions.

On the concave/convex south façade Höger's enjoyment of decoration produced effects which he never managed to repeat on the even surfaces of his later office buildings. Close-set piers separate the window strips, which terminate in round arches to produce the effect of an elongated arcade (compare Poelzig, ill. 17); these piers project, and seen from the side they partly conceal the tall, narrow window sections. As with the steel-skeleton buildings that Mies van der Rohe was to build after he emigrated to the United States, the façade opens and closes to the view of the passer-by. The piers are triangular in section, and in every seventh course one brick is laid sideways, parallel to the wall plane, as if cutting off the point of the pier. Viewed from the side at an angle, this produces an effect of hatching that draws the whole apparently windowless expanse of brick together. The number of different light values appearing simultaneously on the façade at any time of the day Höger calculated to be at least fifty, including shadows and reflections.

Höger was excessively fond of the brick ornamentation which became an architectural cliché throughout Germany. The Chilehaus is a happy exception to the general run of his buildings, for in it the decoration is combined with a convincing plastic volume, and the decoration and volume show each other off to the best advantage. The stepping back of the upper storeys forms a satisfactory termination to the building. The schematic results which Höger's love of 'dreaming, playing and embroidering in small-scale material'[4] could lead to appear in the lumpy Sprinkenhof, diagonally opposite the Chilehaus (ill. 303), which clashes painfully with the relatively delicate articulation of the earlier building. A flat, featureless surface is covered with a net of vitrified bricks, some of them with a gold glaze, and there are coloured motifs in the centre of the diamond patterns. The Gerson brothers' Ballinhaus (ill. 302) is another neighbour of the Chilehaus; with its corner piers which merge into the wall plane in a concave curve, it provides a solid, stable contrast to the Sprinkenhof.

Bernhard Hoetger's early work

The sculptor Bernhard Hoetger (1874–1949) was one of the last to follow the path that the Jugendstil artists had taken and to move from the fine arts to architecture. He claimed that his first architectural attempts were made early.[5] These were, however, probably concerned more with interior decoration, or with the integration of his sculpture into architectural contexts; he did not turn to architecture in practical terms until his forties. The decisive impulse, as with the reformers of the Art Nouveau era, was provided by his desire for a suitable house. Hoetger built his first house, the Brunnenhof (ill. 518), in Worpswede in 1915: a two-storey building of brick, flanked by two towers and placed at right angles in front of an old Lower Saxon farmhouse, it shows the self-assurance – and the financial resources – of this new versatile genius.

Unlike van de Velde and Behrens, as an architect Hoetger remained dependent

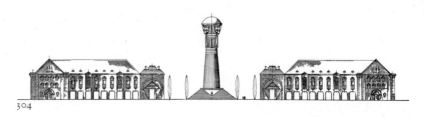
304

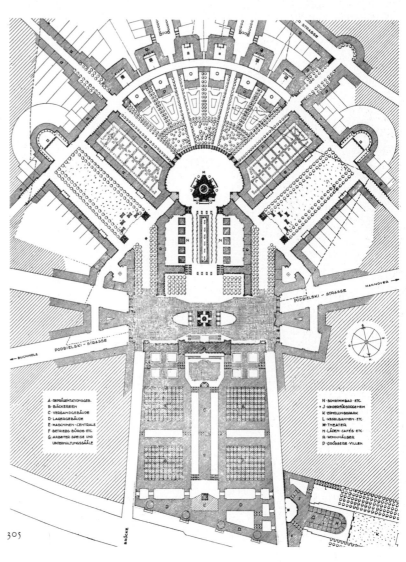
305

306

304–306. Bernhard Hoetger. Project for the TET town, Hanover, 1917.
304. TET square and TET pillar, from the north.
305. Site plan.
306. Show building of the TET factory, from the south.

129

307

308

310

307–310. Bernhard Hoetger. The architect's own house on the Weyerberg, Worpswede, 1921.
307. Exterior.
308. Entrance hall.
309. Bedroom.
310. Plan of the ground floor.

309

throughout his life upon the collaboration of experts. His ideas were expressed not in working drawings which the builders could use, but in rough sketches and clay models. (Even professional architects among the Expressionists found models a favourite means of structuring their sculptural and spatial ideas.) A further means in Hoetger's case was improvisation on the site – by the architect, and also by the craftsmen, whom Hoetger allowed considerable freedom.

The Hanover cake manufacturer Hermann Bahlsen was shown over the Brunnenhof house when he came to see Hoetger in connection with a commission for a piece of sculpture. He immediately felt a complete confidence it its amateur architect:[6] as a collector and patron he had a preference for outsiders and 'difficult' protégés and he was consequently drawn to Hoetger's powerful but curiously hybrid work. Hoetger was that rare phenomenon, a latecomer who was nonetheless original, whose eclecticism in no way damaged the quality of his work. The influences of Rodin and Maillol and of

Nordic, African, Javanese and Chinese art went to produce sculptures that had the impetuousness of Baroque or the hardness and self-sufficiency of idols. His architectural work was characterized by the same lack of uniformity. Kasimir Edschmid saw this as a positive trait: Hoetger 'clings to the dissonance and multiformity of the age, that he may do justice to every possibility and meet every demand'.[7]

It was not only for his artistic gifts that Hoetger interested Bahlsen. Bahlsen's firm, which was planning to build a new factory in conjunction with an extensive residential quarter to the north-east of Hanover, between the Mittellandkanal and the Eilenriede forest, used as its trademark the ancient Egyptian symbol *tet*, a curiously shaped tower symbolizing stability. It thus seemed appropriate to call upon the services of an artist whose sources of inspiration included Egyptian sculpture – and who was, in addition, friendly with a dancer from the Baltic who appeared in Egyptian costume under the stage name of Sent M'Ahesa. Hoetger's mammoth design for the TET town, as it was called (ills. 304–306), was generously provided with squat pyramidal projections, massive ramps, sloping plinths, flat roofs (as in Sant'Elia's projects, surprisingly, the roof decks were to serve as roadways), stepped pyramids used as roof ornaments, obelisks, sphinxes and other sculpted animals. Even the plans of the courts and halls, alternating with thick-set forests of pillars, showed Egyptian influence. 'Primitive and monumental' is how Hoetger himself characterized the project, which he claimed to have conceived 'in humility' as a 'gift of intuition'.[8]

The programme of the TET town was a patriarchal scheme that linked together dwelling and place of work, provided generous cultural and social amenities, but also confronted the inhabitants at every turn of their daily lives with symbols of the power of their lord and master, promoted as works of art. Every principal transverse or radial axis terminated in some emblem of the firm – the great tower that was to conceal the water reservoir and the flue of the heating plant, the palatial administration building, the grotesque TET pillar 35 metres high, or the triangular theatre. The different versions of the site plan reflect Hoetger's efforts to force the asymmetrical site and the arterial road running diagonally across it into an axial system. Shortly before his death in 1919 Hermann Bahlsen admitted that he had been pursuing a chimera.

All of the many critics who reviewed the model when it was exhibited in 1917 were reminded of the buildings of the pharaohs. Hoetger himself, however, claimed an indigenous origin for his project. He pointed to the material specified – unplastered brick – and advanced in justification of his exotic forms a thesis which was bold to the point of absurdity: mountainous country called for the vertical, whereas flat country called for the diagonal. He was clearly serious when he likened the trapezoidal articulations of his TET factory façade to the roofs of traditional Lower Saxon houses.

In his houses of the early twenties Hoetger really fell back on old North German tradition. His second house for himself, on the Weyerberg near Worpswede (ills. 307–310), the Winuwuk Coffee House and Sonnenhof exhibition building in Bad Harzburg, and the Worpswede Café (ill. 313) are all half-timbered; and the timbering, of twisted oak-trunks, is openly exposed on the inside. The hearth, with a massive hood, in each case constitutes the romantic focus of the sculptural architecture. The furniture and

311

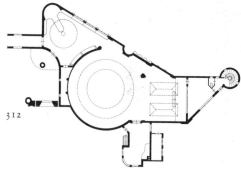

312

313

311, 312. Bernhard Hoetger. Grosse Kunst-schau, Worpswede, 1927. Central hall and plan.
313. Bernhard Hoetger. Worpswede Café, Worpswede, 1925.

many of the beams are held together with dowels, and traces of axe and chisel are visible everywhere. The principle of *horror vacui* seems to have dictated the ornamentation of the supporting members and the treatment of the brick surfaces, where individual bricks project unevenly or are laid in free patterns. Powerful saddleback roofs, hipped and in places continuing right down to the ground, or with gables that project outwards, give a sense of security, but they also recall the witches' houses in fairy tales.

The richness of these extremely wilful creations is a result of the complex interpenetration of parts. Hoetger's own house, for example, features a nave intersected by a kind of transept. In the Worpswede Café three gabled houses are linked by a low building whose roof ridge is more or less at right angles to their own (ill. 313). The convex/concave outer walls sometimes run independently of the post construction. The result is a freedom of plan which, though it uses a completely different formal vocabulary, is not so different from Le Corbusier's *plan libre* – free plastic and spatial composition arising out of a separation between partitional and supporting structures.

The Worpswede Café group was extended in 1927 by the addition of an exhibition building, the Grosse Kunstschau (ills. 311, 312). The whole, loosely linked complex (which was complemented a year later by a smaller private gallery, the Kunsthalle, not far from the Kunstschau) has all the natural respect for terrain, movement and *genius loci* of which Hoetger was capable. Almost the only striking external feature of the Kunstschau is the ruined-looking porch. A circular skylight in the small, irregularly-shaped foyer heralds the great domed hall, also circular in plan (ill. 312). The path of the visitor enters the hall to one side and continues towards a room at the back of the building, which could be used for lectures; a bulge in the outer edge of this path urges one into the domed hall. A shallow, unlit dome – similar to the chimney-cowls in Hoetger's houses – is

suspended freely above it. Light enters the room diagonally through a ring of skylights connecting the lower edge of the dome with the bowl-shaped ceiling of the gallery (ill. 311).

The Böttcherstrasse development

While he was working in Worpswede Hoetger found his second great patron, in the person of Ludwig Roselius, the Bremen coffee-importer, industrialist and banker. Like Bahlsen, Roselius had a strong feeling for art: he felt a certain responsibility for the education of his fellow-citizens, and contrived at the same time to turn his activities as a patron of the arts to good publicity effect. A contemporary racial creed gave an additional impetus to this wish to bring art to the people. Roselius saw himself and his city as mediators 'between the separated tribes beyond the seas' (he meant England and the United States, as Anglo-Saxon countries!) 'and the German tribes of the *Reich*'.[9] The astuteness and flexibility of the import-export merchant dependent upon a network of international contacts went hand in hand, in Roselius' case, with a crankiness that ranted on about Low German *Gemeinschaft*, Germanic emotional consciousness, and the primeval power of a great master-race.

Roselius' activities as a collector, his interest in Prehistoric archaeology (which he called *Väterkunde* – roughly 'the science of ancestry'), and even his commitment to the work of the Worpswede painter Paula Modersohn-Becker, were all governed by this ideology. It was an answer to the defeat of 1918, and an inflammatory one; in place of the pacifism embracing all peoples to which most of the Expressionist artists subscribed, it offered an aggressive nationalistic and racial cult. Hoetger, who exalted the 'strong culture' of 'Nordic man',[10] was the man for Roselius.

Roselius viewed the rebuilding of Böttcherstrasse as an attempt to 'think German'.[11] Böttcherstrasse was a street in the old part of Bremen, between the market

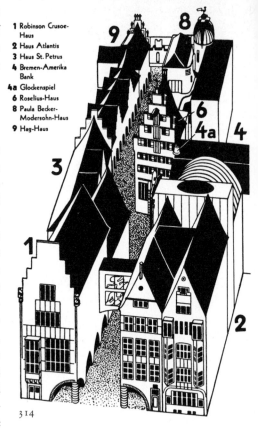

1 Robinson Crusoe-Haus
2 Haus Atlantis
3 Haus St. Petrus
4 Bremen-Amerika Bank
4a Glockenspiel
6 Roselius-Haus
8 Paula Becker-Modersohn-Haus
9 Hag-Haus

314

314. Bernhard Hoetger, Runge & Scotland. Böttcherstrasse, Bremen, 1923–31. Perspective view.
315. Bernhard Hoetger, Runge & Scotland. Böttcherstrasse, Bremen.
316–319. Bernhard Hoetger. Paula-Modersohn-Becker-Haus in Böttcherstrasse, Bremen, 1926–27.
316. View of the upper floors.
317, 318. Plans of the first floor (top) and ground floor.
319. Entrance hall.

315

316

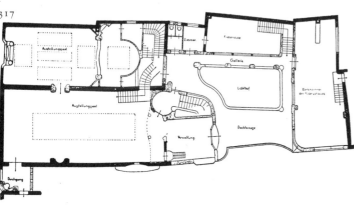

317

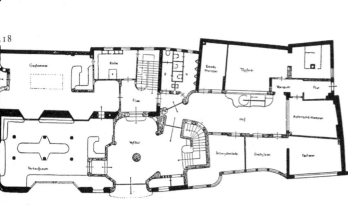

318

319

320

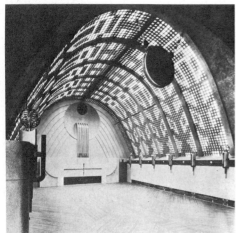

321

and the Weser, where Roselius had bought a fourteenth-century nobleman's house before the war and subsequently either bought or leased the remaining properties. With the exception of the Gothic building now known as the Roselius-Haus, the dilapidated old houses were pulled down and replaced by a new development (ills. 314, 315). The plan of the old street, including the part where it widened out to form a kind of square in front of the Roselius-Haus, was retained. Roselius' programme for Böttcherstrasse provided for commercial and for more or less communal facilities: handicrafts studios and shops, museums, exhibition rooms, banks, restaurants, club meeting rooms, a lecture room and cinema, a library, a gymnasium, and a health clinic. In its mingling of functions the Böttcherstrasse development, for all its ideological extravagance, anticipated the pedestrian streets that were regarded as a miracle formula by town planners after the Second World War.

Roselius had initially entrusted the scheme to a Bremen firm of architects, Runge & Scotland, who submitted a rather tame piece of Gothic. Hoetger was introduced in 1926 because Roselius, rightly, thought that Runge & Scotland's correct but flat façades needed some contrasting modelling. With the Paula-Modersohn-Becker-Haus, the first of his two Böttcherstrasse buildings (ills. 316–319), Hoetger produced not only a contrast to the neighbouring buildings but something unlike any architecture that had ever been seen before.

Conditions were difficult. The fabric of an existing building, the Kunstschau, had to be retained, and there was to be access to the Roselius-Haus. The site available was narrow and overlooked by the backs of neighbouring commercial buildings. These Hoetger hid behind a high wall. Behind this wall on the third floor he provided a new gallery to display paintings by Paula Modersohn-Becker, with top lighting similar to that of the Grosse Kunstschau in Worpswede. A round tower surmounted by a fantastic copper dome

housed the spiral staircase between the second and third floors (ill. 316), and was matched by another tower on the side of the Roselius-Haus. Between a small light well and Böttcherstrasse lay the low, concave workshop wing. Together with an open gallery (walled in after 1945) at the rear of the building, its roof formed a continuous circuit which the curving balustrade kept in constant movement.

The principal alterations that transformed the Kunstschau building into the Paula-Modersohn-Becker-Haus were a deeply hollowed-out vestibule like a mysterious grotto (ill. 319) which gave access to all rooms as well as the workshop court,[12] and a bridge to the new building by Runge & Scotland lying opposite. Hoetger's powerful brick sculpture had the effect of preventing the eye from penetrating the building, thus adding further mystery to the narrow cleft of Böttcherstrasse. For all the fairy-tale effect, however, the grouping of masses corresponds to the functions of the individual parts of the building; although Hoetger did arrange those functions in a completely unorthodox manner.

In the Paula-Modersohn-Becker-Haus Hoetger tried his utmost to exert a psychological influence on the visitor – attracting him from a distance, drawing him in an almost magical way into the cave of the entrance (which makes it so hard for him to continue along the arcade of the north side of Böttcherstrasse), overwhelming him with the weight of the plastic masses, and at the same time using smoothed-off corners and round towers to give a constant sense of movement. So thoroughgoing was Hoetger's design that even the surfaces of his volumes played their part in this variety of spatial and plastic effects. The metal-and-glass patterns, reminiscent of certain French Orphist compositions, and the brick ornamentation appear sometimes as swellings and efflorescences on the walls, sometimes as gashes, dents or other suggestions of weathering and decay.

Hoetger's second Böttcherstrasse building, the Haus Atlantis (ills.

320–322), was different, deriving its effect not from foiling the visitor's every expectation but from the way in which it arbitrarily transforms a given schema. In many respects the Haus Atlantis conforms to the architectural conventions of late-1920s office building: for the first time Hoetger used rolled steel as a building material, and the supporting framework, clad in sheet copper, is clearly distinguished from the infilling, while the load-bearing verticals are also differentiated from the set-back horizontal members. The steel supports of the front and rear façades meet in the roof as parabolic curves. Yet Hoetger treated even this building, apparently so indebted to International Modern, as a solid, fully sculptured mass. A wing is set at right angles to the main street façade: its elevation is like a compressed version of the grid pattern of the street side.

It was against the austere and relatively disciplined façade of the range running parallel to the street that Hoetger and Roselius gave free rein to their *penchant* for Nordic mythology. The entire façade (now replaced by a wall by Ewald Mataré) was covered by a tree of life carved in wood – 'symbol of Nordic self-sacrifice of one man for the good of the people'.[13] Underlying this representation of the crucifixion was the myth of Odin, who died at the summer solstice, and other Germanic sagas of kingly sacrifice. A circle symbolized the cycle of the year and was inscribed with a runic song from the Edda. A solar disc at the top occurs again inside the building in the 'Hall of Heaven' (ill. 320). The wooden window sills (an anachronism in this steel-framed building) with representations of the months, and

the name, Atlantis, are further aspects of a dangerous attempt to mobilize myth.

One feature in the Haus Atlantis would have fulfilled the boldest hopes of Paul Scheerbart's friends: the staircase (ill. 322). The effect Bruno Taut had aimed at in his Glass Pavilion at Cologne here became fascinating reality. The stairs wind their way upward around three pillars in the stair well, which are dematerialized by vertical light fittings. Glass bricks are let into the steps and sides and the whole staircase cylinder is glazed with blue-white glass. Hoetger achieved a similar magical effect in the Hall of Heaven, the parabolic room under the roof of the longitudinal wing (ill. 320). The Art Deco style elements – ceiling lights, wall lights, radiator covers – which lend a rather too obtrusive *chic* to the other halls and clubrooms are here, in these two amply lighted rooms, pleasingly subordinate to the overall effect.

During this phase, which included a studio-annexe to his second house in Worpswede and the Kaffee Hag tower at the Cologne Pressa Exhibition (both in 1928), Hoetger's architecture appears to have been moving in the direction of greater objectivity or neutrality. The international financial crisis, however, and the events which overtook Germany in 1933 meant that Hoetger received scarcely any further commissions, and his development was not fulfilled. About this time Hoetger wrote a letter to a young engineer in which he extolled the latter's profession as the 'finest, most powerful, and most justifiable of all. Today we need only practical things, can enjoy only practical things. Art has taken refuge in the dynamics of the imagination. The

perceptions of our time can be usefully stirred only by this kind of lucid functionalism. And it is right that it should be so – I too am working nowadays under this joyful constraint'.[14]

Despite the studio-annexe, the Kaffee Hag tower, and the Haus Atlantis this is a somewhat surprising admission. It was only a few years since Hoetger had spoken of 'the futile aspiration to *Sachlichkeit*' and of his preference for 'experiencing in all things the transports of our blood'. The contradiction resolves itself in so far as Hoetger drew a distinction between the architect and the artist. As an architect he knew he was governed by the 'joyful constraint' of function. As an artist, however, he would not have been prepared to yield to the need for rational structure and utility: while submitting to the demands of practicality, he felt himself free in the sphere of the 'dynamics of the imagination'. 'Today for the first time it is possible to practise art in true independence. Art should be utterly functionless, should grow out of an inner compulsion . . . like fruit on the tree'.[15] The Haus Atlantis is animated by this conflict between function and imagination; only in the staircase and in the Hall of Heaven does it resolve itself into an imaginative functionalism.

The Haus Atlantis was followed by various designs and models for houses, only one of which was built – Hoetger's third house for his own occupation, in Berlin-Frohnau (1939–40). Hoetger's status as a political outlaw and his considerably reduced circumstances made this a modest project. The application for planning permission bore not his own name but that of a Berlin architect (see p. 206).

The architecture of Rudolf Steiner

'Whatever objections continue to be raised today against this type of architecture, against this style of architecture – it is nonetheless both in type and style the architecture of the future.'

Rudolf Steiner, 'Das Rätsel des Menschen', lecture given on 29 July 1916

The building with a soul

The mood of ideological and religious awakening which contributed so much to Expressionist architecture and which permeated the early Bauhaus, as it did the Liturgical Movement, was also the mainspring of Anthroposophical architecture. Rudolf Steiner (1861–1925), the founder of the Anthroposophical Society, believed in a perception of higher worlds and in the visibility of spiritual states and circumstances behind physical reality, and he was convinced that this transcendental realm was revealed through 'spirit organs' in man. Steiner spoke of 'white magic': by it he meant the careful preparation and training of the powers of the human soul so that it would not be overwhelmed by the powers of the spiritual world, but would find its own way to them.

In Steiner's eyes architecture was an important medium of this white magic. Depending upon the character of the physical world, either favourable or unfavourable connections were formed to 'one sort or another of the spiritual essences . . . that surround us'. According to Steiner the stimulus imparted to the soul by the contemplation and experience of physical forms gave rise to 'thought forms' upon which the transition to these 'spiritual essences' depended. The notion was further differentiated by the hypothesis of an ethereal and an astral world.[1]

For the Anthroposophists it was vitally important to live and teach in houses that fulfilled such criteria. The extraordinary zeal with which the Anthroposophists built – an activity in which they were supported by such wealthy patrons as

Count Otto Lerchenfeld – is explicable not least by their conviction that architecture unlocked the door to higher truths. Steiner even credited architecture with a moral influence when it was experienced through 'inward perception' and not merely through outward observation. The person who experienced the harmony of form would also learn to live in harmony with his fellows. 'Peace and harmony will pour into men's hearts through these forms. Such buildings will be lawgivers.'[2]

If architecture was to fulfil these lofty expectations and stimulate the soul, that stimulus must already be potentially present in the forms employed so that it could become actual in the eye of the beholder. Steiner saw it as a question of 'making the whole building as if possessed of a soul'.[3] The wall, indeed the whole building was regarded as a living thing that thrust forth limbs just as natural organisms do; the building was even credited with human activity. For those capable of reading them, its physiognomical features should represent decipherable signs.

To Steiner's contemporaries this theory of architectural expression was bound up with the aesthetics of Expressionism. In 1919 Paul Fechter quoted as proof of his Expressionist aspirations the following passage from Steiner's collection of essays, *Wie erlangt man Erkenntnisse der höheren Welten?* (1909: English translation, *Knowledge of the Higher Worlds and its Attainment*, 1932): 'The clairvoyant . . . can give for every thought, every natural law a form in which it manifests itself. A vengeful thought for example takes the form of a pointed, arrow-shaped figure; a kindly thought often has the shape of a flower as it opens, and so on. Positive, meaningful thoughts have a regular, symmetrical structure; vague concepts have wobbly outlines!'[4] The quotation might come from Johannes Itten's preliminary course at the Bauhaus.

Rudolf Steiner was a charismatic figure, the sort of man who in an earlier age would have been a saint or the founder of a religious order. He was adored by his

disciples, and often had to rebuke them for their excessive devotion. His knowledge and interests were exceptionally broad and varied. He worked as a natural scientist, mathematician, philologist, doctor of philosophy, artist and writer. In 1902 he was appointed head of the German section of the Theosophical Society, which had been introduced into Germany in 1897. Steiner condemned the spiritualistic practices of the Theosophists, however, and in 1913 he left their ranks and founded the Anthroposophical Society. There he enjoyed an authority that extended to the most diverse fields, and architects accepted his advice as readily as teachers, actors, farmers, chemists and medical men.

Though Steiner counted among his masters Josef Baier, a disciple of Semper, as an architect he must be regarded as self-taught. The major buildings erected at Dornach before his death in 1925 are rightly attributed to him, rather than to the particular architect who carried out the work:[5] Steiner conveyed his plastic and architectural ideas in a variety of ways – through verbal instructions, sketches and models (ills. 334, 341, 342), data concerning plans and dimensions, practical work on the site and in the workshops, and lastly through the famous Dornach *Doktor-Korrekturen* at which he made improvements to his colleagues' designs. The reverence with which Steiner's intentions were adhered to was immense. After his death his followers even worried about whether certain details of his design for the second Goetheanum were deliberate or whether they were merely the result of a slip of the finger during the kneading of the plasticine.

In the history of art Steiner's creations are perplexing, for they stand in virtual isolation. In them, architectural Expressionism was taken to an extreme; but they scarcely show any recognizable origins, and they established no tradition except within the Anthroposophical movement itself. The chief preconditions of Anthroposophical architecture were Steiner's genius and the fact that he was a total outsider. Only an artist who had never had to sit in an architect's office turning out countless drawings of window details could possibly have hit upon the idea of trying to embody 'social conduct and brotherly shoulder-to-shoulder-ness *(Zueinanderstehen)*' in groups of two and three windows inclined towards one another.

When Steiner was studying in Vienna the old masters of Austrian historicism – Theophil Hansen, Friedrich von Schmidt, and Heinrich von Ferstel, all of whom Steiner mentioned with respect – were still alive. Otto Wagner (from whose school there emerged a design for a domed building intended to fulfil a similar function to the Goetheanum, ill. 329) only began teaching in 1894, after Steiner had moved to Weimar. The influence of Henry van de Velde remains conjectural.

During his Berlin period Steiner entertained 'sentiments of affection' towards Paul Scheerbart, whose 'wild fantasy' he subjected to some shrewd criticism.[6] Scheerbart's architectural ideas, however, appear to have made no impression on him. The Anthroposophists' first major building project, the Johannesbau, which

they planned to erect in Munich (see p. 141 and ills. 326, 327), resembles other assembly-room buildings of the time only in the most general way. Both it and the Stadthalle in Hanover (1911–14), by Paul Bonatz and F. E. Scholer, are domed buildings with colonnades surrounded by galleries; but the fundamental architectural concept of the Johannesbau, the interpenetration of two domed rooms of different sizes, and many of the details, are without parallel. Steiner's only contacts must have been with the Theosophists of Lauweriks' circle (see p. 46).

323–325. E. A. Karl Stockmeyer, from suggestions by Rudolf Steiner. Prototype domed building, Malsch near Karlsruhe, 1908–9, completed and restored in 1957.
323. Interior.
324. Plan.
325. Interpenetration of spatial units in the domed building at Malsch (top), compared with the first Goetheanum in Dornach. After Erich Zimmer.

Steiner's first designs

The architectural ideals of the Anthroposophical Society go back to a congress which the European section of the Theosophical Society (of which it was still a part) held in Munich at Whitsun 1907. The Tonhalle in Türkenstrasse, where the congress met, was hung with bright red cloth and decorated with seven columns made of painted boards – the forerunners of the five-faced supports of the Goetheanum. Their capitals represented the signs of the planets, and mounted between the columns were the seven apocalyptic seals. The solemn twilight reigning in the hall made a powerful impression on the followers of Rudolf Steiner. They saw the décor as a summons to start building things themselves.

The first step was taken by a young student, E. A. Karl Stockmeyer. He asked Steiner what architectural conception was suitable for use with such symbols. Steiner sketched an elliptical interior, oriented on an east-west axis. Seven columns on either side of the longitudinal axis were to support a dome in the form of a tri-axial ellipsoid. Around the columns there was

323

324
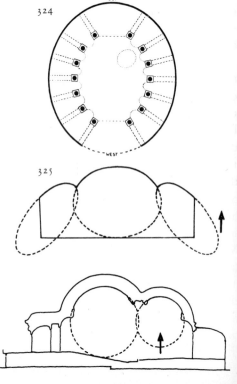
325

an ambulatory, roofed with smaller ellipsoid domes. The only light source was an asymmetrically placed opening in the main dome. Through this opening, at the equinox, the light of the sun was to fall upon a particular point in the interior.

These details were embodied by Stockmeyer in a small prototype which he erected in 1908–9 in Malsch, south of Karlsruhe, on a site belonging to his father (ills. 323–325).[7] The interpenetration of the obliquely-placed ellipsoids in the ambulatory with one another and with the main dome created considerable mathematical, statical and practical problems. The scale Stockmeyer chose made the room barely high enough to stand in, so he lowered the floor level to make it possible to move about inside the tiny interior and retain the illusion of being in a larger building. This miniature temple, which from outside looks like a garden shed or pump house, gives a good idea of Steiner's architectural ideas in 1908. Carl Schmid-Curtius, architect of the Stuttgart branch of the Theosophical Society, knew the prototype and built a variant of it in 1911, with Stockmeyer's help in the cellar of the Society's house in Stuttgart.

Also in 1908, Steiner conceived the idea of a double dome. Two spherical shells side by side took the place of the main ellipsoid, and in a later stage of the design – which became the first Goetheanum (ills. 330–336) – the complex intersections of ellipsoid ambulatory domes with the main dome were also abandoned. The building was now symmetrical in one direction alone, along the line running through the centres of the circular plans of the two spaces. With its two domes, the building was informed with a tension between two spatial poles – as if the subsidiary dome on the east side of the Malsch prototype had gained in importance and its interpenetration with the main dome become the central theme of the building (ill. 325). The practical justification of the new architectural idea lay in the mystery plays which Steiner wrote and the eurythmic performances which called for a division into stage and auditorium.

The dimensions of the two domed sections of the hall, however, and the relationship between them were determined by vastly more important considerations. The larger section, accommodating the audience, was to express the 'physical', while the smaller was to express the 'spiritual-supersensory'. Consequently the shell of the smaller dome did not touch the floor of the building. The point of interpenetration of the domes, their 'state of oscillation', is particularly interesting. A greater distance between the two domes would have meant their isolation from one another and hence of the 'physical' from the 'spiritual'; any closer and they would have lost their identity: the 'physical' would have been swallowed up in the 'spiritual'. Steiner referred to both dangers in terms taken from Anthroposophical esoterism. The 'Ahrimanic' principle (from Ahriman, the Zoroastrian god of darkness) stood for everything that was narrow and shut itself off; the 'Luciferian' principle stood for everything that was enthusiastic and laid itself open. The future building, however, was to embody the principle of reconciliation associated with the figure of Christ. Accordingly the

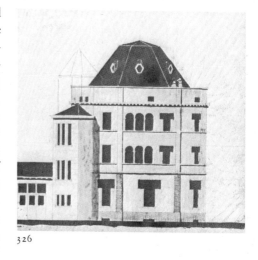

326

326, 327. Rudolf Steiner and Carl Schmid-Curtius. Project for the Johannesbau, Munich-Schwabing.
326. Corner building, 1911. Pen and wash. Goetheanum Archives, Dornach.
327. Bird's-eye view of the complex from the north, 1912. Pen and wash. Goetheanum Archives, Dornach.

327

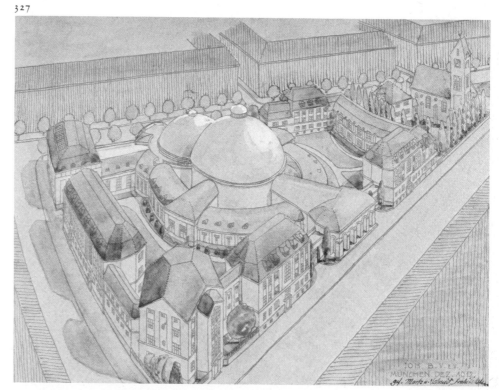

328

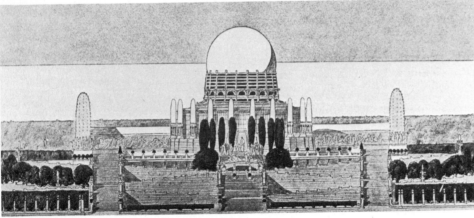

329

figures of Ahriman, Lucifer, and Christ were features in the painting inside the smaller dome of the first Goetheanum as well as in a wooden group intended for the stage and carved by Steiner himself.

This concept of a 'Christian' two-domed structure was the assignment that Steiner laid before the architect. The detailed solution of the plan was provided by a geometrical construction worked out by Schmid-Curtius (ills. 335, 336): the points of intersection and the radii of the two circles, as well as the course of the inner circle of columns, were worked out on the basis of a pentagram construction. The divisions fell into the ratio of the Golden Section. The absolute distance between the centres of auditorium and stage were set by Steiner at 21 metres, thought to be the length of Solomon's Temple.

Steiner later alluded to a different geometrical arrangement for the Goetheanum plan, which would have divided the length of the axis into two, three, four, five, seven and twelve equal parts. The numerical proportions implicit in both plans naturally offered abundant material for meditation. Bruno Taut's speculations on the effect of the numbers three and seven, the numerical mysticism of the early Bauhaus and the two series of measurements incorporated in Le Corbusier's Modulor are amateur compared to the schemes of the Anthroposophists.[8]

Steiner himself emphatically denied that the Goetheanum incorporated any secret mystical allusions. The proportions and forms of the building, he maintained, had grown out of their own intrinsic life, and the people who created them had, in obeying their own artistic perceptions, acted in conformity with the principles of 'the creative cosmic world'. The principle underlying the design of the capitals and bases of the internal supports and the frames of windows and doors was derived from Goethe's morphological studies: basic motifs alter their form, according to the situation and circumstances in which they occur. Steiner did not regard as 'mystical allusions' the fact that the seven pairs of supports in the larger room were meant to evoke the rhythm of human life, the epochs of civilization and the souls of the various peoples on earth, and that the twelve capitals of the smaller room were thought of as symbols of the planets, as cosmological ciphers.

'Nature has neither core/ Nor surface/ Nature is everything all at once.' So runs a passage in one of Goethe's scientific texts which Steiner was editing during his time at Weimar. The sign, the 'surface', was thus not an allegory: it could not be qualitatively distinguished from the thing signified, the 'core'. What strikes the uninitiated as an arbitrary system of interpretation meant to Steiner and his friends the reflection of objective spiritual processes and cosmic laws through the medium of an art that proceeded in the manner of nature. Steiner saw as an all-embracing reality what for others was divided up into symbols and what they stood for. Steiner spoke of a 'homogeneous world . . . in which the material reflects the spirit and the spirit is revealed in the material'.[9]

Dornach

Steiner's two-domed meeting hall – the immediate ancestor of the first Goetheanum – was, as it was planned in 1911–12 for a site in the Munich suburb of Schwabing, a twin-shelled structure of reinforced concrete. It was called the Johannesbau, after a character in one of Steiner's mystery plays. The hall inside was doubly screened from the outside world: once by a foyer with radiating passages, and again by a rather awkward peripheral complex of storehouses and dwellings for Theosophists (ills. 326, 327). The plans were complete and building was about to start when the local authorities objected. An alternative site (already large, and later increased by purchases of land) was offered by Dr Emil Grossheintz at Dornach, near Basel in Switzerland. By the beginning of 1913 plans for the new site were already in progress.

Although the idea of the double dome was retained, the change of site led to a change in the earlier, somewhat inward-looking design. The idea of a hilltop drama festival combined with that of a garden city to suggest the notion of a residential and social community lying in the shadow of the dominant theatre, which would have almost the character of a religious building. The ideal of the Expressionist architects – the abode of man surmounted by the sacred – never came so close to realization as here in this Swiss village. 'At the edge of a grove on the crest of a hill shall this solemn building raise its walls'; so Peter Behrens had written twelve years earlier in connection with a project for an ideal theatre. 'If down below in our familiar environment we had arranged everything to relate to our daily lives, to the logic of our thoughts, and to our material sense of purpose, up here we should be filled with the sense of a higher purpose, a purpose that was merely translated into material terms, a spiritual need, the gratification of our transcendental nature.'[10]

How far the Dornach theatre was in fact regarded as a cult centre is indicated by the

330

name which Steiner gave to the house of Dr Grossheintz, the man who had donated the site – Duldeck (from *dulden*, to tolerate, and *Ecke*, corner or nook), i.e. the secular building that, in the immediate vicinity of the Goetheanum, was only tolerated. The prices of building sites in the projected Anthroposophists' colony were to be governed, among other things, by their distance from the Goetheanum. Steiner recommended that colonists adopt a common architectural style 'as outward expression of a harmony that will become an inner harmony'. From the point of view of organization the garden city of Hellerau, near Dresden, was to serve as model; there too every building required the sanction of a Commission for Architecture and Art such as was projected for Dornach. But in 1914, a year after the foundation stone of the first Goetheanum had been laid, the future Dornach style was still shrouded in uncertainty. 'If . . . colonists cannot find the patience to wait until such time as it may be possible to lay down how this or that house ought best to be built, then nothing useful can be done in this direction.'[11]

The first buildings erected at Dornach do not in fact show any sign of formal

328. Hermann Billing or one of his pupils. Architectural study. From Hermann Billing, ed., *Architektur-Skizzen*, Stuttgart, n.d. (1904).
329. Alois Bastl. Project for a 'Palace of scientific associations for occultism', Paris. From *Wagner-Schule 1902*, Leipzig, n. d.
330. Rudolf Steiner and Carl Schmid-Curtius. Preliminary design for the first Goetheanum, Dornach, 1913. View from the north-west. Charcoal. Goetheanum Archives, Dornach.
331. Schematic site plan for the first Goetheanum, Dornach, 1913.

331

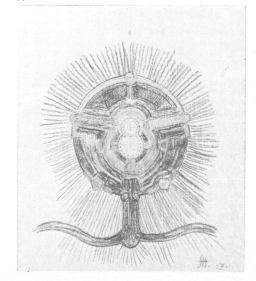

332

333

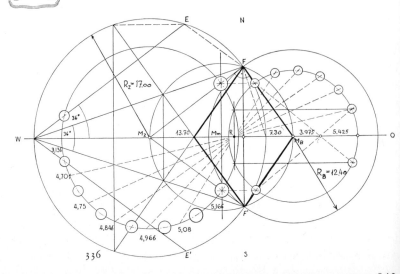

334

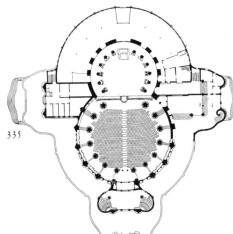

335

332–335. Rudolf Steiner. First Goetheanum, Dornach, 1913–20.

332. View from the south-west.

333. Photograph of the unfinished building, taken on 10 February 1914.

334. Model of the two domed spaces, 1913–14. Wood. Goetheanum Archives, Dornach.

335. Plan of the auditorium.

336. Carl Schmid-Curtius. Geometrical schema for the plan of the first Goetheanum, Dornach, September 1913.

336

homogeneity. The slate-covered domes of the first Goetheanum are treated as stereometrically pure volumes; in the Jura landscape with its smooth contours and precipitous chalk cliffs they are, deliberately, exotic aliens. The semicircular barrel roofs originally planned for the projecting west front of the building and the two side wings were changed at a later stage and made as soft as the brim of a felt hat (ills. 330, 332). The sculptural treatment of detail varied in extent because the lower part of the building was executed in reinforced concrete and only the superstructure, a timber-frame construction, could be thoroughly worked on a delicate scale.

At first a layout in the form of a monstrance was considered for the whole complex (ill. 331), but it was soon decided not to have any fixed plan. The subsidiary buildings are now grouped in a loose wreath around the three sides of the projecting terrace on which the main building stands (ill. 337). Their principal façades all look towards the Goetheanum, though there is not a strict axial connection. The houses are sensibly placed to the south of the Goetheanum, while the other buildings lie to the north.[12]

The two domes of the first Goetheanum led directly to the design of two independent semicircular domes that crown a workshop known as the 'Glashaus', a framed building clad in wooden shingles in which windows similar to those of the Goetheanum were cut (ill. 338). Rather less judicious is the relationship of the boilerhouse (ills. 344, 345) to the main building: its lower storeys are also domical in outline, but even Steiner had trouble in justifying the grotesque chimney like a stem with protruding buds, symbolizing the rising smoke. He maintained that the only alternative would have been an ordinary red factory chimney.

A similarly 'over-produced' effect characterizes the Haus Duldeck (ills. 346, 347, 349, 350), a concrete building with masonry fill in the outside walls. Its dramatic movement is probably due more

337. Rudolf Steiner. The second Goetheanum and surrounding buildings, Dornach. Site plan: 1 second Goetheanum, 2 Eurhythmeum and Brodbeck house, 3 studio building ('Glashaus'), 4 publishing offices, 5 boilerhouse, 6 Schuurman house, 7 temporary carpenters' shop, 8 three houses ('curhythmics houses'), 9 de Jaager house, 10 transformer station, 11 Haus Duldeck (for Dr Grossheintz).

337

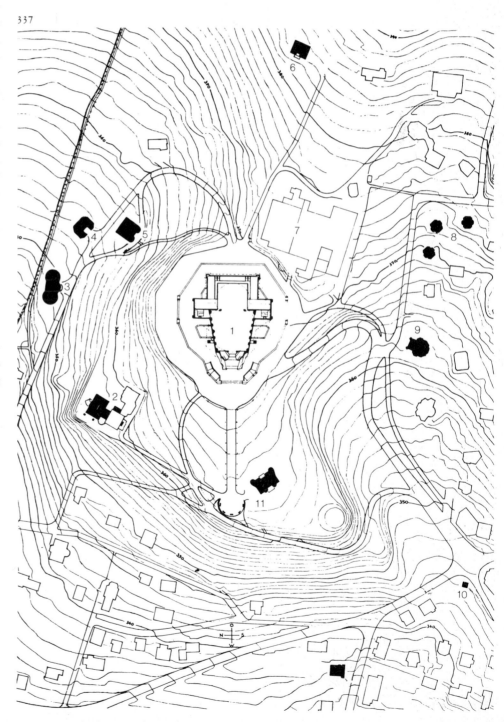

338

339

340

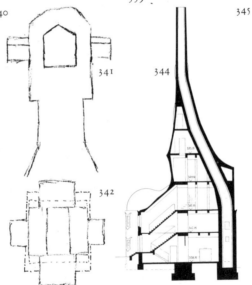

341

342

344

345

343

338. Rudolf Steiner. Studio building ('Glashaus'), Dornach, 1913–14.

339. Rudolf Steiner. Publishing offices, Dornach, 1923–24.

340. Rudolf Steiner with Paul Bay. Transformer station, Dornach, 1921.

341, 342. Rudolf Steiner. Pencil sketches of the transformer station, Dornach, 1921. Partial view and plan.

343. Rudolf Steiner. Eurhythmeum, Dornach, 1923–24. North entrance.

344, 345. Rudolf Steiner with Alfred Hilliger. Boilerhouse, Dornach, 1914–15. Section and view from the south.

to its strategic position on the top of the Goetheanum plateau than to its function as the house of a dental surgeon. The side of the house facing the valley arches out in a convex line, while the side facing the Goetheanum swings inward, as if the force radiating from the cult centre had thrust the mass of the building in upon itself. The powerful yet somehow rather artificial forms of the roof are reminiscent of Gaudí's apartment houses in Barcelona (ill. 348). Stylistically the Haus Duldeck stands midway between the first Goetheanum, with which it is contemporary, and the second Goetheanum.

346

The smaller buildings erected to designs by Steiner just before or at the same time as the second Goetheanum show greater restraint (ills. 339, 343, 358). Their three-dimensional effect derives for the most part from the abrupt meeting of flat planes at acute or obtuse angles or the many refractions in their roof shapes. The little transformer station of 1921 (ills. 340–342) heralds this phase; it is a disciplined composition of roofed prisms of varying sizes which appear to be stuck into and on top of one another; the 'shocking' right-angled changes of direction are meant to express the intake, conversion, and output of electrical power. In the post-war period Steiner clearly felt the need for establishing a hierarchy of forms and keeping the free plastic solution in reserve for the main building.

347

348

349

350

346, 347. Rudolf Steiner with Hermann Moser and Ernst Aisenpreis. Haus Duldeck for Dr Grossheintz, Dornach, 1915–16. Views from the north-east and from the south.

348. Antoni Gaudí. Casa Milá, Barcelona. Detail of the façade.

349, 350. Rudolf Steiner with Hermann Moser and Ernst Aisenpreis. Haus Duldeck for Dr Grossheintz, Dornach, 1915–16. Plan of the ground floor, and north entrance.

45

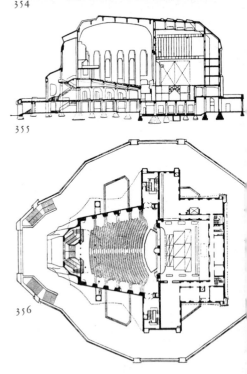

351–357. Rudolf Steiner and his architectural
assistants. Second Goetheanum, Dornach, 1924–2
351. Detail of the auditorium and south transept
above the terrace.
352. South transept.
353. View from the west.
354. View from the east.
355. Section.
356. Plan of the auditorium.
357. Detail of the west façade.

358. Rudolf Steiner with Ernst Aisenpreis. Schuurman house, Dornach, 1924–25. After Erich Zimmer.

The second Goetheanum

Today Dornach and the broad basin of the Birs valley towards Basel are dominated by the powerful concrete sculpture of the second Goetheanum (ills. 351–357). On the night of New Year 1922/23 the first Goetheanum burnt right down to its concrete platform. Its very much larger successor (110,000 instead of 66,000 cubic metres of enclosed space) was opened in 1928, three years after Steiner's death. He had regarded it merely as providing accommodation for the practical work of the college, and as a memorial to the first Goetheanum. A first glance, however, reveals little to remind one of its predecessor. Even the surviving concrete lower storey of the first building was demolished because it did not fit in with the new programme.[13]

There are various reasons for the Anthroposophists' modest assessment of the second Goetheanum. The enormous outlay of artistic commitment and craftsmanship which they had invested in the first building was not something which could be repeated. The complex studies of measurements and proportions, too, were omitted on this occasion. The choice of reinforced concrete as the material for the new building, although it was natural after fire had destroyed the wooden domes, could be interpreted as a surrender. The Dornach artists had been able to handle the living, structured material of the different kinds of wood used in the first Goetheanum to much greater symbolic effect than was possible with an amorphous material like concrete, which could be moulded into any shape quite arbitrarily.

This 'simpler spiritual home', as Steiner's wife called the new building,[14] is in actual fact one of the most magnificent pieces of sculptural architecture of the twentieth century. Its monumentality derives not from absolute dimensions but from the all-inclusive volumetric treatment of the building. The squat exterior and the angled or broken planes leading from one stratum to another appear to be subject to a play of forces partly emerging from within the building and partly bearing upon it from outside. Similarly ambiguous is the relationship between upward and downward movement. The west side towers powerfully upwards (ill. 353), and so do the less sculptural north and south wings (ills. 351, 352); but the pillars flanking the auditorium plunge downwards like aerial roots. The curves and edges of the raw concrete mould the light differently at every moment of the day, from a pale, silvery grey to the deepest, darkest shadow.

In opposition to the prevailing doctrine of the twenties, the most diverse functions are accommodated under one roof: there are lecture rooms, editorial offices, a library, an auditorium seating 1,000 people, and a stage with all the necessary backstage rooms. Not even the high stage tower interrupts the overall shape of the building (ill. 353). The rooms for the various courses given in Dornach were fitted in between the sloping floor of the auditorium and the lower foyers, an arrangement which gave rise to some unhappy spatial relationships. The grandiose effect of the exterior was in fact obtained at the cost of a number of concessions – access to the theatre only from the third level, proscenium stage instead of the linked stage and auditorium of the first Goetheanum, and repeated changes of constructional system (reinforced-concrete frame supports above the stage, trusses of varying depths above the auditorium). The complicated moulding of the warped surfaces made exceptional demands on all concerned in the execution of the building, and in places it was necessary to work with full-sized detail drawings.

Work has gone on at the second Goetheanum ever since the foundation stone was laid. In the five decades of its existence this gigantic mass, with its many almost biological openings, has developed a unique kind of flexibility based not upon the addition of further units, but upon the exploitation of what is already there by the adaptation and conversion of existing rooms and left-over spaces.

Special concerns

11 New churches

'*Now trigger the process off by adding the omninucleus of Christ* (Christ-allkeim), *which must be a clear and purposive liturgical awareness of Christ, and the whole will grow into the new and powerful crystal unity* (Kristalleinheit).'

Johannes van Acken, *Christozentrische Kirchenbaukunst*, Gladbeck, 1922

359

The holy melting-pot

Buildings to serve a faith as yet unknown were designed and dreamt of in their hundreds during the Expressionist years, but they were not actually built. What was built was a variety of churches for existing faiths. A new church-building programme often incorporated meeting rooms, a kindergarten, and sometimes a hall with restaurant facilities; the *Gemeindehaus* or parish hall took on some of the functions associated with the *Volkshaus* or 'house of the people', another favourite Expressionist architectural concept.

The Utopian impulse of the age had its effect on religious architecture, though it was restrained by, and as it were filtered through, considerations of tradition and practicality. The hopes which the men of the Bauhaus placed in the cathedral of socialism were placed by convinced Christians in a renewal of the Church. Otto Bartning, who from his Sternkirche or 'star-church' design of 1922 onwards was the leading Protestant church builder, believed in a Church cleansed of its historical accretions, in the 'holy melting-pot' *(heilige Mischkrug)* of the community of the future.[1] Buildings in which the new brotherhood of men gathered together were to occupy the highest rank in the architectural hierarchy of the *Stadtkrone*. This claim upon the dominant position in the town had been heralded in a number of monumental designs of the pre-war period, for example in Hermann Billing's competition design for the unfinished west front of the cathedral of Freiberg (ill. 360) or in Otto Kohtz's cathedral (ill. 359), which with its brittle concave-

360

359. Otto Kohtz. Project for a cathedral, 1905. From *Gedanken über Architektur*, Berlin, 1909.
360. Hermann Billing. Project for the façade of Freiberg Cathedral, Saxony, 1911.

361

362

convex details is reminiscent of some of the later drawings of Bruno Taut (ills. 155, 156).

Adolf Behne, whose eloquence extended to this field as well, wanted a church to be 'the embodiment of a vast feeling embracing whole multitudes'; he portrayed it in words that seem to spring more from the regret of one born too late than from the ardour of the seer: 'There is a place for everything in this new and mighty work that grows from year to year, everything from a sweet lyricism – incense wafting on feast days through the halls and chapels of the interior, the measureless tenderness of maternal bliss on the altarpieces, exquisite, ardent faces of the Virgin adorning portals and tympanums, hymns that resound in swelling echoes, and the bright light of heaven streaming through stained glass alight with the glow of faith to play upon sculptured stone – everything from this to the heightened architectonics of forms in which everything earthly is silent and there is nothing but the mute, suppressed world-prayer of thousands of people united in complete equality by a feeling of final surrender to the Ultimate.'[2]

Behind Behne's vision stood the Gothic cathedral rather than any image of a new church architecture. The association of the Gothic style with church architecture had become firmly established in the nineteenth century; it was reinforced for Roman Catholics by Pugin's *The True Principles of Pointed or Christian Architecture* (1841) and established for the German

Protestant Church by the sixteen theses of the Eisenach Ruling of 1861. Admittedly, the Ruling's recommendation that the so-called 'Germanic' (read 'Gothic') style was to be preferred came in for increasing criticism. At German Church conferences and in the religious press around 1900 there were many attempts to wean Protestants away from the 'Catholic' Middle Ages and to get them to accept Baroque as the model for Protestant artistic endeavours.[3] Nevertheless the tradition of neo-Gothic church architecture persisted up to the 1920s, and when the Gothic style and cathedrals became topical again for other reasons the tradition received a new lease of life and meaning.

While the forms remained Gothic, the elevation and the treatment of space did not. The division of the interior into nave and aisles, characteristic of earlier neo-Gothic churches, was rejected in both Catholic and Protestant architecture in favour of a single-space interior, or one which at least gave the impression of unity and openness. The chancel, if it was retained at all, was shortened. Transept and apse were often eliminated, and other subsidiary spaces much reduced. Centralized buildings had captured the interest of Protestant architects even before the war; they were now taken up by the Catholic Dominikus Böhm as well. An alternative was an elongated form terminating in a flat or semicircular wall. As the ground plan was simplified and unified, so was the elevation. Pointed or parabolic vaults might spring directly from the level

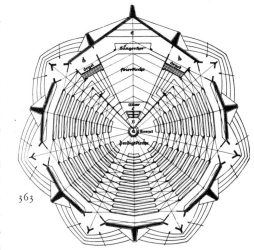

363

of the floor. W. R. Lethaby's little church of All Saints at Brockhampton-by-Ross, Herefordshire (1900–1902), is an early example, and might be regarded as a prelude to Expressionism (ill. 370).[4]

The liturgical grounds for this simplification and unification of the church interior lay in efforts to make worshippers active participants instead of spectators at divine service. A communal celebration was to replace the private exercises of piety that had largely characterized Christian life and worship in the nineteenth century. In the Roman Catholic Church this idea was represented by the Liturgical Movement, which had begun in certain Belgian and German Benedictine monasteries and which appealed to the authority of Pope Pius X. 'The liturgy of the Church . . . consists in . . . we-prayer, not I-prayer' (van Acken).[5] Protestants also showed a desire for a certain visual animation of their liturgy.

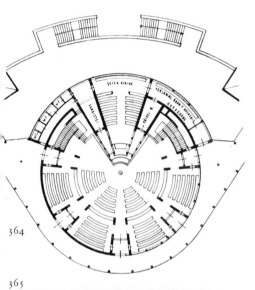

364

365

In terms of church architecture this meant bringing the altar, the focus of liturgical interest, into close contact with the congregational part of the building, and making it visible and accessible to every member of the congregation. The architectural consequences were contradictory: the sanctuary was brought closer to the congregation; but it was set apart as a special area by being raised up on a high platform rather like a stage and illuminated with 'holy' lighting. The designs of Bartning and Dominikus Böhm nevertheless managed to express a new sense of community – the Christian counterpart to the social Utopia of the Expressionists.

Otto Bartning

The 'communion of the mutually guilty, of all men of goodwill, of the loving, of the guilty guiltless in God' – this was how, in 1919, Otto Bartning (1883–1959) expressed his vision of a future, transformed society. The place of those 'who seek the will of the Godhead' was the church, the architectural form of which should present itself as the 'visible and spontaneous gesture of the community'. 'The religious idea, impatient to assume spatial form, would commit itself to the place voluntarily, meaning that the latter would be at all times a wholesome, sacred place seen by every eye and felt in every heart . . . Such a church would be sacred architecture in a new, free, and spiritual sense.'[6]

Bartning's own early work – churches and halls for minority Protestant communities in Austria – led him to the view that contemporary Protestant church architecture had at best produced only aesthetically pleasing utility buildings, preaching-houses which without the preaching were just empty shells, secular buildings despite their sacred purpose. This realization, which struck him on revisiting his first church at Peggau in Steiermark (1906), was a turning point in Bartning's life and work. He knew that the sacred character of the interiors of medieval churches was not something that could be reproduced, particularly not

in a Protestant church which had neither the bodily presence of Christ in the host nor the presence of saints and martyrs through their relics to sanctify it. But in the fact that he and his contemporaries experienced the cathedrals as witnesses to 'the most fervent expression, the ultimate surrender for the sake of redemption' he saw confirmation of the existence of an inner kinship between the two periods.

Bartning believed in a spiritualization of the Church which was to herald the spiritualization of society. This process was not to be brought about by the sermon alone (the central component of the Protestant form of service): Bartning also believed in the possibility of a spiritualization through feeling, which was to arise out of the ceremony of worship, out of the 'active contribution of the individual's emotion as expanded into and absorbed by the collective emotion of the foregathered community.'[7] Here, as Bartning concluded his *Vom neuen Kirchbau*, he laid down his pen and reached impatiently for his drawing pencil.

What Bartning's pencil drew was the Sternkirche or 'star-church' (ills. 361–363), one of the most significant church designs of this century and at the same time one of the most important architectural achievements of its period. Bartning took as his starting point the malaise he felt in Protestant church architecture at the competition between altar and pulpit, and the problematical relationship of each to the building as a whole. The layout of the interior and the orientation of the congregation to these twin focal points almost invariably conflicted. In the eighteenth century the difficulty had frequently been resolved by merging altar and pulpit into one. Bartning went beyond the idea of this pulpit-altar: in his Sternkirche design he did group pulpit and altar together, but he also divided the interior into two corresponding segments, as it were into a church for preaching and a church for worship. The 'preaching' church was centred on the pulpit and on the altar standing behind and above it, while the

366

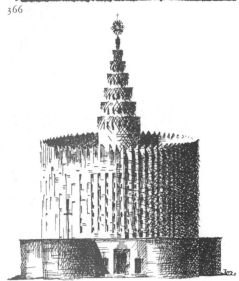

367

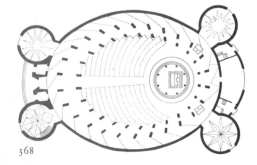

368

366–368. Dominikus Böhm. *Circumstantes* project, 1922. View towards the altar, exterior and plan.

'worship' church was centred exclusively on the altar, the pulpit being lower and consequently remaining hidden behind it. For sacramental services the congregation would leave the 'preaching' church by steps at the sides and move up into the higher 'worship' church, gaining in the process a physical experience of the building.

The plan of the Sternkirche is an almost circular polygon with the pulpit and altar in the middle (ill. 363). The network of timber beams forming pointed arches spanning both segments of the interior was left exposed (ills. 361, 362). Liturgical and spatial centres coincided. The plan made a deep impression at the time. In 1929–30 Bartning was able to put it into practice – somewhat modified, and with a rather more sober formal vocabulary – in the Auferstehungskirche (Church of the Resurrection) in Essen (ills. 364, 365).

Bartning asserted that in designing the Sternkirche his hand was guided in an almost supernatural way. The rings of pews, sunk in the earth, plunge downwards into the 'valley', down to the pulpit, the focal point of the 'preaching' church. The altar on the other hand rears up 'as if on a mountain-top'. Soaring above is the vault of 'heaven', the ribs and cells of the timber vault between which the glazed and latticed arches form crescent moons of light.[8] As in Gaudí's chapel in the Güell colony (ill. 16) and in his church of the Sagrada Familia in Barcelona, the load-bearing members follow the direction of the lines of force. To the eye the complicated geometry of this man-made heaven and earth remains an impenetrable secret; only the plan reveals the seven-part division of the principal formal unit.

The building was meant as an emergency church, like the forty-eight emergency churches Bartning built after the Second World War. Yet just how far he conceived it as a mirror image of the cosmos is clear from a vision which he described in his 'late diary of an early journey': 'The people come up out of the valleys through the forest and pass through the seven low

doors into the loftily vaulted and deeply hollowed-out interior . . . You should see how the vault of the dome and the stepped floor plunge down towards the middle. And the people lining the steps . . . Sun, moon, and stars illuminate the open wreath of the dome turn by turn. And poised inside – . . . the invisible centre. The crystal in which the seven-times-shattered light comes together again.'[9]

Dominikus Böhm

When Bartning produced his Sternkirche design Dominikus Böhm (1880–1955) was already known as the renewer of Roman Catholic church architecture. Immediately after the First World War he had built two small churches on a basilican plan in Offenbach and Dettingen, simple colonnaded structures decked out with every kind of 'triangular modernism'. With his Benedictine abbey at Vaals in southern Holland (ill. 369) he drew upon the whole range of Romantic evocative architecture, from portly round towers, sharp-nosed alcoves and columns of Moorish delicacy in the cloister, right up to crenellations. The Abbot's chapel at Vaals is roofed with a multipartite groin vault, as are the rebuilt church of St

369. Dominikus Böhm. Abbey of St Benedict, Vaals, 1921–23. View from the south.

370. William Richard Lethaby. All Saints, Brockhampton-by-Ross, Herefordshire, 1900–1902.

371, 372. Dominikus Böhm. Parish church, Frielingsdorf near Cologne, 1926–27. Plan and interior.

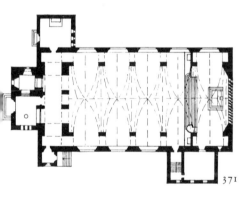

Johannes Baptist in Neu-Ulm (ill. 97) and the village church of Frielingsdorf in the Bergische Land (ills. 371, 372). The white-painted vaults are cast in concrete on an iron mesh suspended beneath the structural girders; with neither base, abutments nor ribs, they give the impression of being made of paper. Their chief task aesthetically was to conduct the light and create prismatically broken surfaces of differing degrees of brightness.

The emphatic centrality of Bartning's Sternkirche was not something Böhm strove for: he was unwilling to give up the path taken by the congregation to the altar, which he saw as symbolic of the way of salvation. In the flower-shaped plan of

one of his two competition designs for the Frauenkirche in Frankfurt and in the circular plan of St Engelbert in the Cologne suburb of Riehl (ill. 375), he put the altar not in the centre but in an apse. When he wanted to incorporate both the idea of the path and the idea of the central altar drawing the congregation together, he chose an elliptical figure for the plan. In his project for a Messopferkirche, or Church of the Mass (ills. 366–368) a tower, from which eight exaggeratedly thin columns extend down into the congregation, casts the maximum light upon the altar, which is situated at the eastern focus of the ellipse. He called the project *Circumstantes* – those gathered around the

Host – and the name is indicative of his new liturgical concept. The wreaths of pillars around the altar with its baldacchino evoke the posture of the faithful: they are themselves *circumstantes*, gathered around the altar of the 'mystic Christ'.

In Bischofsheim, an industrial suburb of Mainz, Böhm struck a sterner note (ill. 373). The parabolic tunnel vault, of unplastered reinforced concrete, embraces congregation and altar in a single oppressive unit of space. 'One loved that vault that shot straight up out of the earth like a fountain, leaving a dark and melancholy interior behind it, and, reaching its lofty apogee, fell back again' (Rudolf Schwarz).[10] Alfred Fischer and J. Hubert

373

374

Pinand, who also used parabolic tunnel vaults, made their naves brighter and varied the light sources in chancel or apse (ill. 374). Böhm, on the other hand, stressed the lightless sanctuary merely by steps and by a quickening rhythm in the parabolic springers at the sides. The entrance façade is divided by a gigantic portal which, in contrast to the parabolic arches of the interior, has the form of a pointed arch. In the later twenties Böhm's exteriors also achieved a more disciplined syntax of broad, unarticulated surfaces, blocky tower forms and flat roofs. Yet in these buildings effective placing of arches, asymmetrical natural lighting and monumental proportions produce the kind of sensuous and emotional effect which Böhm always sought.

The 'path to the hard simplicity of the single, great interior', is how Rudolf Schwarz (1897–1961) characterized Böhm's development;[11] it was a path taken by many architects of the period (ill. 376), and by none with greater determination than by Schwarz himself. Yet even he thought of his religious buildings in terms of graphic symbols, as a 'morphology of the Holy': circle, eruption, thoroughfare, projection or, even more specifically, the open hand or the calyx of the mystic rose. This pictorial approach which had governed many spheres of architectural activity around 1920 remained an intrinsic element of church architecture.

375

376

373. Dominikus Böhm. Christkönigskirche, Mainz-Bischofsheim, 1926. View in the choir showing the altar and gallery for choristers.
374. J. Hubert Pinand. St Marien (Pallotinerkirche), Limburg an der Lahn, 1927.
375. Dominikus Böhm. St Engelbert, Cologne-Riehl, 1930.
376. Clemens Holzmeister. St Adalbert, Linienstrasse, Berlin, 1931–33. View of the apse.

'And if we could make buildings from our hopes, let them be houses – bigger and better houses – skyscrapers!'

Richard Herre, 'Hochhäuser für Stuttgart', in *Wasmuths Monatshefte für Baukunst*, 1922

The house in the landscape

Of all the building actually commissioned during the early post-war years, churches came closest to the Expressionist dream. Tower and crystal, two key images of Expressionist architecture, could be realized in a single building, though the smallness of parish budgets set narrow limits: often an entrance hall based on the German Romanesque westwork had to take the place of a campanile or a façade with towers. Exhibition buildings and monuments offered further opportunities for applying Expressionism's formal principles – exhibition buildings because the fact that they were only temporary lent a boldness of resolution to the people who commissioned them, monuments because the emotional commitment of their promoters made it easier to override convention. For the rest, the architects of Expressionism were thrown back on isolated opportunities. The masterpieces that were built were all the result of exceptional circumstances. Major commissions like the housing programmes of Amsterdam and Vienna were quite untypical of the situation in Central Europe.

The crystal and tower motifs, which in church architecture could be combined, appeared separately in two further building types: the crystal in single houses, and the tower in the tower block. Even here the boldest solutions remained on the drawing board or in model form. No lucky inhabitant ever enjoyed the changing panorama from Max Taut's revolving house on the dunes of the Kurische Nehrung, the great sand-spit north of Königsberg/Kaliningrad (ills. 377, 378). The nearest thing to it that ever was built

was a building with a quite different purpose, the Bastei restaurant in Cologne (ills. 379, 380) by Wilhelm Riphahn (1889–1964). Riphahn's tent of glass and steel projected jauntily out from the base of an old fortification overlooking the Rhine; but it did not revolve.

In the sphere of housing, Hermann Muthesius had often called on architects to give up façade architecture and excessive showiness, illustrating his recommendations mainly with English examples. His advice seemed to be followed in the immediate post-war years by the Luckhardt brothers (ill. 514), the Gropius/Meyer office (ills. 251–256, 266, 267) and Otto Bartning (ills. 387, 388); the plans of their houses, however, are axially symmetrical, and bear no resemblance to the free grouping of the English country house. The Expressionists' fondness for things crystalline led on occasion to multiangular plans of a remarkably impractical nature, though in the hands of the more important architects it also led to polymorphic spatial units which were full of surprises and ceremonial in quality. The dynamic diagonal played a dominant role internally. Externally, the approach was usually not along the principal axes: the resulting oblique views showed off the sculptural quality of the building.

If English domestic architecture did in fact exert an influence, it was for qualities that Muthesius did not much admire – the gloomy, inhospitable and joyless character he noted in certain houses.[1] They were the work of the generation that followed Norman Shaw: architects like W. R. Lethaby, Edgar Wood, E. S. Prior, Sir Edwin Lutyens, and the Scottish circle of Charles Rennie Mackintosh. The bare brick or rough stone, the windows set without trimming into large expanses of wall, the lack of modelled surfaces, the massive chimney-stacks and the peculiar proportions of these buildings conveyed powerful images which in their determined severity made a more lasting impression than many of the villas and town houses of Continental Art Nouveau. Prior's house The Barn in Exmouth, with

377

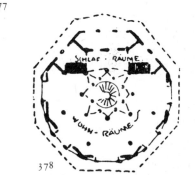
378

379

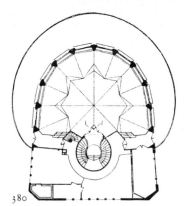
380

377, 378. Max Taut. Revolving house, from *Stadtbaukunst alter und neuer Zeit. Frühlicht*, I, no. 2, 1920. View, and plan of the revolving upper structure.
379, 380. Wilhelm Riphahn. Bastei restaurant, Cologne, 1921–24. View and plan.

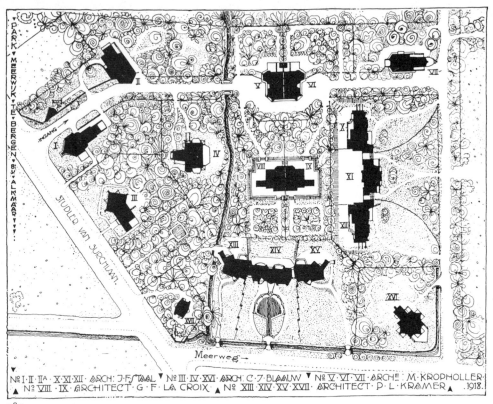

381

382

383

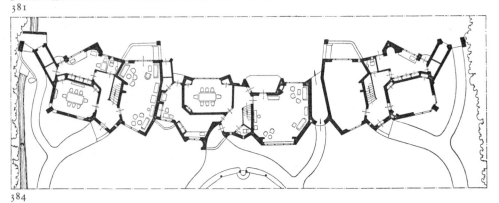

384

385

386

381. Park Meerwijk, Bergen. Site plan, 1918.

382. Margaret Kropholler. Meezennest and Meerlhuis houses, Bergen, 1918–19.

383. Jan Frederik Staal. De Bark house, Bergen, 1916–18.

384, 385. Pieter Lodewijk Kramer. Three linked houses, Bergen (XIII–XV on the site plan, ill. 381), 1915–16. Plan of the ground floor, and entrance front.

386. Jan Frederik Staal. Linked houses, Bergen, 1916–18.

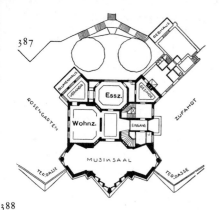

387

388

its two wings meeting at an obtuse angle, was reproduced by Muthesius in the second volume of his *Das englische Haus* in 1910; it appears to have exerted a particularly strong influence, reflected not only in the work of Muthesius himself (e. g. his Freudenberg house in Nicholassee, Berlin, 1907–8) but also in the many plans involving diagonal wings produced by Thilo Schoder, the Luckhardt brothers, Otto Bartning and Bruno Taut.

Where houses were built in the open country, they were treated as an extension and adjunct to nature. Their crystalline forms, in contrast to the planar compositions of the New Architecture, harmonized rather than conflicted with their surroundings. Indeed they appeared to grow out of their environment, like outcrops of rock or powerfully thrusting ridges. An even more thorough fusion of building and landscape was achieved in those houses that evoked an indigenous architectural style: Hoetger's buildings in Worpswede (ills. 307, 313) and the villas in a similar setting, Park Meerwijk near Bergen, built by architects of the school of Amsterdam (ill. 381). Theo Wijde-

veld thought that these designs, too, resembled diamonds in their crystalline clarity,[2] but he was probably thinking only of their three-dimensionality and of the fact that their ground plans were unrelated to traditional formal concepts.

The truth is that the freest and most striking buildings erected in the fashionable Park Meerwijk invite no comparison with crystalline forms whatever. They are either conglomerations of units energetically freeing themselves from the compulsion to form façades, such as the houses of Jan Frederik Staal (ills. 383, 386), or else they are romantic, fairy-tale buildings with thatched roofs that reach almost down to the ground, like the houses of Margaret Kropholler, Cornelis Jonke Blaauw and Piet Kramer (ills. 382, 385). House walls are everywhere extended to form the sides of staircases or garden walls and flow away into the earth, providing, in a quite literal sense, 'roots'.

What distinguishes the Dutch houses from their German counterparts is the warmth of their materials (brick, thatch, weatherboarding) and the feeling of security and intimacy which they communicate. These qualities are not only suggested by the forms employed; they are inherent in the way the different buildings and rooms are arranged. Kramer's loosely linked houses – a middle house with two others facing one another like mirror images (ills. 384, 385) – were perfectly screened from one another.

The functional connection between the house and the space around it was overshadowed by the need for physical and psychological protection. Villas and country houses were seen as partaking in nature, but the relationship was not reciprocal. 'Each room shut off from the outside world, forming in its colourfulness a world of its own and yet still a part of the whole', wrote Ernst Pollak of one of Bartning's major works, the Schuster house at Wylerberg (ills. 387, 388). Bartning himself believed at this time that buildings should satisfy 'feelings of dignity, cosiness, splendour, glory or grief', according to their purpose.[3]

387, 388. Otto Bartning. Schuster house, Wylerberg near Kleve, 1921–24. Plan of the ground floor, and view from the valley.
389. Wilhelm Riphahn. The architect's own house, Cologne-Braunsfeld, 1923–24.
390. Otto Bartning. Water tower, Zeipau, 1922.

389

390

391. Hans Poelzig. *Flughaus*, c. 1918. Charcoal.
Marlene Poelzig Collection, Hamburg.
392. Hermann Obrist. *Monument*, c. 1902. Plaster. Kunstgewerbemuseum, Zurich.
393. Paul Thiersch. *Skyscraper city*, between 1920 and 1925. Pencil. Thiersch Collection, Überlingen.

The 'feeling of cosiness' derived largely from the roof designs. The Wylerberg house owes much of its distinctive appearance to its roof. Together with the chamfered corners of the valley frontage, the planes of the slate roof dramatize the house's topographical position on a slope above the Lower Rhine lowlands. As in the house the Luckhardts built in the Westend district of Berlin (ill. 514), the most important room on the main floor is a music room, symbol of architecture's aspiration to the condition of music.

The architects of this period sought to give their works not only a particular look but an actual 'face', even going as far as to adapt the features of the human face. The big oriel of Wilhelm Riphahn's house in Braunsfeld, Cologne (ill. 389), is like a nose, its windows are like eyes. Bartning's water tower in Zeipau (ill. 390), built two years earlier, may have influenced these forms; in any case his interpretation of his designs for water towers was explicitly anthropomorphic: 'With sharp prows they cleave the clouds and with narrowed eyes peer into the wind.'[4]

391

392

A winged creature in us

The chance to build towers is something that architects and their clients have always seized upon whenever they could. In the nineteenth and early twentieth centuries the opportunity was usually provided by churches, town halls, railway stations, gasometers and water reservoirs. The tower monuments to Kaiser Wilhelm and Bismarck that graced the mountaintops of Germany after their deaths combined the function of memorial with a more 'secular' purpose, in that they served as look-out towers. The tower became the favourite form for monuments. Mammoth statues, like Germania, near Rüdesheim, Hermann or Arminius of the Cherusci in the Teutoburger Wald, and Bismarck in the guise of Roland in Hamburg, became less popular after the turn of the century as purely architectural solutions replaced them. The national competition for a Bismarck monument near Bingerbrück (1909–11) marks the change. The major monuments built in Germany during the twenties were towers: the naval war memorial at Laboe near Kiel took the form of a prow rising up from the land and then falling steeply into the sea, the Tannenberg memorial in East Prussia that of a castle of the dead with ramparts and fortified towers.

During the same period a purely secular type of building, the water tower, also underwent a change and began to assume monumental form. Whereas in the old towers the water container had always been differentiated from the supporting shaft, after about 1910 architects began to treat the whole structure as a unit, giving it a uniform vertical movement (ills. 144–146, 390). The image of the tower became more important than its function. 'Preoccupation with function and the justification of materials should not occupy first place in the designer's thoughts; [he should be concerned with] the general flow, the shape, the outline . . . the elementary, artistically thought-out passage of forces.'[5] This ennoblement of the humble water tower made it possible to

393

introduce other functions; water towers could now accommodate market stalls, flats and offices (ill. 496).

The tower, with its dynamic, upward-thrusting verticality, symbol of the struggle of mind against matter (Magda Révész-Alexander),[6] inevitably caught the fancy of the Expressionists. It appealed to that yearning for the lofty and the exalted; it was closer to the elements, elevated above the mass; it was ecstatic in the etymological sense of the word: it 'stood out'. The tower was an artificial peak, a constructed mountain (see p. 43). Architecture is 'towers, peaks, vaulting of masses out of the bowels of the earth', wrote Walter Müller-Wulckow. Hans Poelzig drew landscapes with towers rising out of them. In one drawing, labelled *Flughaus*, or 'flight house' (ill. 391), paths spiral their way up artificial massifs like

flight paths – or like the spirals on Hermann Obrist's famous maquette for a memorial (ill. 392). 'There is a winged creature in us, rising up and spreading its pinions ever faster as it soars into infinity; it will not be checked, seeking as it does a higher unity'; so Hans Hansen wrote in a text which reads like a commentary on Poelzig's sketch.[7]

In 1918 Josef Ponten wrote a novel entitled *Der babylonische Turm* ('The Tower of Babel'), the hero of which wishes to combine every conceivable cultural and religious function in a single building, from a library and Trappist monastery to a hermit's cell in the topmost turret. 'What matters is that we attain the highest!' Seven years later, in his book *Architektur, die nicht gebaut wurde* ('Architecture which was not built'), Ponten collected together the architectural Utopias of all periods,

394

395

396

including many towers. A psychological commentary on all this tower-mania was supplied by Bruno Taut; in *Die Auflösung der Städte* he proposed a tower in the shape of a giant phallus (ill. 178).

The fact that high-rise building was urged with such emphasis in post-war Europe was due first and foremost to the fascination of the tower. But of course there were also rational arguments in favour of multi-storey office and residential buildings: the more intensive exploitation of a site which inspired the American Raymond Hood to design his narrow service shafts with the mass of the building suspended on them (ill. 397); the saving in both time and travel which it was hoped concentration would bring about; and considerations of the price of land, which those architects who were also social reformers thought should redound to the benefit of the general public. In countries with a bigger housing shortage there was the additional consideration that high-rise buildings would be quicker to clear permission for and to build than low-rise estates. The thought of the endless traffic disasters which would be caused by increasing urban concentration occurred only to those who had actually been to America and looked closely at conditions there.

Irrational motives kept creeping into the most sober analyses of practising architects. The architect and town planner Bruno Möhring, who in 1920 carried out a study of the advantages of tower blocks for the Prussian Academy of Architecture, thought he saw in high-rise building the 'creative yearning for grandeur *(nach Grossem)*' that stirred even the least sensitive. He declared himself in favour of a chain of twenty tower blocks for the centre of Berlin, to run roughly along the line of the River Spree. Max Berg

394. Otto Kohtz. Project for a government building on the Königsplatz (Platz der Republik), Berlin, 1920.
395. Max Berg. Project for an office building next to the town hall, Breslau (Wroclaw), 1920.
396. Hans Poelzig. Project for an exhibition building, Hamburg, 1925.

397

397. Raymond Hood. Project for tower blocks, before 1927.

398. Wilhelm Kreis. Wilhelm-Marx-Haus, Düsseldorf, 1921–24.

399. Paul Bonatz. Stumm building, Düsseldorf, 1921–25.

designed several high-rise buildings for Breslau (ill. 395), and gave his tower blocks a uniform rhythm from top to bottom on the model of the cathedral and the pagoda.[8] The tower block also recommended itself as a means of restoring a skyline to cities that had become so big as to be visually shapeless. But the small towns were given their high-rise buildings too. Paul Thiersch produced *Hochstadt* projects not only for Berlin but also for Halle an der Saale (ill. 393), and Emmanuel Josef Margold planned an office tower as a monumental gate for Darmstadt, which at the time had fewer than 100,000 inhabitants. The goal was the *Stadtkrone*, the Acropolis of labour.

Social considerations took second place to the supposed aesthetic advantages of high-rise building. Wijdeveld merely put as a question what Le Corbusier upheld as an indubitable truth in his 'radiant cities': 'will people find spiritual peace in dwellings which go soaring up into the clouds,

which are conditioned by economics, in which greatness of thought goes hand in hand with the ingenious spatial solution, which promise freedom of life and behaviour, ... which offer *everybody* air and light and sun, leave the land free to bear fruit, and provide gardens and parks and trees and flowers everywhere?'[9] Wijdeveld nevertheless thought he saw in the skyscrapers of the American magnates the first sign of a new life that would replace capitalism.

The tower blocks that were actually built in Europe in the years immediately following the First World War were none of them over twenty storeys high, and they fell far short of competition and ideal designs. They were commissioned as a rule by big concerns rather than by the municipal building societies which ought to have been responsible for them.[10] The results were uneven. There was no trace either of the grandly staggered volumes which Poelzig wanted to pile up on top of the Hamburg railway station or of the truly monumental hall based on a cruciform plan which Otto Kohtz had proposed for a government building in Berlin, in the face of every possible objection from the fire authorities (ills. 394, 396). The best thing about the tower blocks built by Bonatz and Koerfer in Düsseldorf and Cologne (ills. 399, 498) is the way the mass of the building is coordinated by means of vertical articulation. Romantic touches remain in spite of all efforts to achieve a monumental effect – whether breaks in proportion between different units (Bonatz) or in roof superstructures or details of windows and doorways. Other architects such as Eugen Schmohl and Wilhelm Kreis could not yet break away from the horizontal stratification which makes their buildings appear like a series of bits stuck one on top of the other (ill. 398).

The fascination of America

American skyscrapers had reached four times the height of the European tower blocks even before the First World War.

398

399

400

401

400, 401. Hugh Ferriss. Project for a skyscraper based on the New York City zoning law, before 1926.
400. Analysis of the building in terms of light wells.
401. Analysis of the building in terms of its steel framework.

Cass Gilbert's Woolworth Building in New York, with its 55 storeys, was 236 metres high. The overwhelming experience of New York, to which every traveller to America (and there were many) was exposed, was something to which European architects and town planners usually reacted with a reserve which was the saving of their self-respect: the task of Europe, as they saw it, was to refine this great quantitative achievement into a product of the artist's expressive will. Most of the German architects who saw Manhattan would not admit that its vitality derived partly from the lack of any aesthetic planning. Tower blocks must not be allowed to grow wild, they said, but ought to be built where town planners decreed and grouped in administrative clusters. This idea was by no means confined to Europeans: in America the 'civic center' was a common planning concept.

European architects believed that the Zoning Resolution, passed by the city of New York in 1916, showed that Americans were becoming aware of the laws of true architecture. It prescribed a graduated reduction of volumes based on the height of the building, the width of the street, and the coverage laid down for the particular district. The zoning law recommended that buildings be treated not as solid blocks with a façade to the street but rather as terraced masses. Hugh Ferriss compared the spatial concept of the New York law with a matrix of pyramids and conical forms which had to be filled in by the architect of each project.

Ferriss, a trained architect, was a perspective artist, and he illustrated the design stages for a building put up under the provisions of the New York zoning law in some effective and expressive drawings (ills. 400, 401). His book *The Metropolis of Tomorrow*, published in 1929, drew a picture of the future which revealed his obsession with a crystal-hard architecture that glittered in the light. Ferriss could not fail to make an impression in Germany.[11]

13 The cinema

'Give me the cinema and I will move the world.'

Carlo Mierendorff, *Hätte ich das Kino!*, Berlin, 1920

Reform movements

Architects unable to get commissions for real buildings understandably took an interest in a medium where buildings could at least appear to be real. The economic difficulties of the war and post-war years helped rather than hurt the German film industry. The cinema offered all that was lacking in ordinary life – travel, adventure, luxury, high life. The German Ministry of Welfare estimated that three and a half million people went to the cinema every evening.[1] It was not only this enormous demand that stimulated the industry, but also the fact that during the war international competition was temporarily excluded. The emergence at the end of the war of Ufa (Universum-Film AG) and Decla-Bioscop, which later merged, provided an organizational basis for German film companies to operate abroad as well.

The cinema was intriguing for a number of reasons. Film people had as much right as architects to appeal to 'the spirit of a medieval lodge that moved and inspired everone' (Robert Herlth). Most important of all, the cinema reached 'the people'. Here was an audience such as none of the traditional arts had ever brought together: 'Waiters and laundry maids, porters and models, drivers and housewives, painters and milkmaids, jockeys and schoolgirls, delivery boys and hairdressers, furniture removers and domestic servants, ladies in diamonds and butcher boys, stable boys and people passing through town . . . The cinema's audience is the classless audience' (Carlo Mierendorff).[2] Anyone – revolutionary architects included – who wanted to communicate with 'the people' could not possibly ignore the cinema.

The cinema's powers of attraction were perhaps even greater than those of the theatre, which despite all its attempts to win over the working classes still depended for its audience on the upper levels of the bourgeoisie. Among Expressionist architects Poelzig, Bruno Taut, Paul Thiersch and especially Wijdeveld did work for the stage. It was regarded as the elevated, artistically-sanctioned medium, while the cinema's charms were of a coarser, more flamboyant kind. But film was a temptation. Hermann Finsterlin made an outline for a film and, towards the end of the twenties, hoped through the agency of Erich Mendelsohn to contact Fritz Lang, who had seen his drawings in *Wendingen*. Egon Eiermann began his career with an Ufa contract, which he owed to a recommendation from Friedrich Wilhelm Murnau.[3] The project which Bruno Taut eventually proposed to his friends of the Glass Chain as their collective work of art was a film.

Taut's own 'architecture play' *Der Weltbaumeister* was intended for the stage, but it would have been easier to produce on the screen; and the original stimulus may well have come from the film actor and director Paul Wegener.[4] Taut's film project for the Glass Chain was called *Die Galoschen des Glücks* ('The Galoshes of Fortune') after the fairy tale by Hans Christian Andersen: a young couple travel through time and see a great variety of architectural visions. The scenes were tailor-made for the individual members of the Chain: Finsterlin was to produce a 'grown' house, half the work of man and half of nature, Brückmann a flame building, Krayl a ray dome (compare their drawings, ills. 402–404). Hablik promptly offered to build an entire town as well as one or two dwellings for 'single individ-

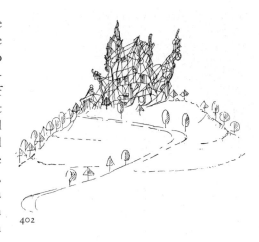

402

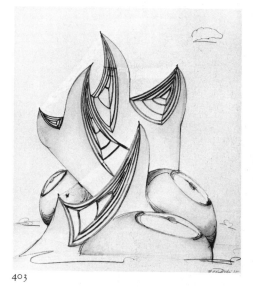

403

402. Carl Krayl. Drawing, from *Stadtbaukunst alter und neuer Zeit*. *Frühlicht*, 1, no. 8, 1920.

403. Hermann Finsterlin. Study V-7, 1917(?). Watercolour.

404. Wilhelm Brückmann. 'Flames', from *Stadtbaukunst alter und neuer Zeit*. *Frühlicht*, 1, no. 9, 1920.

404

405

406

uals' – under water, in the mountains, beneath the ground, and as 'flying houses' in the air.[5] The project shared the fate of similar scenarios collected in Kurt Pinthus' *Kinobuch* (1914): it came to nothing, but it was evidence of the fascination of the new medium for the intelligentsia.

With this project Taut stepped into the ranks of 'cinema reformers'. The coalition of unequal partners which for a few years brought conservatives and progressives together in the field of social and political ideas operated here too (see pp. 28ff.). The austere art historian Konrad Lange, a member of the Dürerbund, had recommended fairy tales as suitable material for the cinema, and expressed the fear that film dramas might overstimulate the imagination. Lange mentioned *Gulliver's Travels* as a possible subject for the cinema; Swift's fantasy was also one of the themes Poelzig treated in his sketch books. The fairy-tale films of Poelzig's friend Paul Wegener were admired by the reformers not only for their quality but also for their subject matter.[6] A group actively engaged in the reform movement was the Film League, which sought to improve the cinema and to provide a link between film and the plastic and graphic arts and literature. It included members of the Deutsche Werkbund, such as Peter Behrens and Bruno Paul.

The thought that such reform might be of doubtful value and might in fact enfeeble the cinema occurred only to outsiders, one or two literary figures with a feeling for *Kintopp* (Berlin slang for 'the flicks'). Pinthus was prepared to accept a reasonable amount of kitsch in the cinema, while Mierendorff applauded the make-believe glamour, naïve fantasy and sentimental pandering to the public that characterized the cinema before it fell into the hands of well-meaning schoolmasters.

The *Golem* town

Even Bruno Taut, with all his doubts about the 'simple instincts of the masses', once thought of using the cinema as an instrument of indoctrination for his Uto-pian 'glass culture', but he was ready enough to renounce the project when he had investigated contemporary film production. Hans Poelzig's involvement with the cinema was more fruitful. His papers show that several times he worked out films based on legends or fairy tales, even without specific commissions. One Poelzig project that was actually carried out was Wegener's second *Golem* film (ills. 407–410); the first version of 1914 had been shot not in a studio but in Hildesheim.

The Golem story, which tells of the magical powers of the great magus Rabbi Löw who brought to life a clay giant (the Golem) and saved the Jewish people of Prague from expulsion from the ghetto, appealed to the taste of the period. It dealt with the desire for salvation, but this was clothed in historical dress; and the setting, in the Jewish quarter of Prague, fitted in perfectly with the contemporary passion for Gothic. On the Tempelhofer Feld in Berlin Poelzig erected an entire town made of reinforced plaster, including the ghetto wall, gateways, fountains, and fifty-four houses. Its crooked alleys with their projecting oriels and leaning gables, its rooms out of a medieval castle – some decorated with stalactite forms in the manner of the Grosse Schauspielhaus – its halls, cellars, corridors, nooks, and spiral staircases winding upwards in complicated convolutions like snail-shells, and all its violently twisted and distorted details spoke a language of their own, even without the actors on the set. Poelzig said that the buildings 'spoke with a Jewish accent'. Round every corner there seemed to lurk a secret. At the same time it was an architecture designed for action: overlapping façades, odd openings, abrupt changes in height, staircases, landings and platforms were invitations to movement. Before the set was built Poelzig made a model, with the aid of Marlene Moeschke, who later became his wife. The layout of the set as a whole and the plastic volumes of the individual buildings interrelate, exerting a mutual influence on each other.

405. Robert Herlth, from designs by Hans Poelzig. Set for *Zur Chronik von Grieshuus* (director: Arthur von Gerlach), 1925. Rough sketch.
406. Robert Herlth and Walter Röhrig, from designs by Hans Poelzig. Set for *Zur Chronik von Grieshuus* (director: Arthur von Gerlach), 1925.
407–410. Hans Poelzig. Set for *Der Golem – wie er in die Welt kam* (director: Paul Wegener), 1920.
407. View looking out from a side street.
408. The ghetto wall.
409. Fire in the ghetto.
410. Synagogue.

The treatment of space in *Golem* is quite different from that in *The Cabinet of Dr Caligari*, where it is suggested artificially by means of canvas backdrops (ills. 411, 412). The latter film is much better known internationally, and its style has led people to believe that the completely three-dimensional set of the *Golem* town was an exception in 1920. In fact even Robert Wiene, the director of *Dr Caligari*, reverted in his next picture but one, *Raskolnikow*, to fully three-dimensional sets by Max Reinhardt's favourite scene designer, Andrei Andrejew (ill. 413); and costlier productions normally followed the example of Italian historical films, with extensive sets either in the open air on in the studio. Indian temples, Egyptian courts, Renaissance palaces, and cathedral interiors big enough to hold several hundred people sprouted up all over Tempelhof and Neubabelsberg. What is remarkable about Poelzig's set is not its three-dimensionality but the fantastic character of his Expressionist Gothic forms and his wealth of spatial invention.

Poelzig was associated with two further films. For *Lebende Buddhas* (a film which lost a great deal of money for Paul Wegener, acting as his own producer) Poelzig in 1924 filled the former Zeppelin hangar at Staaken with a Tibetan landscape complete with temples and houses. It was his bow to the Far East, following his homage to the Gothic world in *Golem*. For *Zur Chronik von Grieshuus*, which had Arthur von Gerlach as director and Robert Herlth and Walter Röhrig in charge of sets, Poelzig did designs for the exteriors, and produced a castle that was a crumbling ruin, dominated by an enormous roof (ills. 405, 406).

411

412

413

414

The object as mirror

Film architecture provided more, during these years, than just the chance to give a temporary reality to architectural ideas which otherwise stood no chance of ever being carried out. Heinrich de Fries commented, 'One [may] almost hope that out of this special development, which is sudden, almost self-willed, and as it were necessary, certain things may emerge which go beyond the needs of film and remain of significant value for the rebirth of architecture at present in progress.'[7]

What made the building of silent-film sets particularly interesting for Expressionist architects was the fact that, in the absence of the spoken word, directors relied on them to convey the drama in clear pictorial terms. 'Objects serve psychologically to mirror the actors' emotions and gestures', noted Taut. Fritz Lang, who was trained as an architect, expressed similar views within the industry itself. He declared one of the principles of film to be the correspondence between thing and person: 'an expressionism of the most subtle kind will bring surroundings, props and action into harmony with one another.'[8] The more powerful the emotions, the more thoroughly the surroundings were harnessed to their expression. Expressionist films (as opposed to ordinary commercial films) were shot without exception on studio sets which excluded all chance incident and allowed only that which was psychologically significant. On some sets, to eliminate naturalism altogether, even light and shadow were represented graphically.

For architects who had pledged themselves to the expressive in art, film was worth studying. It provided an opportunity of investigating the psychological effects of form and space. What were the expressive values of foreground, middleground and distance, of descending or ascending diagonals, of a high and of a low horizon, of the space that sloped downwards and the space that soared upwards; the much foreshortened and distorted yet energetic lines of *The Cabinet of Dr Caligari* as opposed to the clusters of lines flickering nervously over the entire picture in *Von Morgens bis Mitternacht;* bunched, diffused, or single-source lighting; the colliding angles and lines that dominate *Caligari* or the dense, tapestry-like pattern that César Klein designed for *Genuine*?

The stylization of architecture in Expressionist films was accompanied by a corresponding stylization in the costumes and the acting. The same graphic touches used for the sets were often used for the actors' dress and make-up; the performers became part of the set, an indication of the demands which Expressionist architecture placed on people – not only on the screen. In film as in reality, aesthetic success depended upon absolute congruity between the inhabitant and the environment.

The German cinema of the first half of the 1920s produced a system of metaphor in which the motifs of Expressionist architecture assumed fixed meanings. They usually had a negative connotation: narrow Gothic streets and alleys of tall, tightly-packed houses with crooked roofs denoted places where calamity was imminent – in Murnau's *Nosferatu* and *Faust*, for example, or in Fritz Lang's *Metropolis* (ill. 43) where the inventor Rotwang lives in a tiny ancient house in the middle of the highly technical world of the machine age. Cave-like labyrinths were

416

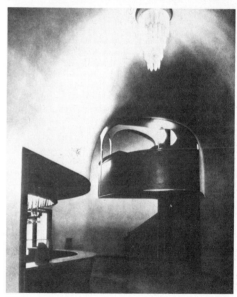

417

411, 412. Walter Reimann, Walter Röhrig and Hermann Warm. Sets for *The Cabinet of Dr Caligari* (director: Robert Wiene), 1919. Escape across the rooftops, and market place.
413. Andrei Andrejew. Set for *Raskolnikow* (director: Robert Wiene), 1922. Street scene.
414. Otto Hunte, Erich Kettelhut and Karl Vollbrecht. Set for *Kriemhilds Rache (Nibelungen*, part 2, director: Fritz Lang). Subterranean passages in Etzel's castle.
415. Otto Hunte, Erich Kettelhut and Karl Vollbrecht. Set for *Metropolis* (director: Fritz Lang), 1926. Section of a street scene.
416, 417. Hans Poelzig. Capitol cinema, Berlin, 1925. Auditorium, and view of one of the staircases with a cloakroom.

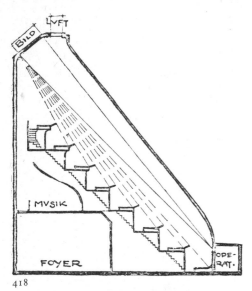

418

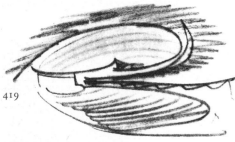

419

418. Bruno Taut. Project for a cinema for a reclining audience, 1924. Section.
419. Erich Mendelsohn. Universum cinema, Berlin, 1926–31. Auditorium. Charcoal. Louise Mendelsohn Collection, San Francisco.

inhabited by dangerous hordes – by the Huns in *Kriemhilds Rache* (ill. 414) and by the rebellious masses in *Metropolis*. Height stood for *hubris:* skyscrapers, which professional architects could defend with so many rational arguments, appeared in *Metropolis* as emblems of Babylonian pride (ill. 415). In *Siegfrieds Tod* and *Nosferatu* the assault of impassably rugged cliffs, in the form of Brünnhilde's and Nosferatu's castles, heralds the downfall or deadly peril of the hero.

From film sets to cinemas

In the latter half of the twenties film-set architecture increasingly became the province of specialists, and ceased to tempt established architects. If they were involved with the film industry at all it was now not for the buildings in which films were shot but for those in which they were shown. One revolutionary, and slightly absurd, proposal was put forward by Bruno Taut. After the failure of his own film plans Taut stated that films had no genuine power to move spectators deeply, and that they should therefore be regarded merely as entertainment. However, he also suggested (in apparent contradiction to his first statement) that films might have a therapeutic value. Taut recommended the cinema to people who 'need intellectual stimulation as a healing impulse',[9] and designed an amphitheatre which, instead of rows of seats, had tiers of accommodation for spectators lying prostrate: invalid cinemagoers would attend the performance on litters and look up at the screen from below. Screen and projection booth thus exchanged their customary places (ill. 418).

Poelzig designed cinemas which involved no radical innovations. In the Deli in Breslau, circle and stalls were linked on both sides of the auditorium by curving staircases, a motif which existed already in Oskar Kaufmann's Cines-Theater on the Nollendorfplatz in Berlin (1911). The way in which the circle (now widened and furnished with rows of seats) was drawn down to the stalls became a frequent feature in cinema and theatre architecture thirty years later. In the Capitol cinema in Berlin there was still a hint of that enigmatic, demon-peopled world which the Expressionist film had conjured up – in the odd curve of the staircases, in their intersections with the tunnel-vaulted passages, and also in the tent-like, fluted ceiling of reinforced plaster (ills. 416, 417). There is the same quality in certain other picture palaces of the period, such as the Titania-Palast in Berlin-Steglitz (1927) by Schöffler, Schlönbach and Jacobi, with its complex play of curves and its staggered parabolic proscenium arches.

Mendelsohn's Universum cinema in Berlin (ill. 419) stands at the end of this development. Here too the fascination of the films themselves was to be suggested by the architecture of the building; but the films for which Mendelsohn was building the Universum were no longer those of the Expressionist era, works of fairy tale and legend steeped in mystery. Mendelsohn formulated a different ideal: 'Real life is genuine, simple and true, so no pose, no stirring it up. Neither in the film, nor on the screen, nor in the building.'[10] Fortunately Mendelsohn did not entirely give up posturing, and it is the rhetorical flourishes that give his building its flavour. Mendelsohn was not satisfied with mere effect. Thinking the plan out afresh, he produced an elongated horseshoe shape that eliminated the seats far to the side from which the screen appeared distorted. The different parts of the building are distinct on the outside, according to their function. The auditorium is lit effectively by horizontal strips, which unlike the indirect lighting of Poelzig's Capitol cinema, clearly declare that the means of persuasion used in this building is light.

Parallels and sequels

14 Futurism

'When people talk about architecture they think of something static. This is wrong.'

Carlo Carrà, *La pittura dei suoni, rumori e odori* ('The Painting of Sounds, Noises and Smells'), 11 August 1913

Universal dynamism

The architecture of Futurism, like that of Expressionism, was an architecture of manifestos and projects. In Central Europe something was actually built here and there which showed what the Expressionist visions and Utopias looked like when translated into reality, but in Italy no building of any size ever demonstrated the possibilities of Futurist architecture. Sant'Elia, Futurism's most important architect, built only a modest country house in the hills above Como (similar to ill. 420),[1] and Mario Chiattone's membership of the Futurist circle was based on his designs, not on his actual buildings.

No other movement of this century has expounded its arguments so consistently and convincingly as Futurism, or so vitally stamped the consciousness of the age. This *tour de force* was due primarily to the organizational ability of the poet Filippo Tomaso Marinetti (1876–1944). Through endless manifestos, books, articles, controversial lectures, exhibitions, tours and discussions Marinetti conducted a campaign that would have been a credit to any public relations office today. The Futurists' ideas, however, developed their full explosive power because the time was ripe.

Few cultural trends of the last half-century do not depend in some way or other on the themes developed by Futurism, from kinetic art to *bruitiste* music and participatory theatre. Its political aspects were no less varied and lively. Anarchism, anticlericalism, chauvinism – ultimately even Fascism, with which Marinetti and his friends came to terms in 1919 – were all aspects of the Futurist movement. These 'primitives of a new sensibility'[2] did more to give their age a new, invigorated awareness, responsive to every facet of change, than all the other groups of modern artists put together. None embraced with less reserve the excitement of the age of technology. The worship of the machine, which had already attracted many converts in the Art Nouveau period, reached a peak in Futurism. In Central Europe the serious belief in crafts as an alternative to technology still had many years to run.

Relations between Futurism and Central European Expressionism were nevertheless close.[3] The Futurists had four rooms in Herwarth Walden's second exhibition at the *Der Sturm* gallery in Berlin in April-May 1912. In Germany, much to the disgust of the critics who were concerned with finer nuances, 'Futurism' was used to designate new art in general. *Der Sturm* printed Futurist manifestos, and a selection of Marinetti's poems appeared. From 1918 Enrico Prampolini acted as link between Berlin and Rome. In 1920 he exhibited in Rome a selection of work by the Novembergruppe artists, including Paul Gösch (who appeared in the exhibition leaflet as 'Gocsh'), from the circle of Bruno Taut.

Umberto Boccioni, who had rehung the Futurist exhibition in Walden's gallery in 1912, criticized German painting on the grounds that it sought support always outside the pictorial field, in philo-

420. Antonio Sant'Elia. A modern country house, from *Le case popolari e le città giardino*, Milan, 1911.

421

422

sophic or emotional content.[4] The Futurist artists preferred construction: within the organism of a literary, pictorial or sculptural work of art, the elements of external reality were indicated in accordance with a law of structural analogies and opposites. This process did not and was not intended to give rise to a single, unambiguous sign language. Shapes and colours that conveyed the impression 'ocean liner' could also convey impressions of a quite different reality, such as 'Galeries Lafayette'. The Futurists saw this ambiguity not as a disadvantage but as a positive advantage. It made possible the representation of a continuum of interreacting objects, of 'universal dynamism', of the 'absolute life-force of matter'. Thus, shapes which intuition had revealed in a dance or in the dancer herself might be rediscovered in the flight of an aeroplane or in the movement of an express train. Through the analogies that had been worked out or established by art, intuition became a bridge between everything and anything. 'We want to encompass the universe within the work of art', wrote Gino Severini.[5]

Severini concluded his 1913 manifesto on the principles of structural analogies with a prophecy: 'I foresee the end of the picture and the statue.' Structural creations, he said, must find fulfilment in architecture. The conclusion was not without consequence. The Futurists maintained that the meaning of a work of art lay in the establishment of connections between apparently incompatible realities, but the purpose was fulfilled and art made unnecessary as soon as the sensibilities of contemporary man could grasp the connections without the work of art as intermediary. A 'complex of dynamic elements', for example a 'moving tram or car + avenue + man going somewhere', need no longer be transmitted through the work of art once the environment was organized in an appropriately dynamic manner and once the eye of the beholder was sufficiently schooled to be able to see and confirm the dynamism of its surroundings. The work of art would then be no more than a constraint upon an individual's creative freedom.

As in Expressionist architecture, though for different reasons, the individual arts were in Futurism to come together in a total restructuring of the environment. Boccioni imagined 'environment sculptures', *sculture d'ambiente*, which projected into space to give it sculptural form, and Severini called for the consummation of art 'in architectural contexts'.[6] The Futurists of course understood by this not the individual *Gesamtkunstwerk*, but the dynamic totality of the 'structured' world.

Apart from asserting this mandate, Futurist writings of the early years contained only hints of a Futurist architecture; the movement as yet had no contacts with architects. The major themes, obviously applicable to architecture as well, were sounded in Marinetti's first manifesto of 1909 – the declaration of war on the past, the hymn of glory to the mass of humanity, and the fascination with speed. Translated into architectural terms, this philosophy implied the abolition of a style-conscious architecture, preference for the metropolis rather than the garden city, and the incorporation of traffic as an integral part of architectural design. Even the distinction between form in movement (relative movement) and movement in form (absolute movement), formulated by Boccioni on a number of occasions, could be carried over from sculpture to architecture. It led to a conception that not only made provision for real paths of movement (traffic routes) but also lent dynamic expression to architecture itself.

The individual building in isolation was not enough. What Boccioni required of painting and sculpture could also be applied to architecture, namely the renunciation of isolated volumes, division into spatial zones and perspective organization, in favour of the interpenetration of masses and planes.[7] Even his demand for the abolition of static balance might have had its consequences. The resulting disturbance of equilibrium was intended to coerce forms into 'total' movement. In

421–423. Antonio Sant'Elia.
421. Railway station (?), 1913. Ink and pencil. Villa Comunale dell'Olmo, Como.
422. Bridge (?), 1913–14. Ink and pencil. Villa Comunale dell'Olmo, Como.
423. Electric power station, 25 February 1914. Coloured ink and pencil. Paride Accetti Collection, Milan.

424. Antonio Sant'Elia. Domed building, 1912
(?). Pencil and coloured pencil. Villa Comunale
dell'Olmo, Como.

425, 426. Emil Hoppe. Sketches, *c.* 1902. From
Wagner-Schule 1902, Leipzig, n.d.

427. Antonio Sant'Elia. Tower, 1913. Ink and
coloured pencil. Villa Comunale dell'Olmo,
Como.

architectural terms, this would have meant relinquishing symmetry, something Sant'Elia and Chiattone found very hard to do. With few exceptions their designs have compositional axes and in many cases they relate to axial systems.

The architecture of the Futurist manifestos was urban architecture. The Futurists drew their emotions from their experience of the city – shafts of light obliterating all hardness of outline, noise of the big city with its roaring engines, screeching trams and the gurgling sounds of water, air and gas passing through metal pipes. 'Our pictures will give expression to the structural equivalents of the colours, sounds and smells of the theatre, the music hall, the cinema, the brothel, the stations, the harbour, the garages, the hospitals, the factories, and so on, and so forth.'[8] In this proclamation by Carlo Carrà, if we subtract brothel and hospital and add bridges and electricity works, we find the principal architectural themes to which Sant'Elia addressed himself.

The Futurists saw the city not just as the container of frenzied activity but as a process and centre of movement, a consideration that did not enter the minds of professional town planners until years later. There was nothing, Marinetti declared, more beautiful than the scaffolding of a building under construction; it symbolized 'burning passion for the coming into existence of things. The finished, executed thing on the other hand disgusts us.' Marinetti valued the process of building positively: he used it as a metaphor for the rhythm and restlessness of life. Durability was no longer a virtue in architecture, but a vice. When in their first manifesto the Futurist artists derided concrete as a material used by building speculators they may have had in mind its indestructibility and consequent opposition to 'the coming into existence of things': 'Let's call a halt to the speculative architecture of the reinforced-concrete contractors!'[9]

Later, of course, Futurist architects refused to accept this condemnation of reinforced concrete by their non-architect colleagues. If any of their designs had been built, both Sant'Elia and Chiattone would have been dependent on this most 'futuristic' of building materials. Yet even Sant'Elia, in his famous catalogue text of 1914, argued against indestructible materials – obviously referring to stone. Sant'Elia's proclamation, demanding buildings of maximum flexibility and describing the city of the future as an enormous noisy building-site, was a logical extension of Marinetti's thought. The concluding passage of *L'architettura futurista*, which Sant'Elia signed, contains a sentence which contemporary critics immediately felt to be sensational: 'Houses have a shorter life-span than we do; every generation will have to build its own city.'[10]

Sant'Elia never translated these thoughts into design terms. Nor, later, did the stage designer and architect Virgilio Marchi. Marchi added to Sant'Elia's ideas the prophetic concept of mobile architecture: recalling the Anglo-Saxon fondness for yachting and camping, he foresaw a time when cities would consist of vast marshalling yards filled with elegant caravans[11] – trailer architecture in 1920. The Futurists, in theory at least, saw expendability and consumer orientation as criteria of modern architecture.

Antonio Sant'Elia

Like every major reform movement of the nineteenth and twentieth centuries, Futurism sought to be all-embracing and to extend its rule over every expression of contemporary culture; literature, grammar, typography, painting, sculpture, politics, drama, music, the position of women, music halls, the 'Art of Noises', and even luxury had appeared in Futurist manifestos before an interest in the architectural environment was stated in professional terms. Five years after the first Futurist proclamation Marinetti, through the agency of Carrà, won over to Futurism the twenty-six-year-old architect Antonio Sant'Elia (1888–1916).

427

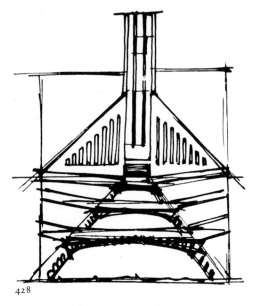

428

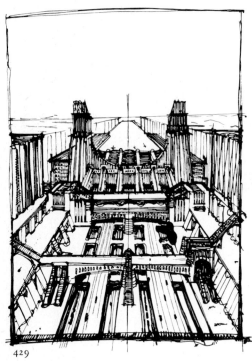

429

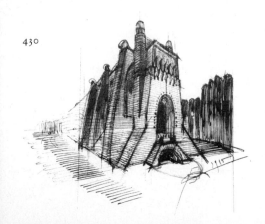

430

Sant'Elia was not unknown to the Futurists. He was a friend of Romolo Romani, one of the signatories of the draft of the *Manifesto dei pittori futuristi*, and he knew Boccioni, Carrà and Russolo. He joined the ranks of the Futurists with the manifesto on Futurist architecture, which appeared as a pamphlet on 11 July 1914 and in the Futurist magazine *Lacerba* a month later. The manifesto is on the whole identical with the text that had been printed in the catalogue of the Nuove Tendenze group of artists. This group, which included both Chiattone and Sant'Elia among its founder-members, had held an exhibition in the Famiglia Artistica rooms on Via Agnello in Milan from 20 May to 10 June 1914; Sant'Elia was represented by sixteen architectural sketches and designs, seven of which the catalogue described as projects for a *città nuova*. In March of the same year the First Exhibition of Lombard Architects in Milan had contained several of his works. In Sant'Elia the Futurists had found their architect.[12]

The two texts published under Sant'Elia's name adhere unswervingly to the earlier Futurist manifestos. The exhortation to blow up every monument and start again from scratch had figured in the first Futurist manifesto; the allusion to a new ideal of beauty capable of inspiring the masses is Marinetti verbatim; the renunciation of a solemn and hierarchical architecture Carrà verbatim.[13] The fact that Sant'Elia, in contradiction to his own designs, denounced vertical and horizontal lines and condemned cubes and pyramids as static, heavy and oppressive can only be explained by the pressures of the Futurist system – or by the work of another hand on the texts. The Futurists' fondness for the spiral emerges in a passage that describes snake-like forms of iron and glass that wind their way up the façades of buildings. For the Futurists the spiral symbolized continuous upward movement; in support of their view they invoked no less an ancestry than Giambattista Vico and Henri Bergson.[14]

428–432. Antonio Sant'Elia.
428. Study for the *Città nuova*, 1914. Ink. Villa Comunale dell'Olmo, Como.
429. Study for the *Città nuova*, 1913–14. Ink. Villa Comunale dell'Olmo, Como.
430. Church (?), 1915. Ink and coloured pencil. Villa Comunale dell'Olmo, Como.
431. Stepped building, 1914. Ink and coloured pencil. Villa Comunale dell'Olmo, Como.
432. Façade study, 1915 (?). Chalk. Sant'Elia Family Collection, Como.

431

Sant'Elia's manifesto and drawings occupy a unique position in the history of European architecture. Individual items can be traced back to particular sources, but their inclusion in a single coherent programme remains without precedent. Thus Frank Lloyd Wright and the English country-house architects (and the Art Nouveau or Jugendstil architects too) had already considered buildings as three-dimensional volumes. The rejection of ornament and detail in favour of the beauty of planes and masses had been anticipated by the Viennese, notably by Adolf Loos. Houses with stepped-back elevations had been designed by Loos in 1910 and were actually built in Paris in 1912–13 by Henri Sauvage. The principle of multi-storey traffic systems went back to Leonardo da Vinci. An example close to hand of the practical requirements of the modern city was Milan railway station, with its elevated platforms and layers of underpasses. In 1912 Sant'Elia did some drawings for the architect Cantoni in the competition for the station façade, designs which inspired him to his incomparably more complex combinations of rail, road and air traffic systems (ill. 429).

The forms of Sant'Elia's work also have precedents. His earliest drawings reflect the atmosphere of Milan after the turn of the century, with its amalgam of fairy-tale historicism, picturesque Art Nouveau, and Symbolism. To this mixture Sant'Elia invariably returned whenever he had to please a particular customer: his colleague Giulio U. Arata commended his competition project for a savings bank in Verona (1913–14, in association with Cantoni) as a 'powerfully evocative synthesis of a historical epoch'.[15] When that compliment was offered Sant'Elia had been designing tall monuments, undecorated volumes and bare structural frames for two years. The originality of these inventions is indisputable, even though the organization of masses appears on occasion to have been influenced by Giuseppe Sommaruga, and though Sant'Elia was obviously impressed by the domes and monumental

432

434

433. Mario Chiattone. Buildings for a modern metropolis, 1914. Ink and watercolour. Istituto di Storia dell'Arte, Pisa.
434. Mario Chiattone. Town-planning study, 1914. Ink and watercolour. Istituto di Storia dell'Arte, Pisa.

433

staircases of Otto Wagner and his school (ills. 329, 425, 426).[16]

Only a few of Sant'Elia's drawings seem to have been based on any precise idea of the internal working of the buildings represented, with the exception of the carefully thought-out studies for a *città nuova* published in the Nuove Tendenze catalogue and in the Futurist architecture manifesto. He drew his buildings like sculpture, from outside. Interiors, sections and ground plans are virtually nonexistent; the function which most of his projects was intended to fulfil is a matter for guesswork. Whenever Sant'Elia suggests a topographical setting it is in the Expressionist tradition of plunging slopes or precipitous cliffs, features which lent themselves to a dramatic development of architectural volumes. The rhetoric of this kind of 'expressive and synthetic art'

is strikingly evident. The scaleless monumentality of Sant'Elia's unused and uninhabited architecture makes it hard to believe that such buildings, in the words of the manifesto, 'have a shorter life-span than we do'. The contradiction struck Sant'Elia's contemporaries.[17]

The Futurists never for a moment accepted architecture as the reflection of function, material and construction, as the materialists of modern architecture, in theory at least, were to do. Sant'Elia's architecture sought to project 'the world of the spirit into the world of things'; it was an architecture of expression. In a famous dictum, he (or his ghostwriter) characterized the Futurist house as a gigantic machine – years before Le Corbusier's 'machine for living in'. It is clear from the context of the remark that he did not mean a mere functional apparatus, rationally and economically designed: the dictum was coloured by the same myth of the machine that characterized Marinetti's desire to reconcile man's flesh with the metal of his engines. Sant'Elia's work is an optimistic parallel to the satanic expression of the machine and science in German Expressionist films, such as *Metropolis* (ill. 43).

How much of Sant'Elia's revolutionary spirit would have survived in practice is difficult to determine. His competition designs indicate that he was flexible. One of his last efforts, a series of projects for monumental buildings – probably churches – suggests a readiness to come to terms with tradition (ill. 430). In the summer of 1915 he was drafted into a cycle battalion and a year later he was killed. So little is known of his work in the last two years of his life that we can only guess at its nature; but we have Marinetti's report that, despite the bitter cold, Sant'Elia kept himself amused at the front by building Futuristic architecture in ice and snow.[18]

Mario Chiattone

The work of Mario Chiattone (1891–1957) enjoyed nothing like the attention which both contemporaries and posterity lavished on the work of Sant'Elia, his friend and three years his senior. Even at the Famiglia Artistica exhibition in 1914 Chiattone provoked little or no comment, whereas Sant'Elia was discussed enthusiastically by a number of critics. Chiattone's life, unlike that of his friend, did not lend itself to legend. No manifesto bore his name; no mountain or magazine was named after him. Although he was a friend of Boccioni, he never joined the Futurists, and consequently he missed the hagiographical treatment that Marinetti gave to Sant'Elia. After the First World War Chiattone returned to the Ticino, and his buildings of later years – country houses, schools, an exhibition pavilion, a market hall – were not of the kind to raise a furore in the publications and exhibitions of the Futurists.

435

436

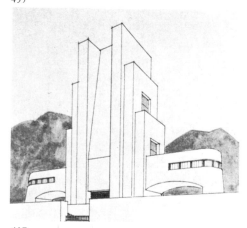

437

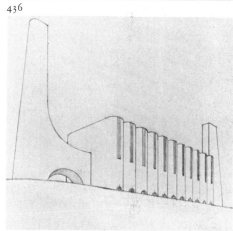

438

439

435–439. Mario Chiattone.
435. Palazzo della Moda, 1914. Pencil and tempera. Istituto di Storia dell'Arte, Pisa.
436. Study, 1914. Pencil, coloured pencil and pastel. Istituto di Storia dell'Arte, Pisa.
437. Head office of a shipping company, 1914. Ink and watercolour. Istituto di Storia dell'Arte, Pisa.
438. Exhibition building III, 1914. Pencil. Istituto di Storia dell'Arte, Pisa.
439. Cathedral I, 1916.

Of Chiattone's surviving drawings only two relate to urban conditions. There is no reason for thinking that others existed, and were destroyed: even in the Famiglia Artistica exhibition, of the three works which Chiattone submitted only one dealt with a city of the future.[19] Problems of urbanism were not his main interest. The two surviving urban studies (ills. 433, 434) are for sites on the water. The lowest of several traffic levels is a canal or a harbour basin, but the organization of buildings in terms of traffic and transport routes is less important than in Sant'Elia's designs. The vast majority of communication elements, particularly vertical ones, appears to be accommodated in the buildings themselves. There are bridges at several levels and one or two steel-frame structures which are perhaps meant to be diagonal cargo-hoists, but the lifts that Sant'Elia designed to climb up the façades are almost entirely absent. Towers and slabs of extravagant slimness, some set back in steps, soar up to a height of seventy storeys, higher than anything that had hitherto been built. The ground plans of these tall slabs are impossible to work out.

Some of Chiattone's works are so close to Sant'Elia's designs in volumetric terms that there are still problems of attribution. Chiattone's work, however, lacks the nervous arresting handwriting, and his perspective lines never cross – a detail that adds to the dynamic impression of Sant'Elia's drawings. Chiattone's buildings are circumscribed by lines that are without life or interest. The coloured grounds with delicately applied shades of apple green, strawberry red, orangy yellow or azure blue betray the former painter. Stylistic parallels are to be found not in Futurist painting but in the trends represented by the magazine *Valori plastici*.

The Futurists attacked *cattedralismo*, but many of Chiattone's projects are for churches. In plan they consist of a nave with single or double aisles and, almost invariably, several choirs or apses. Even his factories, office buildings and exhibition pavilions have an almost religious dignity, with their symmetry, podium structures that seem to set them apart, pairs of bullet-shaped towers, and apse-like sections. They are redolent of the ideals that Carlo Carrà had called a stupid mania in 1913 (and not long afterwards taken up himself): ceremony, solemnity and hierarchy.[20]

Looking back in the last years of his life, Chiattone characterized the aims of the young architects of 1914 as 'free and fresh visions', yet also 'a positive architecture'.[21] For all their air of feasibility, Chiattone's designs went far beyond anything that was being built in his day. His realistic fantasy, which anticipated many later developments, drew upon many sources of inspiration. His sloping skylights had already been used by Mackintosh and van de Velde. The bullet-shaped towers, a favourite motif of the period, had appeared in 1902 in a project by Alois Bastl, a pupil of Wagner, for a 'palace of occultism'; Bastl had described them as beacons 'that remind us of the eternal light' (ill. 329).[22] The clusters of half-cylinders could have come from contemporary illustrations of American silos; Chiattone even applied them to the façades of apartment blocks, giving the proposed apartments remarkably generous bays. Chiattone took the kind of horizontal strip windows that Frank Lloyd Wright used in his prairie houses and Joseph Olbrich in his Hochzeitsturm in Darmstadt and set them in the curved ends of buildings – a device which Erich Mendelsohn was later to use with success.

The movement suggested by Chiattone's designs has of course nothing in common with the vehement dynamics of Mendelsohn. In one or two projects one part of the building thrusts forward, giving a suggestion of sedate motion to the rest of the building against which it seems to be straining (ill. 438). A small pastel sketch of 1914 (ill. 436) reveals a different temperament: it could be the work of Scharoun at the age of fifty. Yet Chiattone's designs remain disciplined volumetric studies. Bathed in lunar light (ill. 439), standing out against a dark ground or suggested with a bare outline, they conjure up the empty silence of the *architettura metafisica* that characterizes de Chirico's paintings of the period. Describing a small, Giotto-like landscape which Carrà painted in 1921, after his Futurist period, Wilhelm Worringer used the phrase 'silent Expressionism'.[23] It applies equally well to Chiattone's architecture.

Virgilio Marchi

The first Futurist design to be translated into reality (a design not otherwise remarkable) came not from the visionaries Sant'Elia or Chiattone but from Virgilio Marchi (1895–1960). It was the conversion of the Casa d'Arte and the Teatro degli Indipendenti in Rome, commissioned in 1921 by the critic and entrepreneur Anton Giulio Bragaglia, and it included a feature which would have appealed to Finsterlin. (Some of Marchi's extraordinarily varied sketches are indeed reminiscent of the Finsterlin/Gaudí tradition.) For Bragaglia he built a theatre bar in the labyrinth of subterranean vaults and passages of the Roman baths in Via degli Avignonesi. He clad the old Roman walls in a concrete shell, exploited the irregularities of the ruins to produce a free plan, and introduced mysterious indirect lighting (ill. 440). Instead of a breakthrough into the new technical era promised by Marinetti and his friends, the first Futurist building was a bizarre medley of cave romanticism and building conversion.

Marchi evolved his aesthetic in two books, *Architettura futurista* (written in 1919) and *Italia nuova architettura nuova* (1931); it is distinguished by changes of emphasis from the canonical writings of Futurism, to which Marchi nonetheless

440–444. Virgilio Marchi.
440. Bar of the Casa Bragaglia, Rome.
441. Hotel.
442. Futurist adaptation of an existing skeleton construction.
443. Building seen from a circling aeroplane.
444. Elevated-railway station.

440

442

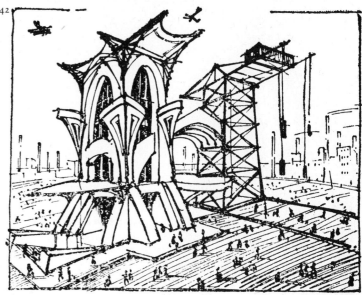

443

441

444

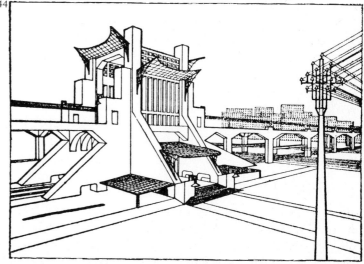

445. Virgilio Marchi. Abstract architecture, from *Architettura futurista*, Foligno, 1924.

continually referred. The *gusto del pratico* ('taste for the practical'), a phrase from the 1914 manifesto, took second place to an architecture intended to mirror the state of the soul. 'It is quite obvious . . . that at the beginning of such investigations the artist is exclusively concerned with finding the new form, and with it himself, without thereby thinking about later possibilities of development. Consequently there should be no pedantry about such studies, which will be naturally nervous, feverish, and even filled with a naïve primitivism.'[24]

Marchi's 'naïve primitivism' echoes the 'primitives of a new sensibility' of the painting manifesto of 1910. But at the same time it involved a new, non-practical idealism. As with the Utopians of the Glass Chain, form was considered independently of its materialization. For the first generation of Futurists architecture was the expression of universal life with its bursting energy and productivity, but Marchi took the Futurist position to imply the right of any man to individual expression. Futurism, he thought, was a style of dynamism and freedom, and hence could only be the particular style of an individual artist.

The formal 'deformations, or better: exaltations' were to arise out of the play of forces of the construction and its materials. But Marchi had in mind neither a logically consistent expression of the 'inner life' of the building nor the kind of symbolic expression practised by the Expressionists. In his book *Architettura futurista* he included an illustration to show how the framework of a steel crane, decorated with scenery flats, could be disguised as Futurist architecture (ill. 442). Marchi justified such fantastic designs, which he described as 'Futurist decoration', by referring to the didactic nature of traditional heraldic ornament. This argument clearly furnished him with yet another reason for later incorporating in his designs for airport buildings and bridgeheads the Fascist symbol of the *fasces*.

Marchi's designs imply criticism of Sant'Elia. He considered that Sant'Elia had stuck too closely to the rectangular forms of American skyscrapers, and countered this with an architecture of curved surfaces, lines of force and free forms that was intended to match every conceivable line of movement both in the vertical and in the horizontal. He justified this as an analogy to the new means of propulsion and new possibilities of experience, for instance from a circling aeroplane (ill. 443). The organization of traffic, however, which was of cardinal importance in Sant'Elia's drawings, did not much interest him. Marchi's drawing of an elevated-railway station, which is reminiscent of Otto Wagner both in its subject matter and in its form (ill. 444), does not even begin to suggest the kind of complex problems that Wagner faced in tackling the Vienna Stadtbahn. Marchi was content to include flimsy and meaningless pedestrian bridges, simply to give his creations a futuristic air (ills. 42, 441). Such sketches seem more like stage designs than like real architecture, and indeed, like Fortunato Depero and Enrico Prampolini, Marchi did work primarily for the theatre.

Stage sets, exhibition pavilions and interiors: these were the main themes that Luigi Colombo Fillía offered in 1928 in his Exhibition of Futurist Architecture. It was the first such exhibition, and it was also the last, despite the hope of many that Futurism might become the national architecture of Fascism.

By 1928 the Futurists had already retreated far from their original positions. They now felt themselves to be the defenders of *classicità*,[25] upholding musicality, inspiration and imagination against the inroads of the younger generation's rationalism; and at the same time they felt themselves threatened by the growing classicism of the Roman traditionalists.

Roots in tradition

Without the Dutch, we should never have known what Expressionist architecture would look like on a large scale. From the time of the First World War into the 1920s, Dutch architects had the same optimistic belief in the future as the Germans. Architecture was to provide the temple 'in which God and man, truly united, perform their common task' (de Bazel). The younger Dutch architects saw themselves as builders of the new humanity. In this atmosphere of anticipation of a new unity, harmony and joy, the 'certainty that knows' and the 'power that can' (Wijdeveld), even such ideas as Taut's *Stadtkrone* appeared half-hearted. 'A light or fire Taut's work is not,' wrote Jan Frederik Staal.[1]

In contrast to the situation in Germany, the Dutch radicals were not only able to but indeed forced to subject their imaginations to the test of reality. The test consisted not in individual commissions of an eccentric and private nature, but in the most urgent architectural task facing Europe – mass housing.

Although Holland had not been directly affected by the war, there was a housing shortage. The uncertainty of the political situation, high interest rates and costs, and a shortage of building materials had severely restricted building activity. In Amsterdam alone in 1918 the shortage of dwellings was estimated at 15,000–16,000. Only about 1,400 homes were built in that year, while the demand rose by 2,700. One of the most extraordinary features of the Dutch scene is the fact that, given these circumstances, the state and local authorities considered aesthetics at all, and did not simply build the big subsidized residential estates of Amsterdam South and West in the most basic way possible.

Dutch architects were able to begin with assumptions which in Germany simply did not exist. In Holland there was widespread acceptance of the need for planning. A country that owed its physical existence to a continuing planning process could not be blind to the fact that architecture and town planning must be thought out as methodically as the business of dike construction and land reclamation. The Dutch housing law of 1901 was an exemplary document for its time. It prescribed loans for communal, public-benefit building cooperatives, charged local authorities with supervising building and laying down long-term planning proposals, and also gave them powers of expropriation.

The repeated revisions of the plan for Amsterdam South under Berlage is an example of how persistently town-planning considerations were pursued in Holland. There seems to have been less hostility to control in Holland than elsewhere. In the Deutsche Werkbund the artists among the architects fought obstinately for their right to free, untrammelled creativity; in Holland there was wide approval for a regulation requiring that housing designs be submitted to fine art commissions.

This sense of the social responsibilities of the architect was matched in the public sphere by a feeling of responsibility towards architecture. In Berlin progressive architects fought constantly against the conservative City Architect Ludwig Hoffmann up until 1924, the year of his retirement. By that time in Holland avantgarde architects held positions of responsibility or were the recipients of important local authority commissions. Berlage, Dudok, van Eesteren, Kramer, Oud, and many others planned and built either directly in the service of or on behalf of the public authorities. The designs put out by the building department of the city of Amsterdam rivalled those of independent architects. Even the excesses of Expressionist architecture were firmly bound up in the Dutch architectural tradition. Architects could count on the traditional brick-building skills of Dutch craftsmen and contractors, on the interest of the public authorities, and on the relatively high standards set by developers and the public.

Dutch architecture is urban architecture. The high density of population in the triangular agglomeration formed by The Hague, Amsterdam and Arnhem ruled out the distinction between town and country architecture, between urbanism and the garden city, that preoccupied German revolutionary architects. The ideal of the garden city was widespread in Holland too, in fact: architects like Jan Gratama and Marinus Jan Granpré Molière used low-rise building for preference, but the predominance of two-storey terraced housing meant that even here relatively high densities were achieved. The street continued to be treated as an integrating element. Even J. J. P. Oud, that early representative of the New Architecture, in his Rotterdam housing-estate projects ranging from Spangen (1918–20) to Kiefhoek (1925–29), rejected the parallel rows of buildings set at right angles to the street that became a town-planning dogma in other countries.

Even in the twenties the major Amsterdam housing developments were based on layouts with grass courtyards. Streets were conceived as spatial units and façades treated as defining not only the buildings themselves but also the streets. The Dutch custom of paving both roadway and pavements with vitrified brick meant that the formal unity of street and wall was expressed in terms of building material as well. The chief difference between Berlage's revised plan for Amsterdam South of 1915 and his version of 1900–1905 lay in the stress on the street and in the elimination of garden-city elements. Berlage did not see this as a surrender to pressures to make more use of the land. In fact he recommended architecturally uniform block develop-

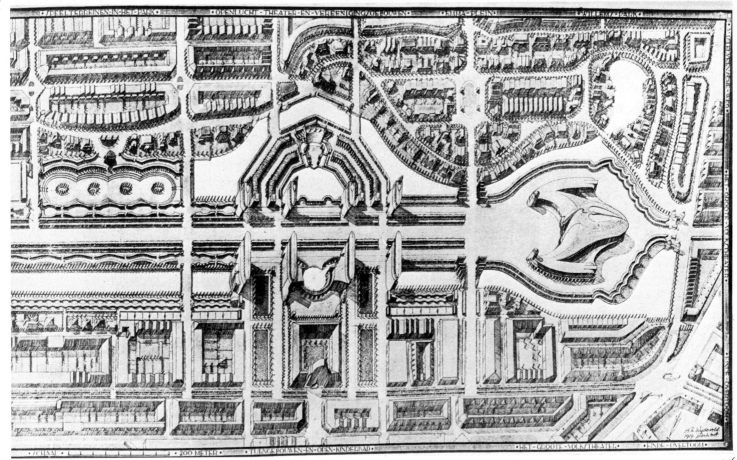

446

446. Hendrikus Theodorus Wijdeveld. Project for the development of the Vondelpark in Amsterdam with tower blocks and theatre (detail), 1919.

ment as a healthy 'reaction against the rampant formal degeneration' that characterized individually conceived detached houses.[2]

The urban tradition and the processes of industrialization and standardization were taken far too much for granted in Holland for there to be any chance of the metropolis-worship of the Italian Futurists, though the proposal by Hendrikus Theodorus Wijdeveld (b. 1885) to turn the Vondelpark in Amsterdam into a boulevard lined with tower blocks and cultural buildings (ill. 446) was dictated by a ruthless passion for metropolitan traffic that recalls Sant'Elia's *città nuova*.[3] The Futurists' adulation of the machine, however, which found a powerful echo among the members of the De Stijl group, was unacceptable to Wijdeveld – as it was to all his contemporaries in the school of Amsterdam.

The lessons of Berlage

In Holland the traditions to which even Expressionist architects were bound were represented by three important established architects: Petrus Josephus Hubertus Cuijpers (1827–1921), Hendrik Petrus Berlage (1856–1934), and, to a lesser extent, Willem Kromhout (1846–1940). Cuijpers' achievement lay in the past. He had freed Dutch architecture from the constraints of historical imitation, if not from historical styles themselves. In his delicately articulated façades, which made free and personal use of Late Gothic and Renaissance features, Dutch brick resumed its old importance, which had been challenged in the stucco buildings of the earlier nineteenth century. Cuijpers used brick surface decoration in a manner that paved the way for the virtuoso performances of the Expressionists.

Berlage occupied an intermediary position: his mature buildings seem original when compared with Cuijpers' work, but historicist when compared with later developments. The heaviness and austere earnestness of his works, from the Amsterdam Exchange (ill. 449) to the Hoenderloo hunting lodge (ills. 451, 452), suggests Romanesque architecture, even when they do not have round arches, arcades, galleries and triforiums. Berlage's 'architecture of the wall' favoured the solid wall surface with holes punched into it. Structurally important points such as springers, keystones and lintels are picked out in stone, in the form of blocks let into the brickwork and not allowed to interrupt the flat surface of the wall.

This surface tensioning, drawing different parts of a building together into a continuum, was one of the ways in which younger architects learned to overcome the problems of extended façades in the new housing estates. It did not rule out sculptural effects – rather the opposite. Berlage's flat surfaces and those of the Amsterdam school are in no way like the clear-cut planar elements of the later De Stijl and International Modern. They were the smoothed-off surfaces of a massive, tangible volume – the wall, which firmly and securely enclosed hollow volumes, the rooms of the interior.

Where freedom in the choice of forms was concerned, Kromhout's lordly arrogance was more sympathetic to the younger generation than Berlage's solidity and discipline. Yet even in Kromhout's American Hotel on the Leidseplein in Amsterdam (ill. 447) uninterrupted surfaces continue across different parts of the building. A similarly smooth transition is effected on the corner of the Noordzee office building in Rotterdam behind fragile, vertical strips of wall (ill. 448).

Berlage remained the great authority right up into the twenties. His buildings were accompanied by a convincing body of theory. His influence went far beyond individual groups and architectural trends (of course many influences were also absorbed into his own later work). His name was invoked as frequently by the De Stijl artists as by their arch-opponents, the architects of the school of Amsterdam. Berlage himself was on the side of the Amsterdam architects; he built with them (Amsterdam West) and saw in them the guarantors of a Dutch national architectural style.[4] The different parties took up particular aspects of his theory. The Expressionists, for example, agreed with his demand for unity in diversity, shared his opinion that architecture would eclipse painting and sculpture in importance in the twentieth century, and even took an interest in his geometrical studies. On the other hand they showed no interest in his belief in the importance of construction as a determinant of design or in his equation of 'style' and 'calm'.

The cautious Berlage in fact went further than his young admirers in the realm of architectural metaphor. In Holland too pictorial associations played an important part in Expressionist architecture: Margaret Kropholler (1891–1966) and her husband Jan Frederik Staal (1879–1940) built houses in Park Meerwijk in Bergen (ills. 382, 383) which suggested ancient ships, and were named 'The Ark' or 'The Longboat'. But no Dutch building of the period is so thoroughly metaphorical as Berlage's Pantheon of Mankind or his hunting lodge at Hoenderloo (ills. 105, 450–452).

The hunting lodge of the Kröller-Müllers is situated in the forest and moorland landscape of the Veluwe on an artificial lake created specially for it. At the request of Mrs Kröller-Müller, the iconographical programme was based on the legend of St Hubert, bishop of Liège.[5] The ground plan in the form of branching antlers (ill. 450) alludes to the stag bearing a crucifix which appeared to Hubert when he was hunting on Good Friday. The building itself is complicated, with a multitude of picturesque views (ill. 451). These have the effect of obscuring its symmetry, particularly since the approaches to the house do not lie along the principal axes, and since from every angle parts of the building overlap other parts.

447

448

447. Willem Kromhout. American Hotel, Amsterdam, 1898–1901.
448. Willem Kromhout. Noordzee building, Rotterdam, 1917–18.

The place of the crucifix between the antlers is taken by a tower thirty metres high which seems to draw the building upwards with it and which dominates the view from a distance.

The rooms inside are fully in accord with the iconographic programme, and suggest a series of carefully planned moods. The sad and solemn hall of exposed brick is intended to evoke Hubert's youth (ill. 452). The main room lying along the terrace is decorated with tile and glass mosaic to symbolize the gay life at court (according to the legend, Hubert lived at the court of King Pepin). The apse terminating the northern side, with its high-set windows, represents a place of contemplation. Its counterpart, the apsidal tea room with large windows facing south, symbolizes the light that illuminated the saint. The adjoining room, Mrs Kröller-Müller's *salon*, was meant to embody the clear conscience – a fact that strikes the modern visitor as somewhat comic. Crucifix and antlers are of course a recurring motif in the interior decoration too, in the linen fabric, chair-covers, and carving of the dresser.

In his work for the Kröller-Müllers, Berlage committed himself for ten years exclusively to the service of a single banking and ship-owning family (though in fact he broke off the relationship prematurely). But he was also a pioneer of social reform, and the fact that the doyen of Dutch architects supported the working-class movement marks the difference between the Dutch and German situations. When the young German architects of 1918 wanted to reform society as well as to renew form, they felt like revolutionaries acting independently. Dutch architects fired with similar ideals could follow a tradition. Their magazine, *Wendingen* (see below), might denounce capitalism and proclaim a communist society: Berlage had already expressed his readiness to combat the social injustice of his time and the pernicious influence of capital more than a decade earlier. For a new style he was prepared to give not only a kingdom but heaven itself, yet when he defined the architecture of the future he ignored style and saw it as 'the material reflection . . . of the emergence of the principle of economic equality'.[6]

Wendingen

The mouthpiece of the Expressionist generation in Holland was *Wendingen*, a connoisseur's magazine presented in Wijdeveld's baffling typography inspired by Lauweriks (ill. 453). Issues were devoted to architecture, interior decoration, the plastic and graphic arts, the theatre, and also to other topics which the editor-in-chief, Wijdeveld, thought particularly stimulating or tropical, such as the crystal or the shell. Illustrations were given much importance. Wijdeveld himself was a persuasive writer, though no theorist; architects like de Klerk and Kramer avoided writing altogether.

In accordance with the Expressionist belief in the individual, *Wendingen* presented architecture in terms of personalities. The young Michel de Klerk (1884–1923) was built up as a mythical hero in Holland – much as Sant'Elia was in Italy – primarily through the propaganda in *Wendingen*. Frank Lloyd Wright, one of the magazine's idols, occupied seven numbers in one year, more than half the year's issues; though there was scepticism concerning Wright's extravagance and warnings against 'the piping of this Pied Piper of architecture' (Oud).[7]

In Germany the publications of architectural Expressionists were the underground of the professional press, appearing as manifestos, privately duplicated letters, or, like *Frühlicht*, as the hobby-horse of a particular individual. *Wendingen* by contrast was published by one of Holland's two architectural associations, Architectura et Amicitia; in 1918, when the magazine was first published, the association had 555 members. The magazine sought to be a forum for all current topics. The word *wendingen* (the plural of *wending*) has the same etymology as the English 'windings', but it would be more

449

449. Hendrik Petrus Berlage. Exchange, Amsterdam, 1898–1903. From *Studies over bouwkunst, stijl en samenleving*, Rotterdam, 1910. Drawing by J. Briedé.
450–452. Hendrik Petrus Berlage. 'St Hubert' hunting lodge, Hoenderloo, 1914–20.
450. Plan of the ground floor: 1 terrace, 2 living room, 3 kitchen, 4 boudoir, 5 hall, 6 apartments.
451. Exterior.
452. Hall.

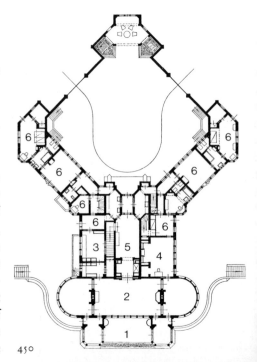

450

451

452

accurately rendered as 'turnings', for in Dutch it suggests 'turning points' and even 'new eras'. The plural was intended – *wendingen* rather than *wending*. In the first issue, Wijdeveld outlined his intention of enabling the reader to 'meander through all these expressions of art, to contemplate with pleasure tendencies which, informed with a powerful impulse, are preparing the way for the harmony of the future.' Wijdeveld left his readers in no doubt, however, as to his preference for an architecture that turned seemingly intractable materials into subtle architectural sculpture. Editorially, the magazine cultivated a very particular type of broadmindedness: it publicized whatever was new, but reduced everything to the common denominator of Amsterdam Expressionism.

Wendingen included the New Architecture, but the space allotted to it was carefully rationed. When a critical appraisal of Wright was needed, even the architects of De Stijl, such as Oud and Jan Wils, were invited to contribute. Before the founding of the magazine *De Stijl*, Wijdeveld had tried to get Theo van Doesburg to work with him.[8] *Wendingen* took syncretism so far as to give one of its issues on Wright a cover designed by, of all people, El Lissitzky. In later years this policy of studied diversity led to meaningless juxtapositions. The twisted romanticism of Rothenburg ob der Tauber might be found next to the manifest functionalism of the van Nelle factory in Rotterdam by Brinkman and van der Vlugt.

Relations between the younger German architects and the members of the

Wendingen group were close. Mendelsohn visited Holland in 1919 and 1923, lectured at the invitation of Architectura et Amicitia, and was friendly with Wijdeveld, with whom at the beginning of the thirties he wanted to found an international 'Académie de la Méditerranée'. Otto Bartning and Bruno Taut reviewed buildings of both the Amsterdam and Rotterdam schools. The 'worthy inn of *Wendingen*', in Finsterlin's phrase, saw many a German 'brother lodger'. Whole issues of the magazine were devoted to Mendelsohn in 1920 and to Finsterlin in 1924. After his 1920 visit Adolf Behne sent in designs by German architects, tried to organize an exhibition of Dutch architecture for the Arbeitsrat für Kunst, and generally made full use of his newly-won contacts for publicity.[9] Four years later Oud pub-

WENDINGEN

MAANDBLAD · VOOR · BOUWEN · EN · SIEREN = VAN · ARCHITECTURA · ET · AMICITIA

HOOFDREDACTEUR ARCHITECT H. TH. WIJDEVELD, VOSSIUSSTRAAT 50, AMSTERDAM. TELEF. 26616
LEDEN DER COMMISSIE VAN REDACTIE: J. G. BOTERENBROOD — H. A. VAN DEN EIJNDE — J. F.
STAAL — P. L. KRAMER — J. L. M. LAUWERIKS — J. B. VAN LOGHEM EN R. N. ROLAND HOLST
WENDINGEN, ORGAAN VAN HET GENOOTSCHAP ARCHITECTURA ET AMICITIA TE AMSTERDAM,
VERSCHIJNT IN DE NEDERLANDSCHE TAAL EN SOMS IN ENGELSCH, FRANSCH OF DUITSCH
WENDINGEN WORDT UITGEGEVEN DOOR DE N. V. UITGEVERS MIJ „DE HOOGE BRUG" AMSTERDAM
GEDRUKT BIJ GERHARD STALLING AKTIEN-GESELLSCHAFT TE OLDENBURG I. O. (DUITSCHLAND)
ABONNEMENT BIJ DE UITGEVERS, OF BIJ DEN BOEKHANDEL

No 6   DIT IS NUMMER 11 EN 12
                    VAN DE 5DE SERIE (1923)
                    EN GEWIJD AAN DE UIT-
                    GEVOERDE PROJECTEN
                    DER ARCHITECTEN EN
                    RIJKSDIENST C. J. BLAAUW
                    J. CROUWEL EN J. M. LUTH-
                    MANN. DE OMSLAG IS EEN
                    HOUTSNEDE DOOR S.
                    JESSURUN DE MESQUITA

453. Hendrikus Theodorus Wijdeveld. Mast-head of *Wendingen*, v, nos. 11–12, 1923.

lished his statement in the *Bauhausbücher* series, a statement that largely determined the verdict of contemporaries and historians on his work. With the opposing viewpoints of its different schools, and its outstanding personalities who offered something for everyone, Dutch architecture remained a subject of constant interest as far as the German architectural press was concerned.

In these exchanges the Dutch found confirmation and the Germans stimulation. Berlage's German publications gave him a tremendous influence in Germany and Switzerland. He assumed a position of moral authority that no one had held in either country since Gottfried Semper. 'Where did Truth ever reveal her body with such purity and innocence before?' asked Taut with reference to Berlage's buildings.[10] The role in Germany of De Stijl and particularly of van Doesburg has often been commented on, but the Amsterdam architects also had an effect. Bruno Taut's Schillerpark estate in Berlin-Wedding (1924–25), with its honestly expressed brick and concrete construction, curious tapering piers above the balconies, and crowded entrances, was redolent of the themes of Amsterdam South and the Spaarndammerplantsoen façades of the Eigen Haard estate.[11]

Façade architecture

The spectacular prelude to Amsterdam's architectural Expressionism was provided by van der Meij's Scheepvaarthuis, or Shipping House (ills. 454–457). Johan Melchior van der Meij (1878–1949) had worked with de Klerk and Pieter Lodewijk Kramer (1881–1961) in the office of Eduard Cuijpers, a nephew of the great Cuijpers, and subsequently for the City Architect's office. He took his two younger colleagues with him as associates for the new office-block project. The Scheepvaarthuis is a framed reinforced-concrete structure with columns organized to create corridor access and very large office areas. The structural grid is expressed on the brick, terracotta and concrete façade in the form of wide piers. With the exception of this feature, however, what distinguishes the building most is the highly inventive, even eccentric, imagination it reveals: the details seem to have been designed deliberately to look like nothing that had ever been seen before.

The integration of plastic and graphic arts in building was something Cuijpers and Berlage had long since sought to achieve. In the case of the Scheepvaarthuis, however, integration is not quite the right word. The construction has the look of a frame over which the exotic trophies of a sculptural architecture have been strewn. Van der Meij's imagination did not stop at façades. The form of the hall that cuts through the building diagonally, and the staircase sides, which are partly open and partly solid, are no less striking.

Iconographically the building is intended to symbolize the world opened up by maritime exploration. Figures representing the Atlantic, Indian and Pacific Oceans and the Mediterranean guard the entrance, and there are many motifs derived from the fittings and equipment of ships. Berlage had used a similar rhetoric in his Exchange, deriving ornamental motifs from different articles of commerce such as tobacco, grapes, rice, and so on.

The Scheepvaarthuis's smallness of detail and its verticality set it apart from the subsequent works of the school of Amsterdam. Even in the buildings which de Klerk and Kramer were designing at the same time (the Hille apartment house, Amsterdam, 1911, by de Klerk, and the Sailors' Union in Den Helder, 1911–14, by Kramer), they reverted to the broader conception of the wall that they had learned from Berlage. The external surfaces were treated like some kind of elastic modelling material and made to look as though they were under tension. There are wave forms on Piet Kramer's monumental but delicately modelled corner structures (ill. 459); the wall surfaces roll together in cylinders towards the entrances in buildings by Margaret Kropholler and Jan Frederik Staal (ill. 461), burst open to form a deep cleft in a porch by Staal (ill. 463); in Jan Boterenbrood's Rijnstraat housing angular oriels project and are squeezed back into the wall (ill. 460).

Certain peculiarities of Dutch apartment houses provided some basis for these antics. In multi-storey buildings each flat often had its own staircase. The large number of house doors and the complex staircase layout led to a concentration of forms around the entrance area which contrasted effectively with the undisturbed surfaces of the façades. The staircases were correspondingly narrow and steep – Amsterdam regulations permitted angles of ascent of up to 50° – so that when people moved house their furniture had to be hauled up the front of the building and taken in through the windows. This required projecting hoists, which were then treated as plastic elements.

The architecture of the new residential quarters of Amsterdam was to a very large extent façade architecture. In order to get their buildings past the Commissie van Vier builders had to call in architects to design their exteriors, but the standard plans remained unchanged. The fact that this procedure degraded the architect's contribution to the level of a cosmetic

454

455

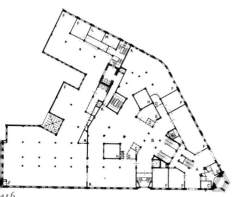

456

454–457. Johan Melchior van der Meij.
Scheepvaarthuis, Amsterdam, 1911–16.
454. Exterior.
455. Main entrance.
456. Plan of the ground floor.
457. Staircase.

457

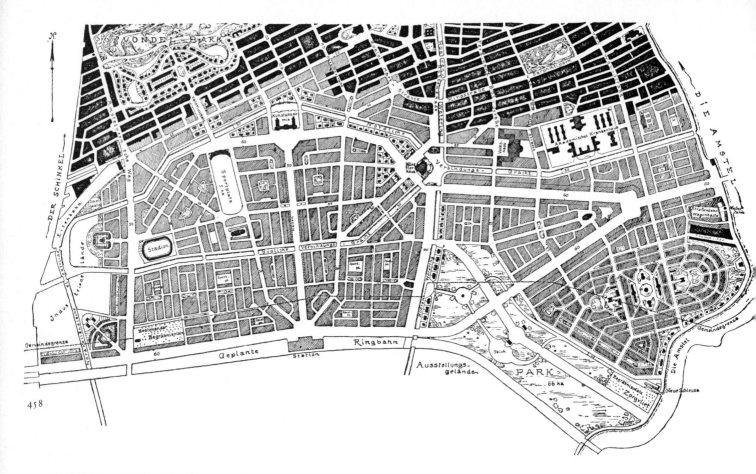

458

458. Hendrik Petrus Berlage. Development plan for Amsterdam South, 1915.
459. Pieter Lodewijk Kramer. Flats, Pieter Lodewijk Takstraat/Burgemeester Tellegenstraat (De Dageraad estate), Amsterdam South, 1918–23.
460. Jan Boterenbrood. Flats, Rijnstraat, Amsterdam South, before 1923.
461. Margaret Kropholler. Flats, Holendrechtstraat, Amsterdam South, 1922.

459

460

461

activity was felt by the Amsterdam architects themselves; yet, as J. P. Mieras asked in *Wendingen*, 'which is better – rotten houses with rotten façades or rotten houses with good façades?'[12]

The adjective 'good' is not one that has often been applied to the façades of Amsterdam South and Amsterdam West since the twenties. The desire for the 'sparklingly new, the sensationally shocking' which de Klerk and his friends regardes as the essence of modernity seems in retrospect to have been excessive.[13] Nevertheless, however subjective the individual solutions may have been, they all merge into a single, homogeneous whole. This harmonious blend of heterogeneous elements was only achieved through the universal acceptance of tradition and an obligation to attain the highest flights of imagination. Their uniformity is the opposite of standardization: it is Berlage's 'unity in diversity'.

This idiosyncratic architecture also had a social significance, in that its individuality appealed to the individual in every citizen. Through purely formal means each street and block in Amsterdam South and Amsterdam West was given a distinctive character with which its inhabitants could identify. Many of the architects concerned, as well as their critics, realized that this achievement clashed with the essence of mass housing, but a strictly functional expression of these suburbs with their many identical plans would have led to monotony.

The Amsterdam school architects rejected monotony as inhuman: 'The twenty-two centimetres of the façade wall must achieve the miracle, must bring deliverance from that which man unconsciously fears – the piling up of houses in a way that kills all illusion, and the inexorable human levelling process that accompanies this.'[14] Their 'fancy-dress architecture', as it was often called, was not solely due to the unfortunate division of labour between architect and builder. It was also the result of a deliberate choice in favour of what, in the circumstances, appeared to be the humanitarian solution.

The development plans for the southern and western extensions to the city were coloured but not dominated by a number of characteristic features. In the revised plan for Amsterdam South (ill. 458) Berlage drew out the principal arterial roads and laid across this system a second east-west system which featured Y-shaped junctions of streets and canals. The superimposition of the two systems gave rise to an alternately tight and open arrangement. Little squares dot the plan like islands. The formal and functional centre of Amsterdam West is the arcaded Mercatorplein, on which Berlage was able to erect one of his towers (ill. 462). Long streets are interrupted or slightly curved in order to avoid endless perspectives.

462. Cornelis Jonke Blaauw. Flats, Orteliusstraat, Amsterdam West, 1925–27. In the background is a tower block by Hendrik Petrus Berlage.

463. Jan Frederik Staal. Flats, John Franklinstraat, Amsterdam West, 1925.

462

463

464

464–466. Michel de Klerk. Flats, Spaarndammerbuurt (Eigen Haard estate), Amsterdam,
1913–19.
464. Flats, Zaanstraat, 1918. Entrance.
465. Site plan.
466. Flats, Hembrugstraat, 1918.

465

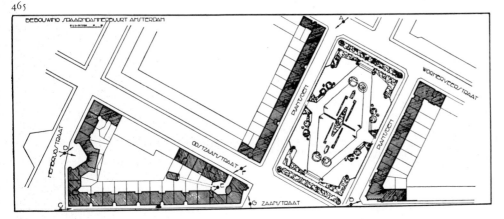

466

Michel de Klerk

No one made fuller use of the scope allowed him than Michel de Klerk, the youthful genius and symbolic figurehead of the school of Amsterdam. Later after his death in 1923 at the age of thirty-nine, he was blamed for all the sins, real and imagined, of the *Wendingen* architects. His associates have left us a portrait of him painted in the most glowing colours – enthusiastic, spontaneous and unconstrained, not without a touch of melancholy; a talented draughtsman and cabinetmaker, a master of sculptural modelling and a virtuoso in matters of detail. 'The power of conviction that radiates from his drawings gives us that curious, happy feeling of being closer to the Almighty', wrote Piet Kramer.[15]

The vision of a better world which friends say inflamed de Klerk was not affected by petty considerations of the way of life of the people for whom he was planning. De Klerk wanted to make people happy not by plans but by forms, for which he sacrificed much. On the estate built for the Eigen Haard ('Own Hearth') housing society in western Amsterdam (a triangle and two sides of a square, ills. 464–468), he broke more than one professional rule. He set bricks vertically or in undulating courses. He clad upper storeys with roof tiles, thus drawing them into the roof zone although they were just as much a part of the vertical wall plane as the lower storeys. On the façade of the flats of the post office building, at the acute angle of the triangular block, he squashed the horizontal lines of windows together, making things very awkward for the inhabitants of these otherwise ordinary rooms (ill. 467).

De Klerk's forms arouse expectations which they do not always fulfil. The exotic obelisk at the base of the isosceles triangle (ill. 466), a distinguishing symbol *par excellence*, in fact distinguishes nothing, unless it be one of the flats which are unusually shaped as a result of the little recess on the Hembrugstraat. De Klerk introduced such effects according to picturesque criteria. The obelisk, for example, was intended as the *point de vue* of an alley running within the block from the post office to a small communal utility building; from Hembrugstraat, the façades of the houses make it look Lilliputian.

The buildings of German Expressionism were generally a symbolic transfiguration of a particular (if idiosyncratically interpreted) functional end. De Klerk freed himself from even this constraint. He created a fantastic environment which had nothing to do with its programmatic purpose beyond the fact that it could be lived in. Nevertheless these wilful expressions of a brilliant talent are characterized in their scale, in their use of ordinary, traditional materials, and in their changing spatial composition by a warm humanity that can be felt at once.

The forms which de Klerk used in his later buildings in Amsterdam South are easier to justify. In comparison with the immense wealth of motifs in the Spaarndammerplantsoen (but only in comparison with that) there is a hint of the self control which even the school of Amsterdam could not ultimately avoid. The balconies linked by semicircular oriels flickering across the long façade wall like a flash of lightning symbolize, on the busy Amstellaan with its heavy traffic, the tempo of modern life (ill. 469). Even from a fast-moving car the bold formal cohesion of the whole is immediately felt. The price paid for this striking motif was the provision of no more than a few flats with south-facing balconies.

On two small squares in the southern part of Amsterdam de Klerk conjured up a totally different atmosphere (ill. 470). Here, where the context allowed an idyllic element, he divided up one side of each square into individual house units to which he gave playful façades. These are not single-family houses, as the exterior suggests, but apartment houses for six tenants each; but the middle-class inhabitants certainly had no objection to the bold deception that made them – in appearance, at least – owners of individual houses.

467, 468. Michel de Klerk. Flats, Spaarndammerbuurt (Eigen Haard estate), Amsterdam.
467. Post office, Zaanstraat/Oostzaanstraat, 1917–18.
468. Flats, Hembrugstraat/Zaanstraat/Oostzaanstraat. View along the internal alley, looking towards the utility building and obelisk.

467

468

Sculptural architecture

The sculptural character that Amsterdam architects tried to give to their street façades was naturally easier to achieve in the case of free-standing buildings. Pieter Vorkink (1878–1960) and his associate J. P. Wormser, who spent most of their time on workers' flats, must have been delighted by the commission to build a rich country house, t'Reigersnest in Oostvoorne (ills. 471, 472). They treated the architecture as an extension of the landscape; the thatched roof of the little pavilion on top of the dunes looked like a hillock. In the main building the division of the plan into a central living area and two wings, one for the kitchen and one for the bedrooms, is countered by the continually rising and falling line of the roof

ridge and the modulated planes of the roof itself. These variations in height also serve to accentuate the individual parts of the building according to their importance.

Powerful roof structures were used again and again in the architecture of the school of Amsterdam to draw together a variety of different functions into one homogeneous building. In the agricultural college at Wageningen (ill. 474), for example, Cornelis Jonke Blaauw (1885–1946) united offices, laboratories and lecture rooms under a single roof. The narrow ends of these elongated buildings are shaped like the prow and stern of the old cog ships of the Hanseatic traders.

Dutch traditions undoubtedly had a beneficial effect on the architecture of these years. Many of the eccentricities of

the *Wendingen* architects would have been unacceptable had they not had a remote similarity to familiar prototypes. The varied mixture of Amsterdam South was not unlike the harmonious blend of different styles along the canals in old Amsterdam. Tradition also had a negative effect, however, for it prevented Dutch architects from exploiting to the full their inclination to treat form sculpturally. With their fixation on brick they deliberately ignored the possibilities of reinforced concrete; though Berlage had, in fact – not without some apprehension – recognized reinforced concrete as the material for the monumental architecture of the future. The country-house architect Adolph Eijbink (b. 1893) had also pointed out the sculptural properties of concrete in an article in *Wendingen*, claiming that its capacity for withstanding pressure and tension from any direction made it not a dead material but a living organism: 'reinforced concrete is therefore . . . on a higher level than other materials used in building.'[16]

In Holland at the time, however, only one architect exploited the monolithic structural properties and the plasticity of reinforced concrete. This was Julius Maria Luthmann (b. 1890) who used the new material for water towers and for an imposing radio station at Kootwijk (ill. 473).

469

470

469. Michel de Klerk. Flats, Amstellaan, Amsterdam South, 1920–22.
470. Michel de Klerk. Flats, Henriette Ronnerplein, Amsterdam South, 1920–21.

471

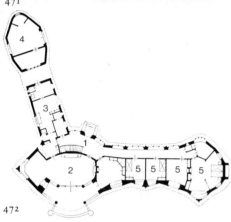

472

473

471, 472. Pieter Vorkink and J. P. Wormser.
'Reigersnest house, Oostvoorne, 1920–21.
View from the garden, and plan of the ground
floor: 1 entrance, 2 living room, 3 kitchen wing,
4 garage, 5 bedroom.
473. Julius Maria Luthmann. Radio station,
Kootwijk, 1920–22.
474. Cornelis Jonke Blaauw. Laboratory for
plant physiology, College of Agriculture,
Wageningen, 1921. Design, modified during
construction.

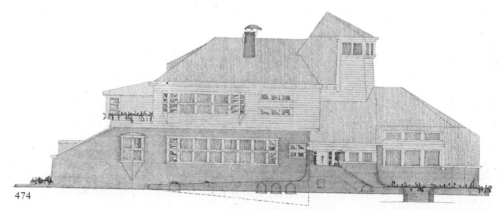

474

16 Expressionism and the New Architecture

'He derided the emperor whom he was committed to serve and from whom he received his pay . . .'

Uriel Birnbaum, *Der Kaiser und der Architekt*, Leipzig and Vienna, 1924

Working with realities

The picture that the Expressionists had of the architect of genius was nowhere more strikingly portrayed than in the tale of *Der Kaiser und der Architekt* (ills. 69, 475, 476) by the Austrian artist and poet Uriel Birnbaum (1894–1956). His book appeared in 1924, when the height of the storm was already past, and it contained not only a description but also a critique of the Expressionist artist: seen from outside, the Messianic attitude of the Expressionists seemed like mischievous caprice, if not indeed inspired by the devil. Birn-

baum's architect has entered the service of an emperor who is consumed with longing for a heavenly city which has appeared to him in a dream. The emperor's subjects regard their lord's architect as part agitator, part fool and part tempter. But the emperor gets him to build one city after another – thirty-three cities in all, representing the entire range of contemporary architectural ideals: cities in yellow, blue, black, white, and rainbow colours; cities of marble, glass (ill. 69), crystal, mother of pearl, silver and gold; a kaleidoscope city that would have delighted the hearts of Scheerbart and Bruno Taut; cities of mountains, of pillars, of terraces, of bridges and of towers.

In none of these creations, built with the blood and sweat of the people, does the emperor recognize the city of his vision. In the end he resigns himself to waiting patiently for the heavenly city in the life hereafter. The architect, however, now a white-haired demon, builds the last and most grandiose city on his own account. The vision of the true heavenly

city dawns, and the tower of the architect's city collapses, burying its creator beneath its ruins.

Most of the architects who had dreamed architectural dreams during and after the First World War subsequently buried the 'demon' in themselves and, like Birnbaum's emperor, gave up trying to build the heavenly Jerusalem on earth. For many the turning-point came between 1922 and 1925. In 1923 Paul Westheim organized an inquiry in *Das Kunstblatt* significantly entitled 'Is Expressionism Dead?'. This was by no means the first article ushering out the young movement: as early as 1919 Kurt Pinthus, in the introduction to his famous anthology *Die Menschheitsdämmerung* ('The Twilight of Mankind'), had appealed to poets to call it a day with their *Chaos, Sturz und Schrei*. In architecture the progressives moved away from the idea of the artist receiving inspiration in a trance of creativity to the idea of architecture as a social service. They sought to hide irrational impulses behind pragmatic argu-

475

476

ments. Cooling off, sobering down, even stylization' were the new key words.

Adolf Behne was one of the first of the architects and architectural critics in Germany to sense the changing climate. Thinking of the De Stijl group in Holland and the avant-garde in France he announced the rejection of crafts, the renunciation of sentimental enthusiasms, and the end of the rule of caprice. His programme was explicitly directed against Expressionism. What had hitherto been celebrated as the expression of a general will now appeared as pure subjectivity. The personal, individualistic work will be more out of place in its surroundings today than ever before . . . Objectivity [is] the highest thing of which we are capable.' A few years later, in his book about Max Taut, Behne defined objectivity *(Sachlichkeit)* as 'the kind of imagination that works with things, with precise data, with realities.'[1] The fact that it was Behne of all people, he who had been one of Expressionism's most eloquent spokesmen, who sounded the retreat was met with a predictable chorus of sarcastic comments.

Behne did not stop at written support of the new movement: he promoted it in deed as well. It was probably he who arranged the first momentous meeting between Theo van Doesburg, the propagandist of De Stijl, and the Bauhaus group. Discussions such as those which went on at the Bauhaus in 1921–22 and which found expression in the Weimar Exhibition of 1923 were going on simultaneously at various other places in Germany. In February 1922 Richard Döcker and Hugo Keuerleber, who wanted to reconstruct the centre of Stuttgart with tower blocks, designed an office building for Königstrasse in the form of a plain rectangular solid with simple, wide windows. A month earlier, on 2 January, the final date for entries in the competition for a tower block at the Friedrichstrasse station in Berlin, the rival sides had already met and clashed. The first prize was in fact awarded for a design which made timid use of the vocabulary of Expressionism (ill.

477). But the second prize went to a project which was well on the way towards the new and more sober approach, a horizontal slab building by the Luckhardt brothers (ill. 478). Of the fantasy of their earlier studies the only trace left is the vaulted superstructures of the tower block and of the low building in front of it. The epoch-making *Chicago Tribune* competition which took place in the same year attracted or inspired a considerable number of designs in the new style.

In housing, which should be regarded as one of the Weimar Republic's greatest achievements,[2] the new trend was felt only two or three years later: no building on any large scale could be undertaken until inflation had been stopped. The requisite financial resources were provided by the controversial new house-rent tax, justified morally by the fact that the house-owners affected had profited from the depreciation of mortgages brought about by inflation. From 1924 onwards the house-rent tax brought in thousands of millions of marks which went to cover loans for housing. The holders of these mortgages were generally the local authorities, who were thus put in a key position; in addition, these authorities had a hand in public cooperatives, built housing on their own account, and could, through their building regulations, influence other construction. The fact that the new style gained ground so rapidly in Germany is due largely to the activity of such towns as Frankfurt am Main, Celle, Dessau, Magdeburg, and, after the appointment of Martin Wagner as City Architect, Berlin.

The administration of the local authorities was mostly in the hands of party politicians of the Weimar coalition, above all Social Democrats like Frankfurt's mayor Ludwig Landmann who were in search of a style for a new era. They found it in an architecture that was sympathetic to technology, open to international influences, and designed for reproduction – an architecture that was diametrically opposed to the glittering

477

478

eccentricities of Expressionism. The *Neues Bauen* or New Architecture, as it was called, commended itself initially more for its quality as a symbol than for any economic advantages which, though promised, were as yet unproven. When in 1923–24 Otto Haesler designed the first housing estate in Germany in the new style, the Italienische Garten in Celle (ill. 479), he chose conventional ground plans and oriented his four-family houses towards the street with no regard for the angle of the sun. What made the houses appear revolutionary was their form – flat roofs, groups of windows continuing around corners, and flat, smooth, painted exterior walls.

Not all the local authorities controlled by the moderate Left embraced the new style. The housing policy introduced in

475, 476. Uriel Birnbaum. Illustrations from *Der Kaiser und der Architekt*, Leipzig and Vienna, 1924.
475. The emperor and the architect.
476. The heavenly city.
477. J. Brahm and R. Kastelleiner. Project for an office building in Friedrichstrasse, Berlin, 1921.
478. Hans and Wassili Luckhardt. Project for an office building in Friedrichstrasse, Berlin, 1921.

479

Vienna in 1923 was more rigorous than anywhere outside the socialist republics of Eastern Europe (ills. 480, 482). As in Germany, a housing shortage forced the Austrian government to introduce legislation to protect tenants. One effect was to discourage private capital from investing in housing. The Social Democratic majority on the Vienna council came to a fairly radical conclusion: they decided to finance out of taxes a municipal housing programme in which tenants were responsible only for maintenance costs. The tenants were selected on a points system which produced a body of people of similar social class and similar political interests. The shortage of building land led to the use of empty sites dotted here and there all over the city; this also allowed a cheaper link-up to mains. The new multi-storey superblocks cut themselves off like fortresses from the existing environment, which was often of a quite different social make-up. The self-sufficiency of these 'popular-housing palaces', which were grouped around inner courtyards and provided with shops, playgrounds, baths, clinics and clubrooms, was reflected in their vast and forbidding façades. As in Amsterdam, the formal display was in grotesque disproportion to the modesty of the flats: originally these had a floor area of between 38 and 48 square metres, increased after 1927 to between 40 and 57 square metres.

The fortress-like character of many of the new buildings may have been prompted by the Vienna council's desire for political self-representation in what was a difficult time. The relaxed layouts of the new housing estates going up in the Weimar Republic would not have been suitable in Vienna either in terms of space or in terms of the reigning political climate. The appropriate architectural reaction to the tense, unsettled situation of the Austrian capital was felt to be Expressionism (here at third hand).

The towers, gates and giant flag-poles of the new buildings, and their symmetry, axial arrangement, and apparently strategic placing around the city led the right-wing opposition to call them 'Red strongholds': the balustrades were rifle stands, the balconies sentry beats, and the projecting angles gun bastions.[3] With bitter irony, in 1934 the Vienna council houses did in fact become the scene of bloody skirmishes between the Heimwehr or local militia of the Dollfuss regime and the Republikanischer Schutzbund of the Socialists (ill. 481).

Differences and similarities

The architects of the New Architecture had been Expressionists themselves, or had at least flirted with Expressionism; once the gulf between the two movements had been made evident, however, it seemed to be unbridgeable. But it should not be overemphasized. Lines of communication ran in both directions. The case of Bernhard Hoetger is typical. He was bitter in his disapproval of T-squares, angles, machines, planes, norms and series; yet the second issue of *Die Böttcherstrasse*, the magazine he co-edited and in which he blindly opposed the tyranny of functionalism, listed among the founders of the modern movement Le Corbusier, Oud and Bruno Taut (though not Gropius or Mies van der Rohe). Conversely, a work by Hoetger was included in the Bauhaus' third portfolio of graphics. *Wendingen* in Holland pursued a similarly liberal policy.

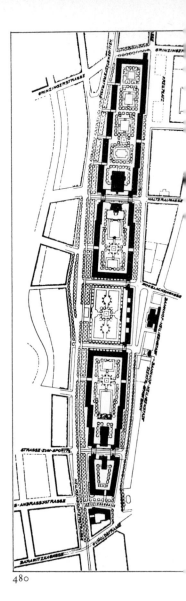

480

479. Otto Haesler. Italienischer Garten estate, Celle, 1923–24.
480. Karl Ehn. Karl-Marx-Hof, Vienna, 1927. Site plan.

481

482

Even the work of individual architects reflected the multiplicity of possibilities. One of the most consistent practitioners of the New Architecture, Mies van der Rohe, in his monument to Karl Liebknecht and Rosa Luxemburg gave heavy, horizontally stratified masses the appearance of being in a constant state of flux (ill. 483). Crimson vitrified brickwork combines with a star (bearing the hammer and sickle) and a flagstaff to form a collage of varied materials. The disciplined restlessness of this architectural sculpture even extended to the bonding system of the brickwork, which follows no traditional pattern. Hoetger's wild brick sculptures (ill. 484) found in Mies' monument a restrained but no less excited and exciting counterpart.

In the later twenties a second wave of conversions occurred among architects who had been associated with Expressionism. Emil Fahrenkamp changed over to an elegant, light-weight Modernism; Wilhelm Kreis tried out the new unfamiliar idiom in his Dresden Museum of Hygiene (1927–30), Peter Behrens tried it in residential blocks and later in a tobacco factory at Linz (1932–34), and Paul Bonatz used it for the Zeppelin building opposite his main station in Stuttgart (1929–31). In Hamburg architects such as Karl Schneider, Friedrich R. Ostermeyer, Gustav Oelsner, Paul A. R. Frank, Hermann Distel and August Grubitz, Hans and Oskar Gerson, Hermann and even Fritz Höger, built a series of residential quarters, mostly under the aegis of the municipal architectural authorities of Hamburg and Altona. In these estates the New Architecture precision of white buildings made of steel, concrete and stucco was translated into brick; occasionally, in the corner details, there is a glimpse of the old drama (ill. 485). The new forms lost a lot of their 'manifesto' character in brick, but the Hamburg architects' distrust of what came to be known as the International Style was so deep that this did not strike them as a disadvantage. Even a man like Fritz Schumacher, who was always anxious to

483. Ludwig Mies van der Rohe. Monument to Karl Liebknecht and Rosa Luxemburg, Berlin, 1926.
484. Bernhard Hoetger. Façade above the entrance to Böttcherstrasse, Bremen, 1927. Measured drawing.

483

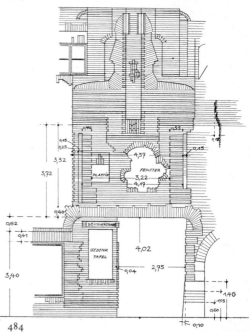

484

481. Book jacket for Josef Schneider and C. Zell, *Der Fall der roten Festung*, Vienna, 1934.
482. Karl Ehn. Karl-Marx-Hof, Vienna, 1927.

485

486

485. Fritz Höger. Flughafen estate, Hamburg-Fuhlsbüttel, 1928.
486. Willem Marinus Dudok. Villa Sevenstijn, The Hague, 1920.
487. Peter Hans Riepert and Dahl. Diagram of the structure and exterior of the Rheinhalle by Wilhelm Kreis, from *Das Stikkleid des Architekten*, Berlin, n.d. (1927).
488. Wilhelm Kreis. Rheinhalle, Düsseldorf, 1925–26.

maintain a balanced view, characterized the New Architecture in less than friendly terms as 'a kind of dogged terseness'.[4]

In Holland the Amsterdam school architects – Luthmann, Margaret Kropholler, Staal and Wijdeveld – changed over to the functionalism which their colleagues in the De Stijl group had long been practising. The international importance at the time of Willem Marinus Dudok (b. 1884) was due to his reconciliation of two apparently irreconcilable schools: that of Amsterdam, to which he had himself belonged, and the Neo-Plasticism of De Stijl. His position as a mediator appears in the harmony of contrasts that characterizes his compositions, almost all of which are resolved by a vertical accent (ill. 486). Hans Poelzig, who sought in his famous speech of 1931 to acknowledge technology but also to defend the 'eternal melody' of architectural creation,[5] may have seen the synthesis he hoped for in such a building as Dudok's head office for IG Farben in Frankfurt am Main (1928–30), at the same time functional and emotive.

The critics who were committed to the New Architecture saw Expressionism in architecture as an evolutionary dead end. Yet with all their difference there was much that the two movements had in common. There is no other way of accounting for such a rapid transformation in the work and outlook of the avant-garde. In many ways Expressionism served as a workshop in which the basic ideals of modern architecture were hammered out.

One of the ideas which can be traced uninterruptedly from the Jugendstil through Expressionism and up into the twenties is the gradual fashioning of the building into a spatially and plastically conceived structure capable of being experienced in every dimension. The architects of Expressionism started in the main from the notion of a substance which was to be treated sculpturally, that is to say modelled, kneaded, cut into, and hollowed out. The clay model played an important part in the design process – with Poelzig, the Luckhardts, Finsterlin,

Hoetger and with the Dutch. The architecture of the later twenties achieved its three-dimensional effects with combinations of one- and two-dimensional or linear and flat components: thin stick-like supports, circular in section, load-bearing partitions, and enclosing surfaces. 'Inside' and 'outside' and 'above' and 'below' were, in complete contrast to Expressionism, abolished. In both cases, however, the key to the experience of the building and its interior lay in the movement of the observer. The principal views, in so far as such a concept survived at all, no longer gave an adequate understanding of the building. 'The artist is constantly looking for fresh stimuli that will activate and attract the observer', wrote Walter Gropius at a time – 1947 – when he had long ceased to be a Romantic and had become the classic representative of the modern movement.[6] His remark also indicates how strongly the modern movement was bound by a compulsion to novelty, a development for which Expressionism, with its cult of the original genius, must take part of the blame.

The New Architecture proved itself better suited to the main architectural task of the twenties, housing, than Expressionist architecture with its theoretical insistence on the uniqueness of every design. Uniqueness was incompatible with the requirements of rationalization. The satisfaction of similar needs called for in mass housing was difficult to reconcile with an individualistic 'artist's architecture'. The kind of composition with similar elements which the New Architecture preached and, to a certain extent, also practised, could easily be extended to produce large complexes. Bruno Taut wrote in 1929, 'Just as [the] individual parts [of the house] coexist through their interaction with one another, so the house coexists with its fellows. It is a product of collective and social intent. Thus repetition, far from being unwanted, is in fact the most important instrument of art.'[7]

In so far as the Expressionists got involved in town planning at all, they conceived the superblock, residential quarter, or *Stadtkrone* or whatever as a unique work rather than as part of an adaptable and extensible structure, thus introducing pressures which then impinged upon the lives of the inhabitants. It can of course be argued, on the other hand, that the rationality of the new estates built in the twenties and after – where the rows of houses are determined by the run of the erection crane, where any kind of tactile interest in materials is denied, and where, if possible, every trace of subjectivity (on the part of architect, landlord, or tenant) is eliminated – implies just as violent an intrusion.

Expression, the cardinal belief of Expressionism, was also present in the New Architecture, in so far as it did not go to extremes and make function the sole determinant of the building. Most of the believers of the New Architecture would have subscribed to Kandinsky's statement of 1912 that form ought to be the outward *expression* of inner content. But there was a change in the constitution of that content. The people, the soul, the Ego, the 'inner visions' – all this was finished. Nor was it any longer permissible to make a building seem to have an organic life of its own, to treat it as 'an independent and in the highest degree alive and active organism' (Heinrich de Fries), or to 'make the whole thing as if possessed of a soul' (Rudolf Steiner).[8] The physical determinants of building – materials and construction – became the important thing that called for expression. They could not convince by their mere presence, for the simple reason that on practical grounds – fire regulations, for example – they were not allowed to appear in their own right. To the Expressionists this had been a matter of indifference, but to the younger generation an offence against the truth of construction was tantamount to a sin against the spirit of architecture (ills. 487, 488).

There was agreement between the two schools on the question of the role of a building in relation to its form. To give suitable and adequate expression to this was an article of belief with most Expressionists as well as with their successors,

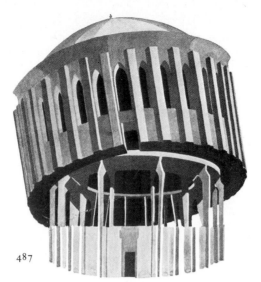

487

488

even when opinions diverged as to means and to the extent to which the architect might go beyond the dictates of economy and function. And there was agreement on what Gropius called 'a struggle for essentials . . . to get at what is at the back of all technique, which is for ever seeking visible expression with its help.'[9] Both Expressionists and New Architecture adherents hoped that architecture would show mankind the way to a new life, whatever their various conceptions of that new life might be. No matter how much else had changed, the yearning for redemption remained. They saw the possibility of a society in which the contradictions of the present should be reconciled. Gropius dreamt of a universalist world in which tension was a thing of the past: 'This dawning recognition of the unity of all things and appearances gives all human creative activity a common meaning, one which resides deep within ourselves.

Nothing exists on its own any more; every creation is the image of a thought that is impatient to emerge from ourselves and take shape, every work a manifestation of our inner being.'[10] In the revolutionary atmosphere of the first months following the end of the war this kind of belief in a new world had seemed wholly intelligible. In 1923, the year of the Ruhr occupation, galloping inflation, and Hitler's Munich *putsch*, it implied a foolhardiness which carried with it all the dangers of violent disillusion.

Like the Expressionists, the architects of the new style looked for universals in number-mysticism. Le Corbusier's concern for 'the rule that orders and connects all things' can be traced back to a visit to Hagen where, as a *passant modeste*, he collected information about the activities of Karl Ernst Osthaus and no doubt also about the design principles of Lauweriks (see pp. 44ff.).[11] Even after the Bauhaus' change of course Gropius referred in the introduction to his *Internationale Architektur* (1924) to proportions as relating to the spiritual world. A tradition going back to Plato and Plotinus held numbers to be the connecting link between the worlds, the guarantee of an ultimate unity.

Nowhere apart from Beuron and Dornach were so many secrets read into numbers as in the Bauhaus. Oskar Schlemmer, who preached *Sachlichkeit* as early as 1921, pursued his fascinated researches into 'the miracle of proportions', 'the splendour of number ratios', and the 'hallowed paths' of mathematical thought. Gropius, Kandinsky, Klee and Schlemmer all adapted their belief in numbers to their new circumstances without apparent effort. The number three, in particular, recurs frequently in the work of the Bauhaus, for example in the triads of form, colour and space; circle, rectangle and triangle; sphere, cube and pyramid; and red, blue and yellow. Now, with the Bauhaus' new social orientation, the number three became the symbol of collectivity: it surmounted both the monomanic Ego

489

and the dualism of opposites. Speculation of this sort (as well as the arts and crafts character of many of the Bauhaus products of the later period) may be what prompted Hannes Meyer, one of the few consistently radical Functionalists, to call Dessau a second Dornach.[12]

Hugo Häring

A connecting link between Expressionism and the New Architecture was provided by the theory evolved by Hugo Häring (1882–1958). Häring, the *éminence grise* of German Modernism, clearly took no part in the activities of the Arbeitsrat für Kunst. A house which he built in Neu-Ulm in 1916 (ill. 489) is remarkable, in spite of its medieval flavour, for the freedom with which its varied parts are put together. Häring had already gone beyond the graphic boldness of Theodor Fischer: the Neu-Ulm house hinted at the possibility of a new kind of spatial relationship and spatial form.

From 1921–22 onwards Häring's projects show that, like Scharoun, he attached great importance to movement and flow. On an alternative design for the existing central station in Leipzig (ills. 490, 491), which Häring did on the basis of the old competition data of 1907, he noted:

'Work out ground plans the way the town planner does paths, roads and squares.' The vaulted projecting entrance and exit pavilions are shaped like flat-irons, a favourite motif with Häring, and the platforms fan out radially to speed access to and from the trains. Häring's entry for the competition for an office building over Berlin's Friedrichstrasse station (see also pp. 41, 195) was no less dramatic than Scharoun's: two delicately modelled sides of a many-sided building meet at Friedrichstrasse in a sharp corner, anticipating the eastern projection of the Chilehaus in Hamburg (ill. 300). Above the firm plan, which should have led to an equally firm volume, Häring placed complex figures made up of many elements, sometimes stretched out in an elastic way, sometimes rectangular. Here for the first time his note about plan as town-plan became reality. Häring's *magnum opus*, the Garkau farm near Lübeck (ill. 492) was admittedly conceived purely as a 'tool'; but the farm buildings (never completed) obey an oscillating movement – following the shoreline at one moment, in contrapuntal opposition to it the next – which evades a purely functional justification.

Häring thought more deeply and more logically about form and function than any other architect working in the new style. He was realistic enough not to assume that there would automatically be harmony between the demand for expression and the demand for functionalism. In the heyday of Expressionism architects had, usually without thinking, set expression above function and left form to the will of the designer. In the era of 'objective' architecture there were three main attitudes: either one denied the existence of any conflict between function and form, or one played it down by using objective, geometrical elements, or the components of expression were subordinated to the demands of usefulness and economy.

Häring, however, took other 'paths to form'.[13] He believed he had found a solution to the dilemma in his attempt to set expression and functionalism 'as equal

489. Hugo Häring. Römer house, Neu-Ulm, 1916–20.
490, 491. Hugo Häring. Main railway station, Leipzig, 1921. Alternative design for the existing building. View and plan. Charcoal. Akademie der Künste, Berlin.
492. Hugo Häring. Garkau farm, near Lübeck, 1924–25. Bird's-eye view showing stables, barn and houses.

490

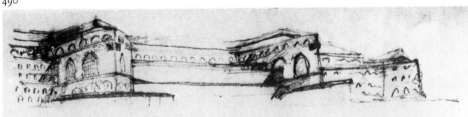

491

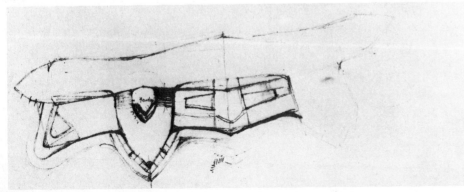

GUT GARKAU

493

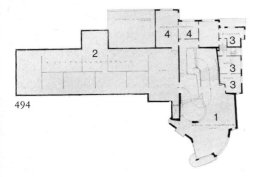

494

493, 494. Hugo Häring. Project for the Berlin Sezession building, 1926.
493. Entrance front.
494. Plan of the first floor: 1 staircase and sculpture room, 2 exhibition rooms, 3 offices, 4 social rooms.

partners on their way'. He talked about finding shape instead of giving shape, of releasing form instead of imposing form from outside. With this principle he placed himself in opposition to Le Corbusier, who seemed to him to represent a geometrical culture.

Häring demanded that the basic forms of architectural creation be drawn not from the world of geometry but from the realm of 'organic formations'. He did not of course mean that the proper repertoire of architecture should consist of prototypes drawn from nature; it was a question rather of hunting down 'the shape imprisoned in the thing', giving it life, and bringing it out. The architect/designer was thus assigned a role which was modest only in appearance; in reality it was extremely grandiose. His task was no less than to assist things to find their right and proper shape and to fashion a second nature, which in terms of its construction was the equivalent of the created world. Such a claim was no less pretentious than the Expressionists' view of the artist as the mouthpiece and prophet of the 'age', the 'cosmic' and the 'essential'.

The 'essence is precisely the purely subjective', wrote the anti-Expressionist Georg Lukács.[14] Was not the 'essence' which in Häring's scheme the architect was to liberate also a subjective assumption? And was this 'essence' fixed for all time? What happened to the form when the functions changed? Moreover, was there not already a conflict of opposed functions at any given moment? Who was to decide between them? It was Häring, the autocratic artist, who decided that in an exhibition building such as that for the Berlin Sezession the 'essential' factor, which would determine the building's appearance, was the vertical circulation of the visitors – and not, for example, the use of the exhibition rooms themselves (ills. 493, 494).[15]

Häring's theory ran the risk of debasing the process of decision in design to the level of an almost horticultural activity in which forms were cultivated, nurtured and developed like prize blooms. It did guard him, however, both against smart modernistic formulas and against the pressures of practice. Häring's work retained a positive will to expression, held in check by a mind that never for a moment overlooked the justification of form.

17 Expressionism and the National Socialists

Triangular modernism

In 1928 the magazine *Die Baugilde* published a satire which mirrored the situation of German architecture at the end of the twenties.[1] It suggested a central clearing-house which would classify customers according to requirements and taste and direct them to one of three departments. In the first department costumed and bewigged architects enthroned on stumps of columns toiled over stylistic imitations. The second was for partisans of the Neue Sachlichkeit or 'New Objectivity', with bald-headed gentlemen (hair being *sub*jective) squatting on cubes. The third studio specialized in 'triangular modernism' and its architects, all wearing goatee beards and triangular spectacles, were perched on pyramid-shaped seating arrangements.

By this time Expressionism had lost its most talented protagonists and had degenerated – if we except Hoetger and the Dornach Anthroposophists – to become 'triangular modernism'. At the same time a majority of the commissions for public and prestige buildings still came its way: in the competitions which, with the onset of boom conditions, were promoted by many firms for head-office buildings and by several cities for city halls, it carried off the lion's share of the prizes. Its attributes were easily imitable

and only concerned the façade: arcades of pointed, triangular or parabolic arches; supports that narrow in section towards the base; portals, doorways, and windows with angled lintels or even triangular in shape; systems of piers set at 45° angles; wall surfaces covered with a net-like pattern of decoration, usually in the form of lozenges; stepped or triangular gables; and, in the case of flat roofs, an attic storey decorated with lacy perforated patterns or with crenellations designed to temper the severity of the horizontal skyline (ills. 495–501).

This repertoire was a pale simulacrum of what had been dynamic, vigorous and challenging forms. The question asked in Kasimir Edschmid's *Timur* (1916) – 'Have you any idea of the teeth (*Zacken*) of torment through which each deed must pass to its accomplishment?' – belonged to another world; so did the raptures which Scheerbart's readers experienced at his multi-facetted ice palaces, glass mountains, and jagged, prismatic domes.

Fascism and the question of style

Expressionism stood even less chance of appealing to the National Socialists than the New Architecture. From the outset the Führer was unlikely to care for any architecture derived from Expressionism: he damned the art which had been avant-garde when he was an aspiring artist as *Kulturbolschewismus*. After the Nazi seizure of power in 1933, despite efforts to save it, Expressionist art was outlawed.

The party's attitude towards modern architecture was originally not negative. The organ of the party, the *Völkischer Beobachter*, applauded standardized and industrialized housing several times between 1927 and 1929 and mentioned with approval architects like Gropius, Le Corbusier, May and Martin Wagner. Remarks made by the Propaganda Minister Joseph Goebbels as late as 1933 can be interpreted as a defence of the New Architecture. That Fascism might tolerate modern architecture seemed as conceivable in Ger-

many for a while as it did in Italy, where the partisans of a rational architecture – the Gruppo 7 and the Movimento italiano per l'architettura razionale – continued to hope for a decision in their favour until well into the thirties.

However, the increasing influence of the 'Blood and Soil' (*Blut-und-Boden*) doctrine, the programme of reagrarianization run by the National Socialist expert Richard Walter Darré, and speculation on petty-bourgeois votes prompted the NSDAP around 1930 to turn to the traditionalist and conservative elements of the architectural profession. Despite revolution and the Bauhaus, Expressionism and International Modern, conventional architects had managed to hold their own right through the twenties, and when National Socialism appealed for a revivalist architecture that was 'true to the homeland', 'of the people', and 'national', it could call on reputable professionals. Paul Schmitthenner and German Bestelmeyer, as well as the unfortunate Paul Schultze-Naumburg, who abandoned his championship of an idyllic bourgeois civilization in the twenties and went over to a militant racialism, beat the party drum in the Nazi Kampfbund (Fighting League) of German Architects and Engineers.

After 1933 it became clear that the colossal ambitions of the Third Reich

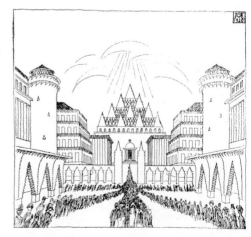

495. Albinmüller. Idea for a *Volkshaus* (community centre), from *Stadtbaukunst alter und neuer Zeit*, I, no. 23, 1920.

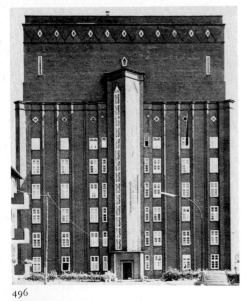

496

497

498

500

499

501

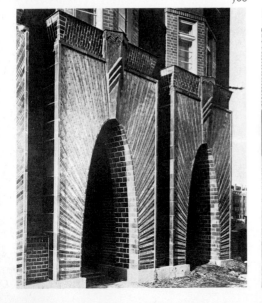

496. Wesermünde City Architect's Department. Flats and water tower, Wesermünde-Wulsdorf, 1927.

497. Hermann Distel and August Grubitz. Montanhof, Hamburg, 1924–26.

498. Paul Bonatz. Stumm building, Düsseldorf, 1921–25.

499. Fritz Höger. Chilehaus, Hamburg, 1923–24. Jeweller's display window on the east corner (sculptor: Richard Kuöhl).

500. Jean Krämer. Flats and tram depot for the Berliner Verkehrsgesellschaft, Berlin, 1926–27.

501. Wilhelm Kreis. Rheinhalle, Düsseldorf, 1925–26. Detail.

502. Clemens Holzmeister. Supreme Court, Ankara, 1933–34. Main entrance.

503. Wilhelm Kreis. Kunstmuseum, Düsseldorf, 1925–26. Corner pavilions.

504. Paul Ludwig Troost. Temple of Honour on Königliche Platz, Munich, 1934.

were not going to be satisfied by the revival of local traditions: neither Schmitthenner nor Schultze-Naumburg was successful, and the Kampfbund failed to make its romantic 'Germanizing' ideas prevail. Instead the Nazis' most prestigious commissions, the so-called 'Führer buildings' and most of the larger party buildings, were executed in a pared-down classicism. The man chiefly responsible for the formulation of this style was the first 'Architect to the Führer', Paul Ludwig Troost.

National Socialist architecture easily acquired a pedigree. The style of its buildings was heterogeneous, ranging from the regionalism of the Hitlerjugend homes to the functionalism of industrial architecture and the pomp and ceremony of the Nuremberg Parteitag installations. Its propagandists could thus claim a variety of respectable sources: these included the rustic modesty of Biedermeier, already recommended by Schultze-Naumburg in his *Kulturarbeiten* (1904–10), as well as the monumentalism of the period around 1910, based in its turn upon Prussian classicism. Honourable men such as Theodor Fischer and Heinrich Tessenow were implicated, men who in the twenties had pursued an architecture of parsimonious dignity without committing themselves to any of the new trends. Albert Speer, later Inspector-General of Building for the Reorganization of the State Capital, was Tessenow's pupil and assistant.

Outside the compass of what historians of modern architecture generally consider to be alone worthy of attention, many buildings were erected during the twenties which seem like anticipations of the later National Socialist party buildings. The Austrian Clemens Holzmeister, who built the memorial to the Nazi martyr Albert Leo Schlageter near Düsseldorf in 1929–31, had begun in 1927 to erect government buildings in the new Turkish capital of Ankara. These are distinguished from the 'Germanic tectonics' of an architect like Troost by their surrealist disregard for any visual differentiation between load and support, but they come close to Troost's style in their arid officialism and in the emphatic quality of their fluted columns (ills. 502, 504). The exhibition and museum buildings which Wilhelm Kreis built in Düsseldorf in 1925–26 for the Gesolei exhibition look like preliminary studies for Nazi designs of ten years later (ills. 503, 505); in 1930 he wrote, 'the marching rhythm that runs through columns of athletes also permeates the rhythm of our art.'[2] Kreis, like Bonatz and Bestelmeyer, received fat commissions from the National Socialists for the projected north-south axis of the capital, along which not only columns of athletes would march (ill. 509). Kreis' career is a depressing example of German continuity – from the Bismarck towers of the young and successful architect of the Wilhelmine era to the 'castles of the dead' of the Board of Works for German War Cemeteries, an organization which was responsible immediately to the Führer.

Of the architects who had been more than superficially involved with Expressionism, the most susceptible to National Socialists ideals were those who had cultivated a Low German variant of it and whose regionalism had been in conscious opposition to the internationalism of the New Architecture. Fritz Höger, whose hobby was collecting objects that reflected 'the spirit of Old Germany' wrote for the Kampfbund magazine, and his contributions reiterate all the phrases of the National Socialist myth-makers, from 'German architecture of German blood' to the 'true and proper soul'.[3]

There is something tragic about Bernhard Hoetger's entanglement with Nazism. In spite of all its exotic influences, his work had been harnessed to the national interest at an early stage; he saw himself as an honest barbarian, a man of ardent emotions among the ice-cold souls of a profit-hungry 'civilized' art. In 1936 he wished in all good faith to identify himself with the National Socialist movement: with the young architect Herbert Helfrich he produced a gigantic model for a 'German Forum', including a cult build-

502

503
504

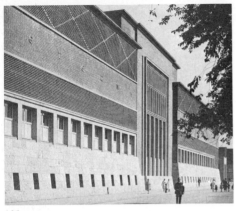

505

506

507

505. Wilhelm Kreis. Kunstmuseum, Düsseldorf, 1925–26.

506. Albert Speer. Grandstand on the Zeppelinfeld, Nuremberg, 1934–37.

507. Title vignette from the pamphlet issued for the Exhibition for Unknown Architects. Arbeitsrat für Kunst, Berlin, 1919.

ing that was swastika-shaped in plan, and exhibited it in Nuremberg, the city of the Parteitag installations. But when he was attacked by the SS newspaper *Das Schwarze Korps* he replied by alleging that he was being boycotted by a Jewish clique of art dealers, and this smacks unpleasantly of opportunism.[4] His obeisance did not pay; the days were past when discussions raged within the party about cultural policy, and when an 'Expressionism of the people' was still a possibility. Hoetger was repeatedly attacked in *Das Schwarze Korps*, forbidden to practise his profession, and even interrogated by the Gestapo. Hitler himself violently condemned 'Böttcherstrasse culture' at the Parteitag in 1936.

The spoilt Utopia

The architects who prepared the way for the National Socialist style were thus not the Expressionists, but those who had a traditionalist or regionalist outlook. There remains the question whether the thinking of the revolutionary architects of 1918–19 contained Fascist elements. Was Alfred Kurella right when in 1937, in the Moscow-based exile periodical *Das Wort*, he maintained that every convinced Expressionist must inevitably go over to Hitler?[5] The Arbeitsrat für Kunst put a swastika on the title page of the pamphlet issued for the Exhibition for Unknown Architects in 1919 (ill. 507), and in January of the same year a swastika adorned the cover of the magazine *Wendingen*. A year later Hitler was having the first swastika flags sewn. Coincidence – or grounds for suspicion?

A number of arguments put forward by Expressionists also figured in the cultural propaganda of the National Socialists. The manifestos of the post-war period had consistently demanded that architecture should take the other arts under its wing: to Hitler architecture seemed, with music, the 'queen of the arts'. Artists had often claimed a role as *Führer* in society and sought to mould life in its 'totality'. Hitler believed that the artist was in-

formed by the same 'authoritarian will' as the professional politician; since he believed himself to be a political and artistic genius, he no doubt considered himself to be the most convincing proof of his thesis.[6]

The Expressionists' demand for a return to crafts (more reactionary than revolutionary) could also be related to the National Socialist postulate of an indigenous architecture. Both Expressionists and National Socialists attacked the soullessness of technology and the big city. In both cases these attacks were challenged, and produced no significant results, with the exception of some suburban housing estates on which food was grown, as promoted by the Third Reich. Expressionists and National Socialists both called for an art rooted in the people, and they shared a belief in the power of architecture to transform society, a power which the National Socialists exploited as a means of psychological conditioning.

In addition to the irrationalism that nourished both movements, there was one concrete town-planning concept, the *Stadtkrone*, that fascinated the men of the NSDAP as it had fascinated the revolutionary architects of Expressionism. In his book *Die Stadtkrone* (ill. 508; see p. 79), Bruno Taut had proposed a hierarchically ascending building complex as the centrepiece of the new city. The lower levels were set aside for such mundane uses as shops, restaurants and cafés. On the higher levels squares and courtyards, a library and a museum were to be disposed around a cruciform core with an opera house, theatre, large community centre and hall. At the highest point was the nonfunctional crystal building, universal symbol and house of prayer for the faith of the future. 'Here at the summit the socially oriented hopes of the people find their fulfilment.' The idea was current at the time: Schmitthenner wrote rather more vaguely than Taut of the heart of the city 'from which all spiritual forces emanate . . . This would have to be a building as powerfully expressive as a Gothic cathedral. At all events it would have to convey the expression of the most sublime feeling.'[7]

Hitler referred to cathedral and acropolis a few years later in a passage of his book *Mein Kampf*. 'What gave the city of antiquity its character was not its private buildings but its public monuments, which gave the impression of having been built not for the moment but for eternity.' He saw no such monumental documents of architecture in the present day: 'Our big cities today have no monuments which dominate the entire urban landscape and which might, as it were, be interpreted as tokens of the age as a whole . . . The result must be a stagnation of which the practical effect will be the complete apathy of the modern citizen with regard to the fate of his city.' In his *Kulturreden*, his speeches on cultural themes, Hitler came back to these ideas again and again. The term *Stadtkrone* was taken over by National Socialism's architectural publicists and complemented by the term *Landskrone*, referring to the NSDAP political training schools which were built in the country.[8]

The *Stadtkrone* as conceived by the Nazis was similar to, and yet different from, the *Stadtkrone* of the Expressionists. Hitler adopted the idea for two reasons. He saw in it the possibility of representing and consolidating his own political power, and he hoped by his monumental buildings to pass on to posterity the message of his own greatness. The party forums were to be incorporated in the new city centres, designed to the scale not of the individual citizen-user but of the march-past. The architectural consequences were the ubiquity of the symbol of party and state, and of impressive axes and parade grounds.

Taut expressly rejected any idea of including in his *Stadtkrone* buildings which embodied the idea of the state. The state and local administration were for him no more than instruments, whose sole purpose was to guarantee satisfactory conditions for existence; he even wanted parliament buildings banned from the heart of the city. 'There is something

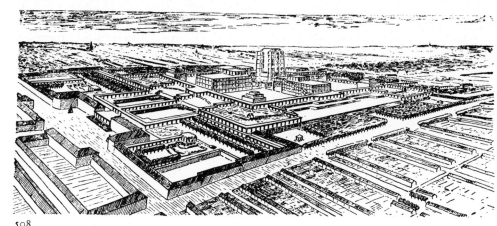

508

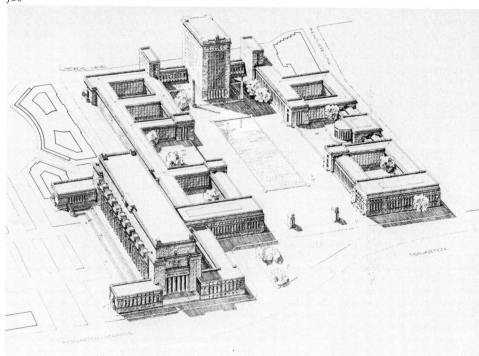

509

508. Bruno Taut. Illustration from *Die Stadtkrone*, Jena, 1919.
509. Wilhelm Kreis. Project for the Army High Command and Soldiers' Hall on the north-south axis, Berlin, 1938.

more than being a citizen and that is being a person,' he quoted. The vertical arrangement of his *Stadtkrone*, with its stairways, ramps and bridges, would have been utterly unsuitable for ostentatious parades of large crowds of people. It furnished a hierarchy of facilities – from strolling and shopping on the lower levels through educational activities and the enjoyment of art to the meditation of the solitary voyager on life's way in the crystal temple, which was tailored to the individual as a voluntary member of the community. The crystal building was to represent a 'symbol of the most sublime serenity, the purest spiritual peace'.[9] To this extent Taut's crystal *Stadtkrone* was the diametrical opposite of the stone parade grounds of the National Socialists.

Yet it is a fact that Expressionism in architecture tended to patterns of thought which lent themselves to infiltration by Fascism. The concern for the individual, by which Taut believed himself to be guided in his project for a new city, gave way in other designs by Taut and his friends to a fascination with size and mass. All the visions of the period tended to be wildly out of scale, with a complete disproportion between the building and the people using it. In Taut's *Die Auflösung der Städte* the workers wend their way like pilgrims to colossal sanctuaries. In the mammoth perspective of his *Alpine Architektur* people appear, if at all, as tiny dots. In the spiral whorls of Finsterlin's cave architecture the human figures are hidden as in a puzzle picture. The Futurists Sant'Elia and Chiattone left people out of their pictures altogether, lest they disturb the solemn majesty of the monuments.

The temptations of aestheticism were something to which almost all the Expressionist architects and their colleagues in other disciplines were exposed. Taut expressed this with unintentional cynicism in *Alpine Architektur*, when he wrote that the workers might for their edification observe from the air the mountain peaks which thanks to their sacrifices had been transformed into crystalline works of art (ills. 180, 181): in a science-fiction text *à la* Scheerbart he had the Federal Chancellor of a united Europe declare in 1993, 'We want . . . to send up as many workers as possible now in big airships and airbuses so that we can maintain their enthusiasm at the old level and fire their strength for the most difficult part [of their work].'[10] End and means have insidiously changed places. The placatory tactics of Taut's rigidly organized worker tourism anticipated the 'Strength Through Pleasure' trips of the National Socialists. Taut clearly proposed such macabre institutions in all purity of heart. But one need only imagine the quotations from Luther, the Bible, Nietzsche and Scheerbart on the vast, illuminated hoardings of his crystal pyramids (ill. 510) replaced by the slogans of reconstruction and perseverance and one would have a first-class tool of totalitarian indoctrination.

The Expressionist architects created vessels for a content which they yearned for without being able to name. They believed that the void of the forms which they designed would fill with meaning as soon as the designs were realized. The National Socialists, on the other hand, built in order to secure the dominion of their own régime. For the Expressionists the revolution had only just begun; for the National Socialists it had been consummated by the seizure of power. For the former it was a question of a groping search for something new, something which there were as yet no words to describe; for the latter it was a question of entrenching a dark and dismal present. No one has the right to doubt the morality of the great awakening signified by Expressionism on the grounds of its later abuse by the Nazis. The reality of the Fascist régime was to the visions of the Expressionist architects as the ghastly implementation to the Utopia.

510. Bruno Taut. Monument to the New Law, 1919. Pen drawing, photocopied. Oswald Mathias Ungers Collection, Cologne.

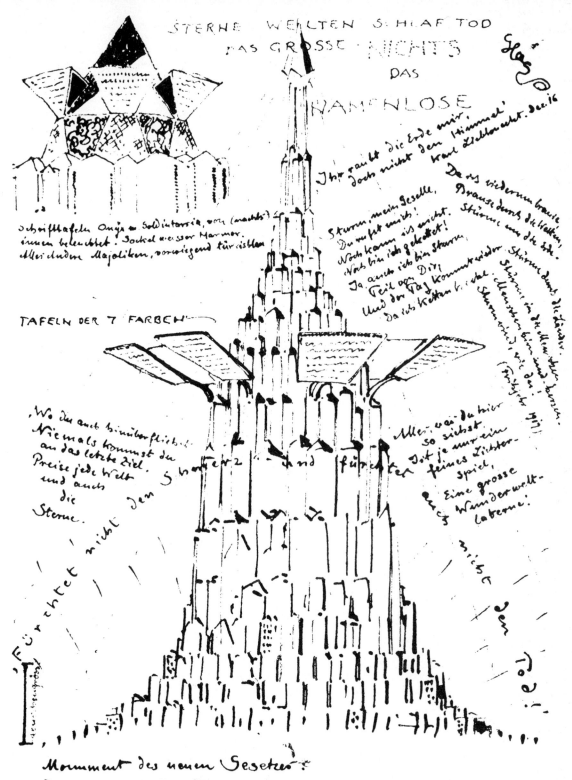

STERNE WELTEN SCHLAF TOD
DAS GROSSE · NICHTS
DAS
NAMENLOSE

Glas

Ihr raubt die Erde mir,
doch nicht den Himmel!
Karl Liebknecht. Dec. 16

Sturm, mein Geselle,
Du rufst mich!
Noch kann ich nicht.
Noch bin ich gekettet!
Ja, auch ich bin Sturm.
Teil aus Dir!
Und der Tag kommt wieder.
Da ich Ketten breche.

Schrifttafeln Onyx u. Goldintarsia, von (nachts) von
innen beleuchtet. Sockel weisser Marmor.
Alles andere Majoliken, vorwiegend türkisblau.

TAFELN DER 7 FARBEN

Wo du auch hinüberfliehst.
Niemals kommst du
an das letzte Ziel.
Preise jede Welt
und auch
die
Sterne.

Fürchtet nicht den Schmerz ... und fürchtet

Aber was du hier
so siehst
ist je nur ein
feines Lichter-
spiel,
Eine grosse
Wunderwelt-
laterne!

nicht den Tod!

Monument des neuen Gesetzes?

Auf Glastafeln geschrieben — man liest gegen den Himmel, Nachts
gegen den von oben kommenden Lichtkegel:
1) Luther: Und wenn die Welt voll Teufel wär ...... 2) Liebknecht: Sturm, mein Geselle ...
3) Nietzsche: Vom neuen Götzen 4) Haggai 1,1-17 5) Scheerbart: Wo Du auch hinüberfliehst.... 6) Offenbar. Joh. 21,9-27. 7) Scheerbart: Lesabéndio: Die Sonne—
Unser Gesetz! ———— Glaskristallpyramide
WEIHNACHTS GRÜSSE !   23.12.19

09

Notes

Foreword
pages 7–12

[1] Nikolaus Pevsner, in Oscar Beyer, ed., *Eric Mendelsohn: Letters of an Architect*, London, New York and Toronto, 1967, p. 14.
[2] H[einrich] de Fries, 'Raumgestaltung im Film', in *Wasmuths Monatshefte für Baukunst*, V (1920–21), nos. 3–4, p. 65.
[3] Theodor Däubler, *Der neue Standpunkt*, 1916, 2nd ed. Dresden, 1957, p. 117. – Wilhelm Worringer, 'Kritische Gedanken zur neuen Kunst', in *Genius*, I (1919), no. 2, p. 228.
[4] Otto Kohtz, *Gedanken über Architektur*, Berlin, 1919, p. 3.
[5] The words 'expressionism' and 'expressionist' (closely related to the word 'impressionism') occur occasionally in the nineteenth century. The painter Julien-Auguste Hervé referred to pictures he exhibited in 1901 and later at the Salon des Indépendants as *expressionismes*. As a collective term denoting a particular stylistic period, however, 'expressionism' seems to have been used first by German art critics. It appears in the catalogue of the Berlin Sezession exhibition of April 1911, and later in the works of Kurt Hiller and Wilhelm Worringer; some say the term was coined by the dealer Paul Cassirer.
See Daniel Henry Kahnweiler, 'Expressionismus', in *Das Kunstblatt*, III (1919), no. 11, p. 351; Fritz Schmalenbach, 'Das Wort Expressionismus', in *Neue Zürcher Zeitung*, no. 899, 12 March 1961, p. 5; Armin Arnold, *Die Literatur des Expressionismus*, Stuttgart, 1966, pp. 9ff.; and Alexander Gosztonyi, *Der Mensch in der modernen Malerei*, Munich, 1970, pp. 52ff.
[6] Adolf Behne, 'Expressionistische Architektur', in *Der Sturm*, V (1914–15), nos. 19–20, p. 135 (pre-publication excerpt from his *Sturmbuch zur neuen Kunst*, Berlin, 1915). – C. Spengemann, 'Die TET-Stadt', in *Reclams Universum*, XXXIII, no. 35, 31 May 1917, p. 686.
[7] Walter Müller-Wulckow, *Aufbau-Architektur!*, Berlin, 1919, p. 16. – Hans Hansen, *Das Erlebnis der Architektur*, Cologne, 1920, p. 91. – Fritz Schumacher, 'Expressionismus und Architektur', in *Dekorative Kunst* (= *Die Kunst*), XLII (1919–20), nos. 1–3, pp. 10ff., 62ff., 80ff. – Henry van de Velde, 'Zukunftsglaube', in *Genius*, II (1920), no. 2, p. 165.

Introduction:
the Theatre of the Five Thousand
pages 13–22

[1] Karl Scheffler, 'Das grosse Schauspielhaus', in *Kunst und Künstler*, XVIII (1919–20), no. 5, p. 238. The 'Theatre of the Five Thousand' is sometimes referred to in the literature of the period, rather more modestly, as the 'Theatre of the Three Thousand'.
[2] The 'Draft for an Addendum to the Contract' which Poelzig sent to the management of the Deutsche Theater explains his task: 'On the basis of discussions held prior to this date you [Poelzig] assume supreme artistic responsibility for the entire conversion of the Zirkus Schumann. This of course comprises the façades, the fitting-out of the auditorium, the corridors, and the whole of the interior with the exception of the stage.' Manuscript, Marlene Poelzig Collection, Hamburg.
[3] Hans Poelzig, 'Festspielhaus in Salzburg', in *Das Kunstblatt*, V (1921), no. 3, pp. 79, 87.
[4] Erich Mendelsohn to Louise Mendelsohn, 17. 6. 1920, in Oskar Beyer, ed., *Eric Mendelsohn: Letters of an Architect*, London, New York and Toronto, 1967, p. 54 (German in Oskar Beyer, ed., *Erich Mendelsohn. Briefe eines Architekten*, Munich, 1961, p. 54).
Poelzig gave reasons for his resignation from the Arbeitsrat in letters to Walter Gropius on 22. 4. and 24. 4. 1919: 'I hereby resign from the Arbeitsrat für Kunst. Reason 1: I am still held in part responsible for the absurdities of that architectural manifesto . . . 2: Taut's behaviour apart from this. I expressed myself a good deal earlier than dear old Taut to the effect that great art in general can only stem from a great and powerful religious will. But this means that I cannot repudiate the attempt to give powerful expression to what modern life demands.' He had written in a similar vein to Walter Curt Behrendt on 27. 1. 1919. (Copies, Marlene Poelzig Collection, Hamburg.) Poelzig later withdrew his resignation.
[5] Bruno Taut ('Glas'), circular letter, 18. 1. 1920, in *Die gläserne Kette. Visionäre Architekturen aus dem Kreis um Bruno Taut 1919–1920*, catalogue of an exhibition at Schloss Morsbroich, Leverkusen, and the Akademie der Künste, Berlin, 1963, pp. 18f.
[6] Peter Behrens, *Feste des Lebens und der Kunst*, Leipzig, 1900, title page. – Helmut Schael, *Idee und Form im Theaterbau des 19. und 20. Jahrhunderts*, dissertation, Cologne, 1956, p. 79.
[7] Romain Rolland, quoted in Kurt Pinthus, 'Möglichkeit zukünftigen Volkstheaters', in *Das Grosse Schauspielhaus. Die Bücher des Deutschen Theaters. I*, Berlin, 1920, p. 45. — Max Reinhardt, 'Denkschrift zur Errichtung eines Festspielhauses in Hellbrunn, 1917', in *Max Reinhardt. Ausgewählte Briefe, Reden, Schriften*, Vienna, 1963, p. 73.
[8] Hans Poelzig to Alfred Roller, 15. 11. 1921. Copy, Marlene Poelzig Collection, Hamburg.
[9] Bruno Taut, 'Zum neuen Theaterbau', in *Das Hohe Ufer*, I (1919), no. 8, p. 205.
[10] Max Reinhardt, in *Hannoverscher Anzeiger*, 13. 1. 1928, quoted in Helmut Schael, *Idee und Form . . .*, op. cit., p. 187.
[11] Walter Gropius, quoted in Sigfried Giedion, *Walter Gropius*, Stuttgart, 1954, p. 154.
[12] Fritz Stahl, 'Das grosse Schauspielhaus in Berlin', in *Wasmuths Monatsheft für Baukunst*, V (1920–21), nos. 1–2, p. 3.
[13] Josef Ponten, *Architektur die nicht gebaut wurde*, vol. 1, Stuttgart, 1925, p. 11. – Otto Bartning, *Erde Geliebte*, Hamburg, 1955, p. 590.
[14] Erich Mendelsohn, 'Das Problem einer neuen Baukunst', 1919, in *Erich Mendelsohn. Das Gesamtschaffen des Architekten*, Berlin, 1930, p. 18. – Karl Scheffler, op. cit., p. 236.
[15] H[einrich] de Fries, 'Raumgestaltung im Film', in *Wasmuths Monatshefte für Baukunst*, V (1920–21), nos. 3–4, p. 65.
[16] Ibid., p. 82. – Bruno Taut, *Alpine Architektur*, Hagen, 1919. – Hans Poelzig, note in a sketchbook, 1918–19. Marlene Poelzig Collection, Hamburg.
[17] Wassili Luckhardt ('Zacken'), circular letter, undated, in *Die gläserne Kette*, op. cit., p. 18.
[18] Hans Poelzig, 'Festspielhaus in Salzburg', op. cit., p. 79.
[19] Bruno Taut, *Die Stadtkrone*, Jena, 1919, p. 87.
[20] Eckart von Sydow, *Die deutsche expressionistische Kultur und Malerei*, Berlin, 1920, p. 53.
[21] Hans Poelzig, 'Bau des Grossen Schauspielhauses', in *Das Grosse Schauspielhaus*, op. cit., p. 119.

1 Politics and society
pages 23–33

[1] See Robert Schmutzler, *Art Nouveau*, New York and London, 1962, pp. 276–77.
[2] William Richard Lethaby, in *The Architectural Association Journal*, 1915, no. 1; reprinted in *Form and Civilization*, London, 1922.
[3] Charles-Edouard Jeanneret, *Etude sur le mouvement d'art décoratif en Allemagne*, La Chaux-de-Fonds, 1912, p. 14.
[4] Karl With, 'Karl Ernst Osthaus', in *Das Kunstblatt*, V (1921), no. 6, p. 169.
[5] Behrens' appointment is attributed both to Emil Rathenau, founder and president of AEG, and to Paul Jordan, an AEG director. See Stanford Owen Anderson, *Peter Behrens and the New Architecture of Germany, 1900–1917*, dissertation, New York, 1968.
[6] Fritz Hoeber, *Peter Behrens*, Munich, 1913, pp. 179ff.
[7] Peter Behrens, 'Kunst und Technik', in *Elektronische Zeitschrift*, XXXI (1910), no. 22, p. 555. – [Albert] H[ofmann], in *Deutsche Bauzeitung*, XLVII (1913), no. 80, p. 721.
[8] Friedrich Naumann, *Der deutsche Stil*, Hellerau, n. d. (1912), p. 13. – Peter Jessen, 'Der Werkbund und die Grossmächte der deutschen Arbeit', in *Jahrbuch des Deutschen Werkbundes 1912*, Jena, 1912, pp. 2ff. – Hermann Muthesius, *Die Zukunft der deutschen Form*, Stuttgart, 1915 (*Der Deutsche Krieg. Politische Flugschriften*, L, p. 36).
[9] See, e.g., Otto Bartning, *Vom neuen Kirchbau*, Berlin, 1919, p. 105; Walter Curt Behrendt, 'Zur Tagung des Deutschen Werkbundes', in *Kunst und Künstler*, XVIII (1919), no. 2, pp. 90ff.; and Paul Mahlberg, 'Vom deutschen Werkbund', in *Kunstchronik*, LV (n. s. XXXI), no. 6, 7. II. 1919, pp. 107ff.
[10] Herbert Kühn, 'Expressionismus und Sozialismus', in *Neue Blätter für Kunst und Dichtung*, II (1919–20), no. 2, p. 29. – Adolf Behne, *Die Wiederkehr der Kunst*, Leipzig, 1919, p. 78.
[11] Kurt Hiller, 'Ortsbestimmung des Aktivismus', in *Die Erhebung. Jahrbuch für neue Dichtung und Wertung*, I (1919), p. 360. – Bruno Taut to Karl Ernst Osthaus, 16. 5. 1919 (Osthaus-Archiv, Hagen): 'The pre-Communist government in Munich wanted to appoint me and Tessenow (or one of us?) to take charge of everything to do with building in Bavaria as a kind of Minister of

Architecture.' The contact man may have been Gustav Landauer, a member of the Bavarian cabinet, whom Taut quotes in his writings.

[12] Walter Gropius to Karl Ernst Osthaus, 23. 12. 1918 and 2. 2. 1919. Osthaus-Archiv, Hagen.

[13] Erich Mendelsohn, 'Notiz auf einer Zeichnung der zwanziger Jahre', in Bruno Zevi, *Erich Mendelsohn. Opera completa*, Milan, 1970, p. 129. – Hans Poelzig, unpublished notes in the Marlene Poelzig Collection, Hamburg. – Bernhard Hoetger, 'Ein Brief an einen Freund', in S.D. Gallwitz, *Dreissig Jahre Worpswede*, Bremen, 1922.

[14] Adolf Behne, in *Ja! Stimmen des Arbeitsrates für Kunst in Berlin*, Berlin, 1919, pp. 13ff.

[15] Walter Gropius to Hans Poelzig, 30. 12. 1918 (Marlene Poelzig Collection, Hamburg); similarly, Gropius to Poelzig, 20. 12. 1917 (Marlene Poelzig Collection, Hamburg), and to Karl Ernst Osthaus, 23. 12. 1918 (Osthaus-Archiv, Hagen). – Bruno Taut to Karl Ernst Osthaus, 11. 2., 28. 4., 16. 5., 2. 8., 25. 10., and 14. 11. 1919 (Osthaus-Archiv).

As late as 1925 Hermann Finsterlin wanted to withdraw to the primeval forest of southern Brazil (Hermann Finsterlin to Erich Mendelsohn, 1. 10. 1924 and 20. 2. 1925, Louise Mendelsohn Collection, San Francisco).

[16] Bruno Taut, circular letter, 24. 11. 1919, in *Die gläserne Kette. Visionäre Architekturen aus dem Kreis um Bruno Taut 1919–1920*, catalogue of an exhibition at Schloss Morsbroich, Leverkusen, and the Akademie der Künste, Berlin, 1963, p. 10 (the date given there is incorrect).

[17] Hans Kampffmeyer, *Wohnungsnot und Heimstättengesetz*, Karlsruhe, 1919, p. 17.

[18] Franz Oppenheimer, *Die soziale Forderung der Stunde. Gedanken und Vorschläge*, Leipzig, 1919. – Jules Méline, *Le Retour à la terre et la surproduction industrielle*, Paris, 1905.

[19] Weilbier, 'Abwanderung der Fabriken aus Städten', in *Die Bauwelt*, x (1919); no. 47, p. 11.

[20] *Die Stadtkrone* is indebted to Kampffmeyer's appeal on many points of detail, and also makes specific reference to it. In the second edition of *Friedenstadt* (Jena, 1918) Kampffmeyer published reactions to the first edition, including a letter from Taut. Significantly, Taut stressed the importance of the 'personality that bears within it the great universal feeling' as being alone capable of producing great work (p. 59).

[21] Fritz Burger, 'Die Kunst des 19. und 20. Jahrhunderts. 1. Einführung in die moderne Kunst', in *Handbuch der Kunstwissenschaft*, Berlin, 1917, p. 14.

[22] Gottfried Feder, 'Das deutsche Siedlungswerk', in *Siedlung und Wirtschaft*, xvi (1934), no. 5, p. 184.

[23] Friedrich Naumann, op. cit., pp. 21f.

[24] Peter Behrens, in 'Kunst und Technik', op. cit., p. 555; in *Protokoll der Vorstandssitzung des Deutschen Werkbundes*, 30. 6. 1919; and in 'Die neue Handwerk-Romantik', in *Die Innendekoration*, xxxiii (1922), no. 10, p. 341.

[25] Otto Bartning, 'Neue Bücher. Heinrich Tessenow: Hausbau und dergleichen', in *Kunst und Künstler*, xvi (1917–18), no. 1, p. 43.

[26] Philipp Scheidemann, 'Was kann uns retten?', Walter Gropius, 'Baukunst im freien Volksstaat', in Ernst Drahn and Ernst Friedegg, eds., *Deut-*

scher Revolutions-Almanach für das Jahr 1919, Hamburg and Berlin, 1919, pp. 14ff., 134ff.

[27] Hans Poelzig, 'Festspielhaus in Salzburg', in *Das Kunstblatt*, v (1921), no. 3, p. 84. – Josef Hoffmann, 'Over de toekomst van Weenen', in *Wendingen*, iii (1920), nos. 8–9, p. 21. Virgilio Marchi, *Architettura futurista*, Foligno, 1924, pp. 92f.

[28] See Nikolaus Pevsner, *Academies of Art, Past and Present*, Cambridge, 1940.

[29] Kurt Eisner, 'Der sozialistische Staat und der Künstler', in *An alle Künstler!*, Berlin, 1919.

[30] Heinrich Tessenow, 'Handwerk und Kleinstadt', in *Das Hohe Ufer*, i (1919), no. 2, p. 41.

[31] Adolf Behne, *Die Wiederkehr der Kunst*, op. cit., pp. 101ff. – Ernst Troeltsch, 'Die geistige Revolution', in *Kunstwart*, xxxiv (1921), no. 4, pp. 228ff. – Eckart von Sydow, *Die deutsche expressionistische Kultur und Malerei*, Berlin, 1920. p. 27.

[32] Tut Schlemmer, ed., *Oskar Schlemmer. Briefe und Tagebücher*, Munich, 1958, p. 132.

[33] 'I am busy putting into practice something which has been haunting me for years – a *Bauhütte!*, with a group of like-minded artists.' Walter Gropius to Karl Ernst Osthaus, 23. 12. 1918, Osthaus-Archiv, Hagen.

Another *Bauhütte* was to be founded in Cologne in connection with the university extensions, with Poelzig at its head. It was to combine under one roof the studios and workshops necessary to artistic architectural creativity. 'If Cologne can manage such a thing, then the first step will have been taken in the direction of a genuine regeneration, because for the first time the academic side will be thoroughly and completely excluded.' Hans Poelzig to Wilhelm Worringer, 16. 1. 1920. Copy, Marlene Poelzig Collection, Hamburg.

[34] See Martin Wagner, *Die Sozialisierung der Baubetriebe*, Berlin, 1919. – Martin Wagner, 'Leitsätze für die Sozialisierung der Baubetriebe', in *Die Bauwelt*, x (1919), no. 28, pp. 5f.

2 Beliefs and writings
pages 34–47

[1] Hermann Obrist, *Ein glückliches Leben*, manuscript, quoted in Siegfried Wichmann, *Hermann Obrist. Wegbereiter der Moderne*, catalogue of an exhibition at the Stuck Villa, Munich, 1968, unpaginated. – Otto Bartning, 'Neue Bücher. Heinrich Tessenow: Hausbau und dergleichen', in *Kunst und Künstler*, xvi (1917–18), no. 1, p. 43; and *Erdball*, Wiesbaden, 1947, p. 82. – Erich Mendelsohn to Louise Mendelsohn, 11. 8. 1917, in Oskar Beyer, ed., *Eric Mendelsohn: Letters of an Architect*, London, New York and Toronto, 1967, p. 41 (German in Oskar Beyer, ed., *Erich Mendelsohn. Briefe eines Architekten*, Munich, 1961, p. 40).

[2] Karl Ernst Osthaus to Bruno Rauecker, 19. 10. 1915. Copy, Osthaus-Archiv, Hagen. – Hans Poelzig, 'Festspielhaus in Salzburg', in *Das Kunstblatt*, v (1921), no. 3, p. 77.

[3] 'Deutsche Architekten', in *Die Bauwelt*, x (1919), no. 23, pp. 5f.

[4] Adolf Behne, 'Bruno Taut', in *Neue Blätter für Kunst und Dichtung*, ii (1919–20), no. 1, p. 14.

[5] Henri Bergson, *Essai sur les données immédiates de*

la conscience, Paris, 1888 (English: *Time and Free Will*).

[6] Ludwig Rubiner, 'Hören Sie!', in *Die Aktion*, vi (1916), nos. 27–28, p. 379. – Ludwig Meidner, 'An alle Künstler, Dichter, Musiker', in *An alle Künstler!*, Berlin, 1919, p. 8.

[7] Adolf Behne, 'Gedanken über Kunst und Zweck, dem Glashause gewidmet', in *Kunstgewerbeblatt*, n.s., xxvii (1915–16), no. 1, p. 4.

[8] Walter Gropius, manuscript. Bauhaus-Archiv, Berlin.

[9] Hans Hansen, *Das Erlebnis der Architektur*, Cologne, 1920, p. 83. – Walter Gropius, manuscript. Bauhaus-Archiv, Berlin.

[10] Bruno Taut, *Die Stadtkrone*, Jena, 1919, p. 69.

[11] Bruno Taut, 'Ex oriente lux. Ein Aufruf an die Architekten', in *Das Hohe Ufer*, i (1919), no. 1, p. 17. – Bruno Taut, *Der Weltbaumeister*, Hagen, 1920, unpaginated. – Hans Poelzig, manuscript. Marlene Poelzig Collection, Hamburg.

[12] Lothar Schreyer, *Erinnerungen an Sturm und Bauhaus*, Munich, 1956, p. 140.

[13] H[endrikus] Th[eodorus] Wijdeveld, 'Natuur, bouwkunst en techniek', in *Wendingen*, v (1923), nos. 8–9, p. 14. – See H[endrikus] Th[eodorus] Wijdeveld, 'Het Park Meerwijk te Bergen', in *Wendingen*, i (1918), no. 8, p. 6.

[14] See Jost Hermand, 'Gralsmotive um die Jahrhundertwende', in *Deutsche Vierteljahrsschrift für Literaturwissenschaft und Geistesgeschichte*, xxxvi (1962), no. 4, pp. 521ff.

[15] *Mies in Berlin. Bauwelt-Archiv record 1*, Berlin, 1964.

[16] Karl Schmidt-Rottluff and César Klein, in *Ja! Stimmen des Arbeitsrates für Kunst*, Berlin, 1919, pp. 91 and 49.

See also Wenzel August Hablik, *Cathedral*, 1923, in *Wenzel A. Hablik*, catalogue of an exhibition at the Lichtwark-Stiftung, Hamburg, 1947, p. 19.

[17] Lothar Schreyer, *Erinnerungen an Sturm und Bauhaus*, op. cit., p. 150. Schreyer's testimony is to be read with caution; he was inclined to see his fellow men surrounded by a mystic aura.

[18] See Sixten Ringbom, 'Art in "the epoch of the Great Spiritual"', in *Journal of the Warburg and Courtauld Institutes*, xxix (1966), pp. 386ff. – See H. L. C. Jaffé, *De Stijl 1917–1931*, Berlin and Frankfurt, 1965, pp. 65 ff.

[19] J. L. Mathieu Lauweriks, 'Einen Beitrag zum Entwerfen auf systematischer Grundlage in der Architektur', in *Ring*, April 1909, p. 34.

[20] J. L. Mathieu Lauweriks, 'Het nut en doel der kunst', in *Theosofia*, 1907; quoted in N. H. M. Tummers, *J. L. Mathieu Lauweriks*, Hilversum, 1968, p. 19.

[21] Friedrich Hugo Kaldenbach, 'Briefe an seine Frau', in *Stadtbaukunst alter und neuer Zeit. Frühlicht*, i (1920), no. 13, p. 208.

3 Art and architecture
pages 48–62

[1] Gottfried Semper, *Der Stil in den technischen und tektonischen Künsten oder Praktische Ästhetik*, Frankfurt, 1860, pp. vf.

[2] Walter Müller-Wulckow, *Aufbau – Architektur!*, Berlin, 1919, pp. 52f.

3 Wilhelm Worringer, 'Künstlerische Zukunftsfragen', in *Kunst und Künstler*, XIII (1916), no. 5, p. 262.
4 Wilhelm Weber, 'Zur Peter-Behrens-Ausstellung', in *Peter Behrens (1868–1940)*, catalogue of an exhibition at the Pfalzgalerie, Kaiserslautern, and elsewhere, 1966–67, p. 16. – Ludwig Coellen, 'Der Kubismus der Ägyptik und sein Bezug zum Expressionismus', in *Das Kunstblatt*, II (1918), no. 9, p. 253.
5 Walter Gropius, 'Die Entwicklung moderner Industriebaukunst', in *Jahrbuch des Deutschen Werkbundes 1913*, Jena, 1913, pp. 21f.
6 Walter Gropius, notes for a speech to Weimar craftsmen, manuscript. Bauhaus-Archiv, Berlin.
7 Wilhelm Worringer, op. cit., p. 260.
8 Herbert Eulenberg, 'Der Gedanke des Hochhauses', in *Das Wilhelm-Marx-Haus Düsseldorf*, Düsseldorf, n.d., p. 10. – Paul Scheerbart, *Glasarchitektur*, Berlin, 1914, p. 79. – Karl Ernst Osthaus, *Grundzüge der Stilentwicklung*, Hagen, 1918, p. 37.
9 Adolf Behne, 'Wiedergeburt der Baukunst', in Bruno Taut, *Die Stadtkrone*, Jena, 1919. pp. 130f., and *Die Wiederkehr der Kunst*, Leipzig, 1919, p. 56.
10 Bruno Taut, 'Ex oriente lux. Ein Aufruf an die Architekten', first published in *Das Hohe Ufer*, I (1919), no. 1, p. 17.
11 Otto Bartning, *Erde Geliebte*, Hamburg, 1955, p. 590. – Walter Gropius, manuscript. Bauhaus-Archiv, Berlin. – Erich Mendelsohn, in *Wendingen*, III (1920), no. 10, p. 2. – Hans Poelzig, 'Festspielhaus in Salzburg', in *Das Kunstblatt*, V (1921), no. 3, p. 83.
12 Bruno Taut, 'Für die neue Baukunst!', in *Das Kunstblatt*, III (1919), no. 1, p. 24.
13 K[arl] Sch[effler], 'Kunstausstellungen. Berlin', in *Kunst und Künstler*, XVIII (1919–20), no. 4, p. 183. – Walter Curt Behrendt, *Der Kampf um den Stil*, Stuttgart and Berlin, 1920, p. 266.
14 Bruno Taut, *Die neue Baukunst in Europa und Amerika*, Stuttgart, 1929, p. 24.
15 Finsterlin, after studying natural science, received his artistic training from Franz Stuck and others; he denies having had any closer contact with Jugendstil artists. 'During the heyday of this kind of art and architecture I was living alone or with a single companion deep in the mountains and had no idea what was going on out in the world or in art . . . Obrist, Endell, and Schmidthals I knew and still know only as names.' Written communication from Hermann Finsterlin, 16. 3. 1968.
16 Hans Poelzig to Walter Gropius, 8. 7. 1919. Copy, Marlene Poelzig Collection, Hamburg.
17 Henry van de Velde, 'Zukunftsglaube' in *Genius*, II (1920), no. 2, p. 165.
18 Wilhelm von Bode, 'Die "Not der geistigen Arbeiter" im Gebiet der Kunstforschung', in *Kunst und Künstler*, XVIII (1920) no. 7, p. 299. – For attitudes to Obrist, see Oscar Beyer, ed., *Eric Mendelsohn: Letters of an Architect*, London, New York and Toronto, 1967, p. 34 (German in Oskar Beyer, ed., *Erich Mendelsohn. Briefe eines Architekten*, Munich, 1961, p. 34); Bruno Taut, 'Glasbau', in *Stadtbaukunst alter und neuer Zeit*, I (1920), no. 8, p. 121; and Kurt Gerstenberg, 'Revolution in der Architektur', in *Der Cicerone*, XI (1919), no. 9, p. 255.

19 Hermann Obrist, in *Ja! Stimmen des Arbeitsrates für Kunst in Berlin*, Berlin, 1919, pp. 61ff.
20 Hermann Obrist, *Neue Möglichkeiten in der bildenden Kunst*, Munich, 1903, p. 161.
21 Hermann Finsterlin, *Gaudí und ich. Mein architektonisches Verhältnis zu Gaudí*, 1967. Duplicated manuscript. – The correspondence has not survived: Gaudí's papers were destroyed in a studio fire in 1936, and Finsterlin's in the Second World War.
22 Pavel Janák's article is included in Jaroslav Vokoun, 'Czech Cubism', in *The Architectural Review*, CXXXIX (1966), no. 829, pp. 229 ff. (reprinted in N. Pevsner and J. M. Richards, eds., *The Anti-Rationalists*, London, 1972).
23 Josef Čapek, 'Moderne Architektur', in *Der Sturm*, V (1914–15), no. 3, p. 18.
24 Peter Jessen, 'Die deutsche Werkbund-Ausstellung Köln 1914', in *Jahrbuch des Deutschen Werkbundes 1915*, Munich, 1915, p. 10. – Josef Čapek, op. cit., p. 18.

4 Around 1910
pages 63–72

1 Hermann Muthesius, 'Wo stehen wir?' in *Jahrbuch des Deutschen Werkbundes 1912*, Jena, 1912, pp. 11ff.
2 Paul Mebes, *Um 1800*, 3rd ed., Munich, 1920, p. 3. Significantly, this book, which mourned the 'efficient, independent craftsman class' and a 'language of art easily accessible to the people', went into second (1918) and third (1920) editions. Many readers appear to have agreed with the author in drawing a parallel between the dark years of the Napoleonic wars and the years following the First World War.
3 Peter Behrens, *Feste des Lebens und der Kunst*, Leipzig, 1900, p. 23, and 'Was ist monumentale Kunst?', in *Kunstgewerbeblatt*, n. s., XX (1908–9), no. 3, p. 46.
4 Probably at least Bruno Schmitz and J. L. Mathieu Lauweriks knew Richardson's work at first hand.
5 Friedrich Tamms, ed., *Paul Bonatz. Arbeiten aus den Jahren 1907 bis 1937*, Stuttgart, 1937, p. 22.
6 Peter Behrens, 'Einfluß von Zeit- und Raumausnutzung auf moderne Formentwicklung', in *Jahrbuch des Deutschen Werkbundes 1914*, Jena, 1914, p. 8.
7 Fritz Hoeber, *Peter Behrens*, Munich, 1913, p. 166.
8 Walter Gropius to Karl Ernst Osthaus, 19. 6. 1913. Osthaus-Archiv, Hagen. For Gropius' stand in the Werkbund dispute, see Peter Stressig, 'Hohenhagen – "Experimentierfeld modernen Bauens"', in Herta Hesse-Frielinghaus, ed., *Karl Ernst Osthaus*, Recklinghausen, 1971, pp. 465ff.
9 Henry van de Velde, *Gegen-Leitsätze*, 1914, quoted in Julius Posener, ed., *Anfänge des Funktionalismus*, Berlin and Frankfurt, 1964, p. 206.
10 Berg and Trauer, 'Zweckmäßigkeit der Verwendung von Eisenbeton oder Eisen für monumentale Hochbau-Konstruktionen', in *Deutsche Bauzeitung. Mitteilungen über Zement-, Beton- und Eisenbetonbau*, X (1913), no. 14, p. 165. – Erich Mendelsohn, 'Das Problem einer neuen Baukunst', 1919, in Erich Mendelsohn, *Das Gesamtschaffen des Architekten*, Berlin, 1930, p. 29.

11 Walter Gropius to Karl Ernst Osthaus, 26. 8. 1913. Osthaus-Archiv, Hagen.
12 Hans Poelzig, 'Der neuzeitliche Fabrikbau', in *Der Industriebau*, II (1911), no. 5, pp. 100ff.
13 In a letter to Karl Ernst Osthaus of 3. 4. 1912, Gropius referred to Poelzig's 'factory in Luban near Posen . . . which I like very much indeed.' Osthaus-Archiv, Hagen.

5 Bruno Taut
pages 73–88

1 Paul Bonatz, *Leben und Bauen*, Stuttgart, 1950, pp. 146ff.
2 Bruno Taut to Karl Ernst Osthaus, 14. 11. and 16. 5. 1919. Osthaus-Archiv, Hagen.
3 Bruno Taut to Ludwig Berger, 13. 10. 1920. Copy, Akademie der Künste, Berlin.
4 Bruno Taut to Karl Ernst Osthaus, 2. 8. 1919. Osthaus-Archiv, Hagen.
5 Bruno Taut to Karl Ernst Osthaus, 11. 2., 28. 4., 16. 5., 2. 8., 25. 10., and 14. 11. 1919. Osthaus-Archiv, Hagen.
6 Adolf Behne, 'Wiedergeburt der Baukunst', in Bruno Taut, *Die Stadtkrone*, Jena, 1919, p. 129, and Adolf Behne, *Die Wiederkehr der Kunst*, Leipzig, 1919, p. 43. For Scheerbart's impact, see Wolfgang Pehnt, 'Paul Scheerbart, ein Dichter der Architekten', in Paul Scheerbart, *Glasarchitektur*, new ed., Munich, 1971, pp. 139ff.
   It would be wrong, however, to assume that Scheerbart's books were familiar to all the members of Taut's circle of friends. Hermann Finsterlin, for example, claims that he did not even hear Scheerbart's name until the end of the twenties; 'nor was I aware that the name Scheerbart had ever come up in conversations within the "*gläserne kette*"' (written communication from Finsterlin, 5. 7. 1967). In actual fact as early as 1919 Gropius had recommended that he read Scheerbart, and Taut had compared Finsterlin and Scheerbart in a circular letter (which was also addressed to Finsterlin) in 1920.
7 Paul Scheerbart, 'Licht und Luft', in *Ver Sacrum*, I (1898), no. 7, pp. 13f. Taut borrowed the argument, which Scheerbart repeated in *Glasarchitektur*, in his book *Die neue Wohnung*, Leipzig, 1924, p. 62.
   Scheerbart's excursion into architectural theory may have been influenced by his controversy with Adolf Loos, in whose circle he had friends. (Letter from Hellmut Draws-Tychsen, 21. 5. 1972.)
8 Bruno Taut, 'Glasbau', in *Stadtbaukunst alter und neuer Zeit*, I (1920), no. 8, p. 120.
9 Bruno Taut, 'Glasbau', in *Die Baugilde*, VII (1925), no. 18, p. 1248.
10 Adolf Behne, *Die Wiederkehr der Kunst*, op. cit., pp. 59f.
11 Paul Scheerbart, 'Glashäuser', in *Technische Monatshefte*, V (1914), no. 4, pp. 8ff. Adolf Behne, *Die Wiederkehr der Kunst*, op. cit., pp. 59f.; and Peter Jessen, 'Die deutsche Werkbund-Ausstellung Köln 1914', in *Jahrbuch des Deutschen Werkbundes 1915*, Munich, 1915, p. 25.
12 Adolf Behne, 'Gedanken über Kunst und Zweck, dem Glashause gewidmet', in *Kunstgewerbeblatt*, n.s., XXVII (1915–16), no. 1, p. 4. Bruno Taut, *Glashaus. Werkbund-Ausstellung Köln 1914*, Berlin, n.d. (1914). See also Bruno Taut, 'Beo-

511. Wenzel August Hablik. Flying estate, from *Cyklus Architektur*, 1925. Etching. Hablik Collection, Itzehoe.
512. Alexander Raymond. *Flash Gordon*, 1934.
513. Oskar Fischer. Façade decoration of the Barasch building, Magdeburg, 1921.

513

bachtungen über Farbenwirkung aus meiner Praxis', in *Die Bauwelt*, x (1919), no. 38, pp. 12f.
13 Bruno Taut, 'Glasbau', in *Die Baugilde*, op. cit., p. 1248.
14 Karl Ernst Osthaus to Walter Gropius, 21. 12. 1918, 9. 1. and 17. 1. 1919. Copies, Osthaus-Archiv, Hagen.
15 Karl Ernst Osthaus to Bruno Taut, 22. 11. 1919 (copy, Osthaus-Archiv, Hagen), and 'Die Folkwang-Schule. Ein Entwurf von Bruno Taut', in *Genius*, II (1920), no. 2, pp. 199ff. See also Bruno Taut, Die Folkwang-Schule in Hagen/Westf., manuscript sent by Taut to Osthaus on 2. 2. 1920. Osthaus-Archiv, Hagen.
16 Bruno Taut, *Die Stadtkrone*, Jena, 1919, pp. 67ff.
17 [Karl Scheffler], 'Bruno Taut', in *Kunst und Künstler*, XVIII (1919–20), no. 10, p. 465.
18 Bruno Taut to Karl Ernst Osthaus, 24. 1. 1920. Osthaus-Archiv, Hagen. When judging the project it is important to remember that Taut's design represents only a site plan. Osthaus originally intended for the individual buildings to be by different architects (Osthaus to Bruno Taut, 22. 11. 1919, copy, Osthaus-Archiv, Hagen).
19 Bruno Taut to Karl Ernst Osthaus, 16. 5. 1919. Osthaus-Archiv, Hagen. – Schmidt-Rottluff produced sculptures strongly influenced by African Negro art, particularly in 1917.
20 Peter Kropotkin. *Fields, Factories and Workshops*, London, 1899, p. 6.
21 Adolf Behne, *Neues Bauen – neues Wohnen*, Leipzig, 1927, p. 74.
22 Otto Kohtz, *Gedanken über Architektur*, Berlin, 1909, pp. 3f.
23 See Manfredi Nicoletti, 'Flash Gordon and the twentieth-century Utopia', in *The Architectural Review*, CXL (1966), no. 834, pp. 87ff. Fantastic dream landscapes with labyrinths and cities in the air had already been visited by Little Nemo, in the series of the same name by Winsor McCay (1905–11). It may have been Lyonel Feininger, himself a designer of comic strips, who brought the new medium to the attention of Berlin artists.
24 Bruno Taut, introduction to *Frühlicht*, no. 1, Autumn 1921, p. 1.

511

512

ONE OF BARIN'S SPEED-CARS WHISKS THEM TOWARD HIS CAPITAL.

"LOOK, FLASH, ARBORIA HAS BEEN REBUILT MORE BEAUTIFUL THAN EVER!"

25 Bruno Taut, 'Mein erstes Jahr "Stadtbaurat"', in *Frühlicht*, no. 4, Summer 1922, pp. 125ff.
26 Bruno Taut, *Ein Wohnhaus*, Stuttgart, 1927, p. 13.
27 Bruno Taut to Ludwig Berger, 11. 2. 1920. Copy, Akademie der Künste, Berlin.
28 Bruno Taut, 'Wiedergeburt der Farbe', lecture given on the occasion of the Deutsche Farbentag (Colour Day) in Hamburg on 15. 4. 1925, in *Die Bauwelt*, XVI (1925), no. 29, p. 676.
29 Kurt Junghanns, *Bruno Taut. 1880–1938*, Berlin, 1970, pp. 16f.
30 Anon., *5. Februar 1919 Spectrum mysticum*, manuscript in the Arbeitsrat für Kunst papers of Walter Gropius. Bauhaus-Archiv, Berlin.
31 Adolf Behne, *Die Wiederkehr der Kunst*, op. cit., p. 102.
32 Walter Curt Behrendt, 'Neue Aufgaben der Baukunst', in *Der Aufbau*, 1919, no. 6, p. 23. – Bruno Taut, 'Wiedergeburt der Farbe', op. cit., p. 674.
33 Hans Poelzig, 'Architekturfragen', lecture given in Berlin on 25. 2. 1922, in *Das Kunstblatt*, VI (1922), no. 5, p. 194. – Fritz Stahl, 'Der gebrochene Bann', in *Berliner Tageblatt*, 10. 2. 1923.
34 Bruno Taut, *Ein Wohnhaus*, op. cit., p. 32.
35 Bruno Taut, *Die neue Baukunst in Europa und Amerika*, Stuttgart, 1929, p. 43.
36 Theo van Doesburg to Anthony Kok, 28. 2. 1922, in *De Stijl*, catalogue of an exhibition at the Stedelijk Museum, Amsterdam, 1951, and in 'Elementarismus', in *De Stijl. 1917–1931*, pp. 15f.
37 Franz Glück, ed., *Adolf Loos. Sämtliche Schriften*, vol. I, Vienna and Munich, 1962, p. 278.

6 Visionary architects
pages 89–106

1 Kurt Hiller, 'Ein deutsches Herrenhaus', in *Tätiger Geist*, quoted in Eva Kolinsky, *Engagierter Expressionismus*, Stuttgart, 1970, p. 117. – Martin Buber, ed., *Gustav Landauer. Sein Lebensgang in Briefen*, vol. II, Frankfurt, 1929, p. 298.
2 Evidence on the date of foundation is contradictory, but the fact that the first meeting of the Novembergruppe on 3. 12. 1918 debated an Arbeitsrat für Kunst motion proposing a merger of the two organizations confirms that it was some time in November. The two groups did not begin to work together until a year later. The financial situation of the Arbeitsrat deteriorated so badly during 1920 that its executive manager, Adolf Behne, worked without pay after 1. 10. 1920, and the report of activities was very meagre (circular from Adolf Behne, 9. 12. 1920). The Arbeitsrat disbanded on 30. 5. 1921.
3 Walter Gropius to Karl Ernst Osthaus, 23. 12. 1918 (Osthaus-Archiv, Hagen), and to Hans Poelzig, 30. 12. 1918 (Marlene Poelzig Collection, Hamburg).
Outside Berlin the activities of the Arbeitsrat für Kunst were much more sceptically received: 'In any case I don't think a lot is going to come of this Arbeitsrat thing and I don't really care much one way or the other.' Hans Poelzig to Franz Seeck, 17. 2. 1919. Copy, Marlene Poelzig Collection, Hamburg.

4 The *Vossische Zeitung* and the *Berliner Tageblatt* published extracts from the manifesto on 11. 12. 1918, the *Mitteilungen des Deutschen Werkbundes* printed in the 4th issue of 1918 (pp. 14f.), and *Die Bauwelt* published it on 26. 12. 1918 (IX, no. 52, p. 5).
Another of the Arbeitsrat's publications was the extensive *Mitteilung an Alle* advertising the projected magazine *Bauen* and probably written by Behne. *Bauen* was to be published in June 1919 by Neumann under Behne's editorship.
5 *Mitteilung an Alle*, prospectus for the magazine *Bauen*, Berlin, n.d. (1919).
6 Walter Gropius, note in the margin of a newspaper report on the Exhibition for Unknown Architects. Bauhaus-Archiv, Berlin. *Die Bauwelt*, X (1919), nos. 2–3, p. 6.
7 Anon., 'Ausstellungen', in *Das Kunstblatt*, III (1919), no. 5, p. 157. Walter Curt Behrendt, 'Berlin', in *Kunst und Künstler*, XVII (1918–19), no. 8, p. 339. A.W., 'Ausstellung für unbekannte Architekten', in *Dekorative Kunst (= Die Kunst)*, XLI (1918–19), no. 9, p. 272.
The most informative reviews are those of Kurt Gerstenberg ('Revolution in der Architektur', in *Der Cicerone*, XI (1919), no. 9, pp. 255ff.), Walter Riezler ('Revolution und Baukunst', in *Mitteilungen des Deutschen Werkbundes*, II (1919–20), no. 1, pp. 18ff.), and Max Osborn (*Vossische Zeitung*, 25. 4. 1919).
8 Adolf Behne, 'Werkstattbesuche. II. Jefim Golyscheff', in *Der Cicerone*, XI (1919), no. 22, pp. 722ff.
9 Hans Luckhardt ('Angkor'), circular letter, 31. 5. 1920, in *Die gläserne Kette. Visionäre Architekturen aus dem Kreis um Bruno Taut. 1919–1920*, catalogue of an exhibition at Schloss Morsbroich, Leverkusen, and the Akademie der Künste, Berlin, 1963, pp. 42ff. – P[aul] W[estheim], 'Neues Bauen', in *Das Kunstblatt*, IV (1920), no. 7, p. 223. – [Karl Scheffler], 'Bruno Taut', in *Kunst und Künstler*, XVIII (1919–20), no. 10, p. 465.
10 Bruno Taut, circular letter, 24. 11. 1919, in *Die gläserne Kette*, op. cit., p. 10 (the date given in the catalogue is wrong). – Walter Gropius to Karl Ernst Osthaus, 2. 2. 1919. Osthaus-Archiv, Hagen. – Hermann Finsterlin to Erich Mendelsohn, 2. 12. 1924. Louise Mendelsohn Collection, San Francisco.
11 Walter Gropius, inaugural lecture to the Arbeitsrat für Kunst, manuscript. Bauhaus-Archiv, Berlin.
12 Bruno Taut to Alfred Brust, 21. 2. 1920. Beinecke Rare Book and Manuscript Library, Yale University, New Haven, Conn. – Alfred Brust, 'Das gläserne Haus', in *Deutsche Allgemeine Zeitung*, 3. 8. 1927.
13 Wenzel August Hablik to Bruno Taut, undated. Copy, Oswald Mathias Ungers Collection, Cologne.
14 Bruno Taut, circular letter, 3. 2. 1920, in *Die gläserne Kette*, op. cit., p. 23.
15 Bruno Taut, 'Baugedanken der Gegenwart', in *Die Bauwelt*, XIV (1923), no. 25, p. 341.
16 Hermann Finsterlin, 'Die Genesis der Weltarchitektur oder die Deszendenz der Dome als Stilspiel', in *Frühlicht*, no. 3, Spring 1922, p. 158.
17 Written communication from Hermann Finsterlin, 16. 3. 1968. Some 300 works were ap-

parently still extant after the end of the Second World War.
18 Hermann Finsterlin to Erich Mendelsohn, 20. 2. 1925. Louise Mendelsohn Collection, San Francisco.
19 Written communication from Hermann Finsterlin, 16. 3. 1968.
20 Paul Gösch, 'Anregungen. Architektonisches', in *Stadtbaukunst alter und neuer Zeit. Frühlicht*, I (1920), no. 14, p. 220.
21 Bruno Taut to Wenzel August Hablik, 20. 12. 1920. Copy, Oswald Mathias Ungers Collection, Cologne.
22 Wassili Luckhardt ('Zacken'), circular letter, undated, in *Die gläserne Kette*, op. cit., p. 18.
23 The man who commissioned the Buchthal house (ill. 514), a wealthy Berlin outfitter, had a remarkable collection of Expressionist paintings. His attention had been drawn to the Luckhardts by the Arbeitsrat für Kunst exhibition of May 1920. (Written communication from Wassili Luckhardt, 2. 1. 1972.)
24 Hans Scharoun ('Hannes'), circular letter, undated, in *Die gläserne Kette*, op. cit., pp. 24f.

514. Hans and Wassili Luckhardt and Alfons Anker. Buchthal house, Berlin-Westend, c. 1922.
515. Hans Scharoun, Suggested modernization of a church, 1910. Charcoal.

514

515

7 The early Bauhaus
pages 107–116

1 Bruno Adler, *Das Weimarer Bauhaus*, Darmstadt, n.d. (1963), unpaginated. – Theo van Doesburg, 'De invloed van de Stijlbeweging in Duitsland', in *Bouwkundig Weekblad*, XLIV (1923), no. 7.
2 Walter Gropius, manuscript. Bauhaus-Archiv, Berlin. See also Walter Gropius to Karl Ernst Osthaus, 2. 2. 1919. Osthaus-Archiv, Hagen.
3 Tomás Maldonado to Walter Gropius, 1. 11. 1963. Gropius replied on 24. 11. 1963: 'An objective appeal to objective work would at that time have failed in its aim, namely to offer young people pregnant with new ideas a broad basis upon which those ideas could be clarified and tried out in practice.' in *Ulm. Zeitschrift der Hochschule für Gestaltung*, nos. 10–11, May 1964, pp. 64ff.
4 Bruno Taut, photocopy, 27. 12. 1919. Oswald Mathias Ungers Collection, Cologne. – Bruno Taut, circular letter, 26. 12. 1919, in *Die gläserne Kette*, *Visionäre Architekturen aus dem Kreis um Bruno Taut. 1919–1920*, catalogue of an exhibition at Schloss Morsbroich, Leverkusen, and the Akademie der Künste, Berlin, 1963, pp. 11 f.
5 Adolf Behne, *Die Wiederkehr der Kunst*, Leipzig, 1919, p. 24.
6 Walter Gropius, 'Baukunst im freien Volksstaat', in Ernst Drahn and Ernst Friedegg, eds., *Deutscher Revolutions-Almanach für das Jahr 1919*, Hamburg and Berlin, 1919, p. 135.
7 Henry van de Velde, memorandum, Weimar, October 1915, unpaginated.
8 Gottfried Semper, *Wissenschaft, Industrie und Kunst*, Brunswick, 1852, p. 39. See Nikolaus Pevsner, *Academies of Art, Past and Present*, Cambridge, 1940.
9 Charles-Edouard Jeanneret, *Etude sur le mouvement d'art décoratif en Allemagne*, La Chaux-de-Fonds, 1912.
10 Otto Bartning, *Ein Unterrichts-Plan*, manuscript with corrections by Gropius. Bauhaus-Archiv, Berlin. Bartning's programme was published, under the title 'Vorschläge zu einem Lehrplan für Handwerker, Architekten und bildende Künstler' in *Mitteilungen des Deutschen Werkbundes*, II (1919–20), no. 2, pp. 42ff. A note in Gropius' handwriting (Bauhaus-Archiv, Berlin), which probably served as an aide-mémoire for a speech during the early days of the Bauhaus, contains the words: 'General reform, plan of the A.f.K.' (Arbeitsrat für Kunst). Gropius himself referred to similar efforts in other schools in a speech on the occasion of the Thuringian Landtag on 9. 7. 1920 (Hans M. Wingler, *Das Bauhaus*, 2nd ed., Bramsche, 1968, pp. 52f.).
11 Max Seliger, head of the Academy for Graphic Arts, Leipzig, at the conference of the League of German Handicrafts Clubs at Brunswick on 20–21. 5. 1904, quoted in 'Kunstgewerbeschule und Lehrwerkstätten', in *Dekorative Kunst*, VI (1904), no. 8, pp. 326ff.
12 'I believe my work is proceeding in a similar direction to your own.' Walter Gropius to Hans Poelzig, 23. 9. 1916. Marlene Poelzig Collection, Hamburg.
Poelzig thought of Gropius for his successor a

21

principal of the Breslau Academy. He praised the 'strict objectivity and beautiful lines' of Gropius' interiors, and – it is now known – was instrumental in getting Gropius appointed at Weimar. Gropius was first considered for the position of principal of the School of Arts and Crafts (hence as van de Velde's successor), but subsequently also for a teaching post at the Art College. As negotiations with Weimar became more and more protracted, Poelzig intervened with his close friend, the painter Richard Engelmann, a professor at the Weimar Academy, in favour of his young colleague. From the correspondence between Engelmann and Poelzig there emerged the idea of appointing Gropius as principal of the Art College. This development led finally to the merging of both Weimar institutes, the Art College and the School of Arts and Crafts, under Gropius' leadership. Poelzig also publicly supported the Bauhaus later, though he felt that Gropius 'had made too much hullabaloo'. (Hans Poelzig to Ministerialdirektor Schmidt, undated; Richard Engelmann to Hans Poelzig, 3. 2. 1919; Hans Poelzig to Ernst Jäckh, 16. 1. 1920. Marlene Poelzig Collection, Hamburg.)

[13] Gunta Stadler-Stölzl, 'In der Textilwerkstatt des Bauhauses 1919 bis 1931', in *werk*, LV (1968), no. 11, p. 745. Of the many sources of information on the early years of the Bauhaus the most graphic are the descriptions by George Adams, Bruno Adler, Alfred Arndt, Paul Citroen, Helmut von Erffa, Werner Graeff, Georg Muche and Lothar Schreyer (see Bibliography, Architecture: individuals . . ., Bauhaus).

[14] Johannes Itten, *Mein Vorkurs am Bauhaus*, Ravensburg, 1963.

[15] Walter Gropius, 'Gibt es eine Wissenschaft der Gestaltung?', 1947, in *Architektur. Wege zu einer optischen Kultur*, Frankfurt, 1956, p. 29.

[16] Walter Gropius, manuscript. Bauhaus-Archiv, Berlin.

[17] Written communication from Fred Forbat, 24. 7. 1969. Forbat began working as an associate in the Gropius/Meyer office in September 1920.

[18] Paul Klopfer, 'Die Gropius-Ausstellung im Staatl. Bauhaus zu Weimar', in *Allgemeine Thüringische Landeszeitung*, supplement *Deutschland*, Weimar, 5. 7. 1922.

[19] Oral communication from Ernst Neufert, 18. 2. 1969.

[20] Walter Gropius to Karl Ernst Osthaus, 2. 2. 1919. Osthaus-Archiv, Hagen.

[21] Walter Gropius, 'Neues Bauen', in *Der Holzbau*, supplement to the *Deutsche Bauzeitung*, issue 2, 1920, p. 5.

[22] Karl Schmidt-Rottluff's 'Pillar of Prayer' was intended for a crystal building by Bruno Taut (see above, p. 152). The design was to be published in the first issue of a new magazine entitled *Bauen* which Behne, Gropius and Taut wanted to bring out together (Bruno Taut to Karl Ernst Osthaus, 28. 4. 1919, Osthaus-Archiv, Hagen). Schmidt-Rottluff himself thinks it possible that Gropius was influenced by his design (written communication, 11. 12. 1970).

[23] Walter Gropius, 'Neues Bauen', op. cit. See also Gropius' answer to the Arbeitsrat's inquiry in *Ja! Stimmen des Arbeitsrates für Kunst in Berlin*, Berlin, 1919, p. 32.

[24] Adolf Meyer to Fred Forbat, 4. 12. 1921. Fred Forbat Collection, Vällingby.

[25] Fred Forbat doubts it; Werner Graeff, one of the first participants in van Doesburg's private courses, thinks it likely (written communication from Fred Forbat, 24. 7. 1969; oral communication from Werner Graeff, 18. 12. 1968).

[26] Written communication from Fred Forbat, 24. 7. 1969.

[27] Walter Gropius, 'Sind beim Bau von Industriegebäuden künstlerische Gesichtspunkte mit praktischen und wirtschaftlichen vereinbar?', in *Der Industriebau*, III (1912), no. 1, pp. 5f. – Walter Gropius, 'Der stilbildende Wert industrieller Bauformen', in *Jahrbuch des Deutschen Werkbundes 1914*, Jena, 1914, pp. 29f. – Walter Gropius, 'Neues Bauen', op. cit. – Walter Gropius to Karl Ernst Osthaus, 12. 3. and 18. 3. 1911. Osthaus-Archiv, Hagen.

[28] Walter Gropius, 'Der stilbildende Wert industrieller Bauformen', op. cit., p. 32.

[29] Walter Gropius, 'Baukunst im freien Volksstaat', op. cit., p. 134.

[30] Walter Gropius, 'Der Baugeist der neuen Volksgemeinde', in *Die Glocke*, X (1924), no. 10, p. 314.

[31] Walter Gropius, manuscript. Bauhaus-Archiv, Berlin. – Walter Gropius to Karl Ernst Osthaus, 2. 2. 1919. Osthaus-Archiv, Hagen.

[32] Theodor Heuss, 'Bilanz von Weimar', in *Stuttgarter Neues Tageblatt*, 10. 10. 1923.

8 Erich Mendelsohn
pages 117–126

[1] The only thing was a chapel for the Jewish cemetery in his home town of Allenstein, which Mendelsohn built in 1911 when he was still a student. In 1914–15 he drew up plans for the conversion of the Becker house in Chemnitz (ill. 516), but the work was never carried out because of the war. (Written communication from Louise Mendelsohn, 21. 12. 1969.)

[2] Erich Mendelsohn, 'My own Contribution to the Development of Contemporary Architecture', lecture given in Los Angeles on 17. 3. 1948, duplicated manuscript.

[3] Richard Neutra, *Auftrag für morgen*, Hamburg, 1962, pp. 169, 171f.

[4] Written communication from Louise Mendelsohn, 21. 12. 1969. 'When [Mendelsohn] moved to Berlin we asked to see [van de Velde's] work in the library and E. was deeply affected.' The two men did not meet until after the war in Berlin.

[5] Erich Mendelsohn to Louise Mendelsohn, 22. 10. 1924, in Oskar Beyer, ed., *Eric Mendelsohn: Letters of an Architect*, London, New York and Toronto, 1967, p. 69 (German in Oskar Beyer, ed., *Erich Mendelsohn. Briefe eines Architekten*, Munich, 1961, p. 34).

[6] Erich Mendelsohn, 'Neue Formprobleme der Baukunst', 1919, manuscript. Louise Mendelsohn Collection, San Francisco. This was the lecture Mendelsohn gave on the occasion of the opening of his exhibition at Paul Cassirer's gallery. He later revised the text, probably for his lectures to the Arbeitsrat für Kunst and in Amsterdam. The revised version was published as 'Das Problem

516. Erich Mendelsohn. Project for the Becker house, Chemnitz, 1914–15. Indian ink.

einer neuen Baukunst', in *Erich Mendelsohn. Das Gesamtschaffen des Architekten*, Berlin, 1930, pp. 7ff.

[7] Erich Mendelsohn, 'Das Problem einer neuen Baukunst', opt. cit. p. 13.

[8] Erich Mendelsohn, 'My own Contribution . . .', op. cit., p. 5. – Erich Mendelsohn to Louise Mendelsohn, 14. 6. 1917, in Oscar Beyer, ed., *Erich Mendelsohn. Briefe . . .*, op. cit., p. 40 (not included in the English selection).

[9] It is unlikely that Mendelsohn saw any of Sant'Elia's drawings before the First World War. In 1911, when Mendelsohn was in Italy and may possibly have been in contact with the Futurists, Sant'Elia was certainly not yet associated with Marinetti and his circle.

[10] Erich Mendelsohn, 'Das Problem einer neuen Baukunst', op. cit., p. 19. Finsterlin called Mendelsohn a 'brotherly comrade' (Hermann Finsterlin to Erich Mendelsohn, 2. 12. 1924, Louise Mendelsohn Collection, San Francisco).

[11] Erich Mendelsohn, 'Die internationale Übereinstimmung des neuen Baugedankens oder Dynamik und Funktion', lecture in Amsterdam, 1923, in *Erich Mendelsohn. Das Gesamtschaffen des Architekten*, op. cit., p. 23.

[12] Hermann Obrist to Erich Mendelsohn, 28. 12. 1914, and 'Gutachten' ('Advice'), a letter to Mendelsohn, undated (early 1915). Louise Mendelsohn Collection, San Francisco.

[13] Erich Mendelsohn to Louise Mendelsohn, 24. 6. 1917, in Oskar Beyer, ed., *Eric Mendelsohn: Letters . . .*, op. cit., p. 40 (German in Beyer, ed., *Erich Mendelsohn. Briefe . . .*, op. cit., p. 40).

[14] Professor Erwin Freundlich, scientist at the Potsdam Observatory and an associate of Einstein, met the architect in 1914 through Louise Maas, later Mendelsohn's wife.

[15] Gustav Adolf Platz, *Die Baukunst der neuesten Zeit*, Berlin, 1927, p. 70.

[16] Jan Frederik Staal, 'Naar anleiding van Erich Mendelsohn's ontwerpen', in *Wendingen*, III (1920), no. 10, p. 3.

[17] Erich Mendelsohn, 'Neue Formprobleme der Baukunst', op. cit. – Erich Mendelsohn to Louise

Mendelsohn, 22. 10. 1924, in Oskar Beyer, ed., *Erich Mendelsohn: Letters . . .*, op. cit., p. 68 (German in Beyer, ed., *Erich Mendelsohn. Briefe . . .*, op. cit., p. 66).

[18] Erich Mendelsohn, 'Die internationale Übereinstimmung . . .', op. cit., p. 26.

[19] Ibid., p. 33.

[20] Reyner Banham, 'Mendelsohn', in *The Architectural Review*, CXVI (1954), no. 692, p. 89.

[21] Erich Mendelsohn to Louise Mendelsohn, 19. 8. 1923, in Oskar Beyer, ed., *Eric Mendelsohn: Letters . . .*, op. cit., p. 60 (German in Beyer, ed., *Erich Mendelsohn. Briefe . . .*, op. cit., p. 57. – See Erich Mendelsohn, 'My own Contribution . . .', op. cit., p. 8.

[22] Erich Mendelsohn, 'Die internationale Übereinstimmung . . .', op. cit., pp. 22f.

[23] Erich Mendelsohn, 'Das Problem einer neuen Baukunst', op. cit., pp. 20f.

[24] Erich Mendelsohn, *Russland Europa Amerika*, Berlin, 1929, p. 217.

517. Fritz Höger. Anzeiger building, Hanover, 1927–28.

518. Bernhard Hoetger. Brunnenhof, Worpswede, 1915.

517

518

9 North German Expressionism

pages 127–136

[1] Fritz Höger, in *Bauwelt*, XVIII (1927), no. 19, p. 489. See also B. Stiefler, 'Durch den Klinker zum deutschen Baustil', in *Die Baugilde*, X (1928), no. 14, p. 1080.

[2] Among the more important designers of the Hamburg *Kontorhaus* were Hermann Distel, the brothers Hans and Oskar Gerson, August Grubitz and Hermann Höger, a brother of Fritz Höger (ills. 302, 497). Fritz Höger himself took the 'Hamburg style' beyond the confines of the city: examples are two tower blocks in Hanover (ill. 517), the Scherk perfumery factory, a church on the Hohenzollernplatz in Berlin, and two other buildings in Berlin.

[3] Rudolf G. Binding, 'Das Chile-Haus in Hamburg', in Carl J. H. Westphal, ed., *Fritz Höger. Der niederdeutsche Backstein-Baumeister*, Wolfshagen-Scharbeutz, 1938, p. 13.

[4] Fritz Höger, 'Backsteinbaukunst', in Westphal, ed., *Fritz Höger . . .*, op. cit. p. 18.

[5] 'As you know, architecture has been a serious concern of mine for many years now, and I have always been interested in working with a rhythm which was admittedly not to your liking, but which you could in fact to some extent appreciate.' Bernhard Hoetger to Max Laeuger, 8. 3. 1917. Copy, Bahlsen-Archiv, Hanover.

[6] 'We have faith in Hoetger's genius, and one should always let a genius have his head, even at the risk that not everything will work out successfully.' Hermann Bahlsen, *Chronik der neuen TET-Stadt*, manuscript. Bahlsen-Archiv, Hanover.

[7] Kasimir Edschmid, 'Bernhard Hoetger', in *Almanach auf das Jahr 1919. Verlag Fritz Gurlitt*, quoted in *Leibniz-Blätter*, Hanover, November 1959, p. 42.

[8] Bernhard Hoetger, *Äusserung zur TET-Stadt*, manuscript. Bahlsen-Archiv, Hanover.

[9] Ludwig Roselius, 'Wir Bremer', 1923, in *Reden und Schriften zur Böttcherstrasse in Bremen*, Bremen, 1932, p. 9.

Hitler had a copy of Roselius' collection of essays: though the political views expressed there were identical with his own, he later condemned the Böttcherstrasse (see above, p. 206; and Hellmut Lehmann-Haupt, *Art under a Dictatorship*, New York, 1954, p. 253).

[10] Bernhard Hoetger, 'Ein Brief an einen Freund', in S. D. Gallwitz, *Dreissig Jahre Worpswede*, Bremen, 1922, p. 90.

[11] Ludwig Roselius, 'Zur Neugestaltung der alten Böttcherstrasse in Bremen', in *Reden und Schriften . . .*, op. cit. p. 19.

[12] Direct access from Böttcherstrasse to the court came only with the rebuilding of the Paula-Modersohn-Becker-Haus by Max Säume and Günter Hafemann.

[13] *Die Böttcherstrasse in Bremen. Praktischer Führer*, Bremen, n.d. (before 1933), unpaginated.

[14] Bernhard Hoetger to Wilhelm Teichmann, 31. 10. 1931. Wilhelm Teichmann Collection, Hamburg.

[15] Bernhard Hoetger, in *Die Böttcherstrasse*, I (1928), no. 2, p. 17. – Bernhard Hoetger to Wilhelm Teichmann, 31. 10. 1931. Wilhelm Teichmann Collection, Hamburg.

10 The architecture of Rudolf Steiner

pages 137–148

[1] Rudolf Steiner, 'Die okkulten Gesichtspunkte des Stuttgarter Baues', lecture given on 15. 10. 1911, printed in *Mitteilungen aus der anthroposophischen Arbeit in Deutschland*, XI (1957), no. 1, pp. 28ff.

[2] Rudolf Steiner, *Wege zu einem neuen Baustil*, Dornach, 1926, pp. 12, 19.

[3] Rudolf Steiner, *Der Baugedanke des Goetheanum* (lecture given on 29. 6. 1921, later published in book form), 2nd ed., Stuttgart, 1958, p. 52.

[4] Paul Fechter, *Der Expressionismus*, 3rd ed., Munich, 1919, p. 59.

[5] The planning of the complex originally intended for Munich was placed in the hands of Dr Carl Schmid-Curtius, of the Stuttgart firm of architects Martz & Schmid, on 3. 3. 1911. Schmid-Curtius was a member of the Anthroposophical Society. He was in charge of the planning and building of the first Goetheanum at Dornach only until Spring 1914. After that time Steiner's suggestions for the buildings at Dornach were worked out by a team of architects, led by Ernst Aisenpreis and including Hermann Ranzenberger and, later, Albert von Baravalle. A few ideas were also contributed by non-architects, such as the sculptor Carl Kemper. The construction of the first Goetheanum was handled by a Basel firm; that of its successor by the Dornach office on its own. The smaller buildings were supervised by various people within the Dornach office.

[6] Rudolf Steiner, *Mein Lebensgang*, 7th ed., Dornach, 1962, pp. 348ff.

[7] Erich Zimmer, 'Der Baugedanke von Malsch', in *Mensch und Baukunst*, XVIII (1969), no. 3, pp. 3ff.; and E. A. Karl Stockmeyer, *Der Modellbau in Malsch*, Malsch, 1969.

[8] See Hilde Raske, ed., *Der Bau. Studien zur Architektur und Plastik des ersten Goetheanum von Carl Kemper*, Stuttgart, 1966, pp. 185ff.

[9] Rudolf Steiner, *Mein Lebensgang*, op. cit., p. 218.

[10] Peter Behrens, *Feste des Lebens und der Kunst*, Leipzig, 1900, pp. 11f.

[11] Rudolf Steiner, *Ausführungen über die Anthroposophen-Kolonie in Dornach*, lecture given on 23. 1. 1914, published as a pamphlet.

[12] See Erich Zimmer, *Rudolf Steiner als Architekt von Wohn- und Zweckbauten*, Stuttgart, n.d. (1971). The following buildings (not discussed in the present work but fully covered by Zimmer) were based on Steiner's suggestions: Vreede house, Dornach (1919–21), van Blommestein house, Dornach (1919), three 'eurhythmics houses', Dornach (1920), de Jaager house, Dornach (1921–22), Eurhythmics School, Stuttgart (1923–24), Eurhythmeum and conversion of the Brodbeck house, Dornach (1923, 1935, ill. 343), publishing offices, Dornach (1923–24), ill. 339), Wegman house, Arlesheim (1924), and Schuurman house, Dornach (1924–25, ill. 358).

[13] The form of the second Goetheanum may have evolved from the portal motif of the old west façade. See Albert von Baravalle, 'Das Baumotiv des II. Goetheanum', in *Das Goetheanum*, XXXI (1952), no. 12, pp. 93ff.

[14] Marie Steiner, foreword to Rudolf Steiner, *Der Baugedanke des Goetheanum*, op. cit., p. 11.

New churches
pages 149–154

Otto Bartning, *Vom neuen Kirchbau*, Berlin, 1919, p. 115.

Adolf Behne, *Die Wiederkehr der Kunst*, Leipzig, 1919, p. 107.

See Richard Bürkner, *Vom protestantischen Kirchenbau. Siebzehnte Flugschrift des Dürer-Bundes*, Munich, 1906, pp. 7ff.

Nikolaus Pevsner, *The Sources of Modern Architecture and Design*, London, 1968, p. 124–25.

J[ohannes] van Acken, *Christozentrische Kirchenkunst. Ein Entwurf zum liturgischen Gesamtkunstwerk*, 2nd ed., Gladbeck i. W., 1923, p. 9. In van Acken's brochure two of Dominikus Böhm's designs – *Lumen Christi* and *Circumstantes* – were published for the first time, as examples of 'Christ-centred' church architecture.

Otto Bartning, op. cit., pp. 113, 119f.

Ibid., pp. 23, 126.

Otto Bartning, 'Zur "Sternkirche"', in Paul Westheim, ed., *Künstlerbekenntnisse*, Berlin, n.d., p. 290ff.

Otto Bartning, *Erde Geliebte*, Hamburg, 1955, p. 602f. Bartning began this diary of his world tour in 1933. The first part was published as *Erdball* in 1947; the whole book came out under the new title eight years later.

Rudolf Schwarz, *Vom Bau der Kirche*, Heidelberg, 1947, p. 114.

Rudolf Schwarz, 'Dominikus Böhm und sein Werk', in *Moderne Bauformen*, XXVI (1927), no. 6, p. 226ff.

Houses and tower blocks
pages 155–162

Hermann Muthesius, *Das englische Haus*, 2nd ed., vol. I, Berlin, 1908, p. 148.

H[endrikus] Th[eodorus] Wijdeveld, 'Het Park Meerwijk te Bergen', in *Wendingen*, I (1918), no. 8, 6.

Ernst Pollak, *Der Baumeister Otto Bartning*, Bonn, 1926, p. 32. – Otto Bartning, 'Säule und Pfeiler', in *Kunst und Künstler*, XV (1916–17), no. 5, 236.

Otto Bartning, *Erde Geliebte*, Hamburg, 1955, 602.

Pelzer, 'Ästhetische und konstruktive Gedanken des Industriebaues, beobachtet bei Wasserturmbauten', in *Mitteilungen über Zement-, Beton- und Eisenbetonbau*, XIV (*Deutsche Bauzeitung*, LI), 24, p. 174.

Magda Révész-Alexander, *Der Turm als Symbol Erlebnis*, The Hague, 1953.

Walter Müller-Wulckow, 'Zukünftige Architektur', in *Das Hohe Ufer*, I (1919), no. 3, p. 35. – Ans Hansen, *Das Erlebnis der Architektur*, Cologne, 1920, p. 99.

The corkscrew movement of Expressionist tower designs is a variant of an archetypal form which includes imaginative reconstructions of the lighthouse at Alexandria and the Tower of Babel and goes back to Trajan's Column.

Bruno Möhring, 'Über die Vorzüge der Turmhäuser und die Voraussetzungen, unter denen sie in Berlin gebaut werden können', in *Stadtbaukunst alter und neuer Zeit*, I (1920), no. 22, p. 353. – Max Berg, 'Hochhäuser im Stadtbild', in *Wasmuths Monatshefte für Baukunst*, VI (1921–22), nos. 4–5, p. 104.

H[endrikus] Th[eodorus] Wijdeveld, 'Inleiding voor de torenhuis-projecten', in *Wendingen*, V (1923), no. 3, p. 3.

See Joachim Schulz, 'Hochhäuser und Citygedanke in Deutschland 1920–1923', in *Deutsche Architektur*, XIII (1964), no. 12, pp. 750ff.

The German architectural historian Herman Sörgel visited Ferriss in New York and published an article on him in the magazine *Baukunst*, of which he was the editor, in 1926 (II, no. 1).

13 The cinema
pages 163–168

[1] Konrad Lange, *Das Kino in Gegenwart und Zukunft*, Stuttgart, 1920, p. 128.

[2] Robert Herlth, *Filmarchitektur*, Munich, 1965, p. 48. – Carlo Mierendorff, *Hätte ich das Kino!*, Berlin, 1920, quoted in Fritz Usinger, ed., *Carlo Mierendorff. Eine Einführung in sein Werk und eine Auswahl*, Wiesbaden, 1965, p. 66.

[3] Hermann Finsterlin to Erich Mendelsohn, 2. 12. 1924. Louise Mendelsohn Collection, San Francisco. – Egon Eiermann et al., 'Architekten und ihr erster Auftrag', in *Baukunst und Werkform*, XII (1959), no. 1, pp. 3 f.

[4] In a lecture which he gave in Berlin on 24. 4. 1916 Paul Wegener developed the idea of a film of 'pure kinetics' and 'optical lyricism'. As in Taut's scenario, forms (not architectural forms, however, but forms derived from nature) were to grow, disappear, become transformed, and break apart. (See Paul Wegener, 'Die künstlerischen Möglichkeiten des Films', in Kai Möller, ed., *Paul Wegener. Sein Leben und seine Rollen*, Hamburg, 1954, pp. 102ff.)

[5] *Die gläserne Kette. Visionäre Architekturen aus dem Kreis um Bruno Taut. 1919–1920*, catalogue of an exhibition at Schloss Morsbroich, Leverkusen, and the Akademie der Künste, Berlin, 1963, pp. 48ff., 57f., 64.

[6] See Konrad Lange, op. cit., pp. 107ff. – Georg Otto Stindt, *Das Lichtspiel als Kunstform*, Bremerhaven, 1924, p. 17.

[7] H[einrich] de Fries, 'Raumgestaltung im Film', in *Wasmuths Monatshefte für Baukunst*, V (1920–21), nos. 3–4, p. 63.

[8] Bruno Taut, 'Die Galoschen des Glücks', in *Die gläserne Kette*, op. cit., p. 49. – Fritz Lang, quoted in Wilhelm Heizer, 'Architektur und Film', in *Baukunst*, II (1926), no. 10, p. 291.

[9] Bruno Taut, 'Bildvorführungen für liegende Zuschauer', in *Bauwelt*, XV (1924), no. 32, p. 743.

[10] Erich Mendelsohn, 'Zur Eröffnung des Kinos "Universum"', 1931, in *Bauwelt*, LII (1961), nos. 41–42, p. 1184.

14 Futurism
pages 169–180

[1] The war memorial by the lake in Como was erected after Sant'Elia's death by Giuseppe and Attilio Terragni, on the basis of one of Sant'Elia's tower designs revised by Enrico Prampolini. It fails to give an adequate impression of the original project.

[2] 'La pittura futurista. Manifesto tecnico', 11. 4. 1910, in Maria Drudi Gambillo and Teresa Fiori, eds., *Archivi del Futurismo*, vol. I, Rome, 1958, p. 67.

[3] See Christa Baumgarth, *Geschichte des Futurismus*, Reinbek bei Hamburg, 1966, pp. 83ff.

[4] Umberto Boccioni, *Pittura scultura futuriste – dinamismo plastico*, Milan, 1914, p. 288.

[5] Gino Severini, 'Le analogie plastiche del dinamismo', September/October 1913, in Gambillo and Fiori, op. cit., pp. 76ff.

[6] Umberto Boccioni, 'La scultura futurista', 11. 4. 1912, in Gambillo and Fiori, op. cit., p. 72. – Gino Severini, op. cit., p. 80.

[7] Umberto Boccioni, *Pittura scultura futuriste . . .*, op. cit., p. 234f.

[8] Carlo Carrà, 'La pittura dei suoni, rumori e odori', 11. 8. 1913, in Gambillo and Fiori, op. cit., p. 75.

[9] 'Manifesto dei pittori futuristi', 11. 2. 1910, in Gambillo and Fiori, op. cit., p. 64.

[10] According to Carlo Carrà, Sant'Elia dissociated himself from this remark, maintaining that it was added by another hand (*La mia vita*, Rome, 1943, pp. 178f.)

[11] Virgilio Marchi, *Architettura futurista*, Foligno, 1924, p. 85.

[12] Whether or not Sant'Elia did belong to the Futurists is a question which is debated with a degree of passion that can only be explained in terms of the psychological situation of Italian architectural criticism. Since Futurism had compromised itself politically, Sant'Elia's prestige after the Second World War seemed to depend on minimizing his connections with the movement. This dubious exercise involved scholars in hunting for 'suspicious' differences between the text of the Nuove Tendenze catalogue, known in the literature of Futurism as the *Messaggio*, and the manifesto. It was asserted that the *Messaggio* was Sant'Elia's original statement, and that it was then added to by Futurists and turned into a Futurist statement, the architecture manifesto.

While this controversy raged on, a different picture emerged from the evidence of people who were involved at the time, particularly Carlo Carrà, Ugo Nebbia and Mario Buggelli. The precise moment at which Sant'Elia decided to join the Futurist movement remains uncertain, but it can now safely be assumed that the manifesto was not a manipulation and adaptation of the catalogue text for Futurist ends. Both texts seem to go back to a single manuscript, in the preparation of which the critic and patron Mario Buggelli played a decisive part. For a summary of the discussion see Luciano Caramel and Alberto Longatti, *Antonio Sant'Elia*, catalogue of an exhibition at the Villa Comunale dell'Olmo, Como, 1962.

[13] See the concordance of points in the text in Caramel and Longatti, op. cit., pp. 51ff.

[14] Gian Pietro Lucini, *Il verso libero*, Milan, 1908, p. 346.

[15] Giulio U. Arata, 'L'esito del concorso per la sistemazione della Piazza Erbe di Verona', in *Pagine d'arte*, III, no. 1, 15. 1. 1915.

16 Joseph August Lux, in the introduction to the album *Wagner-Schule 1902*, which Sant'Elia may have owned, related the designs in the volume to the idea of a 'new city' – a *città nuova*.

17 Giulio U. Arata, 'L'architettura futurista', in *Pagine d' arte*, II, no. 14, 30. 8. 1914.

18 Filippo Tomaso Marinetti, *Primato Italiano. Onoranze all'architetto futurista Antonio Sant' Elia* (pamphlet), Como, September 1930.

19 One of the three drawings could not be identified, but the catalogue description *Forme* does not suggest an urban subject. See also Giulia Veronesi and Gigetta Dalli Regoli, *L'opera di Mario Chiattone*, catalogue of an exhibition at the Istituto di Storia dell'Arte, Pisa, 1965.

20 Carlo Carrà, 'La pittura dei suoni, rumori e odori', in Gambillo and Fiori, op. cit., p. 73.

21 Veronesi and Regoli, op. cit., p. 5.

22 *Wagner-Schule 1902*, Leipzig, n.d., p. 34.

23 Wilhelm Worringer, 'Carlo Carràs Pinie am Meer', in *Neue Schweizer Rundschau*, Zurich, 10. 11. 1925.

24 Virgilio Marchi, op. cit., p. 64.

25 Virgilio Marchi, *Italia nuova architettura nuova*, Foligno and Rome, 1931, p. 6 and *passim*.

15 The school of Amsterdam
pages 181–193

1 K[arel] P[etrus] C[ornelis] de Bazel, 'Onze tijd en het werk van M. de Klerk', in *Wendingen*, II (1919), no. 2, p. 4. – H[endrikus] Th[eodorus] Wijdeveld, 'Natuur, bouwkunst en techniek', in *Wendingen*, V (1923), nos. 8–9, p. 14. – J[an] F[rederik] Staal, 'Die Stadtkrone von Bruno Taut', in *Wendingen*, II (1919), no. 4, p. 10.

2 Hendrik Petrus Berlage, quoted in J[oseph] Stübben, 'Die südliche Stadterweiterung von Amsterdam', in *Deutsche Bauzeitung*, LII (1918), no. 16, p. 73.

3 An exhibition of Futurist pictures was held in Rotterdam in 1913; according to Boccioni it visited Amsterdam and The Hague as well.

4 H[endrik] P[etrus] Berlage, 'Frank Lloyd Wright', in *Wendingen*, IV (1921), no. 11, p. 8.

5 See Salomon van Deventer, *Aus Liebe zur Kunst. Das Museum Kröller-Müller*, Cologne, 1958, pp. 86ff.

6 H[endrik] P[etrus] Berlage, *Gedanken über Stil in der Baukunst*, Leipzig, 1905, pp. 22, 50.

7 J[acobus] J[ohannes] P[ieter] Oud, 'Der Einfluss von Frank Lloyd Wright auf die Architektur Europas', in *Holländische Architektur (Bauhausbücher*, 10), Munich, 1926, p. 80.

8 H[endrikus] Th[eodorus] Wijdeveld, *Mijn contact med Wibaut, de Machtige*, duplicated manuscript, 1968, p. 14.

9 Hermann Finsterlin to Erich Mendelsohn, 22. 3. 1924. Louise Mendelsohn Collection, San Francisco. – Adolf Behne, circular letter, 9. 12. 1920. Copy, Oswald Mathias Ungers Collection, Cologne. Most of these contacts appear to have been initiated by Wijdeveld. Wijdeveld had seen Mendelsohn's exhibition at the Cassirer gallery in 1919 and had, in his own words, 'been the first to discover [Finsterlin] in Munich' (written communication from Hendrikus Theodorus Wijdeveld, 14. 2. 1972).

10 Bruno Taut, *Die neue Baukunst in Europa und Amerika*, Stuttgart, 1929, p. 39.

11 See Kurt Junghanns, *Bruno Taut 1880–1938*, Berlin, 1970, pp. 64f.

12 J. P. Mieras, 'In uitbreiding "Zuid" te Amsterdam', in *Wendingen*, V (1923), no. 4, p. 3.

Apart from Berlage, Boterenbrood, de Klerk, Kramer, Margaret Kropholler, van der Meij and Staal, the architects involved in Amsterdam South and Amsterdam West included the following: Cornelis Jonke Blaauw, Jacobus Johannes Bernardus Franswa, Jan Gratama, Dick Greiner, Dirk Heineke and Evert Kuipers, C. Kruijswijk, Nicolaas Lansdorp, Pieter Lucas Marnette, Willem Noorlander, Jordanus Roodenburgh, Gerrit Jan Rutgers, Philip Anne Warners, Arend Jan Westerman, Hendrikus Theodorus Wijdeveld and Jonke Zietsma.

13 M[ichel] de Klerk, in *Bouwkundig Weekblad*, XXXVI (1916), nos. 44–45.

14 Jan Boterenbrood, 'Inleiding', in *Wendingen*, VIII (1927), nos. 6–7, p. 3.

15 Piet Kramer, 'De bouwwerken van M. de Klerk', in *Wendingen*, VI (1924), nos. 9–10, p. 3.

16 Adolph Eijbink, 'De toepassing van gewapend beton', in *Wendingen*, II (1919), no. 11, p. 3.

16 Expressionism and the New Architecture
pages 194–202

1 Adolf Behne, 'Holländische Baukunst in der Gegenwart', in *Wasmuths Monatshefte für Baukunst*, VI (1921–22), nos. 1–2, p. 4. – Adolf Behne, 'Einige Bemerkungen zum Thema: Moderne Baukunst', in *Max Taut. Bauten und Pläne*, Berlin, 1927, p. 22.

2 For the relationship between architecture and politics in the Weimar Republic, see Barbara Miller-Lane, *Architecture and Politics in Germany, 1918–1945*, Cambridge, Mass., 1968.

3 Josef Schneider and C. Zell, *Der Fall der roten Festung*, Vienna, 1934, pp. 6ff.

4 Fritz Schumacher, 'Architektonische Regungen der Nachkriegszeit', in Architekten- und Ingenieur-Verein zu Hamburg, ed., *Hamburg und seine Bauten 1918–1929*, Hamburg, 1929, p. 124.

5 Hans Poelzig, *Der Architekt* (speech to the Federation of German Architects in Berlin, 4. 6. 1931), Tübingen, 1954.

6 Walter Gropius, 'Design Topics', in *Magazine of Art*, December, 1947.

7 Bruno Taut, *Die neue Baukunst*, Stuttgart, 1929, p. 6.

8 H[einrich] de Fries, 'Raumgestaltung im Film', in *Wasmuths Monatshefte für Baukunst*, V (1920–21), nos. 3–4, p. 75. – Rudolf Steiner, *Der Baugedanke des Goetheanum*, Stuttgart, 1958, p. 52.

9 Walter Gropius, 'The Formal and Technical Problems of Modern Architectural Planning', in *Journal of the Royal Institute of British Architects*, 19. 5. 34, p. 688.

10 Walter Gropius, 'Idee und Aufbau des Staatlichen Bauhauses Weimar', quoted in *Die neue Architektur und das Bauhaus*, Mainz, 1965, p. 28.

11 Le Corbusier to Karl Ernst Osthaus, 27. 3. 1912. Osthaus-Archiv, Hagen. The connection between Lauweriks and Le Corbusier, referred to obscurely in Le Corbusier's *Le Modulor* (3rd ed.,

Boulogne, 1954), has been clarified by N. H. M. Tummers (*J. L. Mathieu Lauweriks*, Hilversum, 1968) and Stanford Owen Anderson (*Peter Behrens and the New Architecture of Germany 1900–1917*, dissertation, New York, 1968).

12 Tut Schlemmer, ed., *Oskar Schlemmer. Briefe und Tagebücher*, Munich, 1958, pp. 116, 150, 202, 207.

13 Hugo Häring, 'Wege zur Form', in *Die Form*, (1925), no. 1, pp. 3ff.

14 Georg Lukács, 'Es geht um den Realismus', quoted in Fritz J. Raddatz, ed., *Marxismus und Literatur*, vol. II, Reinbek bei Hamburg, 1969, p. 71.

15 See Jürgen Joedicke, 'Anmerkungen zum Werk Hugo Härings', in Heinrich Lauterbach and Jürgen Joedicke, eds., *Hugo Häring. Schriften, Entwürfe, Bauten*, Stuttgart, 1965.

17 Expressionism and the National Socialist
pages 203–209

1 G. A. Behrens, 'Architektur-Fliessarbeit', in *Die Baugilde*, X (1928), no. 22, pp. 1670f.

2 Wilhelm Kreis, 'Die Baukunst und der Mensch von heute', in *Die Baugilde*, XII (1930), no. 2, p. 1867.

3 Carl J. H. Westphal, ed., *Fritz Höger. Der niederdeutsche Backstein-Baumeister*, Wolfshagen-Scharbeutz, 1938, pp. 87, 103.

4 See Bernhard Hoetger and Herbert Helfrich, *Deutsches Forum* (leaflet), n.d. (1936?). – *Das Schwarze Korps*, 26. 6. 1935.

5 The connections between Expressionsism and Fascism were fully examined in the so-called 'Expressionism debate' conducted by exiled German-speaking writers in 1937–38. The discussion was sparked off by an essay entitled '"Grösse und Verfall" des Expressionismus' which Georg Lukács had published in *Internationale Literatur* in 1934. Some of the more important contributions appear in Fritz J. Raddatz, ed., *Marxismus und Literatur*, vol. II, Reinbek, 1969.

6 Adolf Hitler, 'Rede auf der Kulturtagung', in *Reden des Führers am Parteitag der Ehre 1936*, Munich, 1936, p. 33.

Hitler's heavy underlining in one book in his library, Josef Ponten's novella *Der Meister* (1919) shows how thoroughly he identified with the contemporary stereotype of the artist as a natural genius (Hellmut Lehmann-Haupt, *Art under Dictatorship*, New York, 1954, pp. 51ff.).

7 Bruno Taut, *Die Stadtkrone*, Jena, 1919, p. 66. Paul Schmitthenner, in Hans Kampffmeyer, *Friedenstadt*, 2nd ed., Jena, 1918, p. 63.

8 Adolf Hitler, *Mein Kampf*, 25th ed., Munich, 1933, pp. 290, 292. – Albert Speer, ed., *Neue deutsche Baukunst*, Berlin, 1941. p. 10. – Gerdy Troost, co-ed., *Das Bauen im neuen Reich*, Bayreuth, 1938 (1939) p. 7.

9 Bruno Taut, op. cit., pp. 69, 85.

10 Bruno Taut, 'Rede des Bundeskanzlers für Europa am 24. April 1993 vor dem europäischen Parlament', in *Sozialistische Monatshefte*, L (1919), nos. 19–20, p. 818.

Bibliography

Further bibliographical references on points of detail will be found in the notes.

Cultural history and art history

An alle Künstler! Berlin, 1919.

Apollonio, Umbro, *Der Futurismus*, Cologne, 1972.

Arnold, Armin, *Die Literatur des Expressionismus*, Stuttgart, 1966.

Bahr, Hermann, *Expressionismus*, 1st ed.,Munich, 1916.

Baumgarth, Christa, *Geschichte des Futurismus*, Reinbek, 1966.

Behne, Adolf, *Zur neuen Kunst. Sturm-Bücher 7*, Berlin, 1915.

Behne, Adolf, *Die Wiederkehr der Kunst*, Leipzig, 1919.

Behrens, Peter, 'Reform der künstlerischen Erziehung', in Reichszentrale für Heimatdienst, *Der Geist der neuen Volksgemeinschaft. Eine Denkschrift für das deutsche Volk*, Berlin, 1919, p. 93 ff.

Boccioni, Umberto, *Pittura scultura futuriste*, Milan, 1914.

Bodenhausen, Eberhard von, *Ein Leben für Kunst und Wirtschaft*, Düsseldorf, 1955.

Carrà, Carlo, *La mia vita*. Rome, 1943.

Drudi Gambillo, Maria, and Teresa Fiori, eds., *Archivi del Futurismo*, 2 vol., Rome, 1958.

Däubler, Theodor, *Der neue Standpunkt*, Dresden, 1916, 2nd ed. Leipzig, 1919, new ed. Dresden, 1957.

Däubler, Theodor, *Im Kampf um die moderne Kunst*, Berlin, 1919.

Edschmid, Kasimir, *Über den Expressionismus in der Literatur und die neue Dichtung*, Berlin, 1919.

L'espressionismo. Pittura, scultura, architettura, catalogue of an exhibition at the Palazzo Strozzi, Florence, 1964.

Fechter, Paul, *Der Expressionismus*, Munich, 1914.

Gay, Peter. *Weimar Culture. The outsider as insider*, New York, 1968.

Gordon, Donald E., 'On the origin of the word "Expressionism"', in *Journal of the Warburg and Courtauld Institutes*, XXIX, London, 1966, pp. 368 ff.

Hausenstein, Wilhelm, *Über Expressionismus in der Malerei*, Berlin, 1919.

Hellwag, Fritz, 'Die Revolutionsprogramme der Künstler', in *Mitteilungen des Deutschen Werkbundes*, II (1919–20), no. 2, pp. 33 ff.

Hofmann, Werner, *Turning points in twentieth-century art, 1890–1917*, New York, 1969.

Jäckh, Ernst, *Der goldene Pflug. Lebensernte eines Weltbürgers*, Stuttgart, 1954.

Kessler, Harry, *Gesichter und Zeiten*, Berlin, 1962.

Kolinsky, Eva, *Engagierter Expressionismus. Politik und Literatur zwischen Weltkrieg und Weimarer Republik*, Stuttgart, 1970.

Kratsch, Gerhard, *Kunstwart und Dürerbund*, Göttingen, 1969.

Mahler-Werfel, Alma, *Mein Leben*, Frankfurt, 1960.

Moeller van den Bruck, Arthur, *Der preussische Stil*, Munich, 1916.

Muche, Goerg, *Blickpunkt. Sturm, Dada, Bauhaus, Gegenwart*, 2nd ed., Tübingen, 1965.

Myers, Bernard S., *The German Expressionists*, New York, 1957.

Naumann, Friedrich, *Der deutsche Stil*, Hellerau, n.d. (1912).

Oppenheimer, Franz, *Die soziale Forderung der Stunde. Gedanken und Vorschläge*, Leipzig, 1919.

Perkins, G. C., *Expressionismus. Eine Bibliographie zeitgenössischer Dokumente. 1910–25*, Zurich, 1971.

Pevsner, Nikolaus, *Academies of Art, Past and Present*, Cambridge, 1940.

Pudor, Heinrich, *Deutsche Qualitätsarbeit. Richtlinien für eine neue Entwicklung der deutschen Industrie*, Leipzig, 1910.

Raabe, Paul, ed., *Expressionismus. Aufzeichnungen und Erinnerungen der Zeitgenossen*, Freiburg, 1965.

Raabe, Paul, ed., *Expressionismus. Der Kampf um eine literarische Bewegung*, Munich, 1965.

Raabe, Paul, ed., *Index Expressionismus. Eine Bibliographie der Beiträge in 103 Zeitschriften des literarischen Expressionismus*, Nendeln, 1972.

Raabe, Paul, and H. L. Greve, eds., *Expressionismus. Literatur und Kunst. 1910–23*, catalogue of an exhibition in the Deutsches Literaturarchiv, Schiller-Nationalmuseum, Marbach, 1960.

Roh, Franz, *Nach-Expressionismus. Magischer Realismus. Probleme der neuesten europäischen Malerei*, Leipzig, 1925.

Samuel, Richard, and R. Hinton Thomas, *Expressionism in German Life, Literature and the Theatre, 1910–1924*, Cambridge, 1939.

Scheffler, Karl, *Der Geist der Gotik*, Leipzig, 1917.

Scheffler, Karl, *Die fetten und die mageren Jahre*, Leipzig and Munich, 1946.

Schlemmer, Tut, ed., *Oskar Schlemmer. Briefe und Tagebücher*, Munich, 1958.

Schmalenbach, Fritz, 'Das Wort "Expressionismus"', in *Neue Zürcher Zeitung*, no. 889, 12. 3. 1961.

Schmidt, Diether, ed., *Manifeste, Manifeste. 1905–1933. Künstlerschriften I*, Dresden, n.d. (1964).

Schreyer, Lothar, *Erinnerungen an Sturm und Bauhaus*, Munich, 1956.

Schultze-Naumburg, Paul, *Kulturarbeiten*, Munich, 1904–10.

Scrivo, Luigi, *Sintesi del futurismo. Storia e documenti*, Rome, 1968.

Sokel, Walter H. *The Writer in extremis. Expressionism in twentieth-century German Literature*, Stanford, 1959.

Steffen, Hans, ed., *Der deutsche Expressionismus. Formen und Gestalten*, Göttingen, 1965.

Sydow, Eckart von, *Die deutsche expressionistische Kultur und Malerei*, Berlin, 1920.

Vogeler, Heinrich, *Erinnerungen*, Berlin, 1952.

Walden, Herwarth, *Einblick in Kunst. Expressionismus Futurismus Kubismus*, Berlin, 1917.

Westheim, Paul, ed., *Künstlerbekenntnisse. Briefe, Tagebuchblätter, Betrachtungen heutiger Künstler*, Berlin, n.d. (1924).

Willett, John, *Expressionism*, London, 1970.

Worringer, Wilhelm, *Abstraktion und Einfühlung*, Munich, 1908, 11th ed. 1921 (English: *Abstraction and Empathy*, London, 1953).

Worringer, Wilhelm, *Künstlerische Zeitfragen*, Munich, 1921.

Ziegler, Leopold, *Volk, Staat und Persönlichkeit*, Berlin, 1917.

Architecture: general

Banham, Reyner, *Theory and Design in the First Machine Age*, London, 1960.

Banham, Reyner, *The Architecture of the Well-Tempered Environment*, London, 1969.

Benevolo, Leonardo, *Storia dell'architettura moderna*, Bari, 1960.

Collins, Peter, *Changing Ideals in Modern Architecture, 1750–1950*, London, 1965.

Conrads, Ulrich, and Hans G. Sperlich, *Phantastische Architektur*, Stuttgart, 1960 (English: *Fantastic Architecture*, London, 1963).

Conrads, Ulrich, *Programme und Manifeste zur Architektur des 20. Jahrhunderts*, Frankfurt and Berlin, 1964.

Durm, Josef, *et al.*, eds., *Handbuch der Architektur*, Darmstadt and elsewhere, 1880 et seq., 4 parts.

Encyclopedia of World Art, New York, Toronto and London, 1959–1968, 15 vol.

Giedion, Sigfried, *Space, Time and Architecture*, Cambridge, Mass., 1941, 3rd ed. 1962.

Hitchcock, Henry-Rusell, *Modern Architecture. Romanticism and Reintegration*, New York, 1929.

Hitchcock, Henry-Russell, *Architecture Nineteenth and Twentieth Centuries*, Harmondsworth, 1958, 2nd ed. 1963, paperback ed. 1971.

Hofmann, Werner, and Udo Kultermann, *Baukunst unserer Zeit*, Essen, 1969 (English: *Modern Architecture in Colour*, London, 1970).

Joedicke, Jürgen, *Geschichte der modernen Architektur*, Stuttgart, 1958 (English: *A History of Modern Architecture*, New York, 1959, London, 1960).

Klopfer, Paul, *Das Wesen der Baukunst*, Leipzig, 1920.

Pehnt, Wolfgang, ed., *Encyclopaedia of Modern Architecture*, London, 1963, New York, 1964.

Pevsner, Nikolaus, *Pioneers of Modern Design*, London, 1936, 2nd ed. New York, 1949, rev. ed. Harmondsworth, 1960.

Pevsner, Nikolaus, *The Sources of Modern Architecture and Design*, London, 1968.

Pevsner, Nikolaus, *Studies in Art, Architecture and Design*, London, 1968, vol. II.

Platz, Gustav Adolf, *Die Baukunst der neuesten Zeit*, Berlin, 1927.

Ponten, Josef, *Architektur die nicht gebaut wurde*, Stuttgart, 1925, 2 vol.

Portoghesi, Paolo, ed., *Dizionario enciclopedico di architettura e urbanistica*, Rome, 1968–69, 6 vol.

Posener, Julius, ed., *Anfänge des Funktionalismus*, Berlin and Frankfurt, 1964.

Schulze, Konrad Werner, *Glas in der Architektur der Gegenwart*, Stuttgart, 1929.

Schumacher, Fritz, *Das Wesen des neuzeitlichen Backsteinbaues*, Munich, n.d. (1917).

Sharp, Dennis, *Sources of Modern Architecture. A bibliography*, London, 1967.

Sörgel, Herman, *Architektur-Ästhetik*, Munich, 1918.

Vischer, Julius, and Ludwig Hilberseimer, *Beton als Gestalter*, Stuttgart, 1928.

Vriend, J[acobus] J[ohannes], *Nieuwere architectuur*, Bussum, 1957.

Wasmuth, Günter, ed., *Wasmuths Lexikon der Baukunst*, Berlin, 1929–37, 5 vol.

Wattjes, J[annes] G[erhardus], *Moderne architectuur*, Amsterdam, 1927.

Whittick, Arnold, *European Architecture in the Twentieth Century*, London, 1950–53, 2 vol.

Zevi, Bruno, *Storia dell'architettura moderna*, Turin, 1953, 3rd ed. 1955.

Architecture: periods

From 1900 to 1914

Behrendt, Walter Curt, *Der Kampf um den Stil im Kunstgewerbe und in der Architektur*, Stuttgart, 1920.

Cürlis, Hans, and H. Stephany, *Die künstlerischen und wirtschaftlichen Irrwege unserer Baukunst*, Munich, 1916.

Jeanneret, Charles-Edouard (Le Corbusier), *Etude sur le mouvement d'art décoratif en Allemagne*, La Chaux-de-Fonds, 1912.

Scheffler, Karl, *Moderne Baukunst*, Leipzig, 1908.

Scheffler, Karl, *Die Architektur der Grossstadt*, Berlin, 1913.

Expressionism

Banham, Reyner, 'The Glass Paradise', in *The Architectural Review*, CXXV (1959), no. 745, pp. 87ff.

Behne, Adolf, 'Wiedergeburt der Baukunst', in Bruno Taut, *Die Stadtkrone*, Jena, 1919.

Borsi, Franco, and Giovanni Klaus König, *Architettura dell'espressionismo*, Genoa, n.d. (1967).

Feuerstein, Günther, 'Architektur des Expressionismus', in *Christliche Kunstblätter*, CV (1967), no. 4, pp. 96ff.

Die gläserne Kette. Visionäre Architekturen aus dem Kreis um Bruno Taut. 1919–1920, catalogue of an exhibition at Schloss Morsbroich, Leverkusen, and the Akademie der Künste, Berlin, 1963.

Gregotti, Vittorio, 'L'architettura dell'espressionismo', in *Casabella*, no. 254, 1961, pp. 24ff.

Hansen, Hans, *Das Erlebnis der Architektur*, Cologne, 1920.

Hoeber, Fritz, 'Architekturaufgaben der Gegenwart', in *Der Cicerone*, XI (1919), no. 11, pp. 320ff.

Joedicke, Jürgen, 'Utopisten der zwanziger Jahre in Deutschland', in *Bauen + Wohnen*, XXII (1967), no. 5, pp. 193ff.

Lindahl, Göran, 'Von der Zukunftskathedrale bis zur Wohnmaschine. Deutsche Architektur und Architekturdebatte nach dem ersten Weltkriege', in *Figura, Acta Universitatis Upsaliensis*, n.s., I (1959), pp. 226ff.

Müller-Wulckow, Walter, *Aufbau – Architektur!*, Berlin, 1919.

Pehnt, Wolfgang, 'Gewissheit des Wunders. Der Expressionismus in der Architektur', in *Das Kunstwerk*, XVII (1964), no. 9, pp. 2ff.

Schumacher, Fritz, '"Expressionismus" und Architektur', in *Dekorative Kunst* (= *Die Kunst*), XLII (1919–20), nos. 1–3, pp. 10ff., 62ff., 80ff.

Sharp, Dennis, *Modern Architecture and Expressionism*, London, 1966

International Style

Behne, Adolf, *Der moderne Zweckbau*, Munich, 1926, new ed. Frankfurt and Berlin, 1964.

Block, Fritz, ed., *Probleme des Bauens*, Potsdam, 1928.

Casteels, Maurice, *Die Sachlichkeit in der modernen Kunst*, Leipzig, 1930.

Gropius, Walter, *Internationale Architektur*, Munich, 1925 (*Bauhausbücher*, 1).

Hilberseimer, Ludwig, *Grosstadtbauten*, Hanover, 1925.

Hilberseimer, Ludwig, *Grosstadtarchitektur*, Stuttgart, 1927.

Hilberseimer, Ludwig, *Internationale Neue Baukunst*, Stuttgart, 1927.

Hitchcock, Henry-Russell, and Philip Johnson, *The International Style. Architecture since 1922*, New York, 1932, new ed. New York, 1966.

Meyer, Peter, *Moderne Architektur und Tradition*, Zurich, 1928.

Rasch, Heinz and Bodo, *Wie bauen?*, Stuttgart n.d. (1927).

Sartoris, Alberto, *Gli elementi dell'architettura funzionale*, Milan, 1932.

Sting, Hellmuth, *Der Kubismus und seine Einwirkung auf die Wegbereiter der modernen Architektur*, dissertation, Aachen, 1965.

Taut, Bruno, *Die neue Baukunst in Europa und Amerika*, Stuttgart and London, 1929.

National Socialism

Brenner, Hildegard, *Die Kunstpolitik des Nationalsozialismus*, Reinbek, 1963.

Lehmann-Haupt, Hellmuth, *Art under a Dictatorship*, New York, 1954.

Speer, Albert, ed., *Neue deutsche Baukunst*, Berlin, 1941.

Speer, Albert, *Erinnerungen*, Berlin, 1969 (English: *Inside the Third Reich*, London, 1970).

Straub, Karl Willy, *Die Architektur im Dritten Reich*, Stuttgart, 1932.

Teut, Anna, *Architektur im Dritten Reich. 1933–1945*, Berlin and Frankfurt, 1967.

Troost, Gerdy, co-ed., *Das Bauen im neuen Reich*, Bayreuth, 1938 (1939).

Architecture: countries

Austria

Graf, Otto Antonia, *Die vergessene Wagnerschule*, Vienna, 1969.

Krauss, Karla, and Joachim Schlandt, 'Der Wiener Gemeindewohnungsbau. Ein sozialdemokratisches Programm', in Hans G. Helms and Jörn Janssen, *Kapitalistischer Städtebau*, Neuwied, 1970, pp. 113ff.

Kunze, Helmut, 'Kommunaler Wohnungsbau im Wien der zwanziger Jahre', in *Bauwelt*, LX (1969), nos. 12–13 (= *Stadtbauwelt*, 21), pp. 44ff.

Musil, Franz, 'Aus der Werkstatt des Stadtbaudirektors', in *Das neue Wien*, vol. III, Vienna, 1927, pp. 4ff.

Uhl, Ottokar, *Moderne Architektur in Wien von Otto Wagner bis heute*, Vienna, 1966.

Weber, Anton, 'Wiener Wohnungs- und Sozial-politik', in *Das neue Wien*, vol. I, Vienna, 1926, pp. 193ff.

Die Wohnungspolitik der Gemeinde Wien, Vienna, 1929.

Czechoslovakia

Benesova, M., 'Architettura cubista in Boemia', in *Casabella*, no. 314 (1967), pp. 62ff.

Czagan, Friedrich, 'Kubistische Architektur in Böhmen', in *Werk*, LVI (1969), no. 2, pp. 75ff.

Pechar, Josef, 'Bauen in der Tschechoslowakei', in *Deutsche Bauzeitung*, CII (1968), no. 5, pp. 320ff.

Vokoun, Jaroslav, 'Czech Cubism', in *The Architectural Review*, CXXXIX (1966), no. 829, pp. 229ff., reprinted in N. Pevsner and J. M. Richards, eds., *The Anti-Rationalists*, London, 1972.

Germany

Architekten- und Ingenieur-Verein zu Hamburg, ed., *Hamburg und seine Bauten. 1918–1929*, Hamburg, 1929.

Berlin und seine Bauten, Berlin, 1964 et seq., 4 vol. to date.

Fries, H[einrich] de, *Junge Baukunst in Deutschland*, Berlin, 1926.

Hajos, Elisabeth Maria, and Leopold Zahn, *Berliner Architektur der Nachkriegszeit*, Berlin, 1928.

Hegemann, Werner, *Das steinerne Berlin*, Berlin, 1930, new ed. Berlin and Frankfurt, 1963.

Hennig-Schefold, Monica, and Inge Schaefer, *Frühe Moderne in Berlin*, Winterthur, 1967.

Hilberseimer, Ludwig, *Berliner Architektur der zwanziger Jahre*, Mainz, 1967.

Klapheck, Richard, *Neue Baukunst in den Rheinlanden*, Düsseldorf, 1928.

Lane, Barbara Miller, *Architecture and Politics in Germany, 1918–1945*, Cambridge, Mass., 1968.

Matthaei, Adelbert, *Deutsche Baukunst. IV. Im 19. Jahrhundert und in der Gegenwart*, 2nd ed., Leipzig and Berlin, 1920.

Müller-Wulckow, Walter, *Deutsche Baukunst der Gegenwart*, Leipzig, 1925–28, 3 vol.

Schinz, Alfred, *Berlin, Stadtschicksal und Städtebau*, Brunswick, 1964.

Schumacher, Fritz, *Strömungen in deutscher Baukunst seit 1800*, Leipzig, 1935, 2nd ed. Cologne, n.d. (1955).

Die zwanziger Jahre in Hannover. 1916–1933, catalogue of an exhibition at the Kunstverein Hanover, Hanover, 1962.

Italy

Meeks, Carroll. L.V., *Italian Architecture, 1750–1914*, New Haven and London, 1966.

The Netherlands

Behne, Adolf, *Holländische Baukunst der Gegenwart*, Berlin, 1922.

Berlage, H. P., W. M. Dudok, Jan Gratama, A. R. Hulshoff, H. van der Kloot Meijburg, J. F. Staal and J. Luthmann, eds., *Moderne bouwkunst in Nederland*, Rotterdam, 1932–35, 20 vol.

Berlage, H[endrik] P[etrus], *De ontwikkeling der moderne bouwkunst in Holland*, Amsterdam, 1925.

Blijstra, R., *Netherlands Architecture since 1900*, Amsterdam, 1960.

Canella, Guido, 'L'epopea borghese della Scuola di Amsterdam', in *Casabella*, no. 215, 1957.

Endt, P. H., 'Amsterdamse School', in *Wendingen*, I (1918), no. 7, pp. 3ff.

Fanelli, Giovanni, *Architettura moderna in Olanda*, Florence, 1968.

Jobst, Gerhard, *Kleinwohnungsbau in Holland*, Berlin, 1922.

Mieras, J. P., and F. R. Yerbury, *Dutch Architecture of the Twentieth Century*, London, 1926.

Oud, J[acobus] J[ohannes] P[ieter], *Holländische Architektur*, Munich, 1926, 2nd ed. 1929 (*Bauhausbücher*, 10).

Stübben, J[oseph], 'Die südliche Stadterweiterung von Amsterdam', in *Deutsche Bauzeitung*, LII (1918), nos. 14–17, pp. 65ff., 73ff., 77ff.

Vriend, J[acobus] J[ohannes], *De bouwkunst van ons land*, Amsterdam, 1938.

Vriend, J[acobus] J[ohannes], *Architectuur van deze eeuw*, Amsterdam, 1959.

Wattjes, J[annes] G[erhardus], *Nieuw-nederlandsche bouwkunst*, Amsterdam, 1924.

Spain

Bohigas, Oriol, *Arquitectura modernista*, Barcelona, 1968.

Cirici-Pellicer, A., *El arte modernista catalán*, Barcelona, 1951.

Flores, Carlos, and Oriol Bohigas, 'Panorama histórico de la arquitectura moderna espanola', in *Zodiac 15*, n.d. (1965).

Architecture: building types, film sets and town planning

Churches

Acken, J[ohannes] van, *Christozentrische Kirchenkunst. Ein Entwurf zum liturgischen Gesamtkunstwerk*, Gladbeck i. W., 1922, 2nd ed. 1923.

Bartning, Otto, *Von neuen Kirchbau*, Berlin, 1919.

Bogler, P. Theodor, *Liturgische Bewegung nach 50 Jahren*, Maria Laach, 1959.

Bürkner, Richard, *Vom protestantischen Kirchenbau. Siebzehnte Flugschrift des Dürer-Bundes*, Munich, 1906.

Lehwess, Walter, 'Der Gedanke des evangelischen Kirchenbaues', in *Stadtbaukunst alter und neuer Zeit*, II (1921–22), no. 11, pp. 161ff.

Lill, Georg, 'Die kirchliche Kunst der Gegenwart und das katholische Volk', in *Die Christliche Kunst*, XXIV (1927), no. 3, pp. 65ff.

Lill, Georg, 'Westdeutsche Kirchenbaukunst', in *Die Christliche Kunst*, XXIV (1927–28), nos. 9–10, pp. 257ff.

Schönhagen, Otto (introduction), *Stätten der Weihe. Neuzeitliche protestantische Kirchen*, Berlin, 1919.

Schwarz, Rudolf, *Von Bau der Kirche*, 2nd ed., Heidelberg, 1947.

Department stores

Wiener, Alfred, *Das Warenhaus. Kauf-, Geschäfts-, Büro-Haus*, Berlin, 1912.

Film sets and cinemas

Barsacq, Léon, *Le Décor de film*, Paris, 1970.

Eisner, Lotte, *L'Ecran démoniaque. Influence de Max Reinhardt et de l'expressionisme*, Paris, 1952 (English: *The Haunted Screen*, London, 1969).

Fries, H[einrich] de, 'Raumgestaltung im Film', in *Wasmuths Monatshefte für Baukunst*, V (1920–21), nos. 3–4, pp. 63ff.

Gregor, Ulrich, and Enno Patalas, *Geschichte des Films*, Gütersloh, 1962.

Heizer, Wilhelm, 'Architektur und Film', in *Baukunst*, II (1926), no. 10, p. 291.

Kaul, Walter, *Schöpferische Filmarchitektur*, Berlin, 1971.

Kracauer, Siegfried, *From Caligari to Hitler. A psychological history of the German film*, London, 1947.

Kurtz, Rudolf, *Expressionismus und Film*, Berlin, 1926, new ed. Zurich, 1965.

Shand, P. Morton, *Modern Theatres and Cinemas*, London, 1930.

Sharp, Dennis, *The Picture Palace and other buildings for the Movies*, London, 1969.

Zucker, Paul, *Theater und Lichtspielhäuser*, Berlin, 1926.

Zucker, Paul, and Georg Otto Stindt, *Lichtspielhäuser. Tonfilmtheater*, Berlin, 1931.

High-rise buildings

Behne, Adolf, 'De duitsche torenhuis bouw', in *Wendingen*, V (1923), no. 3, pp. 15ff.

Behrens, Peter, 'Zur Frage des Hochhauses', in *Stadtbaukunst alter und neuer Zeit*, II (1921–22), no. 24, pp. 369ff.

Berg, Max, 'Der Bau von Geschäftshochhäusern in Breslau zur Linderung der Wohnungsnot', in *Stadtbaukunst alter und neuer Zeit*, I (1920), nos. 7–8, pp. 99ff., 116ff.

Berg, Max, 'Hochhäuser im Stadtbild', in *Wasmuths Monatshefte für Baukunst*, VI (1921–22), nos. 4–5, pp. 101ff.

Hilberseimer, Ludwig, 'Das Hochhaus', in *Das Kunstblatt*, VI (1922), no. 12, pp. 525ff.

H[ofmann, Albert], 'Zur Entwicklung des Hochhauses in Deutschland', in *Deutsche Bauzeitung*, LV (1921), nos. 18–19, pp. 89ff., 93ff.

Mächler, Martin, 'Zum Problem des Wolkenkratzers', in *Wasmuths Monatshefte für Baukunst*, V (1920–21), nos. 7–10, pp. 191ff., 260ff.

Möhring, Bruno, 'Über die Vorzüge der Turmhäuser und die Voraussetzungen, unter denen sie in Berlin gebaut werden können', in *Stadtbaukunst alter und neuer Zeit*, I (1920), nos. 22–24, pp. 353ff., 370ff., 385ff.

Révész-Alexander, Magda, *Der Turm als Symbol und Erlebnis*, The Hague, 1953.

Schulz, Joachim, 'Hochhäuser und Citygedanke in Deutschland. 1920–1923', in *Deutsche Architektur*, XIII (1964), no. 12, pp. 750ff.

Stöhr, Karl F., *Die amerikanischen Turmbauten. Die Gründe ihrer Entstehung, ihre Finanzierung, Konstruktion und Rentabilität*, Munich and Berlin, 1921.

Wijdeveld, H[endrikus] Th[eodorus], 'Inleiding voor de torenhuis-projecten', in *Wendingen*, V (1923), no. 3, p. 3.

Zizler, 'Berechtigung und Bedeutung des Hochhausgedankens', in *Stadtbaukunst alter und neuer Zeit*, II (1921–22), no. 23, pp. 353ff.

Housing

Behrens, Peter, and H[einrich] de Fries, *Vom sparsamen Bauen. Ein Beitrag zur Siedlungsfrage*, Berlin, 1918.

Eberstadt, Rudolf, *Handbuch des Wohnungswesens und der Wohnungsfrage*, 4th ed., Jena, 1920.

Fries, H[einrich] de, *Wohnstädte der Zukunft*, Berlin, 1919.

Fries, H[einrich] de, *Moderne Villen und Landhäuser*, Berlin, 1924.

Gut, Albert, *Der Wohnungsbau in Deutschland nach dem Weltkriege*, Munich, 1928.

Kampffmeyer, Hans, *Wohnungsnot und Heimstättengesetz*, Karlsruhe, 1919.

Klapheck, Richard, ed., *Moderne Villen und Landhäuser*, Berlin, n.d. (1913).

Muthesius, Hermann, *Das englische Haus*, Berlin, 1904–5, 3 vol.

Muthesius, Hermann, *Landhaus und Garten*, Munich, 1907.

Industrial buildings

Gropius, Walter, *Sind beim Bau von Industriegebäuden künstlerische Gesichtspunkte mit praktischen und wirtschaftlichen vereinbar?*, Leipzig, 1911; also in *Der Industriebau*, III (1912), no. 1, pp. 5ff.

Gropius, Walter, 'Die Entwicklung moderner Industriebaukunst', in *Jahrbuch des Deutschen Werkbundes 1913*, Jena, 1913, pp. 17ff.

Gropius, Walter, 'Der stilbildende Wert industrieller Bauformen', in *Jahrbuch des Deutschen Werkbundes 1913*, Jena, 1913, pp. 17ff.

Poelzig, Hans, 'Der neuzeitliche Fabrikbau', in *Der Industriebau*, II (1911), no. 5, pp. 100ff.

Monuments

Dessoir, Max, and Hermann Muthesius, *Das Bismarck-Nationaldenkmal. Eine Erörterung des Wettbewerbes*, Jena, 1912.

Schrade, Hubert, *Das Deutsche Nationaldenkmal. Idee, Geschichte, Aufgabe*, Munich, 1934.

Railway stations

Meeks, Carroll L. V., *The Railroad Station*, New Haven, 1956.

Theatres

Schael, Helmut, *Idee und Form im Theaterbau des 19. und 20. Jahrhunderts*, dissertation, Cologne, 1956.

Taut, Bruno, 'Zum neuen Theaterbau', in *Das Hohe Ufer*, I (1919), no. 8, pp. 204ff.

Fuchs, Georg, *Die Revolution des Theaters*, Munich and Leipzig, 1909.

Rolland, Romain, *Le Théâtre du peuple*, Paris, 1903.

Zucker, Paul, *Theater und Lichtspielhäuser*, Berlin, 1926.

Town planning

Heiligenthal, Roman, *Deutscher Städtebau*, Heidelberg, 1921.

Kampffmeyer, Hans, *Die Gartenstadtbewegung*, Leipzig, 1909.

Unwin, Raymond, *Town Planning in Practice*, London, 1909.

Wolf, Paul, *Städtebau. Das Formproblem der Stadt in Vergangenheit und Zukunft*, Leipzig, 1919.

Volkshaus (community centres)

Bühring, Carl-James, 'Volkshausideen', in *Stadtbaukunst alter und neuer Zeit*, II (1921–22), no. 6, pp. 81ff.

Junghanns, Kurt, and Joachim Schulz, 'Das Volkshaus als Stadtkrone. 1918–1920', in *Deutsche Architektur*, XIII (1964), no. 8, pp. 492ff.

Architecture: individuals and groups

Arbeitsrat für Kunst

— *Programme*, Berlin, 1918, 2nd ed. 1919.

— (Walter Gropius, Bruno Taut, Adolf Behne), Pamphlet issued for the Exhibition for Unknown Architects, Graphisches Kabinett I. B. Neumann, Berlin, 1919.

— *Ja! Stimmen des Arbeitsrates für Kunst in Berlin*, Berlin, 1919.

— *Ruf zum Bauen*, Berlin, 1920.

See also below, Bruno Taut.

Otto Bartning

— 'Von den zwei Bauherren der Siedlung', in *Die Volkswohnung*, I (1919), no. 1, pp. 3f.

— 'Vorschläge zu einem Lehrplan für Handwerker, Architekten und bildende Künstler', in *Mitteilungen des Deutschen Werkbundes*, Berlin, II (1919–20), no. 2, pp. 42ff.

— 'Zur "Sternkirche"', in Paul Westheim, ed., *Künstlerbekenntnisse*, Berlin, n.d. (1924), pp. 290ff.

— *Erdball. Spätes Tagebuch einer frühen Reise*, Wiesbaden, 1947.

— *Erde Geliebte. Spätes Tagebuch einer frühen Reise* (new ed. of *Erdball* with revised first part), Hamburg, 1955.

Mayer, Hans K[arl] F[rederick], *Der Baumeister Otto Bartning und die Wiederentdeckung des Raumes*, Heidelberg, 1951.

Pollak, Ernst, *Der Baumeister Otto Bartning*, Bonn, 1926.

See also above, Building types (churches).

Bauhaus

Gropius, Walter, *Programm des Staatlichen Bauhauses in Weimar*, Weimar, 1919.

Satzungen des Staatlichen Bauhauses zu Weimar, Weimar, 1921, 2nd ed. 1922.

Gropius, Walter, *Idee und Aufbau des Staatlichen Bauhauses Weimar*, Munich and Weimar, 1923.

Staatliches Bauhaus. Weimar 1919–1923, Munich and Weimar, 1923.

Adams, George, 'Memories of a Bauhaus Student', in *The Architectural Review*, CXLIV (1968), no. 859, pp. 192ff.

Adler, Bruno, *Das Weimarer Bauhaus*, Darmstadt, n.d. (1963).

bauhaus, catalogue of an exhibition at the göppinger galerie, Frankfurt, 1964.

Bayer, Herbert, Walter Gropius and Ise Gropius, *Bauhaus 1919–1928*, New York, 1938, 2nd ed. Boston, 1952.

Erffa, Helmut von, 'Bauhaus: First Phase', in *The Architectural Review*, CXXII (1957), no. 727, pp. 103ff.

50 years bauhaus, catalogue of an exhibition at the Royal Academy of Arts, London, 1968.

Franciscono, Marcel, *Walter Gropius and the creation of the Bauhaus in Weimar*, Chicago, 1971.

Hübner, Herbert, *Die soziale Utopie des Bauhauses*, dissertation, Münster, Darmstadt, 1963.

Lang, Lothar, *Das Bauhaus. 1919–1933. Idee und Wirklichkeit*, Berlin, 1965.

Naylor, Gillian, *The Bauhaus*, London, 1968.

Pažitnov, L[eonid Nikolavic], *Das schöpferische Erbe des Bauhauses. 1919–1933*, Berlin, 1963.

Scheidig, Walther, *bauhaus Weimar. 1919–1924. Werkstattarbeiten*, Leipzig, 1966.

Schmidt, Diether, *bauhaus weimar 1919–1925 dessau 1925–1932 berlin 1932–1933*, Dresden, n.d. (1966).

Wingler, Hans M., *Das Bauhaus. 1919–1933. Weimar Dessau Berlin*, Bramsche, 1962, 2nd ed. 1968.

See also below, Walter Gropius.

Karel de Bazel

Reinink, A. W., *K. P. C. de Bazel, architect*, Leiden, 1965.

Peter Behrens

— *Feste des Lebens und der Kunst. Eine Betrachtung des Theaters als höchsten Kultursymbols*, Leipzig, 1900.

— 'Was ist monumentale Kunst?', in *Kunstgewerbeblatt*, n.s., xx (1908–09), no. 3, pp. 46ff.

— 'Einfluss von Zeit- und Raumausnutzung auf moderne Formentwicklung', in *Jahrbuch des Deutschen Werkbundes 1914*, Jena, 1914, pp. 7ff.

— 'Die neue Handwerks-Romantik', in *Die Innendekoration*, xxxiii (1922), no. 10, p. 341.

— 'Stil?', in *Die Form*, i (1922), no. 1, pp. 5ff.

Anderson, Stanford Owen, *Peter Behrens and the New Architecture of Germany, 1900–1917*, dissertation, New York, 1968.

Cremers, Paul Joseph, *Peter Behrens. Sein Werk von 1909 bis zur Gegenwart*, Essen, 1928.

Gregotti, Vittorio, *et al.*, 'Peter Behrens. 1869–1940', in *Casabella*, no. 240, 1960, pp. 1ff.

Hoeber, Fritz, *Peter Behrens*, Munich, 1913.

Peter Behrens (1868–1940), catalogue of an exhibition at the Pfalzgalerie, Kaiserslautern, and elsewhere, 1966–67.

See also above, Cultural history, and Building types (High-rise buildings, Housing).

Max Berg

— 'Die Jahrhunderthalle und das neue Ausstellungsgelände der Stadt Breslau', in *Deutsche Bauzeitung*, XLVII (1913), nos. 42, 51, pp. 385ff., 462ff.

Trauer, 'Die Jahrhunderthalle in Breslau', in *Deutsche Bauzeitung. Mitteilungen über Zement-, Beton- und Eisenbetonbau*, x (1913), nos. 14–15, pp. 105ff., 115ff.

See also above, Building types (High-rise buildings).

Hendrik Petrus Berlage

— *Gedanken über Stil in der Baukunst*, Leipzig, 1905.

— *Grundlagen und Entwicklung der Architektur*, Rotterdam, n.d. (1908).

— *Studies over bouwkunst, stijl en samenleving*, Rotterdam, 1910.

— *Schoonheid in samenleving*, Rotterdam, 1919, 2nd ed. 1924.

Grassi, Giorgio, 'Immagine di Berlage', in *Casabella*, no. 249, 1961, pp. 39ff.

Havelaar, Just, *Dr. H. P. Berlage*, Amsterdam, 1927.

See also above, Countries (The Netherlands).

German Bestelmeyer

Thiersch, Heinz, *German Bestelmeyer. Sein Leben und Wirken für die Baukunst*, Munich, 1961.

Uriel Birnbaum

— *Der Kaiser und der Architekt*, Leipzig and Vienna, 1924.

Dominikus Böhm

Habbel, Josef, ed., *Dominikus Böhm. Ein deutscher Baumeister*, Regensburg, 1943.

Hoff, August (introduction), *Dominikus Böhm*, Berlin, Leipzig and Vienna, 1930.

Hoff, August, *et al.*, *Dominikus Böhm*, Munich and Zurich, 1962.

Paul Bonatz

— *Leben und Bauen*, Stuttgart, 1950, 4th ed. 1958.

Graubner, Gerhard, ed., *Paul Bonatz und seine Schüler*, Stuttgart, n.d. (1931).

Tamms, Friedrich, ed., *Paul Bonatz. Arbeiten aus den Jahren 1907 bis 1937*, Stuttgart, 1937.

Josef Čapek

— 'Moderne Architektur', in *Der Sturm*, v (1914–15), no. 3, pp. 18ff.

Mario Chiattone

Veronesi, Giulia, and Gigetta Dalli Regoli, *L'opera di Chiattone*, catalogue of an exhibition at the Istituto di Storia dell'Arte, Pisa, 1965.

Deutsche Werkbund

—, ed., *Jahrbuch des Deutschen Werkbundes*, Jena, Munich, or Berlin, 1912–20.

—, ed. (text by Theodor Heuss), *Das Haus der Freundschaft in Konstantinopel*, Munich, 1918.

—, ed., *50 Jahre Deutscher Werkbund*, Berlin, 1958.

Willem Marinus Dudok

Friedhoff, G., *W. M. Dudok*, Amsterdam, 1928.

Magnée, R. M. H., ed., *Willem M. Dudok*, Amsterdam, 1954.

Emil Fahrenkamp

Hoff, August (introduction), *Emil Fahrenkamp*, Stuttgart, n.d. (1928).

Hugh Ferriss

— *The Metropolis of To-morrow*, New York, 1929.

Hermann Finsterlin

— 'Der achte Tag', in *Stadtbaukunst alter und neuer Zeit. Frühlicht*, i (1920), no. 11, 171ff.

— 'Die Genesis der Weltarchitektur oder die Deszendenz der Dome als Stilspiel', in *Frühlicht*, issue 3, Spring 1922, pp. 73ff.

Borsi, Franco, ed., *Hermann Finsterlin. Idea dell'architettura. Architektur in seiner Idee*, Florence, 1969.

'Finsterlin. Vormenspel in de architectuur', in *Wendingen*, vi (1924), no. 3, includes Hermann Finsterlin, 'Casa Nova (Zukunftsarchitektur)', pp. 4ff.

Lienemann, Knut, and H. P. C. Weidner, *H. Finsterlin. Architekturen 1917–24*, Stuttgart, n.d.

Sharp, Dennis, *The Works of Hermann Finsterlin*, London, in preparation.

Theodor Fischer

— *Sechs Vorträge über Stadtbaukunst*, Munich, 1920, 2nd ed. 1922.

— *Öffentliche Bauten*, Leipzig, 1922.

Pfister, Rudolf, *Theodor Fischer. Leben und Wirken eines deutschen Baumeisters*, Munich, 1968.

Antoni Gaudí

Bergós, Joan, *Gaudí, l'home i l'obra*, Barcelona, 1954.

Collins, George R[oseborough], *Antonio Gaudí*, New York and London, 1960.

Descharnes, Robert, and Clovis Prévost, *Gaudí the Visionary*, New York, 1971.

Martinell, César, *Gaudí. Su vida su teoria su obra*, Barcelona, 1967.

Ráfols, José F., *Antoni Gaudí*, Barcelona, 1928.

Sweeney, James Johnson, and Josep Lluis Sert, *Antoni Gaudí*, London and New York, 1960.

Hans and Oskar Gerson

Hegemann, Werner (introduction), *Die Architekten Brüder Gerson*, Berlin, Leipzig and Vienna, 1928.

Paul Gösch

— 'Anregungen. Architektonisches', in *Stadtbaukunst alter und neuer Zeit. Frühlicht*, i (1920), nos. 12, 14, pp. 191ff., 220.

W[estheim], P[aul], 'Paul Goesch', in *Das Kunstblatt*, V (1921), no. 9, pp. 264ff.

Walter Gropius

— 'Baukunst im freien Volksstaat', in Ernst Drahn and Ernst Friedegg, eds., *Deutscher Revolutions-Almanach für das Jahr 1919*, Hamburg and Berlin, 1919, pp. 134ff.

— '"Sparsamer Hausrat" und falsche Dürftigkeit', first published in *Die Volkswohnung*, I (1919), no. 8.

— 'Baugeist oder Krämertum?', in *Die Schuhwelt*, nos. 37–39, 1919, pp. 819ff., 858ff., 894ff.

— 'Neues Bauen', in *Der Holzbau*, supplement to the *Deutsche Bauzeitung*, issue 2, 1920, p. 5.

— and Adolf Meyer, *Weimar Bauten*, Berlin, 1924; previously in *Wasmuths Monatshefte für Baukunst*, VII (1922–23). nos. 11–12, pp. 323ff.

— 'Der Baugeist der neuen Volksgemeinde', in *Die Glocke*, X (1924), no. 10, pp. 311ff.

— *The New Architecture and the Bauhaus*, London and New York, 1936.

— *Scope of Total Architecture*, New York, 1943.

— *Apollo in der Demokratie*, Mainz, 1967.

Argan, Giulio Carlo, *Walter Gropius e la Bauhaus*, Turin, 1951.

Behne, Adolf, 'Entwürfe und Bauten von Walter Gropius', in *Zentralblatt der Bauverwaltung*, XLII (1922), no. 104, pp. 637ff.

Fitch, James Marston, *Walter Gropius*, New York and London, 1960.

Giedion, Sigfried, *Walter Gropius, Mensch und Werk*, Stuttgart, 1954.

O'Neal, William B., *Walter Gropius. A bibliography of writings by and about Walter Gropius*, Charlottesville, 1966.

Pehnt, Wolfgang, 'Gropius the Romantic', in *The Art Bulletin*, LIII (1971), no. 3, pp. 379ff.

Weber, Helmut, *Walter Gropius und das Faguswerk*, Munich, 1961.

See also above, Periods (International Style), Building types (Industrial buildings), and this section (Arbeitsrat für Kunst, Bauhaus).

Hugo Häring

— 'Wege zur Form', in *Die Form*, I (1925), no. 1, pp. 3ff.

Joedicke, Jürgen, 'Hugo Häring. Zur Theorie des organhaften Bauens', in *Bauen + Wohnen*, XV (1960), no. 11, pp. 419ff.

Lauterbach, Heinrich, and Jürgen Joedicke, eds., *Hugo Häring. Schriften, Entwürfe, Bauten*, Stuttgart, 1965.

Hans Hertlein

Schmitz, Hermann (introduction), *Neue Industriebauten des Siemenskonzerns von Hans Hertlein*, Berlin, n.d. (1927).

Schmitz, Hermann (introduction), *Siemensbauten von Hans Hertlein*, Berlin, n.d. (1928).

Fritz Höger

Westphal, Carl J. H., ed., *Fritz Höger. Der niederdeutsche Backstein-Baumeister*, Wolfshagen-Scharbeutz, 1938.

Bernhard Hoetger

Bernhard Hoetger, catalogue of an exhibition at Böttcherstrasse, Bremen, and Westfälischer Kunstverein, Münster, 1964.

Ditze, Michael, *Bernhard Hoetger. 1874–1949. Architektur*, seminar paper, Technische Hochschule Stuttgart, 1965.

Müller-Wulckow, Walter, 'Das Haus Bernhard Hoetgers in Worpswede', in *Die Baugilde*, VII (1925), no. 5, pp. 241ff., 257ff.

Müller-Wulckow, Walter, *Das Paula-Becker-Modersohn-Haus. Führer und Plan*, Bremen, 1930.

Die neue TET-Fabrik, Hanover, 1917.

Pfeffer, C. A., *Winuwuk und Sonnenhof*, Bad Harzburg, 1923.

Roselius, Ludwig, *Reden und Schriften zur Böttcherstrasse in Bremen*, Bremen, 1932.

Clemens Holzmeister

— *Bauten, Entwürfe und Handzeichnungen*, Salzburg and Leipzig, 1937.

Johannes Itten

— *Mein Vorkurs am Bauhaus*, Ravensburg, 1963.

Hans Kampffmeyer

— *Friedenstadt. Ein Vorschlag für ein deutsches Kriegsdenkmal*, Jena, 2nd ed. 1918.

See also above, Building types (town planning).

Otto Kohtz

— *Gedanken über Architektur*, Berlin, 1909.

— 'Das Reichhaus am Königsplatz in Berlin', in *Stadtbaukunst alter und neuer Zeit*, I (1920), no. 16, pp. 241ff.

Hegemann, Werner (introduction), *Otto Kohtz*, Berlin, Leipzig and Vienna, 1930.

Jean Krämer

Osborn, Max (introduction), *Jean Krämer*, Berlin, 1927.

Pieter Lodewijk Kramer

Retera, W., *P. Kramer*, Amsterdam, 1927.

Wilhelm Kreis

— *Soldatengräber und Gedenkstätten*, Munich, 1944.

Mayer, H[ans] K[arl] F[rederick], and G[erhard] Rehder, *Wilhelm Kreis*, Essen, 1953.

Osborn, Max, *Neuere Bauten von Architekt Professor Dr. Wilhelm Kreis*, place and date of publication unknown.

Wilhelm Kreis, Berlin, Leipzig and Vienna, 1927.

Das Wilhelm-Marx-Haus in Düsseldorf, Düsseldorf, n.d.

Willem Kromhout

Retera, W., *W. Kromhout*, Amsterdam, 1927.

J. L. Mathieu Lauweriks

— 'Leitmotive', in *Ring*, issue 1, October 1908, pp. 5ff.

— 'Einen Beitrag zum Entwerfen auf systematischer Grundlage in der Architektur', in *Ring*, issue 4, April 1909, pp. 25ff.

Tummers, N. H. M., *J. L. Mathieu Lauweriks. Zijn werk en zijn invloed*, Hilversum, 1968.

Hans and Wassili Luckhardt

Luckhardt, Wassili, 'Vom Entwerfen', in *Stadtbaukunst alter und neuer Zeit*, II (1921), no. 11, pp. 169ff.

Kultermann, Udo, *Wassili und Hans Luckhardt. Bauten und Entwürfe*, Tübingen, 1958.

Virgilio Marchi

— *Architettura futurista*, Foligno, 1924.

— *Italia nuova architettura nuova*, Foligno and Rome, 1931.

Emanuel Josef Margold

Corwegh, Robert, 'Emanuel Josef Margold', in *Wasmuths Monatshefte für Baukunst*, VI (1921–22), nos. 7–8, pp. 241ff.

Erich Mendelsohn

— *Amerika. Bilderbuch eines Architekten*, Berlin, 1926.

— *Russland Europa Amerika*, Berlin, 1929.

Erich Mendelsohn. Das Gesamtschaffen des Architekten, Berlin, 1930; including 'Das Problem einer neuen Baukunst', lecture, 1919, and 'Die internationale Übereinstimmung des neuen Baugedankens oder Dynamik und Funktion', lecture, 1923.

Erich Mendelsohn. Structures and Sketches, London, 1924.

Banham, Reyner, 'Mendelsohn', in *The Architectural Review*, CXVI (1954), no. 692, pp. 84ff.

Beyer, Oskar, ed., *Erich Mendelsohn. Briefe eines Architekten*, Munich, 1961.

Beyer, Oskar, ed., *Eric Mendelsohn: Letters of an Architect*, London, New York and Toronto, 1967 (selection differs from the preceding title).

'Disegni di Erich Mendelsohn', in *L'architettura*, 1962–63 to 1964–65, VIII, nos. 1–3, 5, 6, 8–12; IX, nos. 1–4, 6, 8, 10–12; X, nos. 1–6.

Eckhardt, Wolf von, *Eric Mendelsohn*, New York and London, 1960.

King, Susan, *The Drawings of Eric Mendelsohn*, catalogue of an exhibition at the University Art Museum, Berkeley, California, 1969.

'Mendelsohn', in *Wendingen*, III (1920), no. 10; including Oskar Beyer, 'Architectuur in ijzer en beton', pp. 4ff., Jan Frederik Staal, 'Naar aanleiding van Erich Mendelsohn's ontwerpen', p. 3.

Whittick, Arnold, *Eric Mendelsohn*, London, 1940, 3rd ed. 1965.

Zevi, Bruno, and Julius Posener, *Erich Mendelsohn*, catalogue of an exhibition at the Akademie der Künste, Berlin, 1968.

Zevi, Bruno, *Erich Mendelsohn. Opera completa*, Milan, 1970.

Ludwig Mies van der Rohe

— 'Gelöste Aufgaben. Eine Forderung an unser Bauwesen', in *Die Bauwelt*, XIV (1923), no. 52, p. 719.

Blaser, Werner, *Mies van der Rohe. The Art of Structure*, London, 1965.

Drexler, Arthur, *Ludwig Mies van der Rohe*, New York, 1960.

Hilberseimer, Ludwig, *Mies van der Rohe*, Chicago, 1956.

Johnson, Philip C., *Mies van der Rohe*, New York, 1947, 2nd ed. 1953.

Hermann Muthesius

— *Kultur und Kunst*, Jena and Leipzig, 1904.

— *Kunstgewerbe und Architektur*, Jena, 1906.

— *Landhäuser*, Munich, 1912.

— 'Wo stehen wir?', in *Jahrbuch des Deutschen Werkbundes 1912*, Jena, 1912.

See also above, Building types (Housing, Monuments).

Novembergruppe

Kliemann, Helga, *Die Novembergruppe*, Berlin, 1969.

Hermann Obrist

— *Neue Möglichkeiten in der bildenden Kunst*, Leipzig, 1903.

Wichmann, Siegfried, *Hermann Obrist. Wegbereiter der Moderne*, catalogue of an exhibition at the Stuck Villa, Munich, 1968.

Joseph Maria Olbrich

— *Ideen*, Vienna, 1899, 2nd ed. Leipzig, 1904.

— *Architektur*, Berlin, 1901–14, 30 portfolios.

Lux, Joseph August, *Joseph M. Olbrich*, Berlin, 1919.

Joseph M. Olbrich. 1867–1908. Das Werk des Architekten, catalogue of an exhibition at the Hessisches Landesmuseum, Darmstadt, 1967.

Friedrich Ostendorf

— *Sechs Bücher vom Bauen*, Berlin, 1913–20, 3 vol., 1 supplementary vol.

Karl Ernst Osthaus

— 'Die Gartenvorstadt an der Donnerkuhle', in *Jahrbuch des Deutschen Werkbundes 1912*, Jena, 1912, pp. 93ff.

Hesse-Frielinghaus, Herta, ed., *Karl Ernst Osthaus. Leben und Werk*, Recklinghausen, 1971.

Hans Poelzig

— 'Werkbundaufgaben', speech to the Stuttgart Werkbund conference, 7. 9. 1919, in *Mitteilungen des Deutschen Werkbundes*, II (1919), no. 4, pp. 109ff.

— 'Festspielhaus in Salzburg', in *Das Kunstblatt*, V (1921), no. 3, pp. 77ff.

— 'Vom Bauen unserer Zeit', in *Die Form*, I (1922), no. 1, pp. 16ff.

— 'Architekturfragen', in *Das Kunstblatt*, VI (1922), nos. 4–5, pp. 153ff., 191ff.

— 'Festbauten', in *Das Kunstblatt*, X (1926), no. 5, pp. 197ff.

Das Grosse Schauspielhaus, Berlin, 1920 (*Die Bücher des Deutschen Theaters I*), containing 'Hans Poelzig. Bau des Grossen Schauspielhauses', pp. 117ff.

Heuss, Theodor, *Hans Poelzig. Bauten und Entwürfe. Das Lebensbild eines deutschen Baumeisters*, Berlin, 1939; new ed., *Hans Poelzig. Das Lebensbild eines deutschen Baumeisters*, Tübingen, 1948.

Landsberger, Franz, 'Hans Poelzig – Die Persönlichkeit', in *Das Kunstblatt*, III (1919), no. 4, pp. 109ff.

Posener, Julius, ed., *Hans Poelzig. Gesammelte Schriften und Werke*, Berlin, 1970.

Stahl, Fritz, 'Hans Poelzig', in *Wasmuths Monatshefte für Baukunst*, IV (1919–20), nos. 1–2, pp. 2ff.

Westheim, Paul, 'Architektur', in *Das Kunstblatt*, III (1919), no. 4, pp. 97ff.

Westheim, Paul, 'Eine Filmstadt von Poelzig', in *Das Kunstblatt*, IV (1920), no. 11, pp. 325ff.

See also above, Building types (Industrial buildings).

Wilhelm Riphahn

Fries, H[einrich] de (introduction), *Wilhelm Riphahn*, Berlin, 1927.

Antonio Sant'Elia

— *L'architettura futurista*, Milan, 1914.

Apollonio, Umbro, and Leonardo Mariani, *Antonio Sant'Elia*, Milan, 1958.

Argan, Giulio Carlo, 'Il pensiero critico di Antonio Sant'Elia', in *Dopo Sant'Elia*, Milan, 1935, pp. 45ff.

Banham, Reyner, 'Sant'Elia', in *The Architectural Review*, CXVII (1955), no. 701, pp. 295ff.

Caramel, Luciano, and Alberto Longatti, *Antonio Sant'Elia*, catalogue of an exhibition at the Villa Comunale dell'Olmo, Como, 1962.

Hans Scharoun

Lauterbach, Heinrich (introduction), *Hans Scharoun*, catalogue of an exhibition at the Akademie der Künste, Berlin, 1967.

Staber, Margit, 'Hans Scharoun. Ein Beitrag zum organischen Bauen', in *Zodiac*, 10, n.d. (1962), pp. 52ff.

Staber, Margit, Klaus-Jacob Thiele, Paul Virilio, and Claude Parent, 'Hans Scharoun', in *aujourd'hui*, X (1967), nos. 57–58, pp. 2ff.

Paul Scheerbart

— *Glasarchitektur*, Berlin, 1914; new ed., Munich, 1971.

Hilberseimer, Ludwig, 'Paul Scheerbart und die Architekten, in *Das Kunstblatt*, III (1919), no. 8, pp. 271ff.

Fritz Schumacher

— *Stufen des Lebens. Erinnerungen eines Baumeisters*, Stuttgart, 1949.

See also above, General, Periods (Expressionism) and Countries (Germany).

Rudolf Steiner

— *Mein Lebensgang*, Dornach, 1925, 7th ed. 1962.

— *Wege zu einem neuen Baustil*, Dornach, 1926, 2nd ed. Stuttgart, 1957 (English: *Ways to a New Style in Architecture*, 1928).

— *Der Baugedanke des Goetheanum*, Dornach, 1932.

— *Stilformen des Organisch-Lebendigen* (2 lectures, 1921), Dornach, 1933.

— *Der Dornacher Bau als Wahrzeichen geschichtlichen Werdens und künstlerischer Umwandlungsimpulse* (5 lectures, 1914), Dornach, 1937.

— *Der Baugedanke von Dornach* (3 lectures, 1920), Dornach, 1942.

Baravalle, Albert, 'Das Goetheanum in Dornach', in *Schweizerische Technische Zeitschrift*, no. 42, 1945.

Baravalle, Albert, 'Das Baumotiv des II. Goetheanum', in *Das Goetheanum. Wochenschrift für Anthroposophie*, XXXI (1952), no. 12, pp. 93ff.

Brunati, Mario, and Sandro Mendini, 'Kultur espressionista', in *L'architettura*, VI (1960–61), nos. 1–4, pp. 58ff., 130ff., 202ff., 276ff.

Raab, Rex, *Sprechender Beton*, in preparation.

Raske, Hilde, ed., *Der Bau. Studien zur Architektur und Plastik des ersten Goetheanum von Carl Kemper*, Stuttgart, 1966.

Stockmeyer, E. A. Karl, 'Von Vorläufern des Goetheanums', in *Mitteilungen aus der anthroposophischen Arbeit in Deutschland*, no. 10, 1949, pp. 13ff.

Stockmeyer, E. A. Karl, *Der Modellbau in Malsch*, Malsch, 1969.

Zimmer, Erich, 'Der Baugedanke von Malsch', in *Mensch und Baukunst*, XVIII (1969), no. 3, pp. 3ff.

Zimmer, Erich, *Rudolf Steiner als Architekt von Wohn- und Zweckbauten*, Stuttgart, n.d. (1971).

Bruno Taut

— 'Eine Notwendigkeit', in *Der Sturm*, IV (1913–14), nos. 196–197, pp. 174ff.

— *Glashaus. Werkbund-Ausstellung Cöln 1914*, Berlin, n.d. (1914).

— *Ein Architekturprogramm*, first pamphlet of the Arbeitsrat für Kunst, Berlin, 1918, 2nd ed. 1919.

— *Alpine Architektur*, Hagen, 1919.

— 'Beobachtungen über Farbenwirkung aus meiner Praxis', first published in *Die Bauwelt*, X (1919), no. 38, pp. 12ff.

— 'Die Erde eine gute Wohnung', in *Die Volkswohnung*, I (1919), no. 4, pp. 45ff.

— 'Ex oriente lux. Ein Aufruf an die Architekten', first published in *Das Hohe Ufer*, I (1919), no. 1, pp. 15ff.

— 'Für die neue Baukunst!', in *Das Kunstblatt*, III (1919), no. 1, pp. 16ff.

— 'Rede des Bundeskanzlers von Europa am 24. April 1993 vor dem europäischen Parlament', in *Sozialistische Monatshefte*, LIII (1919), nos. 19–20, pp. 816ff.

— *Die Stadtkrone*, Jena, 1919.

— 'Zuviel Gerede vom Architektur-Unterricht', in *Die Bauwelt*, X (1919), no. 32, pp. 9ff.

— *Die Auflösung der Städte oder die Erde eine gute Wohnung oder auch der Weg zur Alpinen Architektur*, Hagen, 1920.

— 'Glasbau', in *Stadtbaukunst alter und neuer Zeit*, I (1920), no. 8, pp. 120ff.

— 'Künstlerisches Filmprogramm', in *Das Hohe Ufer*, II (1920), nos. 5–6, pp. 86ff.

— 'Mein Weltbild', first published in *Das Hohe Ufer*, II (1920), nos. 10–12, pp. 152ff.

— *Der Weltbaumeister. Architekturschauspiel für symphonische Musik*, Hagen, 1920.

—, ed., *Frühlicht*, supplement to *Stadtbaukunst alter und neuer Zeit*, I (1920), nos. 1–14; as an independent publication, Magdeburg, 1921–22, 4 issues; new ed. (selection), Berlin and Frankfurt, 1963.

— 'Baugedanken der Gegenwart', in *Die Bauwelt*, XIV (1923), no. 25, pp. 341ff.

— 'Glasarchitektur', in *Die Bauwelt*, XV (1924), no. 10, pp. 183f.

— *Die neue Wohnung. Die Frau als Schöpferin*, Leipzig, 1924, 5th ed. 1928.

— 'Glasbau', in *Die Baugilde*, VII (1925), no. 18, p. 1248.

— 'Wiedergeburt der Farbe', in *Die Bauwelt*, XVI (1925), no. 29, p. 676.

— *Bauen. Der neue Wohnbau*, Leipzig, 1927.

— *Ein Wohnhaus*, Stuttgart, 1927.

Behne, Adolf, 'Bruno Taut', in *Neue Blätter für Kunst und Dichtung*, II (1919–20), no. 1, pp. 13ff.

Junghanns, Kurt, *Bruno Taut. 1880–1938*, Berlin, 1970.

Rühl, Konrad, 'Erinnerungen an Bruno Taut', in *Baukunst und Werkform*, XII (1959), no. 9, pp. 485ff.

See also above, Periods (International Style), Building types (Theatres), and this section (Arbeitsrat für Kunst).

Max Taut

Behne, Adolf (introduction), *Max Taut. Bauten und Pläne*, Berlin, 1927.

Fehling, Hermann, and Julius Posener, *Max Taut*, catalogue of an exhibition at the Akademie der Künste, Berlin, 1964.

Heinrich Tessenow

— *Hausbau und dergleichen*, Berlin, 1916, 2nd ed. 1920, 3rd ed. 1928.

— *Handwerk und Kleinstadt*, Berlin, 1919.

Paul Thiersch

Fahrner, Rudolf, ed., *Paul Thiersch. Leben und Werk*, Berlin, 1970.

Henry van de Velde

— *Geschichte meines Lebens*, Munich, 1962.

Hammacher, A. M., *Die Welt Henry van de Veldes*, Antwerp and Cologne, 1967.

'Henry van de Velde', in *Casabella*, no. 237, 1960; including Ernesto N. Rogers, 'Henry van de Velde o dell'evoluzione', pp. 3ff.

Henry van de Velde. 1863–1957, catalogue of an exhibition at the Rijksmuseum Kröller-Müller, Otterlo, 1964.

Hüter, Karl-Heinz, *Henry van de Velde. Sein Werk bis zum Ende seiner Tätigkeit in Deutschland*, Berlin, 1967.

Osthaus, Karl Ernst, *Van de Velde*, Hagen, 1920.

Werkbund, see Deutsche Werkbund

Hendrikus Theodorus Wijdeveld

— 'Natuur, bouwkunst en techniek', in *Wendingen*, V (1923), no.s 8–9, pp. 12ff.

— *Cultuur en kunst. Verzamelde opstellen. 1917–1929*, Amsterdam, 1929.

Tummers, N. H. M., 'H. Th. Wijdeveld', in *Bouwkundig Weekblad*, LXXXIII (1965), no. 19, pp. 1ff.

Index

Sources of illustrations

Amsterdam: Gemeentelijke Dienstvolkhuusvesting 461, 470

Barcelona: Archivos Amigos de Gaudí 16; Escuela Superior de Arquitectura 119; Foto Mas 120, 348
Berlin: Bauhaus-Archiv 249, 250, 254, 256; Deutsche Kinemathek e.V. 405, 414; Reinhard Friedrich 7, 103, 238, 240; Monica Hennig-Schefold 284–286, 291; Walter Köster 56, 57; Staatsbibliothek 273, 275
Bonn: Theo Schafgans 388
Bremen: Hed. Wiesner 313

Cologne: Henry Maitek 379; Hugo Schmölz 369, 373, 375
Como: Ghizzoni di Scotti 423, 424, 430–432
Copenhagen: Jorgen Watz 98, 99

Dornach: Heydebrand-Osthoff 332
Düsseldorf: Oskar Söhn 503; Stadtarchiv 29, 399, 498, 505; Dr Franz Stoedtner 20, 38, 50, 128, 161, 165–167, 308, 309, 497, 500
Dyckerhoff & Widmann KG, company archives 140

Essen: Manfred Hanisch 15; Städtische Bildstelle 365

Frankfurt am Main: Farbwerke Hoechst AG, company archives 136, 137
Freiburg: Foto Stober 323

Gelsenkirchen: Ilse Pässler 78

Hagen: Franz Gröl 81
Hamburg: Fischer-Daber 302, 303, 499; Staatliche Landesbildstelle 300
Hanover: Hans Wagner 122

Laren: Doeser Fotos 451
Levallois-Perret: Michel Moch 14
London: Eric de Maré 370

Maartensdijk: Hans Sibbelee 382, 383, 447, 452, 454, 455, 457, 459, 466–469, 474

Marburg: Bildarchiv Foto Marburg 27, 33, 34, 93, 130
Munich: Bayerische Staatsgemäldesammlung 109; S. R. Gnamm 116; Staatliche Graphische Sammlung 114

New York: Museum of Modern Art 72

Pisa: Istituto di Storia dell'Arte 433–439
Prague: Antonin Vodák 123–125

Rodenkirchen: Wolfgang Pehnt 338–340, 343, 345–347, 350–354, 357, 488, 501

Stuttgart: Landesbildstelle Württemberg 132; Helga Schmidt-Glassner 372

Vienna: Photoatelier Gerlach 482

Wiesbaden: Deutsches Institut für Filmkunde e.V. 406, 411–413, 415

Zurich: Michael Wolgensinger 104, 106

We are grateful for permission to reproduce illustrations from the following recent publications:

Rudolf Fahrner, ed., *Paul Thiersch. Leben und Werk*, Berlin, 1970: 79, 175
Die gläserne Kette. Visionäre Architekturen aus dem Kreis um Bruno Taut. 1919–1920, catalogue of an exhibition at Schloss Morsbroich, Leverkusen, and the Akademie der Künste, Berlin, 1963: 225, 226, 235, 236
Bernhard Hoetger, catalogue of an exhibition at Böttcherstrasse, Bremen, and the Westfälischer Kunstverein, Münster, 1964: 484
August Hoff et al., *Dominikus Böhm*, Munich and Zurich, 1962: 366–368, 371
César Martinelli, *Gaudí. Su vida su teoria su obra*, Barcelona, 1967: 121
Hans-Wolfgang Müller, *Ägyptische Kunst*, Frankfurt am Main, 1970: 92
Erich Zimmer, *Rudolf Steiner als Architekt von Wohn- und Zweckbauten*, Stuttgart, n. d. (1971): 337, 341, 342, 344, 349, 358

The remaining illustrations come from publications of the time.